Quantitative Studies on
Production and Prices

Quantitative Studies on
Production and Prices

Edited by
W. Eichhorn, R. Henn, K. Neumann, and R.W. Shephard †
at the Universities of Karlsruhe/Germany and Berkeley/U.S.A.

Physica-Verlag · Würzburg–Wien
1983

CIP-Kurztitelaufnahme der Deutschen Bibliothek

Quantitative studies on production and prices /
ed. by W. Eichhorn .... – Würzburg ; Wien : Physica-Verlag, 1983.
ISBN 3-7908-0275-1

NE: Eichhorn, Wolfgang [Hrsg.]

Composed and printed by repro-druck „Journalfranz“ Arnulf Liebing GmbH + Co., Würzburg.

Printed in Germany

ISBN 3 7908 0275 1

Ronald W. Shephard †

Ronald William Shephard †

Ronald W. Shephard, co-editor of this book, passed away on July 22, 1982. We have lost a great scholar, teacher, colleague and, above all, our beloved friend.

He was by nature kind, compassionate, considerate and humourous, though occasional seen by some as tough, absolutely unbending and unyielding to the extent of being stubborn and opinionated.

About five years ago, the Administration of his University (Berkeley) in its infinite wisdom, decided that the fourth floor of Etcheverry Hall needed to have its doors painted in various bright colors. Only one door, Ronald Shephard's, was not painted. The painters would have had to physically move him out of the way, as he would not tolerate an expenditure for paint for his door at the same time budgets for educational programs were limited.

The welfare of the students and the University was always uppermost in his mind. We remember him as someone who caused the Administration great annoyance, as he steadfastly clung to the now-radical but really traditional notion that staff and administrators existed to serve the faculty.

Ronald Shephard must be remembered as a man of tradition and history, possessing an almost romantic vision of the University. He was a living link with the University's past for the students, as he would frequently entertain them with stories of his career – stories of putting himself through California during the depression by caddying golf and selling newspapers; of having to stay out of school one semester because he could not raise $ 25 for tuition; stories of working with his teacher Griffith Evans as a graduate student; of roping a blackboard to the roof of his car, driving to Evans' house in the Berkeley Hills, interrupting a garden party, and the two of them sorting out a difficult theoretical problem with the blackboard set up in Evans' garage.

The human touch of his philosophizing and reminiscing in the classroom and in research meetings was well known and highly praised.

We must also remember him as a man of tremendous energy and courage. In his last years his hands were badly bruised and discolored, his spine was terribly curved, his breath very short. Even in his last days he still continued to write and work with his graduate students.

Ronald Shephard is for us what the University is all about, and why we are proud to be members of universities.

He deeply believed in the ideals that belong perhaps to a bygone era: the superiority of the intellect, the pursuit of truth and beauty, honour and duty, the rights of an individual and more importantly his obligations. With his foresight and intellectual prowess, he developed Production Theory as his keen perception of truth led him, little concerned about how far he was leaving the rest of us behind. He was relentless in upholding the excellence of scholarship and the duty of higher education, treated his students as equal as colleagues, and challenged them accordingly to fight tooth and nail for what they believe to be true. He was far-sighted and pioneered the organization of Operations Research as a graduate field of study. Around 1960, he set up in Industrial Engineering the Operations Research area and invited three of us (Dantzig, Jewell, Oliver) to join him. The O.R. center at Berkeley became a research laboratory of the Department of Industrial

Engineering chaired by him. Today the graduates of his pioneering effort dominate the field.

There are many experts who see Ronald Shephard as the foremost production theorist ever. His success as a theorist, however, grew out of practical insights into real world problems. The classic work on duality theory, essentially stating that under certain conditions a production unit can be modelled either in the primal (factor) space or in the dual (price) space, grew out of his observation that production data are most frequently presented in monetary terms. His work on duality theory published in the book "Cost and Production Functions" (Princeton University Press 1953), has been called by Dale Jorgensen, in the preface of a reprint of the book, "the most original contribution to economic theory of all time".

Ronald Shephard's interest in the planning of production made him raise the question: "What can be obtained when expenditures are given?" To answer this question, he developed an axiomatic theory of indirect production functions. In the book "Indirect Production Functions" (Mathematical Systems in Economics, No. 10, Anton Hain, Meisenheim 1974) he showed the relationships between production functions, indirect production functions and cost-benefit analysis. He also developed the logic of accounting (shadow) prices as proxies for market prices.

"Imagine that you visit a shipyard" he stated in the preface to the monograph "Dynamic Theory of Production Correspondences" written by him and Rolf Färe (Mathematical Systems in Economics, No. 50, Anton Hain, Meisenheim 1980). "Day by day a tremendous amount of production activity of great variety is carried on, yet no ships are turned out. This goes on for a long time. Eventually a ship emerges. What is being produced day by day all during this time? It is clear that the daily, weekly, monthly outputs of the system were intermediate products. The shipbuilding production system, like construction, is a dynamically evolving process. Thus . . . I was prompted to undertake the development of a dynamic theory of production correspondences". The monograph represents an essential progress in the theory of production. By working in a function space of input and output rate histories, the crucial notion of time was successfully incorporated into production theory.

Among his papers, Ronald Shephard liked "Proof of the Law of Diminishing Returns" (Zeitschrift für Nationalökonomie **30**, 1970, 7–34) most. It was judged by Oskar Morgenstern as a benchmark in theoretical economics. Ronald Shephard's approach to prove this law, initially formulated by Turgot in 1767, established a fundamental set of axioms for production theory.

For a long time he did not receive the recognition that his continuous contributions to the foundations of Production Theory deserve. However, at the end of his life he was honoured not only by praising remarks on his work as mentioned above. In 1980, he was awarded a Ph. D. honoris causa by the Faculty of Economics of the University of Karlsruhe, where he had held several Visiting Research Scholarships in the years before.

Our sympathies go to his wife, Mrs. Hilda Shephard. We shall never forget him.

George B. Dantzig
Wolfgang Eichhorn
Rolf Färe
William S. Jewell
Robert C. Leachman
King-Tim Mak
Robert M. Oliver

Preface

This book consists of 18 contributions that can be classified as quantitative studies on production and prices. Oral presentations and discussions of several of the topics first took place at a symposium held at the University of Karlsruhe, June 23 – July 4, 1980. This symposium focussed on *Natural Resources and Production*, but there was a group of scholars known throughout the world participating who concentrated on topics concerning production and prices rather than natural resources. Since their contributions are very worth reading, we take the liberty and have the privilege of editing them in this volume.

As far as the natural resources topic is concerned, a substantial part of the symposium proceedings on this subject is contained in a book entitled *Economic Theory of Natural Resources*, which was issued by the same editors and publisher.

Each paper has been reviewed by two anonymous referees. Consequently, the articles of this book are revisions or, in many cases, revised revisions of the original papers.

The contributions are organized in four parts. Part I contains five papers on production correspondences and laws of returns.

The five papers of Part II are devoted to dynamic structures of production. In two of them optimization problems are treated.

Turning next to topics of measurement and aggregation in the context of production and prices, Part III consists of four contributions involving single and multiple output production technologies as well as input price subindexes.

The concluding Part IV consists of four econometric studies whose underlying models are implemented by data of the U.S. or (West) German economy.

We take this opportunity to acknowledge indebtedness to Stiftung Volkswagenwerk (Volkswagen Foundation), Alfried Krupp von Bohlen und Halbach-Stiftung (Krupp Foundation) and Fritz Thyssen Stiftung (Thyssen Foundation) for providing the financial means to carry out the symposium. In addition, the Karlsruher Hochschulvereinigung (including alumni and friends of the University of Karlsruhe) provided the funds that made publication of this book possible. To all sponsors we express our sincere appreciation for their support.

Karlsruhe und Berkeley
June 1981

W. Eichhorn, R. Henn
K. Neumann, R.W. Shephard
Editors

Contents

Part I
Structure of Technologies and Laws of Returns

Quantitative Studies on Production and Prices © Physica-Verlag, Würzburg–Wien, 1983.

On Strictly Monotonic Production Correspondences

Rolf Färe

1. Introduction

This paper is concerned with strictly monotonic production correspondences and the role they play for certain economic concepts like joint production functions, isoquants and efficient subsets.

It is frequently assumed that production (and utility) functions are strictly increasing along rays, i.e., $\phi: R_+^N \to R_+$, satisfies the condition $\phi(\lambda \cdot x) > \phi(x)$, for $\lambda > 1$ and $x \neq 0$. This implies that the output correspondence $P(x) := \{u \in R_+ : \phi(x) \geqslant u\}$ has disjoint isoquants for proportional increases in the factors, i.e., $\text{Isoq}\, P(\lambda \cdot x) = \phi(\lambda \cdot x) \neq \neq \phi(x) = \text{Isoq}\, P(x)$. However, this assumption does not imply that the inverse (input) correspondence has disjoint isoquants for different output levels. (See example 3.4.) In this paper we will explore production functions and correspondences having disjoint input and output isoquants or efficient subsets. This captures the idea of strict monotonicity for correspondences.

In section 3 a characterization of lower semi-continuity in terms of disjoint input isoquants is proven. This result is used to analyze two definitions of the isoquant used in economic literature. In sections 4 and 5 two different joint production functions are defined and shown to exist under certain conditions. These existence theorems are stated in terms of disjoint input and output isoquants and efficient subsets, respectively. The last section shows when these joint production functions coincide. Notations and basic properties are introduced in section 2.

2. Notation

In section 3 a function $\phi: R_+^N \to U$ is used. $U = \{u \in R_+ : 0 \leqq u \leqq \bar{\bar{u}}\}$ with $\phi(0) = 0$ and $\sup_{x \in R_+^N} \phi(x) = \bar{\bar{u}}$. Corresponding to this production (utility) function there is an input correspondence $L(u) := \{x \in R_+^N : \phi(x) \geqslant u\}$ and an output correspondence $P(x) := \{u \in R_+ : \phi(x) \geqq u\}$. Clearly, $x \in L(u)$ if and only if $u \in P(x)$ and the function ϕ is defined by $\phi(x) = \sup\{u : x \in L(u)\} = \sup\{u : u \in P(x)\}$. Supremum is used since it is not assumed that $P(x)$ is closed. Additional properties on ϕ are introduced in section 3.

The function ϕ is said to be lower semi-continuous on R_+^N if for each $x^0 \in R_+^N$ and each sequence $x^n \to x^0$, $\liminf_{n\to\infty} \phi(x^n) \geqslant \phi(x^0)$ or equivalently, the set $V(u) := \{x \in R_+^N : \phi(x) > u\}$ is open for each $u > 0$.

The remaining sections deals input and output correspondences as mappings between $2^{R_+^M}$ and $2^{R_+^N}$. The output correspondences denoted by P maps $P: R_+^N \to P(x) \in 2^{R_+^M}$ and $P(x) :=$ {output vectors in R_+^M obtainable from $x \in R_+^N$}. The inverse input correspondence L, maps $L: R_+^M \to L(u) \in 2^{R_+^N}$ and $L(u) :=$ {input vectors in R_+^N, yielding at least output $u \in R_+^M$}. One has that $x \in L(u)$ if and only if $u \in P(x)$.

It will be assumed that in sections 4–6, the output correspondence P satisfies the following subset of axioms, suggested by *Shephard* [1970].

P.1 $P(0) = \{0\}$,
P.2 $P(x)$ is bounded for $x \in R_+^N$,
P.3 $P(\lambda \cdot x) \supseteqq P(x)$ for $\lambda \geqq 1$, (weak disposability of inputs)
P.4 P is a closed correspondence,
P.5 $u \in P(x)$ implies that $\{v: v = \theta \cdot u, \theta \in [0, 1]\} \subseteqq P(x)$, (weak disposability of outputs).

In places, stronger assumptions than P.3 and P.5 are needed. These assumptions are:

P.3.S $x'' \geqq x'$ implies $P(x'') \supseteqq P(x')$, (strong disposability of inputs),
P.5.S $u'' \leqq u' \in P(x)$ imply $u'' \in P(x)$, (strong disposability of outputs).

The following vector inequalities are used, $\geqq, \geqslant$, and $>$. $\geqslant$ means $\geqq$ but $\neq$. $>$ means strictly larger in each component.

3. On Two Definitions of the Input Isoquant

Given a production function ϕ, the following two definitions of the input isoquants are used in the literature.

Definition 3.1: [*Shephard*] The Input Isoquant for the output level u is given by Isoq $L(u) := \{x: x \in L(u)$ and $\nexists\, 0 \leqq \lambda < 1$ such that $\lambda \cdot x \in L(u)\}$, Isoq $L(0) := \{0\}$.

Definition 3.2: The Input Isoquant for the output level u is given by $I(u) := \{x: \phi(x) = u\}$.

In general these two isoquants do not coincide, not even under rather strong assumptions on the production function ϕ. For example consider:

$$\phi(x) := \begin{cases} x & \text{for } x \in [0, 1) \\ x + 1 & \text{for } x \in [1, +\infty). \end{cases} \quad \text{and} \tag{3.3}$$

This production function is strictly increasing and upper semi-continuous, however, Isoq $L(1\ 1/2) = \{1\}$ and $I(1\ 1/2)$ is empty.

As a second example, consider:

$$\phi(x) := \begin{cases} x & \text{for } x \in [0, 1] \\ 1 & \text{for } x \in [1, 2] \\ x - 1 & \text{for } x \in [2, +\infty). \end{cases} \tag{3.4}$$

This production function is nondecreasing and continuous, however, Isoq $L(1) = \{1\}$ and $I(1) = \{x: x \in [1, 2]\}$.

In this section, given a nondecreasing upper semi-continuous production function, necessary and sufficient conditions for Isoq $L(u)$ to equal $I(u)$ are shown. For this purpose the following lemma is useful.

Lemma 3.5:[1] [*Färe/Primont*] Let $\phi: R_+^N \to U$ be a nondecreasing production function (i.e., $x'' \geqq x' \Rightarrow \phi(x'') \geqq \phi(x')$). ϕ is lower semi-continuous if and only if Isoq $L(v) \cap$ Isoq $L(u)$ is empty for all $u \neq v$, u and $v \in U$ and $\min\{u, v\} > 0$.

Proof: Let ϕ be lower semi-continuous. We have to prove that Isoq $L(u) \cap$ Isoq $L(v) = \emptyset$ for all $u \neq v$. Let $u \neq v$, u, $v \in U$, and without loss of generality let $u > v$. Then $x \in$ Isoq $L(u)$, if $\lambda \cdot x \notin L(u)$ for all $0 \leqq \lambda < 1$. We define a function $g: R_+ \to U$ by $\lambda \mapsto \phi(\lambda \cdot x)$. Since, by assumption, g is lower semi-continuous and nondecreasing, for $\delta := u - v$ there exists an $0 < \epsilon < 1$ such that $g(\lambda) > g(1) - \delta$, implying $\phi(\lambda \cdot x) > v$, for all $1 - \epsilon < \lambda$. Hence, $x \notin$ Isoq $L(v)$.

To prove the converse, observe that ϕ is lower semi-continuous if and only if the sets $V(u) := \{x: \phi(x) > u\}$ are open for all $u \in R$. Without loss of generality let $u \geqq 0$, and let $x \in V(u)$. Then $v := \phi(x) > u$. Hence $x \geqslant 0$. We distinguish the following cases:

a) $x \in$ Isoq $L(v)$. By assumption $x \notin$ Isoq $L(u^0)$ for an $u < u^0 < v$. Since $x \in L(u^0)$, there exists an $0 \leqq \lambda < 1$ with $\lambda \cdot x \in L(u^0)$. Now there exists an open set W contained in $\{y: y \geqq \lambda \cdot x\}$ with $x \in W$. By assumption $\phi(y) \geqq u^0 > u$ for all $y \in W$. Hence $V(u)$ is open.

b) $x \notin$ Isoq $L(v)$. Hence, there exists a $0 \leqq \lambda < 1$ with $\lambda \cdot x \in L(v)$. Then the rest of proof is the same as in case a). QED

A complete characterization of an upper semi-continuous, nondecreasing production function ϕ for which Isoq $L(u) = I(u)$, $u > 0$, can now be proved.

Proposition 3.6: Let $\phi: R_+^N \to U$ be a nondecreasing, upper semi-continuous production function. ϕ is lower semi-continuous and ray strictly increasing (i.e., $\phi(\lambda \cdot x) > \phi(x)$, $\lambda > 1$) if and only if Isoq $L(u) = I(u)$, $u > 0$.

Proof: Clearly, Isoq $L(u) \subseteqq \{x: \phi(x) \geqq u\}$, $u > 0$. Let $x^0 \in \{x: \phi(x) > u\}$. Since ϕ is continuous, (upper and lower semi-continuous), the set $\{\lambda: \phi(\lambda \cdot x^0) > u\} \subseteqq R_+$ is open, implying that $x^0 \notin$ Isoq $L(u)$. Hence Isoq $L(u) \subseteqq I(u)$. Next assume that $x^0 \notin$ Isoq $L(u)$, $u > 0$, then since ϕ is ray strictly increasing, if $x^0 \in L(u)$, there is a $\lambda < 1$ such that $\phi(\lambda \cdot x^0) = u$ implying that $x^0 \notin I(u)$.

---

[1]) This proof was suggested by an anonymous referee.

Conversely, assume Isoq $L(u) = I(u)$, $u > 0$. Let $u > v > 0$, then (Isoq $L(u) \cap$ Isoq $L(v)) = (I(u) \cap I(v))$ is empty, since if $x^0 \in I(u)$ and $x^0 \in I(v)$, $\phi(x^0) = u > v = \phi(x^0)$, impossible. Thus, by Lemma 3.5, ϕ is lower semi-continuous. Finally, if $x \in$ Isoq $L(u) = I(u)$, $\phi(x) = u$ and since $x \in$ Isoq $L(u)$, $\phi(\lambda \cdot x) < \phi(x)$, $\lambda < 1$. Thus, $\phi(\mu \cdot y) > \phi(y)$, $\mu = 1/\lambda$, $y = \lambda \cdot x$.
QED

One notes that in the proof of obtaining Isoq $L(u) = I(u)$ the nondecreasency of ϕ was not involved. It is also clear that if ϕ is nondecreasing and positive ray strictly increasing, then $\phi(x'') > \phi(x')$ for $x'' > x'$.

4. The Joint (Isoquant) Production Function

Joint production functions are frequently used in economics to model production technologies with multi input and multi output. A joint production function, relating input isoquants to output isoquants (production possibility curves) has been defined by *Shephard* [1970] as:

Definition 4.1: The function $F: R_+^M x R_+^N \to R_+$ such that

(1) for $u^0 \geqslant 0$, Isoq $L(u^0) = \{x: F(u^0, x) = 0\}$, $L(u^0)$ nonempty,
(2) for $x^0 \geqslant 0$, Isoq $P(x^0) = \{u: F(u, x^0) = 0\}$, $P(x^0) \neq 0$,

is called a Joint (Isoquant) Production Function.

The input isoquant for $u \in R_+^M$ is defined like in definition 3.1, while the output isoquant is given by

Definition 4.2: The (Output) Isoquant for the input vector $x \in R_+^N$ is given by
Isoq $P(x) := \{u \in P(x)$ and $\exists\, \theta > 1$ such that $\theta \cdot u \in P(x)\}$, $P(x) \neq \{0\}$.

Bol/Moeschlin [1975] gave the following characterization of a joint production function.

Lemma 4.3: A joint (isoquant) production function $F(u, x)$ exists if and only if for all $x \geqslant 0$, $P(x) \neq \{0\}$ and $u \geqslant 0$, $L(u)$ nonempty, $u \in$ Isoq $P(x) \Leftrightarrow x \in$ Isoq $L(u)$.

Examples (3.3) and (3.4) show that in general there need not exist a joint production function. For example, in (3.3), $1\ 1/2 \notin$ Isoq $P(1)$ but $1 \in$ Isoq $L(1\ 1/2)$, and in (3.4), $1 \in$ Isoq $P(1\ 1/2)$ but $1\ 1/2 \notin$ Isoq $L(1)$.

Next, consider the following properties of the input and output correspondences.

Definition 4.4: For all $x \geqslant 0$, $u \geqslant 0$ such that $P(x) \neq \{0\}$ and $L(u)$ nonempty, define:

I:1 Isoq $L(\theta \cdot u) \cap$ Isoq $L(u)$ empty for $\theta \neq 1$,
I:2 Isoq $P(\lambda \cdot x) \cap$ Isoq $P(x)$ empty for $\lambda \neq 1$,

II:1 $x \in$ Isoq $L(u)$ implies $u \in$ Isoq $P(x)$,
II:2 $u \in$ Isoq $P(x)$ implies $x \in$ Isoq $L(u)$.

The following relationships between the above properties of the input and output correspondences are valid.

Lemma 4.5: I:1 $\Leftrightarrow$ II:1 and I:2 $\Leftrightarrow$ II:2.

Proof: Assume $x \in (\text{Isoq}\, L\,(\theta \cdot u) \cap \text{Isoq}\, L\,(u))$, $\theta \neq 1$, then $(\theta \cdot u)$ and $u \in P\,(x)$ implying that $(\theta \cdot u)$ or u does not belong to Isoq $P\,(x)$, proving that II:1 implies I:1.

Conversely, assume that $x \in \text{Isoq}\, L\,(u)$ but $u \notin \text{Isoq}\, P\,(x)$. Clearly, $u \in P\,(x)$. Thus there is a $\theta > 1$ such that $(\theta \cdot u) \in \text{Isoq}\, P\,(x)$, and $x \in L\,(\theta \cdot u)$. Since $\theta > 1$, $L\,(\theta \cdot u) \subseteqq L\,(u)$ by weak disposability of outputs. Thus $x \in \text{Isoq}\, L\,(\theta \cdot u)$ since $x \in \text{Isoq}\, L\,(u)$. However, this contradicts I:1. Therefore, I:1 implies II:1.

Similar arguments apply to show that I:2 is equivalent to II:2. QED

The following proposition is clear from lemmata 4.3 and 4.5.

Proposition 4.6: [*Al-Ayat/Färe*] A joint (isoquant) production function $F\,(u, x)$ exists if and only if I:1 and I:2 hold.

This proposition shows that isoquant ray strict monotonicity of the input and output correspondences is necessary and sufficient for the existence of a joint (isoquant) production function.

5. The Joint Efficiency Production Function

In the same manner as the common joint (isoquant) production function is defined, a joint efficiency production function can be defined. This function will relate efficient input vectors to efficient output vectors.

The efficient input and output sets are defined, respectively as:

Definition 5.1: The Efficient Input Set for the output vector $u \in R_+^M$ is given by $\text{Eff}\, L\,(u) := \{x\colon x \in L\,(u) \text{ and } \nexists\, y \leqslant x \text{ such that } y \in L\,(u)\}$, $\text{Eff}\, L\,(0) := \{0\}$.

Definition 5.2: The Efficient Output Set for the input vector $x \in R_+^N$ is given by $\text{Eff}\, P\,(x) := \{u\colon u \in P\,(x), \nexists\, v \geqslant u \text{ such that } v \in P\,(x)\}$, $\text{Eff}\, P\,(0) := \{0\}$.

The joint efficiency production function is next defined in a similar way as the common joint (isoquant) function.

Definition 5.3: The function $E\colon R_+^M \times R_+^N \to R_+$ such that

(1) for $u^0 \geqslant 0$, $\text{Eff}\, L\,(u^0) = \{x\colon E\,(u^0, x) = 0\}$, $L\,(u^0)$ nonempty,
(2) for $x^0 \geqslant 0$, $\text{Eff}\, P\,(x^0) = \{u\colon E\,(u, x^0) = 0\}$, $P\,(x^0) \neq \{0\}$,

is called a Joint Efficiency Production Function.

The following characterization, useful later, can be proven.

Lemma 5.4: A joint efficiency production function $E(u, x)$ exists if and only if for all $x \geqslant 0, u \geqslant 0, P(x) \neq \{0\}$ and $L(u)$ nonempty, $u \in \text{Eff } P(x) \Leftrightarrow x \in \text{Eff } L(u)$.

Proof: If a joint efficiency production function exists, then $x \in \text{Eff } L(u) \Leftrightarrow E(u, x) = 0 \Leftrightarrow u \in \text{Eff } P(x)$ hold. Conversely, assume that $u \in \text{Eff } P(x) \Leftrightarrow x \in \text{Eff } L(u)$ and consider the sets

$$\{(u, x): x \geqslant 0, u \geqslant 0, P(x) \neq \{0\}, u \in \text{Eff } P(x)\}$$

and

$$\{(u, x): x \geqslant 0, u \geqslant 0, P(x) \neq \{0\}, x \in \text{Eff } L(u)\}.$$

Clearly these sets are equal. Call them A, and define

$$E(u, x) = \begin{cases} 0 & (u, x) \in A \\ 0 & u = 0 \text{ and } P(x) = \{0\} \\ 1 & \text{otherwise.} \end{cases}$$

Then clearly, $E(u, x)$ is a joint efficiency production function. QED

In general there exists no joint efficiency production function as shown by the following example.

$$\left.\begin{array}{l} P(x) := \{u \in R_+: \min\{x_1, x_2\} \geqslant u\} \\ \text{and} \\ L(x) := \{x \in R_+^2: \min\{x_1, x_2\} \geqslant u\}. \end{array}\right\} \quad (5.5)$$

In this sample, $u = 1 \in \text{Eff } P(1, 2)$, but $(1, 2) \notin \text{Eff } L(1)$. To prove a necessary and sufficient condition for the existence of a joint efficiency production function, introduce:

Definition 5.6: For all $x \geqslant 0, u \geqslant 0$ such that $P(x) \neq \{0\}$ and $L(u)$ nonempty, define:

III:1 $u \geqslant v \geqslant 0$ implies $\text{Eff } L(u) \cap \text{Eff } L(v)$ empty,
III:2 $x \geqslant y \geqslant 0$ implies $\text{Eff } P(x) \cap \text{Eff } P(y)$ empty,
IV:1 $x \in \text{Eff } L(u)$ implies $u \in \text{Eff } P(x)$,
IV:2 $u \in \text{Eff } P(x)$ implies $x \in \text{Eff } L(u)$.

The following relationships are valid for a production technology with inputs and outputs strongly disposable:

Lemma 5.7: [*Färe*] Let $x'' \geqq x'$ imply $P(x'') \subseteqq P(x')$ and $u'' \geqq u' \in P(x)$ imply $u'' \in P(x)$. III:1 $\Leftrightarrow$ IV:1 and III:2 $\Leftrightarrow$ IV:2.

Proof: Assume III:1 holds, but there is an $x \in \text{Eff } L(u), u \geqslant 0$, such that $u \notin \text{Eff } P(x)$. Then there is a $v \geqslant u$ with $v \in \text{Eff } P(x)$ implying that $x \in L(v)$. Since $v \geqslant u$, $L(v) \subseteqq L(u)$ by strong disposability of outputs. Thus $x \in \text{Eff } L(v)$. However, this contradicts III:1.

Conversely, assume IV:1 holds but $x \in \text{Eff } L(u) \cap \text{Eff } L(v), u \geqslant v \geqslant 0$. Then by IV:1, $u \in \text{Eff } P(x)$ and $v \in \text{Eff } P(x)$. However, $u \geqslant v$. This contradicts the definition of output efficiency.

Similar arguments apply to show that III:2 $\Leftrightarrow$ IV:2. QED

The following proposition is a direct consequence of lemmata 5.4 and 5.7.

Proposition 5.8: If inputs and outputs are freely disposable, there exists a joint efficiency production function if and only if III:1 and III:2 hold.

This proposition shows that efficient strict monotonicity of the input and the output correspondences is necessary and sufficient for a joint efficiency production function to exist.

6. On the Equivalence Between the Joint (Isoquant) and the Joint Efficiency Production Functions

In this section, conditions are given such that the above two joint production functions coincide. This task is pursued by showing sufficient conditions for the input and output isoquants to equal the input and output efficient subsets. In general, of course, these sets are not equal, see e.g. (5.5). It should be noted that it is of importance for measuring technical input and output efficiency to know when Isoq $L(u) = \text{Eff } L(u)$ and when Isoq $P(x) = \text{Eff } P(x)$, see *Färe/Lovell* [1978].

Definition 6.1: For all $x \geqslant 0, v \geqslant 0$ such that $P(x) \neq \{0\}$ and $L(u)$ nonempty, define:

V:1 $u \geqslant v \geqslant 0$ imply Isoq $L(u) \cap$ Isoq $L(v)$ empty,
V:2 $x \geqslant y \geqslant 0$ imply Isoq $P(x) \cap$ Isoq $P(y)$ empty,

VI:1 Eff $L(u) =$ Isoq $L(u)$,
VI:2 Eff $P(x) =$ Isoq $P(x)$.

The following relationships can be proven.

Lemma 6.2: V:1 and V:2 imply VI:1 and VI:2.

Proof: It is first shown that V:1 and V:2 imply VI:1. Since in general, Eff $L(u) \subseteqq$ Isoq $L(u)$, it is sufficient to show that Isoq $L(u) \subseteqq$ Eff $L(u)$. Therefore, assume $x \notin$ Eff $L(u)$. If $x \notin L(u)$ then $x \notin$ Isoq $L(u)$ and we are done. Thus assume $x \in L(u)$. Then there is a $y \leqslant x$, $y \in$ Eff $L(u)$. Since Eff $L(u) \subseteqq$ Isoq $L(u)$, $y \in$ Isoq $L(u)$. It now follows from V:1 and lemma 4.5 that $u \in$ Isoq $P(y)$. Hence by V:2, $u \notin$ Isoq $P(x)$. Since V:1 holds, so does I:1 equivalent to II:1, thus $x \notin$ Isoq $L(u)$. This shows that Isoq $L(u) \subseteqq$ Eff $L(u)$.

A similar argument can be used to show that V:1 and V:2 also imply II:2. QED

From this lemma the following proposition is clear, noting that $F(u, x) = 1$ if $(u, x) \notin A$ or $u = 0$ and $P(x) = \{0\}$, see proof of lemma 5.4.

Proposition 6.4: If properties V:1 and V:2 hold then $F(u, x) = E(u, x)$.

It is also of interest to investigate the converse of lemma 6.2. Here one has:

Proposition 6.5: II:2 and VI:1 imply V:2. II:1 and VI:2 imply V:1.

Proof: Let $x \geqslant y \geqslant 0$ and $u \in \text{Isoq}\, P(x)$. It has to be shown that $u \notin \text{Isoq}\, P(y)$. Since $u \in \text{Isoq}\, P(x)$ it follows from II:2 that $x \in \text{Isoq}\, L(u)$. Now $y \leqslant x$ and thus $y \notin L(u)$ by VI:1. Since $y \notin L(u)$ if and only if $u \notin P(y)$, $u \notin \text{Isoq}\, P(y)$, proving the first part.

A similar argument can be used to prove the second part. QED

It is next shown that VI:1 by itself does not imply V:2. Let $P(x) := \{u \in R_+ : \phi(x) \geqq u\}$, where ϕ is given by example (3.3). Then $P(x)$ satisfies P.1, P.2, P.3.S, P.4 and P.5.S and clearly, $\text{Isoq}\, L(u) = \text{Eff}\, L(u)$ for all $u \in R_+$. However, $\text{Isoq}\, P(1\ 1/2) = \text{Isoq}\, P(2)$.

To show that IV:2 does not imply V:1, define $P(x)$ with the use of example (3.4). Then again, $P(x)$ satisfies the required properties and $\text{Isoq}\, P(x) = \text{Eff}\, P(x)$ for all $x \in R_+$. However, $\text{Isoq}\, L(1\ 1/2) = \text{Isoq}\, L(2)$.

References

Al-Ayat, R., and *R. Färe*: On the Existence of Joint Production Functions. Naval Research Logistics Quarterly **26**, 1979, 627–630.

Bol, G., and *O. Moeschlin*: Isoquants of Continuous Production Correspondences. Naval Research Logistics Quarterly **22**, 1975, 391–398.

Färe, R.: Simultaneous Input and Output Efficiency. Operations Research Verfahren, 1980, forthcoming.

Färe, R., and *C.A.K. Lovell*: Measuring the Technical Efficiency of Production. Journal of Economic Theory **19**, 1978, 150–162.

Färe, R., and *D. Primont*: Continuous Enough. Department of Economics. Southern Illinois University, Carbondale 1980.

Shephard, R.W.: Theory of Cost and Production Functions. Princeton 1970.

Quantitative Studies on Production and Prices © Physica-Verlag, Würzburg–Wien, 1983.

A Functional Inequality and the Law of Diminishing Returns

King-Tim Mak [1])

A functional inequality is used in the formulation of a regularity condition on the scaling of production. This functional inequality is characterized and then applied to: (i) deduce a law of diminishing return; (ii) derive a bound on the growth of an open economy.

1. Introduction

Functional equations have always been an important area in mathematics, and have found much applications in the physical sciences. Functional equations have become a useful technique in economic analysis; for example, in the study of aggregation, technical progress, structures of utility functions, price indices and scaling of production, etc. [see *Eichhorn*].

In the study of scaling of production, functional equations are used to formulate notions of homogeneity, homotheticity and semi-homogeneity etc. [again, see *Eichhorn*]. This approach was extended to the formulation of ray-homotheticity [*Färe/Shephard*] and general-homotheticity [*Mak*, 1980]. In this paper, a different approach is taken. A simple functional inequality is proposed as a general condition on scaling, called *regular scaling*. This functional inequality is then characterized. Finally, the notion of regular scaling is applied to: (i) deduce a law of diminishing returns, (ii) derive a bound on the speed of growth of an open economy.

2. Regular Scaling and a Functional Inequality

(2.1) *Definition*: A function $\phi : \mathbf{R}_+^n \rightarrow \mathbf{R}_+$ satisfies *regular scaling* if for every $\lambda \in \mathbf{R}_{++}$ there is a scalar $f(\lambda) \in \mathbf{R}_{++}$ such that

$$\phi(\lambda \cdot x) \leqslant f(\lambda) \cdot \phi(x), \quad x \in \mathbf{R}_+^n. \tag{2.2}$$

Note that the condition of regular scaling is satisfied for homogeneous and sub-homogeneous functions. Furthermore, it is easy to show that the condition also holds for all "polynomials" of the form

[1]) The author is indebted to Professor Wolfgang Eichhorn whose question concerning the size of the class of functions which satisfy regular scaling prompted the writing of this paper. The author is also grateful to Professor Ronald W. Shephard for his many helpful suggestions.

$$\phi(x) = \sum_{k=1}^{K} \left(\prod_{i=1}^{n} a_{ki} x_i^{\alpha_{ki}}\right), \ x \in \mathbf{R}^n_+, K < +\infty,$$

if $\phi(x) > 0$ on $\mathbf{R}^n_{++}$.

To see how large is the class of functions which satisfy the functional inequality (2.2), it is convenient first to restrict the domain of ϕ to $\mathbf{R}_+$. With this specialization, the following function

$$\phi(x) = 3 + \sin x, \ x \in \mathbf{R}_+$$

shows that a regular scaling function may go up and down in value. Hence, it seems useful to delimit the class of functions further since we are mainly interested in production functions. The following properties (they are part of *Shephard's* [1974] weak axioms for production) will be imposed:

ϕ.1 $\phi(0) = 0$.
ϕ.2 $\phi(x)$ is bounded if x is bounded.
ϕ.3 ϕ is non-decreasing (on $\mathbf{R}_+$).
ϕ.4 ϕ is upper-semi-continuous.

In the following, a characterization of the class of $\phi : \mathbf{R}_+ \to \mathbf{R}_+$ satisfying regular scaling is given. But, first note that

$$\text{if } \phi : \mathbf{R}_+ \to \mathbf{R}_+ \text{ satisfies regular scaling and } \phi.1 \text{ but } \phi(x) = 0 \text{ for some } x > 0, \text{ then } \phi \equiv 0. \tag{2.3}$$

When ϕ is taken as a production function, (2.3) may be somewhat too restrictive a condition. However, the properties of a production function already imply much of regular scaling in the following sense:

(2.4) *Proposition*: Suppose $\phi : \mathbf{R}_+ \to \mathbf{R}_+$ satisfies ϕ.2, ϕ.3 and ϕ.4. If $\phi(x)$ is positive over a compact interval $[a, b]$ where $a > 0$, then for each $\lambda \in \mathbf{R}_{++}$ there exists a scalar $f(\lambda) \in \mathbf{R}_{++}$ such that (2.2) holds for all $x \in [a, b]$.

Proof: To use contra-positive argument, suppose for a $\lambda_o \in \mathbf{R}_{++}$ there is an infinite sequence $\{x^k\} \subset [a, b]$ with $\phi(\lambda_o \cdot x^k) / \phi(x^k) \uparrow +\infty$. Since $[a, b]$ is compact, there is a subsequence $\{x^j\} \subset \{x^k\}$ with $\{x^j\} \to x^o \in [a, b]$. Clearly, $\{\lambda_o \cdot x^j\} \to \lambda_o \cdot x^o$. Since $\phi(a) > 0$ by assumption and ϕ.3 and ϕ.4 hold,

$$+\infty = \limsup \frac{\phi(\lambda_o \cdot x^j)}{\phi(x^j)} \leqslant \frac{1}{\phi(a)} \limsup \phi(\lambda_o \cdot x^j) \leqslant \frac{\phi(\lambda_o \cdot x^o)}{\phi(a)}.$$

This contradicts the boundedness assumption ϕ.2. □

Note that if $\phi \not\equiv 0$, say $\phi(z) > 0$, then by the monotonicity of ϕ, ϕ is positive on every interval $[z, y]$ where $y > z$. Hence, every non-trivial production function $\phi : \mathbf{R}_+ \to \mathbf{R}_+$ satisfies regular scaling at least over a certain range.

(2.5) *Theorem*: Suppose $\phi : \mathbf{R}_+ \to \mathbf{R}_+$ satisfies ϕ.1 and ϕ.3. Then ϕ satisfies regular scaling if and only if for some scaling factor $\lambda_o \in \mathbf{R}_{++}$, and $x_o \in \mathbf{R}_{++}$, there is a scalar $\theta \in \mathbf{R}_{++}$ such that

$$\phi(\lambda_o^{j+1} \cdot x_o) \leqslant \theta \cdot \phi(\lambda_o^j \cdot x_o) \qquad \text{for all } j \in \{0, \pm 1, \pm 2, \ldots\}. \tag{2.5.1}$$

Proof: Without loss of generality, we assume $\lambda_o > 1$.

The "only if" part follows directly from the definition of regular scaling.

To show the "if" part, first observe that due to ϕ.1 and ϕ.3, if $\phi(x_o) = 0$, then $\phi \equiv 0$. This is consistent with condition (2.3). Next, note that it suffices to consider only those $x \in \mathbf{R}_{++}$ since ϕ.1 is assumed. Also, $\theta \geqslant 1$ because λ_o is taken to be > 1.

Consider an arbitrary $x \in \mathbf{R}_{++}$. Let $p \in \{0, \pm 1, \pm 2, \ldots\}$ be the largest integer such that $\lambda_o^p \cdot x_o \leqq x$. Since λ_o is assumed to be larger than 1, $\lambda_o \cdot x \in [\lambda_o^p \cdot x_o, \lambda_o^{p+2} \cdot x_o]$. Thus

$$\frac{\phi(\lambda_o \cdot x)}{\phi(x)} \leqq \frac{\phi(\lambda_o^{p+2} \cdot x_o)}{\phi(\lambda_o^p \cdot x_o)} = \frac{\phi(\lambda_o^{p+2} \cdot x_o)}{\phi(\lambda_o^{p+1} \cdot x_o)} \cdot \frac{\phi(\lambda_o^{p+1} \cdot x_o)}{\phi(\lambda_o^p \cdot x_o)} \leqq \theta^2 < +\infty.$$

Note that the above inequality is independent of the arbitrarily chosen x. Hence, by letting $f(\lambda_o) := \theta^2$, the functional inequality (2.2) holds for λ_o.

To show (2.2) holds for all $\lambda \in \mathbf{R}_{++}$, first suppose $\lambda < \lambda_o$. It follows from ϕ.3 that

$$\sup_{x \in \mathbf{R}_{++}} \frac{\phi(\lambda \cdot x)}{\phi(x)} \leqq \sup_{x \in \mathbf{R}_{++}} \frac{\phi(\lambda_o \cdot x)}{\phi(x)} \leqq f(\lambda_o) < +\infty.$$

Hence (2.2) holds for all $\lambda < \lambda_o$. Now, suppose $\lambda > \lambda_o$. For an arbitrary $x \in \mathbf{R}_{++}$, again let p be the largest integer with $\lambda_o^p \cdot x_o \leqq x$. Let m be the smallest integer such that $\lambda \cdot x \leqq \lambda_o^m \cdot x_o$. It may be easily shown that for $\lambda \in [\lambda_o^k, \lambda_o^{k+1})$ (where $k \in \{1, 2, \ldots\}$), the integers p and m associated with x is related by: $m - p \leqslant 2 + k$. Then by ϕ.3 and the regular scaling hypothesis on x_o with scaling factor λ_o

$$\frac{\phi(\lambda \cdot x)}{\phi(x)} \leqq \frac{\phi(\lambda_o^m \cdot x_o)}{\phi(\lambda_o^p \cdot x_o)} \leqq \frac{\theta^{m-p} \cdot \phi(\lambda_o^p \cdot x_o)}{\phi(\lambda_o^p \cdot x_o)} \leqq \theta^{2+k}.$$

Since the inequality on $(m - p)$ depends only on λ and not on the arbitrarily chosen x, by letting $f(\lambda) := \theta^{2+k}$ (where k is the integer depending on λ), the functional inequality (2.2) holds.

□

Theorem (2.5) is quite remarkable in demonstrating that a single scaling factor λ_o and a single sequence of points $\{\ldots, (1/\lambda_o) \cdot x_o, x_o, \lambda_o x_o, \ldots\}$ is necessary and sufficient to test if regular scaling prevails.

With the domain of ϕ taken to be $\mathbf{R}_+^n$, property ϕ.3 (which is the assumption on input disposability when ϕ is a production function) is modified to

ϕ.3′ $\quad \phi(\lambda \cdot x) \geqq \phi(x)$ if $\lambda \geqq 1, x \in \mathbf{R}_+^n$; or

ϕ.3.S $\quad x \geqq y$ implies $\phi(x) \geqq \phi(y)$.

The following propositions are concerned with function ϕ having domain $\mathbf{R}_+^n$. The first two are direct analogs of (2.4) and (2.5), hence proof will be omitted.

(2.6) *Proposition*: Suppose $\phi : \mathbf{R}_+^n \to \mathbf{R}_+$ satisfies $\phi.2$, $\phi.3'$ and $\phi.4$. Let K be a compact subset of $\mathbf{R}_+^n$. If $\mathrm{Inf}\,\{\phi(x) \mid x \in K\} > 0$, then for each $\lambda \in \mathbf{R}_{++}$ there is a scalar $f(\lambda) \in \mathbf{R}_{++}$ such that (2.2) holds for all $x \in K$.

(2.7) *Proposition*: Suppose $\phi : \mathbf{R}_+^n \to \mathbf{R}_+$ satisfies $\phi.1$ and $\phi.3'$. Then ϕ satisfies regular scaling if and only if for some scaling factor $\lambda_o \in \mathbf{R}_{++}$, there is a scalar $\theta \in \mathbf{R}_{++}$ such that

$$\phi\left(\lambda_o^{j+1} \cdot \frac{x}{\|x\|}\right) \leqq \theta \cdot \phi\left(\lambda_o^{j} \cdot \frac{x}{\|x\|}\right)$$

for all $j \in \{0, \pm1, \pm2, \ldots\}$ and each mix $x/\|x\|$.

The above characterization of regular scaling hinges on the existence of a scalar θ for which the functional inequality holds for each mix $x/\|x\|$. The author has not been able to establish conditions under which such a scalar θ exists. However, the following proposition relating the regular scaling of one mix to another is of some interest. First, as notation, for a function $\phi : \mathbf{R}_+^n \to \mathbf{R}_+$ and a mix $x/\|x\| \in \mathbf{R}_{++}^n$, define the function

$$\alpha \in \mathbf{R}_+ \mapsto \phi(\alpha \mid x/\|x\|) := \phi(\alpha \cdot x/\|x\|)\,.$$

(2.8) *Proposition*: If $\phi.3.S$ holds for a function $\phi : \mathbf{R}_+^n \to \mathbf{R}_+$ and for some mix $x/\|x\| > 0$, the function $\phi(\cdot \mid x/\|x\|) \not\equiv 0$ and satisfies regular scaling, then $\phi(\cdot \mid y/\|y\|)$ also satisfies regular scaling for every mix $y/\|y\| > 0$.

Proof: Suppose the mix $x/\|x\| > 0$ has $\phi(\cdot \mid x/\|x\|)$ satisfying regular scaling while the mix $y/\|y\| > 0$ has $\phi(\cdot \mid y/\|y\|)$ violating regular scaling. For each $\beta > 0$ representing an element on the ray $\{\tilde{\beta} \cdot y/\|y\| \mid \tilde{\beta} > 0\}$, define

$$\alpha^1(\beta) := \max\,\{\sigma > 0 \mid \sigma \cdot x/\|x\| \leqq \beta \cdot y/\|y\|\};$$

$$\alpha^2(\beta) := \min\,\{\sigma > 0 \mid \sigma \cdot x/\|x\| \geqq \beta \cdot y/\|y\|\}.$$

Since $x/\|x\| > 0$ and $y/\|y\| > 0$, $\alpha^1(\beta)$ and $\alpha^2(\beta)$ are well defined for $\beta > 0$. Furthermore, it is a simple geometric fact that the ratio $\Delta := \alpha^2(\beta) / \alpha^1(\beta)$ is independent of β.

Since the function $\phi(\cdot \mid y/\|y\|)$ violates regular scaling, there exists $\lambda^* > 1$ with

$$\sup_{\beta > 0} \frac{\phi(\lambda^* \beta \mid y/\|y\|)}{\phi(\beta \mid y/\|y\|)} = +\infty. \tag{2.8.1}$$

Since $\phi(\cdot \mid x/\|x\|)$ satisfies regular scaling, for the scaling factor $\lambda^*\Delta$, there is a scalar $f(\lambda^*\Delta)$ such that

$$\phi(\lambda^*\Delta\sigma \mid x/\|x\|) \leqq f(\lambda^*\Delta) \cdot \phi(\sigma \mid x/\|x\|), \qquad \forall \sigma > 0. \tag{2.8.2}$$

Now (2.8.1) implies the existence of a $\beta^* > 0$ with $\phi(\lambda^*\beta^* \mid y/\|y\|) > f(\lambda^*\Delta) \cdot \phi(\beta^* \mid y/\|y\|)$. But by construction and $\phi.3.S$

$$\phi(\alpha^1(\beta^*) \cdot x/\|x\|) \leqq \phi(\beta^* \cdot y/\|y\|),$$

and

$$\phi(\lambda^*\alpha^2(\beta^*) \cdot x/\|x\|) \geqq \phi(\lambda^*\beta^* \cdot y/\|y\|).$$

Hence letting $\sigma := \alpha^1(\lambda^*)$,

$$\frac{\phi(\lambda^*\Delta\alpha^1(\lambda^*)\cdot x/\|x\|)}{\phi(\alpha^1(\lambda^*)\cdot x/\|x\|)} = \frac{\phi(\lambda^*\alpha^2(\lambda^*)\cdot x/\|x\|)}{\phi(\alpha^1(\lambda^*)\cdot x/\|x\|)} \geqq \frac{\phi(\lambda^*\beta^*\cdot y/\|y\|)}{\phi(\beta^*\cdot y/\|y\|)} > f(\lambda^*\Delta).$$

This contradicts (2.8.2), and the proof is completed. □

3. Application

(A.1) *A Law of Diminishing Returns*

Suppose $\phi : \mathbf{R}^n_+ \to \mathbf{R}_+$ is a production function. The input level sets induced by ϕ are given by

$$u \in \mathbf{R}_+ \mapsto L(u) := \{x \in \mathbf{R}^n_+ \mid \phi(x) \geqq u\}.$$

The technical efficient subsets of the technology are

$$E(u) := \{x \in L(u) \mid y \leqslant x \Rightarrow y \notin L(u)\}, \quad u \in \mathbf{R}_+.$$

In addition to $\phi.1$, $\phi.2$, $\phi.3'$, $\phi.4$, *Shephard's* [1974] weak axioms for production impose the following on the production technology:

$\phi.5$ If $\phi(\bar{x}) \geqq \bar{u} > 0$, then for every $\theta > 0$ there is a $\lambda_\theta > 0$ with $\phi(\lambda_\theta \cdot \bar{x}) \geqq \theta \cdot \bar{u}$.
E $E(u)$ is bounded for each $u \in \mathbf{R}_+$.

An input factor combination $I \subset\subset \{1, \ldots, n\}$ is said to be *essential* for production if $\phi(x) = 0$ for every input x with $x_I = 0$ [2]). An input factor combination $I \subset\subset \{1, \ldots, n\}$ is *strong limitational* for output if for every bound $B \in \mathbf{R}_{++}$ on x_I, $\sup\{\phi(x) \mid \|x_I\| \leqq B\} < +\infty$.

(3.1) *Proposition*: Suppose a production function ϕ satisfies Shephard's weak axioms and regular scaling. Then an input factor combination $I \subset\subset \{1, \ldots, n\}$ is strong limitational for output if and only if it is essential.

The above proposition in general is not true without the assumption of regular scaling [see *Shephard*, 1970]. A proof of the proposition may be found in *Mak* [1982] in this volume.

(A.2) *A Limit on the Growth of an Economy*

Suppose an economy has a single manufactured commodity which is used both as consumption goods (u) and as inputs to production (y). The production technology of this economy is represented by a production function ϕ. The other inputs (q) to production are exogenous to the economy and *primary* (i.e. essential). The stream of exogenous resources is given as $(q_0, q_1, \ldots, q_t, \ldots)$. The initial endownment of the manufactured commodity is $\bar{y}$. The evolution of the economy is characterized by a *program* $\{(u_t, y_t); t = 0, 1, \ldots\}$:

---

[2]) x_I denotes the components $\{x_i, i \in I\}$ of a vector x.

$$u_0 + y_0 = \phi(\bar{y}, q_0),$$
$$u_t + y_t = \phi(y_{t-1}, q_t), \qquad t = 1, 2, \ldots \tag{3.2}$$

Assumption: The production function ϕ of the economy satisfies regular scaling. Moreover, there exists $K \in \mathbf{R}_{++}$ such that the scaling factor $f(\lambda)$ in the functional inequality (2.2) satisfies $f(\lambda) \leqq K\lambda$ for all $\lambda > 0$.

(3.3) *Proposition* [analog to *Radner*, Theorem 2.1]: Suppose the production technology ϕ of an economy satisfies ϕ.2, ϕ.4 and the above Assumption. If for some $\alpha > 0$ the sequence of exogenous primary resources satisfies $\|q_t\| \leqq \alpha^t \|q_0\|$, then given the endowment $\bar{y}$, for every program $\{(u_t, y_t)\}$ which is feasible (i.e. satisfies (3.2)), the sequence $\{(u_t + y_t)/\alpha^t\}$ is bounded.

Proof: Suppose to the contrary that $(u_t + y_t)/\alpha^t$ is not bounded. Then there is a subsequence of indices S such that

$$\lim_{t \in S} \alpha^t / (u_t + y_t) = 0; \text{ and}$$
$$0 < \frac{u_{t-1} + y_{t-1}}{\alpha^{t-1}} \leqq \frac{u_t + y_t}{\alpha^t}, \qquad \text{for all } t \in S. \tag{3.3.1}$$

Denoting $x_t := (y_{t-1}, q_t)$, it follows that

$$\frac{\|x_t\|}{u_t + y_t} \leqq \frac{y_{t-1}}{u_t + y_t} + \frac{\|q_t\|}{u_t + y_t} \leqq \frac{1}{\alpha} + \frac{\alpha^t \|q_0\|}{u_t + y_t}. \tag{3.3.2}$$

Thus, $\{x_t/(u_t + y_t)\}$ is a bounded sequence and has a subsequence (with index set SS) converging to some input x^*.

By rearranging the functional inequality (2.2), it follows from the Assumption that for each t

$$\phi\left(\frac{x_t}{u_t + y_t}\right) \geqq \frac{\phi(x_t)}{f(u_t + y_t)} \geqq \frac{\phi(x_t)}{K \cdot (u_t + y_t)} = \frac{1}{K} > 0$$

where $f(\cdot)$ denotes the appropriate scaling factor. Then, by ϕ.4 (the upper-semi-continuity of ϕ), $\phi(x^*) > 0$. Let $x^* \equiv (y^*, q^*)$. The exogenous resource component q^* of the limit point x^* has

$$\|q^*\| \leqq \limsup_{t \in SS} \frac{\|q_t\|}{u_t + y_t} \leqq \lim_{t \in SS} \frac{\alpha^t \|q_0\|}{u_t + y_t} = 0.$$

This contradicts the fact that exogenous resources are primary (essential). □

Remark: Proposition (3.3) generalizes the cited theorem in *Radner* [1967, Theorem 2.1] in the sense that the technology of the economy is not assumed to be homogeneous. Although a production function was used, the notion of regular scaling may be extended to the case of production correspondences and the result of (3.3) will remain essentially unchanged.

References

Eichhorn, W.: Functional Equations in Economics. Reading, MA, 1978.

Färe, R., and *R.W. Shephard*: Ray-homothetic Production Functions. Econometrica **45**, 1977, 133–146.

Mak, K.: General Homothetic Production Correspondences. ORC 80–7, Operations Research Center, University of California, Berkeley 1980.

– : Dynamic Laws of Returns under Uncertainty. Quantitative Studies on Production and Prices. Ed. by W. Eichhorn et al. Würzburg–Wien 1982 (this volume).

Radner, R.: Dynamic Programming of Economic Growth. Activity Analysis in the Theory of Growth and Planning. Ed. by E. Malinvaud and M.O.L. Bacharach. New York 1967.

Shephard, R.W.: Proof of the Law of Diminishing Returns. Zeitschrift für Nationalökonomie **30**, 1970, 7–34.

– : Semi-homogeneous Production Functions and Scaling of Production. Lecture Notes in Economics and Mathematical Systems 99, Berlin 1974.

Quantitative Studies on Production and Prices © Physica-Verlag, Würzburg–Wien, 1983.

Dynamic Laws of Returns under Uncertainty

King-Tim Mak

An abstract model of dynamic stochastic production correspondences and a model of production policies are outlined. They are used, together with the notion of essentiality of input factors and a new deduction for strong limitationality, to give formulations of dynamic laws of returns under uncertainty. The formulations given serve to indicate the relationship between technology, information and production policy in a stochastic model of production.

1. Introduction

The study of the effect of resource constraints (limitations) on production has always been an important topic in the theory of production. *Turgot* [1967] introduced into economic thought a proposition which has come to be known as the Law of Diminishing Returns at the intensive margin. The original spirit of the law was concerned with the restraint on agricultural production imposed by the scarcity of land. From this viewpoint, the particular formulation of the law in terms of diminishing product increments is nonessential to its significance. In bare form, the issue is: whether a bound on the inputs of a proper subset of factors leads to bounded outputs, when the other inputs may be applied in unlimited amounts. This more basic formulation of the law is described by *Menger* [1936] as an intersecting assertion.

Shephard [1970b] gave a meta-economic proof of an intersecting assertion of the law of returns for production with scalar output, using the theoretical steady state framework of production introduced in *Shephard* [1967, 1970a]. Subsequently, other formulations of the law (both steady state and dynamic, single and multiple products) had been offered along the same line. See *Färe* [1972, 1978, 1980], *Shephard/Färe* [1974] and *Shephard/Färe* [1980, Chapter 3].

This paper extends the formulation of the laws of returns to allow for uncertainty in the production processes. This extension is meaningful since the limitation of resource may be relevant only under certain production environment; depending, for instance, on the weather conditions, machine failures etc. Furthermore, the impact of resource limitation is contingent upon (a) the availability of substitutable resources; (b) the development of alternative production techniques; typically neither contingency is foreseen with certainty.

The formulation of laws of returns under uncertainty to be given brings out to a certain extent the interrelationship between the underlying technology and the information structures of the producers. It is found that for production under uncertainty, the information structures play a role in limiting outputs, leading to a notion of diminishing returns in information.

The organization of this paper is as follows: Both Section 2 and 3 contains background materials. Section 2 outlines a model of stochastic dynamic production correspondences, and a model of production policies. Section 3 introduces the notions necessary for the formulation of laws of returns. Finally, Section 4 formulates some dynamic laws of returns under uncertainty.

2. Stochastic Production Correspondences and Production Policies

Based on *Shephard/Färe's* [1980] framework of dynamic production correspondences, an abstract model of stochastic dynamic production correspondences is given herein. A production technology involving uncertainty is modelled by a mapping (output correspondence):

$$P : (L_\infty)^n_+ \times S \to 2^{(L_\infty)^m_+}; \tag{2.1}$$

where $(L_\infty)^n_+$ and $(L_\infty)^m_+$ are the input and output space respectively, and S is a state space whose members completely characterize the possible states of the production environment. The true state of the production environment is not controllable by any producer and is not known with certainty. More precisely, the state space is taken to be a probability space $(S, \mathbf{S}, \Pr)$. Concretely, the map set $P(x, s)$ is the collection of all technically feasible output histories obtainable from an input history $x \in (L_\infty)^n_+$ if the true state is $s \in S$. Alternatively, the same production technology may be modelled by a mapping (input correspondence) L which is inversely related to P:

$$L : (L_\infty)^m_+ \times S \to 2^{(L_\infty)^n_+}; \quad x \in L(u, s) \quad \text{iff } u \in P(x, s). \tag{2.2}$$

A study of the production correspondences P and L may be found in *Mak* [1981]. Here, for the study of the laws of returns, it suffices to list those axioms imposed on the technology (via the input correspondences L) needed in later sections:

L1 For each state $s \in S$, $L(u = 0, s) = (L_\infty)^n_+$; if $u \neq 0$, $0 \notin L(u, s)$.

L2 For each state $s \in S$, and each infinite sequence of outputs $\{u^k\} \subset (L_\infty)^m_+$ with $\|u^k\| \to +\infty$, $\bigcap_k L(u^k, s)$ is empty.

L3 For each state $s \in S$, every $u \in (L_\infty)^m_+$, $x \in L(u, s)$ implies $\lambda \cdot x \in L(u, s)$ for all $\lambda \in [1, +\infty)$.

L4.1 For each $i \in \{1, \ldots, m\}$, there is an output $u \in U$ with $u_i \neq 0$ and an event $A \in \mathbf{S}$ with $\Pr(A) > 0$ such that $\bigcap_{s \in A} L(u, s) \neq \emptyset$.

L4.2 For each $s \in S$ and each $u \in U$, if $x \in L(u, s)$ and $x \neq 0$, then $L(\theta \cdot u, s) \cap \{\lambda \cdot x \mid \lambda \in \mathbf{R}_+\}$ is not empty, all $\theta \in \mathbf{R}_{++}$.

L5 For each $s \in S$, the graph of the correspondence $u \in (L_\infty)^m_+ \mapsto L_s(u) := L(u, s)$ is closed.

L6.S For each $s \in S$ and each $u \in (L_\infty)^n_+$, $x \in L(u, s)$ and $v \leqq u$ implies $x \in L(v, s)$.

Among all the inputs x which may yield output u under state s, those that are technically efficient are of special interest. Define for all $u \in (L_\infty)_+^m$ and $s \in S$, the *technical efficient subsets:*

$$E(u, s) := \{x \in L(u, s) \mid y \leqslant x \Rightarrow y \notin L(u, s)\}. \tag{2.3}$$

Intuitively speaking, technical efficiency cannot prevail when inputs of infinitely large size are used to yield a finite output. This notion is formalized by the following axiom on the input correspondences:

Axiom E: For each state $s \in S$ and $u \in (L_\infty)_+^m$, $L(u, s)$ is bounded.

Note that for each $s \in S$, the axioms imposed on the correspondence $u \in (L_\infty)_+^n \mapsto L_s(u) \equiv L(u, s)$ is that of *Shephard/Färe* [1980]. Thus, if the true state of nature is known, one may regard the technology as deterministic.

It is to be emphasized that the above model of technology follows the viewpoint of *Shephard* [1967]: – that in a general theory of production, technical feasibility is to be modelled as unconstrained production. Later on, the particularities of a producer (e.g. his short-run plant capacity limit, his organizational structure, etc.) are to be imposed on the underlying technology as constraints.

In a deterministic production model, a production policy may be taken simply as an input-output pair (x, u) with $u \in P(x)$. With the introduction of uncertainty, it is intuitively obvious that any reasonably well-defined production policy must be concerned with any "information" on the unknown production environment. The model of information introduced in the following is that of *Radner* [1968]:

$\boldsymbol{V}$ is a *partition* of $(S, \boldsymbol{S})$ if $\boldsymbol{V} \equiv \{V_\alpha\}$ is a collection of pairwise disjoint element of the σ-algebra $\boldsymbol{S}$ with $\bigcup_\alpha V_\alpha = S$. For two partitions $\boldsymbol{W}$ and $\boldsymbol{V}$ of $(S, \boldsymbol{S})$, $\boldsymbol{W}$ is said to be *as fine as* (or *as informative as*) $\boldsymbol{V}$ if for every $W \in \boldsymbol{W}$ and $V \in \boldsymbol{V}$, either $W \subset V$ or $W \cap V = \emptyset$.

Based on a periodic-review scheme, an *information structure* (of a producer) is an infinite-tuple $\boldsymbol{I} = (\boldsymbol{I}_1, \boldsymbol{I}_2, \ldots, \boldsymbol{I}_t, \ldots)$ where each $\boldsymbol{I}_t$ is a partition of the state space $(S, \boldsymbol{S})$. The "fineness" of the partition $\boldsymbol{I}_t$ indicates how informed a producer is at time t concerning the true state of the production environment: two states s' and s'' with $s', s'' \in I_t \in \boldsymbol{I}_t$ may be interpreted as signaling the same information to the producer (see *Radner* [1968] for a more detailed interpretation). Furthermore, the notion of "as fine as" provides a partial ordering which will be used in Section 4 to define a notion of boundedness of information.

The information structure of a producer, when imposed on the underlying stochastic technology (which is independent of the producer), restricts the production policies (options) open to him. Abstractly, at time t, with the information $\boldsymbol{I}_t$ available, a producer engages in production by taking certain *actions* (procures inputs, allocates resources, commences certain production operations, etc.). Referring to the collection of possible actions as $\boldsymbol{A}$, the choice of action (production decision) over time is a mapping

$$D : S \to \boldsymbol{A} \tag{2.4}$$

$$s \in S \to D(s) \equiv (D_1(s), D_2(s), \ldots, D_t(s), \ldots) \in \boldsymbol{A}$$

where $D_t(s)$ denotes the action at time t. To be consistent with the information available, the following condition on the decision D holds:

$$s', s'' \in I_t \in \mathscr{I}_t \Rightarrow D_t(s') = D_t(s''); \tag{2.5}$$

i.e., the action taken at time t, in essence, depends only on the information available.

Looking at a production unit from a system theoretical point of view, the production decision of a producer is manifested by the input used and the output obtained under the various states of production environment. Explicitly, associated with a decision D are the input and output mappings $\underline{x}$ and $\underline{u}$.

$$(D(s), s) \rightarrow (\underline{x}(s), \underline{u}(s)) \in (L_\infty)_+^n \times (L_\infty)_+^m. \tag{2.6}$$

In order that production is technically feasible, the following condition on the mappings $\underline{x}$ and $\underline{u}$ must hold:

$$\underline{u}(s) \in P(\underline{x}(s), s), \quad (s \in S, D(s) \in A). \tag{2.7}$$

The *information consistency* and the *technical feasibility* conditions (2.5) and (2.7), jointly (via (2.6)) restrict the class of input and output mappings $(\underline{x}, \underline{u})$ which may be meaningfully taken as the consequence of a production policy. When there is no danger of confusion, we shall simply call an $(\underline{x}, \underline{u})$ pair derived via (2.6) from a decision D which is consistent with information structure $\mathscr{I}$ a production policy consistent with $\mathscr{I}$.

The purpose of the above somewhat abstract and sketchy discussion is simply to indicate the role of information in the formulation of production policies. It should be remarked here that there does not appear to be any general characterization of the space of decision A, which is usually specific to individual production technology. Fortunately, in the formulation of laws of returns in Section 4, all that is required is a rather general condition relating the fineness of an information structure $\mathscr{I}$ and the $(\underline{x}, \underline{u})$ pairs consistent with it, without explicit characterization of the decision space A.

3. Essentiality and Limitationality

The purpose of this section is to introduce the notions necessary for the formulation of laws of returns. These notions are stated in a deterministic framework of production (where S may be taken as a singleton). The definitions used are basically modifications of those originally used by *Shephard* [1970b] and extended in the already cited references, so is the deduction for weak-limitationality. A new deduction for strong-limitationality is given. For simplicity of exposition, *the output space is specialized to* $(L_\infty)_+$. *Strong disposal of output, i.e., Axiom L6.S is assumed, and Axiom L5 (closure of the graph* L_S*) is stated with the weak* topology on the input space.*

As indicated in the introduction, we are interested in the effect of the boundedness of input factors on the level of outputs attainable. In a dynamic framework, it is convenient, for production planning purposes, to specify the time periods over which the bounds on inputs are relevant. Let $I \subset\subset \{1, \ldots, n\}$ denote a proper subset of the n input factors. The time period (support) over which an input factor $i \in I$ is limited is taken as an element $S_i \in \Sigma_i$ with a positive measure (Σ_i being the σ-field on $\mathbf{R}_+$ for the i-th input history, see *Shephard/Färe* [1980]). Collectively for the factor group I, the relevant time periods (supports) of the input-bound is denoted by a family

$$SI \equiv \{S_i; S_i \in \Sigma_i, i \in I\}. \tag{3.1}$$

Focusing attention to the support SI, define for a vector input history $x \in (L_\infty)^n_+$,

$$x_{SI} := (\tilde{x}_1, \tilde{x}_2, \ldots, \tilde{x}_n) \in (L_\infty)^n_+ \tag{3.2}$$

where

$$\tilde{x}_i(t) := \begin{cases} 0 & \text{if } t \notin S_i \text{ or } i \notin I; \\ x_i(t) & \text{if } t \in S_i \text{ and } i \in I. \end{cases}$$

The partial ordering of vector inequality may be restricted to apply only on the support SI:

$$x_{SI} \leqq y_{SI} \text{ if and only if } (\tilde{x}_1, \ldots, \tilde{x}_n) \leqq (\tilde{y}_1, \ldots, \tilde{y}_n), \quad x, y \in (L_\infty)^n_+. \tag{3.3}$$

The "truncated" input history x_{SI} defined in (3.2) may be interpreted alternatively as a subvector, i.e., as a component of the original vector x. With this notation, a bound on an input factor group I over a support SI may be modelled by restricting inputs to

$$\{x \in (L_\infty)^n_+ \mid x_{SI} \leqq x^o_{SI}\}, x^o \in (L_\infty)^n_+, x^o_{SI} \geqslant 0 \tag{3.4}$$

where the subvector x^o_{SI} acts as a bound on inputs.

Similarly, let SO (which is an element of the σ-field of the single output history) specify the time period (support) over which bounds on outputs are relevant. The output restricted to SO, denoted u_{SO}, is defined as in (3.2) with analogous definition of a partial ordering as (3.4), and the interpretation as subvectors.

A remark is in order concerning the relationship between SI and SO. Since future inputs cannot affect past outputs, it is necessary to postulate that

$$\begin{aligned} &\text{Inf } \{t \in \mathbf{R}_+ \mid t \in S_i \text{ for some } i \in I\} \leqq \text{Inf } \{t \in \mathbf{R}_+ \mid t \in SO\}; \\ &\text{Sup } \{t \in \mathbf{R}_+ \mid t \in S_i \text{ for some } i \in I\} \leqq \text{Sup } \{t \in \mathbf{R}_+ \mid t \in SO\}. \end{aligned} \tag{3.5}$$

For SI and SO satisfying (3.5), the following formulation of a law of returns is meaningful:

(3.6) Definition: An input factor group $I \subset\subset \{1, \ldots, n\}$ over support SI is *weak-limitational* for outputs over support SO if for every output (reference) subvector $u^o_{SO} > 0$, there exists an input bound $x^o_{SI} \geqslant 0$ such that $L(u) \cap \{x \in (L_\infty)^n_+ \mid x_{SI} \leqq x^o_{SI}\}$ is empty for all output u with $u_{SO} \geqq u^o_{SO}$.

(3.7) Definition: An input factor group $I \subset\subset \{1, \ldots, n\}$ over support SI is *essential* for outputs over support SO if for every output u with $u_{SO} > 0$ and $L(u)$ not empty, $L(u) \cap \{x \in (L_\infty)^n_+ \mid x_{SI} = 0\}$ is empty.

(3.8) Proposition: For an input factor group $I \subset\subset \{1, \ldots, n\}$ over support SI to be weak-limitational over support SO, it is necessary and sufficient that (I, SI) is essential for SO.

Proposition (3.8) may be proved along the same line as the one given in *Shephard/Färe* [1980, Proposition (3.3-1)].

It is conceivable that although (I, SI) is essential for output on SO and x_{SI} is bounded by some x^o_{SI}, via appropriate factor and time substitution, any bound u^o_{SO} on the output may be exceeded. For example, inputs (I, SI) may be needed only to initiate a new production process which otherwise does not require input factors I in its subsequent operations. To formulate a stronger version of limitationality, define:

(3.9) Definition: An input factor group $I \subset\subset \{1, \ldots, n\}$ over support SI is *strong-limitational* for outputs over support SO if for every input bound $x^o_{SI} \geqslant 0$ there exists a bound $u^o_{SO} > 0$ on the output such that $L(u) \cap \{x \mid x_{SI} \leqq x^o_{SI}\}$ is empty for all output u with $u_{SO} \geqq u^o_{SO}$.

In the steady state framework of production, *Färe* [1972, 1980] and *Shephard/Färe* [1974] gave sufficient conditions for strong limitationality. In the following, a further sufficient condition for strong-limitationality is given via a regularity assumption on the scaling of production.

With a single output history, a dynamic production correspondence $P\colon (L_\infty)^n_+ \to 2^{(L_\infty)_+}$ may be represented by the following functionals:

$$\Phi(x \mid w) := \operatorname{Max} \{\alpha \in \mathbf{R}_+ \mid \alpha \cdot w \in P(x)\}, \ x \in (L_\infty)^n_+, w \in (L_\infty)_+, \| w \| = 1. \tag{3.10}$$

Note that because of Axiom L5, $\Phi(\cdot \mid w)$ is well-defined for each w; furthermore, by L4.2, either $\Phi(\cdot \mid w) \equiv 0$ or $\Phi(\cdot \mid w)$ has the range $[0, +\infty)$. In a sense, $\Phi(\cdot \mid w)$ is a production functional which gives the maximal scale of an output "time-pattern" w attainable.

(3.11) Definition: A dynamic production structure $P\colon (L_\infty)^n_+ \to 2^{(L_\infty)_+}$ satisfies *regular scaling* if

(a) there exists a $B \in \mathbf{R}_{++}$ such that for all $x \in (L_\infty)^n_+$ and all output pattern $w \in (L_\infty)_+$, $\| w \| = 1$, defining

$$\sigma^*_x(w) := \begin{cases} 0 & \text{if } \Phi(\alpha \cdot x \mid w) = 0 \text{ for all } \alpha \in \mathbf{R}_{++}, \\ \operatorname{Inf}\{\sigma > 0 \mid \Phi(\sigma \cdot x \mid w) > 0\} & \text{if otherwise;} \end{cases}$$

it is true that $\Phi(\sigma^*_x(w) \cdot x \mid w) \leqq B$; and

(b) for every $\lambda \in \mathbf{R}_{++}$, there exists $\theta_\lambda \in \mathbf{R}_{++}$ such that for each $w \in (L_\infty)_+$, $\| w \| = 1$, the following functional inequality holds:

$$\Phi(\lambda \cdot x \mid w) \leqq \theta_\lambda \cdot \Phi(x \mid w) \quad \text{for all } x \in (L_\infty)^n_+ \text{ with } \Phi(x \mid w) > 0. \tag{3.12}$$

It is important to note that regular scaling allows the output sets $P(\lambda \cdot x)$ to span different output time patterns as λ changes; as would be the case where increased inputs allows for more production possibilities.

Regular scaling appears to be a rather mild and reasonable regularity condition on a production technology. The class of functionals which satisfy the functional inequality (3.12) appears to be rather large. Clearly, homogeneous and sub-homogeneous functionals satisfy (3.12). In fact, the postulate of regular scaling was inspired by *Eichhorn* [1968] who used the homogeneity of production functions to derive the law of diminishing incremental returns over the whole range of inputs. This class of functional is characterized in *Mak* [1982]. Here, regular scaling is used to establish:

(3.13) Proposition: Suppose a production structure satisfies regular scaling, then an input factor group $I \subset\subset \{1, \ldots, n\}$ over support SI is strong-limitational for outputs over support SO if (I, SI) is essential for outputs over SO.

The reasoning underlying this proposition is actually very simple: – if an input bound x^o_{SI} does not bound outputs on SO, factors I on SI must be "infinitely substitutable" by the other factors on SI and other input supports. Then because of the assumed boundedness of the efficient subsets (Axiom E in Section 2), this is possible only if (I, SI) is not essential for outputs on SO.

Proof of Proposition (3.13)

Suppose (I, SI) is not strong-limitational for SO. Then there exists an input bound $x^o_{SI} \geqslant 0$ such that for all output bound $u^o_{SO} > 0$, there is an input x with $x_{SI} \leqq x^o_{SI}$ and an output $u \in P(x)$ with $u_{SO} \geqq u^o_{SO}$. In particular, consider a sequence of output bounds $\{v^k := \alpha^k \cdot 1_{SO}\}$ where $\alpha^k \geqq 1$ and $\{\alpha^k\} \to +\infty$. Let $\{x^k\}$ and $\{u^k\}$ be sequences of inputs and outputs such that $x^k_{SI} \leqq x^o_{SI}$, $u^k \in P(x^k)$ and $u^k_{SO} \geqq v^k$. Considering the indicator function 1_{SO} as an output history, it follows from L6.S that $x^k \in L(1_{SO})$ for all k. Define an infinite sequence of scalars by

$$\gamma^k := \min \{\alpha \in \mathbf{R}_+ \mid \alpha \cdot x^k \in L(1_{SO})\}, \qquad k = 1, 2, \ldots$$

The γ^k's are well-defined because of Axiom L5 and L4.2.

Claim: There exists a scalar $K \geqslant 1$ such that $\Phi(\gamma^k \cdot x^k \mid 1_{SO}) \leqq K$ for all index k. To prove this claim, first note that by construction, $\Phi(\gamma^k \cdot x^k \mid 1_{SO}) \geqq 1$. If $\Phi(\gamma^k \cdot x^k \mid 1_{SO}) = 1$ for all k, then the claim is trivially true by taking K to be 1. So, let $\Phi(\gamma^k \cdot x^k \mid 1_{SO}) > 1$ for some indices. Consider arbitrarily such an index k. Clearly, either there exists $\theta \in (0, 1)$ with $\Phi(\theta\gamma^k \cdot x^k \mid 1_{SO}) \in (0, 1)$; i.e., $\gamma^k \cdot x^k$ is a point of discontinuity of $\Phi(\cdot \mid 1_{SO})$ along the ray $\{\lambda \cdot x^k \mid \lambda \geqslant 0\}$ but not a first jump point to a positive scaling of 1_{SO}; or $\gamma^k \cdot x^k$ is in fact a first jump point.

Now use contra-positive argument: Suppose there does not exist a positive scalar K such that $\Phi(\gamma^k \cdot x^k \mid 1_{SO}) \leqq K$ for all k. Then there is an infinite subsequence

$\{\gamma^j \cdot x^j\} \subset \{\gamma^k \cdot x^k\}$, such that $\{\Phi(\gamma^j \cdot x^j \mid 1_{SO})\}$ diverges to $+\infty$. If in the sequence $\{\gamma^j \cdot x^j\}$, there is an infinite subsequence of first jump points, then condition (3.11a) is violated. On the other hand, if such a subsequence does not exist, one may as well assume none of the points $\gamma^j \cdot x^j$ is a first jump point. Fix an arbitrary $\lambda^* \in (0, 1)$. Since $\gamma^j \cdot x^j$ is not a first jump point, there exists an input vector $z^j \in \{\lambda \cdot x^j \mid \lambda \in [\lambda^* \gamma^j, \gamma^j)\}$ such that $1 > \Phi(z^j \mid 1_{SO}) > 0$. Consider the sequence $\{z^j\}$ thus chosen. Because $\lambda^* \in (0, 1)$, $\gamma^j \leqq 1$ for all j by definition, and $\Phi(\cdot \mid 1_{SO})$ is monotone along rays (Axiom L3).

$$\frac{\Phi(z^j/\lambda^* \mid 1_{SO})}{\Phi(z^j \mid 1_{SO})} \geqq \frac{\Phi(\gamma^j \cdot x^j \mid 1_{SO})}{\Phi(z^j \mid 1_{SO})} \geqq \Phi(\gamma^j \cdot x^j \mid 1_{SO}) \xrightarrow{j} +\infty.$$

Hence condition (3.11b) does not hold for the scaling factor $1/\lambda^*$. This contradicts the hypothesis of regular scaling, thus establishing the claim.

Next, it is shown that $\operatorname{Inf}\{\gamma^k\} = 0$. Suppose otherwise, then there exists a $\epsilon > 0$ such that $\gamma^k \geqq \epsilon$ for all k. Then by the monotonicity of $\Phi(\cdot \mid 1_{SO})$ along rays and the hypothesis of regular scaling

$$0 < \Phi(x^k \mid 1_{SO}) = \Phi\left(\frac{1}{\gamma^k} \cdot \gamma^k \cdot x^k \mid 1_{SO}\right) \leqq \Phi\left(\frac{1}{\epsilon} \cdot \gamma^k \cdot x^k \mid 1_{SO}\right)$$

$$\leqq \theta_{1/\epsilon} \cdot \Phi(\gamma^k \cdot x^k) \leqq \theta_{1/\epsilon} \cdot K < +\infty$$

where K is the bound on $\{\Phi(\gamma^k \cdot x^k \mid 1_{SO})\}$ established in the earlier claim. This contradicts the original assumption that $\{\Phi(x^k \mid 1_{SO})\} \to +\infty$.

Since $\operatorname{Inf}\{\gamma^k\} = 0$, there is a subsequence $\{\gamma^p\} \subset \{\gamma^k\}$ with $\{\gamma^p\} \downarrow 0$. For each index p, $\gamma^p \cdot x^p \in L(1_{SO})$, hence an input $z^p \leqq \gamma^p \cdot x^p$ may be constructed such that z^p belongs to the efficient subset $E(1_{SO})$ [for detail, see *Mak*, 1981a]. So by construction, $z^p_{SI} \leqq \gamma^p \cdot x^p_{SI}$. Since $\{\gamma^p\} \downarrow 0$, it is seen that

$$\operatorname{Inf}\{\|z - y\| \mid z \in \overline{E(1_{SO})^*}, x \in (L_\infty)^n_+ \text{ with } x_{SI} = 0\} = 0.$$

Since $E(1_{SO})$ is bounded by assumption (Axiom E), its weak* closure is weak* compact. Furthermore, since the sup-norm $\|\cdot\|$ is lower-semi-continuous with respect to the weak* topology on $(L_\infty)^n_+$, [refer to *Yosida*, Thm. 9, p. 125], it follows that the infimum above is actually attained, implying that $\overline{E(1_{SO})^*} \cap \{x \in (L_\infty)^n_+ \mid x_{SI} = 0\} \neq \emptyset$. Finally, by Axiom L5 as stated under the weak* topology, $\overline{E(1_{SO})^*} \subset L(1_{SO})$. Hence (I, SI) cannot be essential for SO, completing the contra-positive proof. □

4. Laws of Returns under Uncertainty

As in the deterministic case, the issue is whether a bound on some input factors will limit outputs. In a deterministic model of production, since every feasible input-output combination (x, u) with $u \in P(x)$ may be regarded as the manifestation (from a system point of view) of some production policy, laws of returns may be deduced strictly from the properties of the deterministic technology without explicit mention of production policies. With the introduction of uncertainty, the attainability of outputs is a direct consequence of the production policy of the producers. Thus, there is the question of the role played by information structures on the laws of returns.

The consistency condition (2.5) clearly indicates that, broadly speaking, an information structure acts as a constraint on the choice of production decisions. In this sense, it may be taken as a bound on the information available for formulating production policies.

One may be interested only in the information available at certain time points; for instance, it may be important to know the availability of new production techniques when investment decisions have to be made on new plant capacities. Consider a subset $T \subset \{1, 2, \ldots\}$ of decision time points; and let

$$I_T^o \equiv \{I_t^o\}_{t \in T}$$

denote the "restriction" of a particular information structure I^o to the set T. A bound on information is formulated by using the partial ordering:

$$I_T \precsim I_T^o \text{ if } I_t^o \text{ is as fine as } I_t \text{ for all } t \in T. \tag{4.1}$$

When the information structure I of a producer is such that $I_T \precsim I_T^o$, his information is said to be limited by I_T^o over the time period T. Later on, the special case of "perfect information" I_T^p defined by:

$$I_t \text{ is a singleton for all } I_t \in I_t^p, \; (t \in T);$$

is useful. Note that every information structure I has $I_T \precsim I_T^p$; i.e., bounded by I_T^p over T.

With respect to the input and output mappings, $\underline{x}$ and $\underline{u}$, associated with a production policy, the input support SI (for factors I) and the output support SO are defined as in the deterministic case; and for each state s, the subvectors $\underline{x}_{SI}(s)$, $\underline{u}_{SI}(s)$ have the same meaning as in (3.2). Since in general, limitation on input depends on the true state of nature, bounds on input and output should be taken as functions, respectively:

$$\begin{aligned} &s \in S \mapsto \underline{x}_{SI}^o(s); \\ &s \in S \mapsto \underline{u}_{SI}^o(s); \end{aligned} \tag{4.2}$$

where for each state $s \in S$, the partial ordering (3.3) of subvectors is valid. However, for simplicity, henceforth the input bound $\underline{x}_{SI}^o(\cdot)$ will be taken to be a constant function over S, and denoted by its value x_{SI}^o when an input bound is to be specified for the formulation of the laws of returns.

With the definition of the time points T, supports SI and SO, bounds I_T^o, $x_{SI}^o(\cdot)$ and $u_{SO}^o(\cdot)$, the following notion of limitationality on output is meaningful for a state $s^* \in S$:

(4.3) There exists an output bound $u_{SO}^o > 0$ such that limited by the information I_T^o, there does not exist an information structure I with $I_T \precsim I_T^o$ under which a production policy may be formulated (i.e., (2.5) holds) and whose associated (via (2.6)) input and output mapping $s \mapsto (\underline{x}(s), \underline{u}(s))$ not only satisfies technical feasibility (2.7), but also has $\underline{x}_{SI}(s) \equiv (\underline{x}(s))_{SI} \leqslant x^o_{SI}$, all $s \in S$; and the output at state s^* is such that $\underline{u}_{SO}(s^*) \equiv (\underline{u}(s^*))_{SO} \geqq u^o_{SO}$.

The above formulation may be interpreted as follows: – as long as the available information is bounded by I^o_T, then irrespective of possible availability of better (finer) information at other times (i.e., time points not in the set T), no production policy may be formulated such that the resultant input employed is bounded by x^o_{SO} while the output bound u^o_{SO} is exceeded if the true state of nature is s^*, even though there is no limitation on the increased application of other inputs (factors not in I), or increased application of inputs at other times (outside support SI). That is, the unrestricted increased application of inputs and the solicitation of finer information jointly have, in the sense of Menger's intersecting assertion, diminishing returns [*Menger*, 1954].

Corresponding to the notion of strong and weak limitationality in the deterministic case, laws of returns under uncertainty may be formulated by either one of the following:

F1 For each bound $x^o_{SI} \geqslant 0$ on (I, SI) and each bound I^o_T on information, (4.3) holds.

F2 There exists a bound $x^o_{SI} \geqslant 0$ on (I, SI) such that for each bound I^o_T on information, (4.3) holds.

F3 For each bound I^o_T on information, there exists a bound $x^o_{SI} \geqslant 0$ on (I, SI) such that (4.3) holds.

F4 There exists a bound I^o_T on information such that for each bound $x^o_{SI} \geqslant 0$ on (I, SI), (4.3) holds.

F5 For each bound $x^o_{SI} \geqslant 0$ on (I, SI), there exists a bound I^o_T on information such that (4.3) holds.

F6 There exists a bound $x^o_{SI} \geqslant 0$ on (I, SI) and a bound I^o_T on information such that (4.3) holds.

Note that F1 to F6 are related by:

$$\begin{array}{ccccccc} & \nearrow & F2 & \Rightarrow & F3 & \searrow & \\ F1 & & & & & & F6 \\ & \searrow & F4 & \Rightarrow & F5 & \nearrow & \end{array}$$

The interplay between the bounds on information and the bounds on inputs will be made clear later by the characterization of F1 to F6. Offhandedly, by observing that an information bound I^o_T may be as fine as the perfect information I^p_T, and the input bound x^o_{SI} may be arbitrarily large, one may see intuitively that in F2 and F3, it is the bound on the inputs; while in F4 and F5 it is the bound on information; which plays the key role in limiting outputs.

To give alternative characterization of F1 to F6, the following will be assumed:

(A.1) output support SO is a finite subset of $\{1, 2, \ldots\}$.

As a consequence of (A.1) and the reasoning of (3.5), supports T and SI are also finite.

With respect to production policies, the following condition is imposed:

(A.2) If there is perfect information at all times (i.e., $T \equiv \{1, 2, \ldots\}$ and $I \equiv I_T^p$), then for each state $s \in S$ and input-output pair $(x_s, u_s) \in (L_\infty)_+^n \times (L_\infty)_+$ with $u_s \in P(x_s, s)$, there exists a production policy whose associated input and output mappings has $\underline{x}(s) = x_s$ and $\underline{u}(s) = u_s$.

The above condition merely asserts that with perfect information, a producer may plan for production as in the deterministic case. The next two definitions address the case where perfect information is not available.

(4.4) Definition: Two states s' and s'' are *indistinguishable* under I_T^o if for each $t \in T$ there is an element I_t in I_T^o which contains both s' and s''.

(4.5) Definition: Information over time points T on $s', s'' \in S$ is *instrumental* for outputs over SO if for every information structure I^o for which s' and s'' are indistinguishable under its restriction I_T^o to T, there exists a bound $B \in \mathbf{R}_{++}$ such that all production policy consistent with the information structure I^o (i.e., the decision choice satisfies (2.5)) results in an output mapping $s \in S \mapsto \underline{u}(s)$ (via (2.6)) satisfying $\|\underline{u}_{SO}(s') - \underline{u}_{SO}(s'')\| \leqq B$.

The above definition models the situation where due to lack of sufficiently "timely" information (information rich enough to distinguish state s' from s''), the choice of production policy is so restricted that the resulting outputs under state s' and s'' cannot be of arbitrary large difference. This is the condition relating the fineness of information structure I and the production policy $(\underline{x}, \underline{u})$ consistent with it alluded to at the end of Section 2. This condition will be used in the next proposition to capture the following production phenomenon: Given that inputs (I, SI) are bounded by x_{SI}^o. Suppose under this input bound, it is still technically feasible to attain arbitrary large output (on SO) if the state of nature is s''; but only bounded output is technically possible if the state is s'. If the true state of nature is known with certainty to be s'', then by (A.2), appropriate production policies may be chosen so that arbitrary large output may be attained. On the other hand, if the information available is not fine enough to distinguish s' from s'', then it may be the case that to guarantee the satisfaction of the input bound under both states s' and s'', the choice of consistent policies are so restricted that the output obtained when the true state is actually s'' is bounded as a consequence.

With all the preliminary notions defined, the following proposition gives the characterization of F1 to F6:

(4.6) Proposition: Suppose a stochastic production technology satisfies the stochastic axioms L1 to L5, E and L6.S; and Assumptions (A.1) and (A.2) are enforced. Consider a state $s^* \in S$:

(i) If the output correspondences $x \mapsto P_{s^*}(x) := P(x, s^*)$ satisfies regular scaling (3.11), then F1 is equivalent to : – (I, SI) is essential for SO under s^*; i.e., (3.7) holds for the correspondences P_{s^*}.

(ii) F2 is equivalent to : – (I, SI) is essential for SO under s^*.

(iii) F3 is equivalent to : – for each bound I_T^o on the information, there exists a state s' which is indistinguishable from s^* under I_T^o, information on s' and s^* is instrumental for SO, and (I, SI) is essential for SO under s'.

(iv) Suppose the output correspondences $x \mapsto P_s(x) := P(x, s)$ satisfy regular scaling for each $s \in S$, then F4 is equivalent to: – there exists a bound I_T^o on information under which there exists a state s' indistinguishable from s^*, information on s' and s^* is instrumental for SO, and (I, SI) is essential for SO under s'.

(v) and (vi) F5 (F6) is equivalent to : – for every bound $x_{SI}^o \geqslant 0$ on (I, SI) (there exists a bound $x_{SI}^o \geqslant 0$ on (I, SI)), there exists a bound I_T^o on information under which exists a state s' indistinguishable from s^*, information on s' and s^* is instrumental for SO and there exists an output bound u_{SO}^o such that $u \notin P(x, s')$ for all input x with $x_{SI} \leqq x_{SI}^o$ and output u with $u_{SO} \geqq u_{SO}^o$.

Proof:

(i) Suppose (I, SI) is essential for SO under s^* and the output correspondence P_{s^*} satisfies regular scaling, then by Proposition (3.13) there exists for each input bound x_{SI}^o an output bound $u_{SO}^o > 0$ such that $x_{SI} \leqq x_{SI}^o$ implies $u \notin P(x, s^*)$ if $u_{SO} \geqq u_{SO}^o$. Then F1 follows from the technical feasibility condition (2.7). To show the converse, suppose (I, SI) is not essential for SO under s^*. Then there is an input $\bar{x}$ with $\bar{x}_{SI} = 0$ and output $\bar{u} \in P(\bar{x}, s^*)$ with $\bar{u}_{SO} > 0$. Then by the scaling Axiom L4.2 and (A.1), for every bound $u_{SO}^o > 0$ there is a scalar θ such that $(\theta \cdot \bar{u})_{SO} \geqq u_{SO}^o$ and a scalar λ_θ such that $\theta \cdot \bar{u} \in P(\lambda_\theta \cdot \bar{x}, s^*)$. Finally, with I_T^o taken as the perfect information I_T^p, (A.2) implies F1 does not hold.

(ii) May be established as in (i) using Proposition (3.8).

(iii) Suppose (I, SI) is essential for SO under s'. Then by (2.7) and Proposition (3.8), there exists a bound $x_{SI}^o \geqslant 0$ on (I, SI) and a bound $u_{SO}^o > 0$ such that every production policy has $\underline{u}(s') \ngeq u_{SO}^o$. If s' is indistinguishable from s^* and information on s' and s^* is instrumental for outputs on SO, then F3 follows directly. Conversely, assume contra-positively that there is an information bound I_T^o under which no state s' which is indistinguishable from s^* satisfies either: (a) (I, SI) essential for SO under s'; or (b) information on s' and s^* is instrumental for SO. If such an I_T^o exists, clearly one may as well take $I_T^o \equiv I_T^p$. Since s^* is indistinguishable from itself and s^* and itself is instrumental for SO, (I, SI) is not essential for SO under s^*. Then as argued in the latter part of (i), F3 does not hold.

(iv), (v) and (vi) may be established using similar arguments. In (iv), Proposition (3.13) is used to establish the existence of an output bound. In (v), the existence of output bound is assumed directly. That (v) is a weaker assertion than (iv) is due to the possibility that if the input bound x_{SI}^o is relaxed (i.e., made larger), a less fine I_T^o bound on information may be needed to locate a state s' under which output is limited. □

Formulations F1 to F6, of course, are not the only possible formulations of laws of returns under uncertainty. In fact, they are the simplest formulations possible. Formulations may be extended to the cases: (a) bounds are expressed in terms of norms; (b) output bounds u^o_{SO} are taken as functions on S instead of focusing attention on a state s^*; (c) input bounds x^o_{SI} are taken as functions; etc. However, it is hoped that the formulations offered here have succeeded in indicating the complexity of dynamic production under uncertainty, in particular the interplay between information, technology and production policies.

References

Eichhorn, W.: Deduktion der Ertragsgesetze aus Prämissen. Zeitschrift für Nationalökonomie **28**, 1968, 191–205.

– : Functional Equations in Economics. Reading, MA, 1978.

Färe, R.: Strong Limitationality of Essential Proper Subsets of Factors of Production. Zeitschrift für Nationalökonomie **32**, 1972, 417–424.

– : A Dynamic Formulation of the Law of Diminishing Returns. Symposium on Production Theory. Stockholm 1978.

– : Laws of Diminishing Returns. Vol. 176, Lecture Notes in Economics and Mathematical Systems. Berlin 1980.

Mak, K.: A Stochastic Theory of Production Correspondences. ORC 81-6, Operations Research Center, University of California, Berkeley, 1981.

– : A Functional Inequality, with Applications to Production Theory. Quantitative Studies on Production and Prices. Ed. by W. Eichhorn et al. Würzburg–Wien 1982 (this volume).

Menger, K.: Bemerkungen zu den Ertragsgesetzen. Zeitschrift für Nationalökonomie **7**, 1936, 25–56.

– : Weitere Bemerkungen zu den Ertragsgesetzen. Zeitschrift für Nationalökonomie 7, 1936, 388–397.

– : The Logic of the Laws of Returns. A Study in Metaeconomics. Economic Activity Analysis. Ed. by O. Morgenstern. New York 1954.

Radner, R.: Competitive Equilibrium Under Uncertainty. Econometrica **36**, 1968, 31–58.

Shephard, R.W.: The Notion of a Production Function. Unternehmensforschung **11**, 1967, 209–232.

– : Theory of Cost and Production Functions. Princeton, N.J., 1970a.

– : Proof of the Law of Diminishing Returns. Zeitschrift für Nationalökonomie **30**, 1970b, 7–34.

Shephard, R.W., and *R. Färe*: The Law of Diminishing Returns. Zeitschrift für Nationalökonomie **34**, 1974, 69–90.

– : Dynamic Theory of Production Correspondences. Vol. 50, Mathematical Systems in Economics. Meisenheim 1980.

Turgot, A.R.J.: Sur le Memoire de M. de Saint-Puruvy. Oeuvres de Turgot. Ed. by Daire, Vol. 1, Paris 1967, 418–483.

Yosida, K.: Functional Analysis. 2nd Ed. Berlin 1968.

References

Quantitative Studies on Production and Prices

Analysis and Construction of Uniformly Compact Production Correspondences

Wolfgang Teusch

This paper is concerned with stepwise construction methods of production correspondences and the adaptability of these methods to the estimation of production models. As to the structure of production technologies used here, we shall closely follow Shephard [1970, 1974].

1. Introduction

According to our point of view, the complexity of a technology set is in general prohibitive for its global and at the same time transparent description. But while the technology set as a whole may be highly complex, it may have constituent parts which have a relatively simple structure and which allow for descriptions by quite transparent production models. Following this line of thought, a closer analysis of the question as to how the production of the whole technology set relates to the production models of the parts would be very rewarding.

The following inquiry into this idea has been inspired by the composition of a linear activity model. Here, given a finite set D of activities (the parts), the global model of the technology set is connected to the parts via two operations: nonnegative scalar multiplication and addition of vectors.

In this paper, some (simple) production correspondences play the role of the activities in D, and we define three construction methods – the so-called maximal closure, the convolution (comparable to addition of vectors) and the saturation (comparable to nonnegative scalar multiplication). As we shall see later on, the assumption of uniformly compact production correspondences will play an important role at this point.

In section 2, some notation relating to special correspondences is introduced and the three methods for the construction of new correspondences (maximal closure, convolution and saturation) are rigorously defined. In addition, we derive results concerning uniformly compact correspondences which prove useful for the subsequent sections, and we establish a connection to strictly bounded correspondences, which were introduced by *Afriat* [1974] into economic literature.

In section 3, we analyse uniformly compact output correspondences. It is proven that output correspondences which describe the production of a single good or which satisfy the axiom of strong disposability of inputs, are always uniformly compact. Furthermore, an equivalent characterization of an uniformly compact output correspondence in terms of the saturation of its inverse (input) correspondence is given.

The consideration of the saturation of an input correspondence has been inspired by *Färe* [1975], who introduced this concept into economic analysis in the case of the production of a single good.

In section 4, we prove that the maximal closure of input (output) correspondences is an input (output) correspondence. In the case where only a single good is produced, a formula for the production function corresponding to a maximal closure is developed.

Section 5 deals with the convolution of production correspondences. This operation was introduced by *Ruys* [1974] under more restrictive assumptions than ours. In this section, the main result is that the convolution of $2 \leqq k$ output correspondences is an output correspondence if, and only if, the given k output correspondences are uniformly compact. In addition, we analyse the convolution of input correspondences and, in the single output case, we derive a formula for the production function corresponding to a convolution. A comparison of the convolution and the maximal closure concludes this section.

In section 6, we estimate input correspondences and production functions satisfying four different sets of regularity conditions on the basis of a given finite data set of output vectors and corresponding input vectors. As estimation methods we apply the maximal closure and the convolution. The approaches we suggest are nonparametric in the sense that parametric production models are not used for the estimation procedure. Hence, our method is related to the approaches of *Afriat* [1972], *Diewert/Parkan* [1982], *Farrell* [1957] and *Hanoch/Rothschild* [1972]. The work of these authors and the present study differ in (i) the kind of the estimation procedure, (ii) the production model to be estimated, and (iii) the use of regularity conditions.

ad (i): According to our point of view presented at the beginning of this section, we carry out the estimation procedure in two steps. In the first step, we derive for each observation of the data set an input correspondence. The second step consists of applying the maximal closure or the convolution; the choice of either one depends upon which regularity conditions are assumed. Whereas the above authors – except for *Hanoch/Rothschild* [1972] – estimate the production model in a global manner, our stepwise estimation procedure gives more insight into the genesis and the structure of a technology set.

ad (ii): As stated before, we estimate only production correspondences of Shephard's type. In contrast, the above authors use more general models, which makes estimation easier. On the other hand, the price for using Shephard's production models is the restriction that we can only estimate linear homogeneous production correspondences. Except for *Hanoch/Rothschild* [1972], the other studies estimate production functions, even in the multiple output case, whereas in this last case we estimate production correspondences.

ad (iii): As in *Farrell* [1957] and partly also in *Afriat* [1972], the underlying principle here is to estimate a production correspondence so that each observation belongs to the technology set and is as near to the boundary of the technology set as possible. In contrast, *Diewert/Parkan* [1982] and *Hanoch/Rothschild* [1972] always assume all the data to be on the boundary of the estimated technology set. Furthermore, the only properties which will be the common core of our regularity conditions are the properties of linear homogeneity and strong disposability of inputs. The sets of regularity conditions differ according to whether we assume the technology set to be convex and/or to satisfy strong disposability of outputs or not. This distinguishes our analysis from the work of *Hanoch/ Rothschild* [1972] who assume convexity from the outset.

2. Preliminaries

This section contains some definitions and results concerning correspondences (point-to-set mappings) and deals particularly with production correspondences and production functions, suggested by *Shephard* [1970]. In the following let X, Y be metric spaces.

Definition 2.1: Let $F: X \to Y$ be a correspondence.

(i) F is said to be *regular*, if $F(x) \neq \emptyset$ for all $x \in X$.
(ii) F is called *closed*, if Graph $(F) := \{(x, y) \in X \times Y \mid y \in F(x)\}$ is a closed subset of $X \times Y$.
(iii) F is said to be *uniformly compact* [for the notion cp. *Hogan*, p. 594], if for each $x \in X$ there is a neighbourhood U of x, such that $\overline{F(U)}$ [1]) is compact.
(iv) In the case where X and Y are contained in $\mathbf{R}^n$ and $\mathbf{R}^m$ respectively, F is called *strictly bounded* [cf. *Afriat*, 1974, p. 13], if $F(B)$ is a bounded subset of Y for all bounded subsets B of X.

In the following two theorems, the interrelations between closed, uniformly compact and strictly bounded correspondences will be established. They are very useful for the analysis in the subsequent sections.

Theorem 2.1:

(i) Let $F: X \to Y$ be a closed correspondence. If $K \subset X$ is compact, then $F(K)$ is a closed subset of Y.
(ii) If $F: X \to Y$ is a closed uniformly compact correspondence, then $F(K)$ is compact for all compact subsets K of X.

Proof: Let $K \subset X$ be a compact subset of X.

ad (i): Let $\{y_\nu\} \subset F(K)$ be a sequence converging to y_0. We have points k_ν in K satisfying $y_\nu \in F(k_\nu)$ for all $\nu \in \mathbf{N}$. The compactness of K leads to a convergent subsequence $\{l_\nu\}$ of $\{k_\nu\}$ with a limit k_0 in K. Since F is closed the point (k_0, y_0) lies in Graph (F). Therefore $y_0 \in F(k_0) \subset F(K)$.

ad (ii): For each k in K there is a neighbourhood $U(k)$ such that $\overline{F(U(k))}$ is compact. The compactness of K accordingly assures us of a finite number of points $k_1, \dots, k_n$ in K such that K is contained in $\bigcup_{i=1}^{n} U_i$, where $U_i := U(k_i)$. Hence $F(K) \subset F(\bigcup_{i=1}^{n} U_i) \subset \bigcup_{i=1}^{n} \overline{F(U_i)}$. In this relation the last set is compact, by as-

---

[1]) For $B \subset Y$ $\bar{B}$ denotes the closure of B.

sumption. According to part (i) $F(K)$ is closed. Since a closed subset of a compact set is compact, $F(K)$ therefore is compact, as was to be proved. □

Theorem 2.2: Let X, Y be closed subsets of $\mathbf{R}^n$, $\mathbf{R}^m$ respectively. A correspondence $F: X \to Y$ is uniformly compact if, and only if, F is strictly bounded.

Proof: Let B a bounded subset of X. Consequently $K := \bar{B}$ is compact. Since $F(B) \subset F(K)$, $F(B)$ is bounded, because by Theorem 2.1 $F(K)$ is compact. To prove the converse, let $x \in X$. Clearly, a bounded neighbourhood U of x exists. By hypothesis $F(U)$ is bounded. Therefore, $\overline{F(U)}$ is compact, and the theorem is established. □

In the later sections we shall be concerned with some special correspondences which we shall now define. Let $\mathbf{R}^n_+ := \{x \in \mathbf{R}^n \mid x \geqq 0\}$.

Definition 2.2: Let $F, F_1, \ldots, F_k: \mathbf{R}^m_+ \to \mathbf{R}^n_+$ be correspondences.

(i) F is called (positively) *linearly homogeneous*, if $F(\lambda x) = \lambda F(x)$ for all $x \in \mathbf{R}^m_+$ and $\lambda > 0$.

(ii) F is said to be *concave*, if $\lambda F(x) + (1-\lambda) F(w) \subset F(\lambda x + (1-\lambda) w)$ for all $x, w \in \mathbf{R}^m_+$, $0 \leqq \lambda \leqq 1$.

(iii) The correspondence $F_s: \mathbf{R}^m_+ \to \mathbf{R}^n_+$, defined by $F_s(x) := F(x) + \mathbf{R}^n_+$ [2]), is called the *saturation of F*.

(iv) The correspondence $mx(F_1, \ldots, F_k): \mathbf{R}^m_+ \to \mathbf{R}^n_+$, defined by

$$\mathrm{mx}(F_1, \ldots, F_k)(x) := \bigcup_{i=1}^{k} F_i(x),$$ is called the *maximal closure of* $F_1, \ldots, F_k$.

(v) The correspondence $F_1 \square \ldots \square F_k: \mathbf{R}^m_+ \to \mathbf{R}^n_+$, defined by

$$F_1 \square \ldots \square F_k(x) := \bigcup_{\sum_{i=1}^{k} x_i = x,\, x_i \geqq 0} \; \sum_{i=1}^{k} F_i(x_i),$$ is called the *convolution of* $F_1, \ldots, F_k$ [cp. *Ruys*, p. 245].

(vi) F is called *superadditive*, if $F(x_1) + F(x_2) \subset F(x_1 + x_2)$ for all $x_1, x_2 \in \mathbf{R}^m_+$.

Remark 2.1: F is concave if, and only if, Graph (F) is a convex subset of $\mathbf{R}^m_+ \times \mathbf{R}^n_+$. If F is concave and linearly homogeneous, then it is superadditive.

The rest of this section contains the production theoretical framework with which we deal later on.

Definition 2.3:

(i) A regular correspondence $P: \mathbf{R}^n_+ \to \mathbf{R}^m_+$ is called an *output correspondence* (OC), if it satisfies the following conditions [cf. *Shephard*, 1974, 255–259]:

P1 $P(0) = \{0\}$.

P2 $P(x)$ is bounded for every $x \in \mathbf{R}^n_+$.

P3 $P(x) \subset P(\lambda x)$ for all $\lambda \geqq 1$ and all $x \in \mathbf{R}^n_+$ (weak disposability of inputs).

---

[2]) If $F(x)$ is empty we put $F_s(x) := \emptyset$.

P4 (i) There are $u \geqslant 0$ [3]) and $x \geqslant 0$, such that $u \in P(x)$.
(ii) If $u \in P(x)$ with $u \geqslant 0$ and $x \geqslant 0$, then for all $\theta > 0$ there is a $\lambda > 0$ with $\theta u \in P(\lambda x)$.

P5 P is closed.

P6 $u \in P(x)$ implies $\theta u \in P(x)$ for all $0 \leqq \theta \leqq 1$ (weak disposability of outputs).

(ii) The inverse correspondence $L: \mathbf{R}_+^m \to \mathbf{R}_+^n$ of an OC P, defined by $L(u) := \{x \in \mathbf{R}_+^n \mid u \in P(x)\}$, is called an *input correspondence* (IC) corresponding to P.

(iii) A correspondence is said to be a *production correspondence* (PC), if it is an OC or an IC.

The next theorem reveals the relation between an OC, P, and its corresponding IC, L.

Theorem 2.3 [*Shephard*, 1970]:

(i) If $P: \mathbf{R}_+^n \to \mathbf{R}_+^m$ is an OC, then the corresponding IC $L: \mathbf{R}_+^m \to \mathbf{R}_+^n$ has the following properties:

L1 $L(0) = \mathbf{R}_+^n$ and $0 \notin L(u)$ for all $u \neq 0$.

L2 $|u^\nu|$ [4]) $\to \infty$ for $\nu \to \infty$ ($\nu \in \mathbf{N}$) implies $\bigcap_{\nu=1}^{\infty} L(u^\nu) = \emptyset$.

L3 $x \in L(u)$ implies $\lambda x \in L(u)$ for all $\lambda \geqq 1$.

L4 (i) $\exists\, u \geqslant 0 : L(u) \neq \emptyset$.
(ii) If $x \in L(u)$ with $u \geqslant 0$ and $x \geqslant 0$, then $\{\lambda x \mid \lambda \geqq 0\} \cap L(\theta u) \neq \emptyset$ for all $\theta \geqq 0$.

L5 L is closed.

L6 $L(\theta u) \subset L(u)$ for all $\theta \geqq 1$ and all $u \in \mathbf{R}_+^m$.

(ii) If a correspondence $L: \mathbf{R}_+^m \to \mathbf{R}_+^n$ satisfies *L1*, . . . , *L6*, then the inverse correspondence $P: \mathbf{R}_+^n \to \mathbf{R}_+^m$ of L, defined by $P(x) := \{u \mid x \in L(u)\}$, is an OC.

Proof: [*Shephard*, 1970, 189–192]. □

Sometimes, additional conditions can be assumed about an OC $P: \mathbf{R}_+^n \to \mathbf{R}_+^m$:

P3s $P(x) \subset P(y)$ for all $x \leqq y$ (strong disposability of inputs).
P4(i)s There are $u > 0$ and $x \geqslant 0$, such that $u \in P(x)$.
P6s $u \in P(x)$ implies $[0, u]$ [5]) $\subset P(x)$ (strong disposability of outputs).

The corresponding equivalent properties of the IC $L: \mathbf{R}_+^m \to \mathbf{R}_+^n$ are:

L3s $x \in L(u)$ and $x \leqq y$ imply $y \in L(u)$.
L4(i)s $\exists\, u > 0$ such that $L(u) \neq \emptyset$.
L6s $L(v) \subset L(u)$ for all $u \leqq v$.

---

[3]) Let $u, v \in \mathbf{R}^n$. $u \leqslant v :\Leftrightarrow u \leqq v$ and $u \neq v$.
$u < v :\Leftrightarrow u_i < v_i \quad (i = 1, \ldots, n)$.

[4]) For $u \in \mathbf{R}^m$ $|u|$ denotes the euclidean norm of the vector u.

[5]) Let $u, v \in \mathbf{R}^n$. $[u, v] := \{w \in \mathbf{R}^n \mid u \leqq w \leqq v\}$,
$[u, v[:= \{w \in \mathbf{R}^n \mid u \leqq w < v\}$.

In the single product case, i.e. $m = 1$, the following theorem holds:

Theorem 2.4 [*Shephard*, 1970]:

(i) If $P\colon \mathbf{R}^n_+ \to \mathbf{R}_+$ is an OC and $L\colon \mathbf{R}_+ \to \mathbf{R}^n_+$ the corresponding IC, then there exists a so-called *production function* (PF) $\pi\colon \mathbf{R}^n_+ \to \mathbf{R}_+$, which satisfies the following conditions:
A1 $\pi(0) = 0$, and there is a $x \geqslant 0$, such that $\pi(x) > 0$.
A2 $\pi(x) \leqq \pi(\lambda x)$ for all $\lambda \geqq 1$ and all $x \in \mathbf{R}^n_+$.
A3 $\pi(x) > 0$ implies $\lim_{\lambda \to \infty} \pi(\lambda x) = \infty$.
A4 π is upper semi-continuous on $\mathbf{R}^n_+$.
*A** $P(x) = [0, \pi(x)]$ and $\max \{u \mid x \in L(u)\} = \pi(x)$.

(ii) If $\pi\colon \mathbf{R}^n_+ \to \mathbf{R}_+$ is a PF, then the correspondences $P\colon \mathbf{R}^n_+ \to \mathbf{R}_+$ and $L\colon \mathbf{R}_+ \to \mathbf{R}^n_+$, defined by $P(x) := [0, \pi(x)]$ and $L(u) := \{x \mid \pi(x) \geqq u\}$, are an OC and an IC respectively.

Proof: [*Shephard*, 1970, 20–22, 192–196]. □

3. Uniformly Compact OC's and Saturations of IC's

Let P be an OC and L the corresponding IC. In this section, we shall prove that uniform compactness of P is a necessary and sufficient condition for the saturation L_s of L to be an IC.

The uniform compactness of an OC means economically that it is impossible to get an unbounded set of output vectors with a bounded set of input vectors (cp. Theorems 2.1 and 2.2). Therefore, uniformly compact OC's constitute an important class of OC's and are of interest in their own right. For the single output case the saturation of an IC was introduced by *Färe* [1975, 319–321]. We shall begin our considerations with this situation.

Theorem 3.1: Every OC $P\colon \mathbf{R}^n_+ \to \mathbf{R}_+$ is uniformly compact.

Proof: Theorem 2.4 implies the existence of an upper semi-continuous function π: $\mathbf{R}^n_+ \to \mathbf{R}_+$ with $P(x) = [0, \pi(x)]$. Let $\emptyset \neq B \subset \mathbf{R}^n_+$ be a bounded set. Then $K := \overline{B}$ is compact. According to the upper semi-continuity of π we can select [for a proof cp. *Bourbaki*, chap. IV, § 6.2, theorem 3, p. 361] a point k in K, such that

$$\pi(k) = \sup_{x \in K} \pi(x). \tag{3.1}$$

Therefore $P(B) \subset P(K) = [0, \pi(k)]$. Consequently $P(B)$ is a bounded set. Combining this result with Theorem 2.2, we obtain Theorem 3.1. □

The following result gives a sufficient condition for an OC to be uniformly compact and is due to *Afriat* [1974, p. 14].

Theorem 3.2: Each OC which satisfies *P3s* is uniformly compact.

Proof: Let the OC P: $\mathbf{R}_+^n \to \mathbf{R}_+^m$ satisfy *P3s*, and let $x = (x_1, \ldots, x_n)' \in \mathbf{R}_+^n$. Then for $y := (x_1 + 1, \ldots, x_n + 1)'$, the set $[0, y[$ is a neighbourhood of x. By virtue of *P3s*, we have $P(z) \subset P(y)$ for all $z \in [0, y]$ and hence also $P([0, y[) \subset P(y)$. *P2, P5* and Theorem 2.1 imply the compactness of $P(y)$. Consequently, $\overline{P([0, y[)}$ is compact, as was to be proved. □

The next theorem establishes the connection between uniformly compact OC's and saturations of IC's. Our result is an extension of that put forward by *Färe* [1975, 319–321].

Theorem 3.3: Let P: $\mathbf{R}_+^n \to \mathbf{R}_+^m$ be an OC, and L: $\mathbf{R}_+^m \to \mathbf{R}_+^n$ its corresponding IC. Then the saturation L_s of L is an IC, which satisfies *L3s*, if, and only if, P is uniformly compact.

Proof: Observe that, by definition of L_s,

$$L(u) \subset L_s(u) = L_s(u) + \mathbf{R}_+^n \qquad \text{for all } u \in \mathbf{R}_+^m. \tag{3.2}$$

If P is uniformly compact, we have to prove, that L_s is an IC, which satisfies *L3s*.

ad *L1*: $L_s(0) = L(0) + \mathbf{R}_+^n = \mathbf{R}_+^n + \mathbf{R}_+^n = \mathbf{R}_+^n$. Let $u \geqslant 0$, and $x \in L_s(u)$. Then there are $x_1 \in L(u), y \in \mathbf{R}_+^n$ with $x = x_1 + y$. Consequently $x \geqq x_1$. By hypothesis, $x_1 \geqslant 0$, which implies $x \geqslant 0$. We have accordingly $0 \notin L_s(u)$.

ad *L2*: Select a sequence $\{u^\nu\} \subset \mathbf{R}_+^n$ with $|u^\nu| \to \infty$ for $\nu \to \infty$. Suppose that the conclusion is false, i.e. there exists a point x in $\cap L_s(u^\nu)$. Then, for every integer ν, there are vectors x^ν in $L(u^\nu)$ and y^ν in $\mathbf{R}_+^n$ such that $x = x^\nu + y^\nu$. Hence $x^\nu \in [0, x]$ for all $\nu \in \mathbf{N}$, and consequently $u^\nu \in P([0, x])$ for all ν. Since by virtue of Theorem 2.1 $P([0, x])$ is compact, this implies that $\{u^\nu\}$ is bounded, contrary to our hypothesis that $|u^\nu| \to \infty$ for $\nu \to \infty$.

ad *L3s* and *L6*. Both follow immediately from (3.2).

ad *L4*. (i) By virtue of our hypothesis, there exists a point $u \geqslant 0$ such that $L(u) \neq \emptyset$. Then (3.2) implies $L_s(u) \neq \emptyset$.

(ii) If $x \geqslant 0, u \geqslant 0$ and $x \in L_s(u)$, then x can be expressed in the form $x = x_1 + y$, where $x_1 \in L(u)$ and $y \in \mathbf{R}_+^n$. Let $\theta \geqq 0$. Since L is an IC, there is a scalar $\lambda \geqq 0$ such that $\lambda x_1 \in L(\theta u)$. Therefore $\lambda x = \lambda x_1 + \lambda y \in L_s(u)$.

ad *L5*. Let $\{(u^\nu, x^\nu)\} \subset \text{Graph}(L_s)$ be a sequence converging to (u^0, x^0). Since $x^\nu \in L_s(u^\nu)$, x^ν can be expressed as a sum $x^\nu = z^\nu + y^\nu$, where $z^\nu \in L(u^\nu)$ and $y^\nu \in \mathbf{R}_+^n$. Observe that $\{x^\nu\}$ converges only if $\{z^\nu\}$ and $\{y^\nu\}$ are bounded, because $z^\nu, y^\nu \in \mathbf{R}_+^n$ for all ν. It follows that the sequence $\{(z^\nu, y^\nu)\}$ has a subsequence $\{(w^\nu, v^\nu)\}$ converging to a point (z^0, y^0). Since L is closed, we have $z^0 \in L(u^0)$. In addition, $y^0 \in \mathbf{R}_+^n$. Consequently $x^0 = z^0 + y^0 \in L(u^0) + \mathbf{R}_+^n = L_s(u^0)$. Hence $(u^0, x^0) \in \text{Graph}(L_s)$.

To prove the converse, let L_s be an IC. If ${}_sP$ denotes the OC corresponding to L_s, then it follows from (3.2) that $P(x) \subset {}_sP(x)$ for all $x \in \mathbf{R}_+^n$. Combining this result with Theorem 3.2, we obtain Theorem 3.3. □

4. The Maximal Closure of IC's and OC's

The aim of this section is to prove that the maximal closure of IC's (OC's) is an IC (OC). Furthermore, we investigate the maximal closure of special IC's.

Throughout this section let $k \geqq 2$ be an integer and $L_1, \ldots, L_k$: $\mathbf{R}_+^m \to \mathbf{R}_+^n$ IC's. By $P_1, \ldots, P_k$ and, if $m = 1$, by $\pi_1, \ldots, \pi_k$ we denote the corresponding OC's and PF's.

Theorem 4.1: The correspondence $mx\,(L_1, \ldots, L_k)$ is an IC and the corresponding OC is the maximal closure of $P_1, \ldots, P_k$. In the case of $m = 1$, the PF $mx\,(\pi_1, \ldots, \pi_k)$ corresponding to the IC $mx\,(L_1, \ldots, L_k)$, which by virtue of Theorem 1.4 exists, has the form

$$mx\,(\pi_1, \ldots, \pi_k)\,(x) = \max_{i=1,\ldots,k} \pi_i\,(x) \qquad \text{for all } x \in \mathbf{R}_+^n. \tag{4.1}$$

Proof: Let $L := mx\,(L_1, \ldots, L_k)$.

ad *L1, L3, L4* and *L6*. Each proof is straightforward.

ad *L2*. Let $\{u^\nu\} \subset \mathbf{R}_+^n$ be a sequence with $|u^\nu| \to \infty$ for $\nu \to \infty$. Then property *L2* holds, since $\bigcap_{\nu=1}^{\infty} L\,(u^\nu) = \bigcap_{\nu=1}^{\infty} \bigcup_{i=1}^{k} L_i\,(u^\nu) = \bigcup_{i=1}^{k} \bigcap_{\nu=1}^{\infty} L_i\,(u^\nu) = \emptyset$ because $\bigcap_{\nu=1}^{\infty} L_i\,(u^\nu) = \emptyset$ for all i.

ad *L5*. As a first step in the proof of this result, observe that

$$\text{Graph}\,(L) = \bigcup_{i=1}^{k} \text{Graph}\,(L_i). \tag{4.2}$$

Hence Graph (L) is closed as a finite union of closed sets.

The second conclusion follows immediately from (4.2).

If $m = 1$, put $\pi\,(x) := \max_{i=1,\ldots,k} \pi_i\,(x)$ and $\widetilde{L}\,(u) := \{x \mid \pi\,(x) \geqq u\}$. Then we have to show $L = \widetilde{L}$. Let $(u, x) \in$ Graph $(\widetilde{L})$. Then $x \in \widetilde{L}\,(u)$, consequently $\pi\,(x) \geqq u$. Hence, there exists an index i such that $\pi_i\,(x) \geqq u$, whence $x \in L_i\,(u)$ or $(u, x) \in$ Graph (L_i). By virtue of (4.2) Graph (L_i) is a subset of Graph (L). Hence Graph $(\widetilde{L}) \subset$ Graph (L). In a similar way we can prove Graph $(L) \subset$ Graph $(\widetilde{L})$. Combining both inclusions, we obtain (4.1). This proves Theorem 4.1. □

The following lemma is concerned with properties of $L_1, \ldots, L_k$ which remain invariant under the operation of maximal closure. To this end, let (*LE*) denote one of the following properties: linear homogeneity, *L3s, L4(i)s* and *L6s.*

Lemma 4.2: If all $L_1, \ldots, L_k$ satisfy (*LE*), so does their maximal closure.

Proof: Obvious. □

5. The Convolution of Uniformly Compact OC's

In this section, we prove that the convolution of more than two OC's is an OC if, and only if, the given OC's are uniformly compact. Furthermore, we analyse the convolution of special OC's and finally we establish a connection between the convolution and the maximal closure of uniformly compact OC's.

Using the same notation as at the beginning of section 4, we put $P := P_1 \square \ldots \square P_k$, L the inverse correspondence of P and, if $m = 1$, π the function, defined by $\pi(x) := \sup \{u \mid x \in L(u)\}$.

Theorem 5.1:

(i) If all $P_1, \ldots, P_k$ are uniformly compact, then P is an uniformly compact OC.
(ii) If P is an OC, then all $P_1, \ldots, P_k$ are uniformly compact.
(iii) If P is an OC, then L is the convolution of $L_1, \ldots, L_k$, i.e. $L = L_1 \square \ldots \square L_k$ [6]).
(iv) In the case of $m = 1$, P is always an OC and the corresponding PF π which exists by virtue of Theorem 2.4 has the form

$$\pi(x) = \sup \{\sum_{i=1}^{k} \pi_i(x^i) \mid x = \sum_{i=1}^{k} x^i, x^i \geqq 0\}. \tag{5.1}$$

Proof: (i) Since $x \geqq 0$, observe that the relation $P_i(x) \subset P(x)$ holds for all i. Consequently, P is regular.

ad *P1, P3, P4* and *P6*. Each proof is easily verified.

ad *P2*. For $x \geqq 0$, each $P_i([0, x])$ is compact by virtue of Theorem 2.1, whence the compactness of $R(x) := \sum_{i=1}^{k} P_i([0, x])$. Since $\sum_{i=1}^{k} P_i(x^i) \subset R(x)$ for all $x^i \geqq 0$ such that $\Sigma x^i = x$, we have $P(x) \subset R(x)$. Therefore, $P(x)$ is bounded.

ad *P5*. Let $\{(x^\nu, u^\nu)\} \subset \text{Graph}(P)$ be a sequence converging to the point (x^0, u^0). Since $u^\nu \in P(x^\nu)$, x^ν and u^ν can be expressed as sums $x^\nu = \sum_{i=1}^{k} x^{\nu i}$ and $u^\nu = \sum_{i=1}^{k} u^{\nu i}$, where $x^{\nu i} \in \mathbf{R}_+^n$ and $u^{\nu i} \in P_i(x^{\nu i})$. Observe that $\{(x^\nu, u^\nu)\}$ converges only if $\{z^\nu := (x^{\nu 1}, \ldots, x^{\nu k}, u^{\nu 1}, \ldots, u^{\nu k})\}$ is bounded, because $z^\nu \geqq 0$ for all ν. It follows that the sequence $\{z^\nu\}$ has a subsequence converging to a point $z^0 := (x^{01}, \ldots, x^{0k}, u^{01}, \ldots, u^{0k})$. Then, $u^{0i} \in P_i(x^{0i})$ for all i follows from $P_1, \ldots, P_k$ being closed. Thus, $u^0 = \sum_{i=1}^{k} u^{0i} \in \sum_{i=1}^{k} P_i(x^{0i}) \subset P(x^0)$. Consequently, $(x^0, u^0) \in \text{Graph}(P)$.

It remains to be shown that P is uniformly compact. Let $K \subset \mathbf{R}_+^n$ be compact. Clearly, a point $x \geqq 0$ exists such that $K \subset [0, x]$. Hence, $P_i(y) \subset P_i([0, x])$ for all $y \in K$. Therefore $P(K) \subset \sum_{i=1}^{k} P_i([0, x]) =: R(x)$. Recalling the proof of *P2*, we obtain that $P(K)$ is bounded. Hence, $P(K)$ is compact since P is closed.

(ii) Let $K \subset \mathbf{R}_+^n$ be compact. Obviously, a point $x \geqq 0$ exists such that $K \subset [0, x]$. Therefore, together with $k \geqq 2$, the relation $P_i(K) \subset P_i([0, x]) \subset P(x)$ holds for all i. Hence, with $P(x)$ being compact, the conclusion follows.

(iii) The proof is straightforward.

(iv) Observe that, if $m = 1$, then by virtue of Theorem 3.1 $P_1, \ldots, P_k$ are uniformly

---

[6]) By virtue of Theorem 3.3 we can restate this part of the Theorem in the following form: L as a convolution of the IC's $L_1, \ldots, L_k$ is an IC if, and only if, the saturations of all $L_1, \ldots, L_k$ are IC's.

compact, whence according to part (i) P is an OC. To establish the conclusion (5.1), let $\tilde{\pi}(x)$ be defined by the right side of (5.1) and $\tilde{L}(u) := \{x \mid \tilde{\pi}(x) \geqq u\}$. Let $x \in \tilde{L}(u)$. Since the set $K(x) := \{(x^1, \ldots, x^k) \in (\mathbf{R}^n_+)^k \mid x = \sum_{i=1}^k x^i\}$ is compact, the upper semi-continuity of $\pi_1, \ldots, \pi_k$ ensures[7]) that there is a point $(y^1, \ldots, y^k)$ in $K(x)$ leading to $\tilde{\pi}(x) = \sum_{i=1}^k \pi_i(y^i)$ Setting $u^i := \pi_i(y^i)$ we have $x = \sum_{i=1}^k y^i \in \sum_{i=1}^k L_i(u^i) \subset L_1 \,\square \ldots \square\, L_k(\tilde{\pi}(x)) = L(\tilde{\pi}(x)) \subset L(u)$. Hence $\tilde{L}(u) \subset L(u)$. To prove the converse, let $x \in L(u)$. By virtue of (iii) there are points $x^i \in L(u^i)$ with $\sum_{i=1}^k x^i = x$ and $u = \sum_{i=1}^k u^i$. Hence, $\tilde{\pi}(x) \geqq \sum_{i=1}^k \pi_i(x^i) \geqq \sum_{i=1}^k u^i = u$, which proves $L(u) \subset \tilde{L}(u)$. □

Remark 5.1: Part (iv) of Theorem 5.1 justifies our naming the operation □ a convolution: There, the formal structure of the PF agrees precisely with what is called a convolution in convex analysis [cp. *Rockafellar*, 33–34].

The economic implications of the convolution of uniformly compact OC's are obvious: Given a production system consisting of $k \geqq 2$ production subsystems, each of them represented by an OC, and given an input vector x, a vector u of commodities is obtainable from x in the production system if, and only if, it is possible to divide x into input vectors x^i $(i = 1, \ldots, k)$, such that u can be expressed as a sum of contributions u^i, where u^i is an output vector obtainable with x^i in the i-th production subsystem. If only a single commodity is produced, the determination of the maximal output u obtainable with x in the production system consists in a division of x into input vectors x^i, in such a way that the sum of the maximal outputs obtainable with x^i in the i-th production subsystem leads to the output u.

Similary, in an activity model, the description of a production system as a convolution assumes the noninteraction between the simultaneous operations of the different production subsystems.

In the following lemma, we analyse whether the convolution of given uniformly compact OC's has a special property if all OC's have this property. To this end, let *(PE)* denote one of the properties: linear homogeneity, concavity, *P3s*, and *P6s*.

Lemma 5.2: If $P_1, \ldots, P_k$ satisfy *(PE)*, so does their convolution.

Proof: We give the proof only for *(PE)* = *P3s*. If $x \leqq y$, then $P_i(x) \leqq P_i(y)$ for all i. Let $x^i \geqq 0$ such that $x = \sum_{i=1}^k x^i$. Setting $y^i := x^i$ for $i = 1, \ldots, k-1$ and $y^k := y - (x - x^k)$, we have $x^i \leqq y^i$ for all i. Consequently $\sum_{i=1}^k P_i(x^i) \subset \sum_{i=1}^k P_i(y^i)$. Therefore $P(x) \subset P(y)$, as was to be proved. □

Turning to the relationship between the convolution and the maximal closure of uniformly compact OC's the following result is easily verified.

Lemma 5.3: $mx(P_1, \ldots, P_k)(x) \subset P_1 \,\square \ldots \square\, P_k(x)$ for all input vectors x.

[7]) For a proof, combine Proposition 2, p. 362, with Theorem 3, p. 361, of *Bourbaki* [1966], chap. IV, § 6.2.

6. Farrell's Procedure to Estimate Linearly Homogeneous IC's and PF's

6.1 The Frontier Concept and the Data Set

In 1957 Farrell established a procedure to estimate so-called Frontier PF's on the basis of a given set $D := \{(v^1, y^1), \ldots, (v^k, y^k)\} \subset \mathbf{R}_+^m \times \mathbf{R}_+^n$ of data, $k \geqq 2$. Each point (activity) $(v^i, y^i) \in D$ describes a production operation v^i being the output vector obtainable with the input vector y^i. Throughout this section, D always denotes the above specified sample of activities. As we deal with Frontier PC's and PF's in the sequal, let us introduce these terms rigorously at the outset.

Definition 6.1: If there exists an IC L with $y^i \in L\ (v^i)$ for all i, then L is said to be a *Frontier IC w.r.t. D*, and the corresponding OC is called a *Frontier OC w.r.t. D*. If we consider the production of a single good the corresponding PF is called a *Frontier PF w.r.t. D.*

In this section, we generalize Farrell's procedure to estimate linearly homogeneous Frontier IC's and PF's on the basis of a given sample D. To this end, we apply the operations proposed in the preceeding sections for the construction of the desired IC's.

Throughout this section we assume the data set D to satisfy the condition DA:

$$DA \quad \text{(i)} \quad \sum_{j=1}^{m} v_{ij} > 0 \qquad i = 1, \ldots, k$$

$$\text{(ii)} \quad \sum_{r=1}^{n} y_{ir} > 0 \qquad i = 1, \ldots, k$$

where $v^i := (v_{i1}, \ldots, v_{im})'$ and $y^i := (y_{i1}, \ldots, y_{in})'$ $\quad i = 1, \ldots, k$.

6.2 Four Sets of Regularity Conditions on the IC

To carry out the estimation procedure, in this subsection we impose four sets of regularity conditions on the IC partly suggested by Farrell [cf. *Farrell*, 253–255; *Afriat*, 1972, 576–579]. Then we shall prove that each regularity set is compatible with the data set D, i.e. for each regularity set we can construct (estimate) a Frontier IC w.r.t. D satisfying the demanded set of regularity conditions.

Let L denote the IC to be estimated. We shall consider the following regularity conditions:

Conditions 1:

F.1 (i) Let L be a Frontier IC w.r.t. D.
(ii) Let L be linearly homogeneous.
(iii) Let L satisfy *L3s*.
(iv) Let L be concave.

FU.1 There is no other IC $\tilde{L}$ different from L and satisfying *F.1* such that $\tilde{L}\ (u) \subset L\ (u)$ for all $u \in \mathbf{R}_+^m$.

Conditions 2:

F.2 Let L satisfy *F.1* and *L6s.*
FU.2 Defined like *FU.1* by replacing condition *F.1* by *F.2.*

Conditions 3:

F.3 Let L satisfy *F.1* (i)–(iii).
FU.3 Defined like *FU.1* by replacing condition *F.1* by *F.3.*

Conditions 4:

F.4 Let L satisfy *F.1* (i)–(iii) and *L6s.*
FU.4 Defined like *FU.1* by replacing condition *F.1* by *F.4.*

As will be shown in the following two subsections, the estimation procedure for concave IC's (as with Conditions 1 and 2) necessarily involves an application of the convolution, whereas in the case of estimating nonconvex technology sets (as with Conditions 3 and 4), we have to apply the maximal closure.[8])

Before starting with the estimation procedures, let us make a remark as to the existence and uniqueness of an IC satisfying *F.i* and *FU.i*, $i = 1, \ldots, 4$. We shall call such an IC an *estimation in Farrell's sense.*

Remark 6.1: For $i \in \{1, \ldots, 4\}$ let

$$\Phi(i) \text{ denote the set of all IC's satisfying } F.i. \tag{6.1}$$

If we can prove that $\Phi(i)$ is nonempty, then an estimation in Farrell's sense exists. In fact, if $L_1, L_2 \in \Phi(i)$, then it is easy to show that $L_1 \cap L_2 \in \Phi(i)$, where $(L_1 \cap L_2)(u) := L_1(u) \cap L_2(u)$. Hence, by virtue of *FU.i*:

$$L := \bigcap_{\tilde{L} \in \Phi(i)} \tilde{L} \tag{6.2}$$

is the unique (!) estimation in Farrell's sense.

6.3 The Convolution and the Estimation of Concave IC's

In this subsection, we derive an estimation in Farrell's sense satisfying Conditions 1 or 2. We carry out the estimation procedure in two stages. In the first stage, we consider a single observation, and then on the basis of this single activity we find an IC satisfying *F.1* (*F.2*) and *FU.1* (*FU.2*). This stage, when carried out for all points in D, leads to k IC's which we denote by $L_1, \ldots, L_k$.

In the second stage, we take into consideration all elements of the sample D simultaneously. To this end, we put $\tilde{L}$ the convolution of $L_1, \ldots, L_k$. Finally, we proceed to prove that $\tilde{L}$ is the desired estimation in Farrell's sense.

---

[8]) In contrast to *Hanoch/Rothschild* [1972, 267–270], we do not assume convexity of the technology set in Conditions 3 and 4 and consider instead property *L6s.*

ad Conditions 1: Let (v^i, y^i) be the i-th activity in D. Next, we show that there is an IC L_i of the following form satisfying *F.1* and *FU.1*:

$$L_i(u) = \begin{cases} \{x \mid x \geqq \lambda y^i\} & \text{if } u = \lambda v^i \text{ for some } \lambda \geqq 0 \\ \emptyset & \text{otherwise.} \end{cases} \tag{6.3}$$

Proof: We denote the correspondence defined by (6.3) by $\widetilde{L}_i$. First, we show that $\widetilde{L}_i$ is an IC satisfying *F.1*. Then, by virtue of Remark 6.1, the estimation L_i in Farrell's sense exists. In order to establish the conclusion, we finally have to prove that the relation $\widetilde{L}_i(u) \subset L_i(u)$ is true for all $u \in \mathbf{R}^m_+$.

To show that $\widetilde{L}_i$ is an IC satisfying *F.1*, observe that Graph $(\widetilde{L}_i) = \{\lambda(v^i, y^i) \mid \lambda \geqq 0\} + \{0\} \times \mathbf{R}^n_+$. Using this fact, the conclusion is easily verified.

It remains to be shown that $\widetilde{L}_i(u) \subset L_i(u)$ for all $u \in \mathbf{R}^m_+$. By *F.1*(i) we have $(v^i, y^i) \in$ Graph (L_i). *F.1*(ii) and (iii) imply $\{\lambda(v^i, y^i) \mid \lambda \geqq 0\} + \{0\} \times \mathbf{R}^n_+ \subset$ Graph (L_i) for all $\lambda \geqq 0$. Hence, Graph $(\widetilde{L}_i) \subset$ Graph (L_i), as was to be shown. □

Since each L_i $(i = 1, \ldots, k)$ satisfies *L3s*, The following correspondence

$$\widetilde{L} := L_1 \,\square \ldots \square\, L_k \tag{6.4}$$

is an IC because of the Theorems 3.3 and 5.1. If we can show that $\widetilde{L}$ satisfies *F.1*, then the set $\Phi(1)$ defined by (6.1) is nonempty and according to Remark 6.1 the (unique) estimation in Farrell's sense exists and is given by (6.2).

We are now in a position to establish

Theorem 6.1: The IC $\widetilde{L}$ defined by (6.4) is the estimation in Farrell's sense, satisfying *F.1* and *FU.1*. If, in addition, the sample D satisfies the relation $\sum_{i=1}^{k} v^i > 0$ then $\widetilde{L}$ satisfies *L4(i)s*.

Proof: The scheme of the proof is the same as that used for the claim with respect to (6.3).

Let us show that $\widetilde{L}$ satisfies *F.1*. The properties *F.1*(ii), (iii) and (iv) follow directly from Lemma 5.2. To show *F.1*(i), let $1 \leqq i \leqq k$ be a fixed integer. Setting

$$u^j := \begin{cases} v^i & \text{if } i \neq j \\ 0 & \text{otherwise,} \end{cases}$$

we have $\sum_{j=1}^{k} L_j(u^j) = L_i(v^i) \subset \widetilde{L}(v^i)$ by virtue of *F.1*(iii). Hence, $y^i \in \widetilde{L}(v^i)$, since $y^i \in L_i(v^i)$.

Let us denote by L the estimation in Farrell's sense which exists and is uniquely determined by Remark 6.1. We have to show that $\widetilde{L}(u) \subset L(u)$ for all $u \in \mathbf{R}^m_+$. Since L satisfies *L3s*, we have $L_i(v^i) \subset L(v^i)$ for all $i = 1, \ldots, k$. Hence, by virtue of *F.1*(ii) and (iv) and Remark 2.1 it follows that

$$\sum_{i=1}^{k} \lambda_i L_i(v^i) \subset L\left(\sum_{i=1}^{k} \lambda_i v^i\right) \qquad \text{for all } \lambda_1, \ldots, \lambda_k > 0. \tag{6.5}$$

Let C_1 be the convex hull of $v^1, \ldots, v^k$, $C := \{\lambda u \mid \lambda > 0, u \in C_1\}$ and C^k the k-fold Cartesian product of C. Hence, for $u \geqslant 0$, (6.3) implies

$$\tilde{L}(u) = \bigcup_{\substack{(u^1,\ldots,u^k)\in C^k \\ \sum_{i=1}^k u^i = u}} \sum_{i=1}^{k} L_i(u^i) = \bigcup_{\substack{(\lambda_1,\ldots,\lambda_k)>0 \\ \sum_{i=1}^k \lambda_i v^i = u}} \sum_{i=1}^{k} L_i(\lambda_i v^i) \subset L(u). \quad (6.5)$$

The proof of the second claim is obvious. □

In the following theorem, we derive a form of the IC (6.4) which shows directly where the sample D appears. To this end, we put the matrices

$$A := (y^1, \ldots, y^k) \quad \text{and} \quad B := (v^1, \ldots, v^k). \quad (6.6)$$

Theorem 6.2: The estimated IC L in Farrell's sense – represented by (6.4) – has the form

$$L(u) = \{x \in \mathbf{R}_+^n \mid \exists\, z \geqq 0 : Bz = u, Az \leqq x\}. \quad (6.7)$$

If only a single good is produced, the PF π corresponding to L, which exists by virtue of Theorem 2.4, is equal to

$$\pi(x) = \max\, \{Bz \mid Az \leqq x\}. \quad (6.8)$$

Proof: Let us denote by $\tilde{L}$ the correspondence defined by (6.7). We have to show that $L = \tilde{L}$. To prove $L(u) \subset \tilde{L}(u)$ for all $u \in \mathbf{R}_+^m$, let $u \geqq 0$ and $x \in L(u)$. By Theorem 6.1, there exists $x^i \geqq 0$ and $u^i \geqq 0$ such that $x = \sum_{i=1}^k x^i$, $u = \sum_{i=1}^k u^i$, and $x^i \in L_i(u^i)$ for all i. The u^i's can be expressed as $u^i = \lambda_i v^i$ by virtue of (6.3). Setting $z := (\lambda_1, \ldots, \lambda_k)'$, we have $Bz = \Sigma \lambda_i v^i = \Sigma u^i = u$ and $Az = \Sigma \lambda_i y^i \leqq \Sigma x^i = x$. Hence $L(u) \subset \tilde{L}(u)$.

To prove the converse relation, let $u \geqq 0$ and $x \in \tilde{L}(u)$. By hypothesis, there exists $z \geqq 0$ such that $Bz = u$ and $Az \leqq x$. Setting $u^i = z_i v^i$ and $\tilde{x}^i = z_i y^i$, we have $\tilde{x} := \Sigma \tilde{x}^i = Az \leqq x$. Putting $x^j := (1/k)(x - \tilde{x}) + \tilde{x}^j$ we have $\Sigma x^j = x - \tilde{x} + \tilde{x} = x$. Therefore, since $x^i \geqq z_i y^i$, $x^i \in L_i(z_i v^i) = L_i(u^i)$. Consequently, $x = \Sigma x^i \in L(u)$.

To prove the second claim, let $\tilde{L}(u) := \{x \mid \tilde{\pi}(x) \geqq u\}$, where $\tilde{\pi}$ is defined by (6.8). Then, we have to show that $\tilde{L} = L$. For $u = 0$ there is nothing to prove. If $u > 0$ and $x \in \tilde{L}(u)$, then there exists $z \geqslant 0$ such that $Bz \geqq u$ and $Az \leqq x$. Setting $\lambda := u/Bz$ and $\tilde{z} := \lambda z$, we have $0 < \lambda \leqq 1$, $B\tilde{z} = u$, and $A\tilde{z} \leqq Az \leqq x$. Hence $x \in L(u)$. Consequently $\tilde{L}(u) \subset L(u)$.

To prove the converse, let $u > 0$ and $x \in L(u)$. By hypothesis, there exists $z \geqq 0$ such that $Bz = u$, and $Az \leqq x$. Therefore $\tilde{\pi}(x) \geqq u$, i.e. $x \in \tilde{L}(u)$. Accordingly $L(u) \subset \tilde{L}(u)$, as was to be proved. □

ad Conditions 2: Let (v^i, y^i) be the i-th activity in D and B_i denote the set of all vectors $u \in \mathbf{R}_+^m$ with $u \leqq v^i$ but not $u < v^i$. In a manner, analogous to the verification of (6.3), we can prove that the IC L_i satisfying *F.2* and *FU.2* is in the following form:

$$L_i(u) = \begin{cases} \mathbf{R}^n_+ & \text{if } u = 0 \\ \{\lambda y^i\} + \mathbf{R}^n_+ & \text{if } \lambda^{-1} u \in B_i \text{ for some } \lambda > 0 \\ \emptyset & \text{otherwise.} \end{cases} \tag{6.9}$$

We are now in a position to establish a result which can be proved in the manner of Theorems 6.1 and 6.2.

Theorem 6.3: The estimation L in Farrell's sense satisfying *F.2* and *FU.2* can be expressed in the following form

$$L = L_1 \,\square \ldots \square\, L_k, \tag{6.10}$$

where $L_1, \ldots, L_k$ are given by (6.9). Furthermore, L can be expressed as

$$L(u) := \{x \in \mathbf{R}^n_+ \mid \exists\, z \geqq 0 : Bz \geqq u,\ Az \leqq x\}, \tag{6.11}$$

where the matrices A and B are given by (6.6).[9])

6.4 The Maximal Closure and the Estimation of Nonconcave IC's

In this subsection we derive an estimation in Farrell's sense satisfying Conditions 3 or 4. Once again, we state our results without proof, because these can be given in a manner, analogous to the verification of the Theorems 6.1 and 6.2.

ad Conditions 3:
Theorem 6.4: The estimation L in Farrell's sense satisfying *F.3* and *FU.3* can be expressed in the following form

$$L = mx\,(L_1, \ldots, L_k), \tag{6.12}$$

where again $L_1, \ldots, L_k$ are given by (6.3). In the single output case the PF π corresponding to L which exists by virtue of Theorem 2.4 is equal to

$$\pi(x) = \max_{i=1,\ldots,k} \pi_i(x) \tag{6.13}$$

because of Theorem 4.1, where π_i is the PF corresponding to L_i and satisfies the equation

$$\pi_i(x) = \max\,\{\lambda y^i \mid \lambda v^i \leqq x,\ \lambda \geqq 0\}. \tag{6.14}$$

ad Conditions 4:
Theorem 6.5: The estimation L in Farrell's sense satisfying *F.4* and *FU.4* can be expressed in the following form

$$L = mx\,(L_1, \ldots, L_k), \tag{6.15}$$

where again $L_1, \ldots, L_k$ are given by (6.9).[10])

---

[9]) Clearly, in the single output case a formula for the PF is superfluous, because then the IC's (6.7) and (6.10) coincide.

[10]) As in Theorem 6.3 a formula for the PF is superfluous.

References

Afriat, S.N.: Efficiency Estimation of Production Functions. International Economic Review **13**, 1972, 568–598.

– : Production Duality and the von Neumann Theory of Growth and Interest. Meisenheim am Glan 1974.

Bourbaki, N.: General Topology, Part 1. Paris 1966.

Diewert, W.E., and *C. Parkan*: Linear Programming Tests of Regularity Conditions for Production Functions. Quantitative Studies on Production and Prices. Würzburg–Wien 1982 (this volume).

Färe, R.: Efficiency and Production Function. Zeitschrift für Nationalökonomie **35**, 1975, 317–324.

Farrell, M.J.: The Measurement of Productive Efficiency. Journal of the Royal Statistical Society. Series A General **120**, 1957, 253–290.

Hanoch, G., and *M. Rothschild*: Testing the Assumptions of Production Theory: A Nonparametric Approach. Journal of Political Economy **80**, 1972, 256–275.

Hogan, W.W.: Point-to-Set Maps in Mathematical Programming. SIAM Review **15**, 1973, 591–603.

Rockafellar, R.T.: Convex Analysis. Princeton, N.J., 1970.

Ruys, P.H.M.: Production Correspondences and Convex Algebra. Production Theory. Ed. by W. Eichhorn et al. Berlin–Heidelberg–New York 1974, 231–252.

Shephard, R.W.: Theory of Cost and Production Functions. Princeton, N.J., 1970.

– : Semi-Homogeneous Production Functions and Scaling of Production. Production Theory. Ed. by W. Eichhorn et al. Berlin–Heidelberg–New York 1974, 253–285.

Quantitative Studies on Production and Prices © Physica-Verlag, Würzburg–Wien, 1983.

On the Structure of Technologies of an Input-Limited Unit

Kimberly D. Zieschang[1])

The axiomatic approach to modelling technologies of a limited unit of Shephard and Färe is used to characterize the minimal axiom set, the scaling properties, and the functional structure of input correspondences with fixed input subset. Representability of limited unit models by a distance function is shown to depend critically on certain disposal properties, stronger than weak disposal and weaker than strong disposal, of the global technology in the variable inputs. It is shown that the property that nonzero output requires nonzero variable input implies essentially of fixed input, while attainability implies nonessentiality of fixed input. Given representability, the scaling law of the limited unit correspondence may be analyzed via the scaling function, defined as a ratio of distance functions. Independence of the scaling function of certain of its arguments is shown to generate various kinds of separable structures for the unrestricted technical correspondences.

1. Introductory Remarks

Technologies of an input-limited unit, characterized by a bounded subset of the global vector of inputs, are of interest because production activities often take place under constraints on the quantities of inputs procurable over finite periods. If an organization produces a vector of outputs, the part of that vector representing by-products such as pollutants may also be constrained by storage limitations or by government regulations. In this case production takes place with an output-limited unit.

In this paper, the structure of a stationary state technology of a unit with a fixed input vector is analyzed. Sections 2 and 3 to follow are concerned with, respectively, (i) the structure of the input-partial model arising from the unrestricted model characterized by the axioms of *Shephard* [1974], and (ii) the additional structure imposed on the partial and unrestricted models by the form of the input scaling function of the input-partial model. Under (i), it is shown that the partial model is not in general characterized by the same axiom system as the unrestricted model, unless assumptions concerning the disposability of variable inputs and the essentiality of fixed and variable inputs are made. Under (ii) invariance of the partial input scaling function to variations in, for example, fixed inputs, is shown to imply a form of near separability of fixed inputs from variable inputs. Further restrictions on the form of the partial distance function imply the usual type of separable structures.

[1]) The views expressed are those of the author and do not reflect the policies of the Bureau of Labor Statistics or the views of other BLS staff members.

2. Basic Structure

2.1 The Unrestricted Model

Consider a production unit producing a vector of output rates $u := (u_1, \ldots, u_m) \in R_+^m$ with a vector of input rates $x := (x_1, \ldots, x_n) \in R_+^n$. Denote by $L(u)$ the set $\{x \in R_+^n$: x can produce $u\}$, so that $L: R_+^m \to 2R_+^n$ is a correspondence mapping outputs into sets of inputs in R_+^n for which those outputs are feasible. This input correspondence is assumed to be characterized by the following properties:

L.1 $L(0) = R_+^n$ and $0 \notin L(u)$ for $u \geqslant 0$.

L.2 For $\{|u^n|\} \to +\infty$, $\bigcap_{n=1}^{\infty} L(u^n) = \emptyset$, where $\emptyset$ is the null set.

L.3 If $x \in L(u)$, $\lambda x \in L(u)$ for $\lambda \in [1, +\infty)$.

L.4 If $x \geqslant 0$ and $\bar{\lambda} x \in L(\bar{u})$ for some $\bar{\lambda} \in (0, +\infty)$, the ray $\{\lambda x | \lambda \in [0, +\infty)\}$ intersects all input sets $L(\theta u)$, $\theta \in [0, +\infty)$.

L.5 $L(u)$ is a closed set, $u \in R_+^m$.

L.6 $L(\theta u) \subset L(u)$, $\theta \in [1, +\infty)$.

L.A Eff $L(u) := \{x \in R_+^n: x \in L(u), y \leqslant x, y \notin L(u)\}$ is bounded.

L.A is termed the "asymmetric postulate" by *Shephard* [1970] and is an important concept regarding limitationality of inputs, as demonstrated by Shephard and Färe.

The correspondence $u \to L(u)$ may be inverted to obtain the output correspondence $x \to P(x)$ with $P(x) := \{u \in R_+^m : x \in L(u)\}$. $P(x)$ may be viewed as the set-valued analog of a production function, where, specifically, if $m = 1$, the production function may be defined as $\Phi(x) := \max \{u \in R_+ : u \in P(x)\}$. Since $L(u)$ satisfies L.1–L.6, $P(x)$ satisfies

P.1 $P(0) = \{0\}$ and there exists $x \geqslant 0$ such that $u \in P(x)$ for some $u > 0$.

P.2 $P(x)$ is bounded for finite $x \in R_+^n$.

P.3 $P(\theta x) \supset P(x)$ for $\theta \in [1, +\infty)$, $x \in R_+^n$.

P.4 If $x \geqslant 0$ and there exists $\bar{u} \geqslant 0$, $\bar{\lambda} \in (0, +\infty)$ such that $\bar{u} \in P(\bar{\lambda} x)$, then for all $\theta \in (0, +\infty)$ there exists $\lambda_\theta \in (0, +\infty)$ such that $\theta \bar{u} \in P(\lambda_\theta x)$.

P.5 $P(x)$ is a closed set, $x \in R_+^n$.

P.6 If $u \in P(x)$, $\{\theta u: \theta \in [0, 1]\} \subset P(x)$.

The distance function of a correspondence $u \to L(u)$ allows the correspondence to be expressed implicitly in the form of a real scalar valued function. For the input correspondence, the distance function is

$$\Psi(u, x) = \begin{cases} 0 \text{ if } \{\lambda x: \lambda \in [0, \infty)\} \cap L(u) = \emptyset \\ [\min \{\lambda: \lambda x \in L(u)\}]^{-1} \quad \text{otherwise,} \end{cases}$$

where $\Psi(u, x)$ is a bounded, nonnegative function for bounded, nonnegative (u, x) and nonzero u which is (i) upper semicontinuous and nonincreasing along rays in $u \in R^m_+$, (ii) positively linear homogeneous in $x \in R^n_+$, and (iii) which satisfies the boundary conditions $\Psi(0, x) = +\infty$, $x \in R^n_+$, and $\Psi(u, 0) = 0$, $u \geqslant 0$. Under L.1–L.6, $L(u) = \{x \in R_+ : \Psi(u, x) \geqq 1\}$ and $P(x) = \{u \in R^m : \Psi(u, x) \geqq 1\}$.

2.2 The Unrestricted Input Scaling Function

Consider $x \in L(u)$. In what follows, it will be of interest to know by how much x must be scaled when output is varied, so that the scaled input vector maintains its relative position in the input set of the new output vector. By 'maintained position in', it is meant that the scaled input vector yields the same value of the distance function at the new output as the initial input vector yielded at the initial output. This condition may be written

$$\Psi(u, x) = \Psi(u', \lambda x)$$

where $\lambda > 0$ is some factor applied to inputs x, u is the initial output, and u' is the terminal output. Using the homogeneity property of $\Psi(u, x)$, the derivation of the input scaling function is direct:

$$\Psi(u, x) = \lambda \Psi(u', x),$$

$$\lambda(u, u', x) = \frac{\Psi(u, x)}{\Psi(u', x)}.$$

$\lambda(u, u', x)$ is the input scaling function for $u \to L(u)$ satisfying L.1–L.6, yielding the scaling factor which, when applied to $x \in L(u)$, results in the correspondent input $\lambda(u, u', x)\, x \in L(u')$. From the properties of $\Psi(u, x)$, $\lambda(u, u', x)$ is a nonnegative function which is (i) zero homogeneous in $x \geqslant 0$, and (ii) upper (lower) semicontinuous and nonincreasing (nondecreasing) along rays in $u \geqslant 0$ ($u' \geqslant 0$). Defining $L(u, (x/|x|)) :=$ $L(u) \cap \{\lambda x : \lambda \geqslant 0\}$, some $x \in R^n_+$, $x \geqslant 0$, we have

$$L\left(u' \,\middle|\, \frac{x}{|x|}\right) = \lambda\left(u, u', \frac{x}{|x|}\right) L\left(u \,\middle|\, \frac{x}{|x|}\right).$$

2.3 Partial Input Technologies

A partial input technology is defined by a correspondence, input or output, for which all inputs are free to vary except some proper subset. Let $x^0 = (x_{\nu_1}, \ldots, x_{\nu_k}) \in R^k_+$ and let $x^1 = (x_{\nu_{k+1}}, \ldots, x_{\nu_n}) \in R^{n-k}_+$ where $\{\nu_1, \ldots, \nu_n\}$ is a permutation of the index set $\{1, \ldots, n\}$.

2.3.1 Definition

The partial input correspondence is defined

$$L(u|x^0) := \{x^1 : (x^0, x^1) \in L(u), x^1 \in R_+^{n-k}\},$$

with $x^0 \in R_+^k$ being a subset of inputs which is being held fixed, the Cartesian order of $L(u)$ having been appropriately rearranged. Define the distance function for the input correspondence as follows:

$$\Psi(u, x^1|x^0) := \begin{cases} 0 \text{ if } \{\lambda x^1 : \lambda \in [0, \infty)\} \cap L(u|x^0) = \emptyset \\ [\min \{\lambda : \lambda x^1 \in L(u|x^0)\}]^{-1} \text{ otherwise.} \end{cases}$$

Earlier it was noted that $L(u) := \{x : \Psi(u, x) \geqq 1\}$, or $x \in L(u)$ iff $\Psi(u, x) \geqq 1$. In the input partial case, this is not true without an additional condition. For example, if $L(u) = \{x \in R_+^n : x = \lambda u(x^0, x^1); \lambda \geqq 1\}$, with $u \to L(u)$ satisfying L.1–L.6, $L(u|x^0) = \{(x^0, x^1)\}$, a single point. Therefore, $\Psi(u, \lambda x^1|x^0) \geqq 1$ for $\lambda \geqq 1$, but $(\lambda x, x^0) \in L(u|x^0)$ only if $\lambda = 1$. To make the partial correspondence representable by a distance function, the following is introduced

2.3.2 Lemma

If $x^1 \in L(u|x^0)$ implies $\lambda x^1 \in L(u|x^0)$, $\lambda \geqq 1$, or equivalently, if $(x^0, x^1) \in L(u)$ implies $(x^0, \lambda x^1) \in L(u)$, $\lambda \geqq 1$, then $x^1 \in L(u|x^0)$ iff $\Psi(u, x^1|x^0) \geqq 1$.

Proof: Trivial in light of the definitions of $L(u|x^0)$ and $\Psi(u, x^1|x^0)$.

2.3.3 Proposition

If $u \to L(u)$ satisfies, in addition to L.1–L.6

L.3P If $(x^0, x^1) \in L(u)$, then $(x^0, \lambda x^1) \in L(u)$, $\lambda \geqq 1$,

then its x^0-partial correspondence satisfies

$L^0.1$ $L(0|x^0) = R_+^{n-k}$,

$L^0.2$ $\bigcap_{n=1}^{\infty} L(u^n|x^0) = \emptyset$ for $\{|u^n|\} \to +\infty$,

$L^0.3$ If $x^1 \in L(u|x^0)$, then $\lambda x^1 \in L(u|x^0)$, $\lambda \geqq 1$,

$L^0.5$ $L(u|x^0)$ is closed, $u \in R_+^m$, $x^0 \in R_+^k$,

$L^0.6$ $L(\theta u|x^0) \subset L(u|x^0)$ for $\theta \geqq 1$.

Proof: Note that by definition $L(u|x^0)$ may be implicitly defined by

$$(x^0, L(u|x^0)) = R(x^0) \cap L(u),$$

where $R(x^0) = \{(q^0, q^1) \in R_+^k \times R_+^{n-k} : q^0 = x^0, q^1 \in R_+^{n-k}\}$. By L.1, $L(0) = R_+^n$, so $R(x^0) \cap L(0) = R(x^0) \cap R_+^n = (x^0, R_+^{n-k})$, and $L(0|x^0) = R_+^{n-k}$. By L.2, $\bigcap_{n=1}^{\infty} L(u^n) = \emptyset$ for $\{|u^n|\} \to +\infty$, so $\bigcap_{n=1}^{\infty} [R(x^0) \cap L(u^n)] = R(x^0) \cap \emptyset = \emptyset$ for $\{|u^n|\} \to +\infty$. $L^0.5$ follows from $L^0.3$. By L.6, $L(\theta u) \subset L(u)$ for $\theta \geqq 1$ and therefore $R(x^0) \cap L(\theta u) \subset R(x^0) \cap L(u)$, establishing $L^0.6$. Q.E.D.

Note that the conditions for $u \to L(u|x^0)$ are very similar to those for $u \to L(u)$ with the exception of an abbreviated first axiom (L.1 vs. $L^0.1$) and the lack of an attainability axiom $L^0.4$. Specifically, we have

$L^0.1E$ $L(0|x^0) = R_+^{n-k}$ and $0 \notin L(u|x^0)$, $u \geqslant 0$.

$L^0.4$ If $\lambda x^1 \in L(u|x^0)$, some $\lambda > 0$, then for every $\theta > 0$, there exists a $\lambda_\theta > 0$ such that $\lambda_\theta x^1 \in L(\theta u|x^0)$.

To explain, it may be that $0 \in L(u|x^0)$ for some $u \geqslant 0$, and that if $\lambda > 0$ such that $\lambda x^1 \in L(u|x^0)$, there does not exist for every (for instance, sufficiently large) $\theta > 0$ a $\lambda_\theta > 0$ such that $\lambda_\theta x^1 \in L(\theta u|x^0)$. On this see *Shephard* [1970, p. 40]. Whether the partial input technology has an extended $L^0.1$ and an $L^0.4$ depends on the essentiality of x^0 and x^1. From Shephard and Färe we appeal to the following three definitions:

2.3.4 Definition

A proper subset $\{\nu_1, \ldots, \nu_k\}$ (representing indices with $1 \leqq k < n$) of n inputs is weakly essential for a subset $\{\pi_1, \ldots, \pi_l\}$ of m outputs if and only if output vectors with $(u_{\pi_1}, \ldots, u_{\pi_l}) > 0$ are feasible for some input and

$$D(\nu_1, \ldots, \nu_k) \cap L(u) = \emptyset$$

for all $u \in \{u: u \in R_+^m, (u_{\pi_1}, \ldots, u_{\pi_l}) > 0\}$, with

$$D(\nu_1, \ldots, \nu_k) := \{x: x \geqslant 0, x_{\nu_i} = 0, i = 1, \ldots, k\}.$$

2.3.5 Definition

A proper subset $\{\nu_1, \ldots, \nu_k\}$ (representing indices with $1 \leqq k < n$) of n inputs is strongly essential for a subset $\{\pi_1, \ldots, \pi_l\}$ of m outputs if and only if it is weakly essential for every set of outputs whose indices are a subset of $\{\pi_1, \ldots, \pi_l\}$.
It follows that an input combination is nonessential for an output subvector if it is not weakly essential.

2.3.6 Definition

A subset $\{\nu_1, \ldots, \nu_k\}$ (representing indices with $1 \leqq k < n$) of n inputs is weakly limitational for a subset $\Gamma = \{\pi_1, \ldots, \pi_l\}$ (representing indices with $1 \leqq l \leqq m$) of m outputs if and only if there exists a positive bound $(x_{\nu_1}^0, \ldots, x_{\nu_k}^0)$ such that the subvector $u(\Gamma)$ is bounded for $x \in R^{00} = \{x: x \in R_+^n, (x_{\nu_1}, \ldots, x_{\nu_k}) \leqq (x_{\nu_1}^0, \ldots, x_{\nu_k}^0)\}$.

Weak limitationality of inputs $\{\nu_1, \ldots, \nu_k\}$ (corresponding to x^0) for output subvector Γ means that if they are bounded at certain (for instance, sufficiently low) levels, outputs with indices in Γ are also bounded or limited. The same can be said of the inputs $\{\nu_{k+1}, \ldots, \nu_n\}$ (corresponding to x^1) if they are weakly limitational for output subvector Γ. Strong essentiality and weak limitationality are linked by

2.3.7 Proposition [*Shephard/Färe*, Proposition 7.2, p. 85]

A subset $\{\nu_1, \ldots, \nu_k\}$ (of indices with $1 \leqq k < n$) of n inputs is weakly limitational for every subset of a subset $\Gamma = \{\pi_1, \ldots, \pi_l\}$, $1 \leqq l \leqq m$ of m outputs if and only if it is strongly essential for Γ.

2.3.8 Proposition

Let $u \to L(u)$ Satisfy L.1–L.6 and L.A. L^0.1E holds for $u \to L(u|x^0)$ for $x^0 \in R^k_+$ if and only if $L(u) \cap D(\nu_{k+1}, \ldots, \nu_n) = \emptyset$ for $u \in R^m_+$, $u \neq 0$ (x^1 is strongly essential for output index set $\{1, 2, \ldots, m\}$).

Proof: Suppose $L(u) \cap D(\nu_{k+1}, \ldots, \nu_n) \neq \emptyset$, some $u \geqslant 0$, $u \in R^m_+$. Then there exists a point $(x^0, 0) \in L(u) \cap D(\nu_{k+1}, \ldots, \nu_n)$ with $x^0 \geqslant 0$, contradicting, L^0.1E. Q.E.D.

Before considering L^0.4, the following is introduced:

2.3.9 Definition

A set S is aureole-connected if, for $x_1, x_2 \in S$ there exists a $\lambda^* > 0$ such that for $\lambda \geqq \lambda^*$, $\lambda[x_1, x_2] \subset S$.

2.3.10 Proposition

Let $u \to L(u)$ satisfy L.1–L.6 and L.A. If $D(\nu_1, \ldots, \nu_k) \cap L(u) \neq \emptyset$, $u \in R^m_+$, $u \neq 0$ *and* $L(u)$ is aureole-connected, $u \in R^m_+$, then $u \to L(u|x^0)$ satisfies L^0.4 for $x^0 \in R^m_+$.

Proof: Consider $u \geqslant 0$, $u \in R^m_+$ with $0 < |u| < \eta$ arbitrarily small. Let $z = (z^0, z^1) \in L(u) - D(\nu_1, \ldots, \nu_k)$ where $z^0/|z^0| = x^0/|x^0|$. Let $y = (0, y^1) \in L(u) \cap D(\nu_1, \ldots, \nu_k) \neq \emptyset$ where $y^1/|y^1| = z^1/|z^1|$. By aureole-connectedness of $L(u)$, there exists an λ^* such that for $\lambda \geqq \lambda^*$, the interval $\lambda[z, y] \subset L(u)$. Let $R(x^0) :=$ $\{(q^0, q^1) R^k_+ \times R^{n-k}_+ : q^0 = x^0, q^1 \in R^{n-k}_+\}$ and chose λ^0 such that $\lambda^0 z^0 \geqq x^0$. Then $\lambda^0 [z, y] \cap R(x^0) \neq \emptyset$. Let $x^* \in \lambda^0 [z, y] \cap R(x^0)$. By L.3, $x^* \in L(u)$. By L.4 and L.6, for $\theta \geqq 1$, $\lambda_\theta \geqq 1$ such that $\lambda_\theta x_* L(\theta u)$. Consider the interval $\lambda_\theta [x_*, y] \subset L(\theta u)$ with $\lambda_\theta [x_*, y] \cap R(x^0) \neq \emptyset$. Choose $x_{2*} \in \lambda_\theta [x_*, y] \cap R(x^0) \cap L(\theta u)$. By construction, $x^0_{2*} = x^0_* = x^0$ and $x^1_{2*}/|x^1_{2*}| = x^1_*/|x^1_*| = y/|y|$. Hence there is a $\lambda^* \geqq 1$ such that $x_{2*} = (x^0, x^1_{2*}) = (x^0, \lambda^* x^1_*)$ with $(x^0, \lambda^* x^1_*) \in L(\theta u) \cap R(x^0)$ if $(x^0, x^1_*) \in L(u) \cap R(x^0)$. Hence, starting with $|u|$ as small as you like, if $\{\theta_n\}$ is a nondecreasing sequence of positive scalars greater than one, there exists a nondecreasing scalar sequence $\{\lambda_{\theta n}\}$, $\lambda_{\theta n} \geqq 1$ such that if $(x^0, x^1) \in L(u)$, then $(x^0, \lambda_{\theta n} x^1) \in L(\theta_n u)$, establishing L^0.4. Q.E.D.

2.3.11 Proposition

Let $u \to L(u)$ satisfy L.1–L.6 and L.A. If L^0.4 holds for $x^0 \in R^n_+$ then $D(\nu_1, \ldots, \nu_k) \cap L(u) \neq \emptyset$, $u \in R^m_+$.

Proof: Let $x^0 = 0$. The result follows trivially. Q.E.D.

2.3.12 Proposition

Let $u \to L(u)$ satisfy L.1–L.6 and L.A. and let $L(u)$ be aureole-connected for $u \in R^m_+$. Then L^0.4 holds for $u \to L(u|x^0)$ if and only if $D(v_1, \ldots, v_k) \cap L(u) \neq \emptyset$ for $u \in R^m_+$, $u \neq 0$ (x^0 is nonessential for output index set $\{1, 2, \ldots, m\}$).

Proof: Proposition 2.3.12 follows directly from 2.3.10–11. Q.E.D.

2.3.9 implies that the necessary and sufficient conditions for L^0.4 and extended L^0.1 given in 2.3.8 and 12 also are necessary and sufficient for, respectively, x^0 to be nonlimitational for all output subsets, x^1 to be weakly limitational for all output subsets. In commenting on this result, it seems desirable to eliminate attainability L^0.4 as a maintained hypothesis for the partial input technology in order not to preclude the possibility of limitationality of fixed inputs. The extended first axiom L^0.1E may be eliminated as a maintained hypothesis if essentiality of variable inputs is not also desired as an implied maintained hypothesis.

3. Partial Scaling and Structure

3.1 The Partial Input Scaling Function

The partial input scaling function is that neutral scaling factor which, when applied to $x^1 \in L(u|x^0)$ yields an input $\lambda x^1 \in L(u'|x^0)$ with the same input partial distance function value (relative position) in $L(u'|x^0)$ as x^1 has in $L(u|x^0)$. Therefore

$$\lambda\left(u, u', \frac{x^1}{|x^1|}\bigg|x^0\right) = \frac{\Psi(u, x^1|x^0)}{\Psi(u', x^1|x^0)},$$

and the following relationship holds:

$$L\left(u', \frac{x^1}{|x^1|}\bigg|x^0\right) = \lambda\left(u, u', \frac{x^1}{|x^1|}\bigg|x^0\right) \cdot L\left(u, \frac{x^1}{|x^1|}\bigg|x^0\right),$$

representing the ray scaling law of the partial input correspondence $u \to L(u|x^0)$.

3.2 The Partial Input Scaling Function and the Functional Structure of Technology

Suppose that the input scaling law of the partial technology $u \to L(u|x^0)$ is invariant with respect to (i) fixed inputs x^0, (ii) to variable inputs mix $x^1/|x^1|$, or (iii) to both.

3.2.1 Lemma

(i) $\lambda(u, u', x^1/|x^1||x^0) = \lambda(u, u', x^1/|x^1|)$

(ii) $\quad = \lambda(u, u'|x^0)$

(iii) $\quad = \lambda(u, u')$

if and only if

(i) $\Psi(u, x^1 | x^0) = \Psi(u, x^1)\,\omega(x^0, x^1/|x^1|)$
(ii) $\qquad = \phi(u, x^0)\, h(x^1, x^0)$
(iii) $\qquad = \epsilon(u)\, h(x^1, x^0)$
with $\psi(u, \cdot)$ and $h(\cdot, x^0)$ positively linear homogeneous (p.l.h.).

Independence of the partial scaling function to variations in all or part of the input vector has powerful structural implications for the distance function of the partial input correspondence. Proof of the Lemma is as follows:

Proof:

(i) By definition and rearrangement

$$\Psi(u, x^1 | x^0) = \lambda\left(u, u', \frac{x^1}{|x^1|}\right) \Psi(u', x^1 | x^0).$$

Treating $(x^1/|x^1|)$ as a parameter, define $f(u, u') = \lambda(u, u', (x^1/|x^1|))$ and $\Psi(u, (x^1/|x^1|) \,|\, x^0) = g(u, x^0)$, so that $g(u, x^0) = f(u, u')\, g(u', x^0)$. But this is a Sincov functional equation with solution according to *Aczel* [1970, Theorem 2, p. 303],

$$g(u; x^0) = H(u)\, G(x^0) = \psi\left(u, \frac{x^1}{|x^1|}\right) \omega\left(x^0, \frac{x^1}{|x^1|}\right)$$

$$f(u; u') = H(u)/H(u') = \psi\left(u, \frac{x^1}{|x^1|}\right) \quad \psi\left(u', \frac{x^1}{|x^1|}\right),$$

and

$$\Psi(u, x^1 | x^0) = \psi(u, x^1)\, \omega\left(x^0, \frac{x^1}{|x^1|}\right)$$

with ψ p.l.h. in x^1. Ψ of this form clearly satisfies the functional equation and (i) is established.

(ii) We have

$$\Psi(u, x^1 | x^0) = \lambda(u, u' | x^0)\, \Psi(u', x^1 | x^0),$$

which resolves to a Sincov equation when x^0 is treated as a parameter, leading to the solution (ii) in a manner exactly analogous to the above.

(iii) We have

$$\Psi(u, x^1 | x^0) = \lambda(u, u')\, \Psi(u', x^1 | x^0),$$

which is a Sincov equation in u and (x^1, x^0), the solution of which leads directly to the proof of (iii).

Q.E.D.

According to Lemma 3.2.1, when the input partial input ray scaling function is independent of the fixed input vector x^0, x^0 is separable from rays of the variable input vector; that is, variable input vectors having the same mix $(x^1/|x^1|)$. Simultaneously imposing variable input mix independence and fixed input independence has the effect of making output separable from both inputs, as in Lemma 3.2.1. From *Färe/Shephard's* [1977]

Proposition 5, mix independence of the ray scaling function implies that the technology has radial expansion path structure. Hence Lemma 3.2.1 highlights the fact that radiality of the partial technology does not by itself insure that variable inputs are homothetically separable from fixed inputs, as it would intuitively seem.

The results of Lemmas 3.2.1 have implications for the functional structure of the output correspondence as given in

3.2.2 Proposition

If

(i) $\lambda\left(u, u', \frac{x^1}{|x^1|} \middle| x^0\right) = \lambda\left(u, u', \frac{x^1}{|x^1|}\right)$

(ii) $= \lambda(u, u'|x^0)$

(iii) $= \lambda(u, u')$

then $x \to P(x)$ is characterized by

(i) $P(x^0, x^1) = P^*\left(\omega\left(x^0, \frac{x^1}{|x^1|}\right) \cdot x^1\right)$

(ii) $= P^{**}(x^0, h(x^0, x^1))$

(iii) $= P^{***}(h(x^0, x^1))$

where

$$P^*: R_+^{n-k} \to 2^{R_+^m}, \quad P^{**}: R_+^{k+1} \to 2^{R_+^m}, \quad P^{***}: R_+ \to 2^{R_+^m}$$

$$\omega: R_+^n \to R_+, \quad h: R_+^n \to R_+ \text{ with } h(x^0, \lambda x^1) = \lambda h(x^0, x^1).$$

Proof: "$\to$"

(i) From 3.2.1 $\lambda\left(u, u^1, \frac{x^1}{|x^1|} \middle| x^0\right) = \lambda\left(u, u', \frac{x^1}{|x^1|}\right)$ iff $\psi(u, x^1|x^0) =$

$\psi(u, x^1)\,\omega\left(x^0, \frac{x^1}{|x^1|}\right)$.

$$P(x^0, x^1) = \left\{u \in R_+^m : \psi(u, x^1)\,\omega\left(x^0, \frac{x^1}{|x^1|}\right) \geqq 1\right\}$$

$$= \left\{u \in R_+^m : \psi\left(u, \omega\left(x^0, \frac{x^1}{|x^1|}\right) \cdot x^1\right) \geqq 1\right\}$$

$$= P^*\left(\omega\left(x^0, \frac{x^1}{|x^1|}\right) \cdot x^1\right).$$

(ii) From 3.2.1 $\lambda\left(u, u', \frac{x^1}{|x^1|}\middle| x^0\right) = \lambda(u, u'|x^0)$ iff $\Psi(u, x^1|x^0) = \phi(u, x^0)\, h(x^0, x^1)$.

$$\begin{aligned} P(x^0, x^1) &= \{u \in R_+^m : \phi(u, x^0)\, h(x^0, x^1) \geqq 1\} \\ &= \{u \in R_+^m : \phi^*(u, x^0, h(x^0, x^1)) \geqq 1\} \\ &= P^{**}(x^0, h(x^0, x^1)). \end{aligned}$$

(iii) From 3.2.1 $\lambda\left(u, u', \frac{x^1}{|x^1|}\middle| x^0\right) = \lambda(\mathrm{u}, \mathrm{u}')$ iff $\Psi(u, x^1|x^0) = \epsilon(u)\, h(x^0, x^1)$.

$$\begin{aligned} P(x^0, x^1) &= \{u \in R_+^m : \epsilon(u)\, h(x^0, x^1) \geqq 1\} \\ &= \{u \in R_+^m : \epsilon^*(u, h(x^0, x^1)) \geqq 1\} \\ &= P^{***}(h(x^0, x^1)) \end{aligned}$$

"←"

(i) $$\begin{aligned} P^*\left(\omega\left(x^0, \frac{x^1}{|x^1|}\right)\cdot x^1\right) &= \left\{u : \psi\left(u, \omega\left(x^0, \frac{x^1}{|x^1|}\right)\cdot x^1\right) \geqq 1\right\} \\ &= \left\{u : \psi(u, x^1)\, \omega\left(x^0, \frac{x^1}{|x^1|}\right) \geqq 1\right\} \end{aligned}$$

by homogeneity of the distance function ψ. So

$$\Psi(u, x^1|x^0) = \psi(u, x^1)\, \omega\left(x^0, \frac{x^1}{|x^1|}\right).$$

(ii) $P^{**}(x^0, h(x^0, x^1)) = \{u : \phi^*(u, x^0, h(x^0, x^1)) \geqq 1\}$

Let $h(x^0, x^1) = z$. Since

$\phi^*(u, x^0, h(x^0, \lambda x^1)) = \lambda\phi^*(u, x^0, h(x^0, x^1))$ and $h(x^0, \lambda x^1) = \lambda h(x^0, x^1)$,

$\phi^*(u, x^0, \lambda z) = \lambda\phi^*(u, x^0, z)$

with $z \in R_+$. Hence $\phi^*(u, x^0, z) = \phi(u, x^0)\, z$ and

$$\begin{aligned} \Psi(u, x^1|x^0) &= \phi^*(u, x^0, h(x^0, x^1)) \\ &= \phi(u, x^0)\, h(x^0, x^1). \end{aligned}$$

(iii) $$\begin{aligned} P^{***}(h(x^0, x^1)) &= \{u : f(u, h(x^0, x^1)) \geqq 1\} \\ &= \{u : f(u, 1)\, h(x^0, x^1) \geqq 1\} \\ &= \{u ; \epsilon(u)\, h(x^0, x^1) \geqq 1\} \end{aligned}$$

and

$\Psi(u, x^1|x^0) = \epsilon(u)\, h(x^0, x^1)$. Q.E.D.

As expected, the last two scaling function invariances imply and are implied by output correspondences which are input ray-homothetic (but not necessarily output ray homothetic) in x^1 conditional on x^0. If the partial input scaling function is independent of fixed input x^0, x^0 is implied to be separable in the output correspondence from rays of variable inputs x^1 in the partial distance function. When u is a scalar, we can define the production function

$$\Phi(x^0, x^1) = \max \{u \in R_+ : \Psi(u, x^1 | x^0) \geqq 1\},$$

in which case, the production function is homothetic in x^1 conditional on x^0 under scaling invariances (ii) and (iii).

In cases (i) and (iii) it is possible to identify interesting specific structures for the unrestricted distance function. The following concept will be useful:

3.2.3 Definition

A function $f: R^n \to R$ is said to be super-homogeneous of degree k if for $\lambda \geqq 1$, $f(\lambda x) \geqq \lambda^k f(x)$ and $f(\lambda^{-1} \cdot x) \leqq \lambda^{-k} f(x)$. f is said to be strictly super-homogeneous of degree k if, additionally, for $\lambda > 1$, $f(\lambda x) > \lambda^k f(x)$ and $f(\lambda^{-1} x) < \lambda^{-k} f(x)$.

3.2.4 Proposition

If

(i) $\Psi(u, x^1 | x^0) = \psi(u, x^1)\, \omega(x^0, x^1/|x^1|)$

(ii) $\qquad = \epsilon(u)\, h(x^1, x^0)$

with ψ and h p.l.h. in x^1, and ω and h strictly super-homogeneous of degree -1 in x^0, then $\Psi(u, x^0, x^1)$, the unrestricted distance function, is characterized by

(i) $\Psi(u, x^0, x^1) = q(x^0, \psi(u, x^1), x^1/|x^1|)$

(ii) $\qquad = \beta(x^0, \epsilon(u)\, |x^1|, x^1/|x^1|)$

with q p.l.h. in $(x^0, \psi(\cdot,\cdot))$, β p.l.h. in $(x^0, \epsilon(\cdot)\, |\cdot|)$, q strictly increasing in ψ, and β strictly increasing in $\epsilon(\cdot)\, |\cdot|$.

Proof:

(i) $\Psi(u, x^0, x^1) = \{\lambda^{-1} : \Psi(u, \lambda x^1 | \lambda x^0) = 1\}$

$\qquad = \{\lambda^{-1} : \psi(u, \lambda x^1)\, \omega(\lambda x^0, x^1/|x^1|) = 1\}$

$\qquad = \{\lambda^{-1} : \lambda^{-1}/\omega(\lambda x^0, x^1/|x^1|) = \psi(u, x^1)\}$.

Let $q^{-1}(\lambda^{-1}, x^0, x^1/|x^1|) := \lambda^{-1}/\omega(\lambda x^0, x^1/|x^1|)$ and let q^{-1} be strictly monotonic in λ^{-1}.

Then

$\Psi(u, x^0, x^1) = \lambda^{-1} = q(x^0, \psi(u, x^1), x^1/|x^1|)$

with q p.l.h. in $(x^0, \psi(\cdot,\cdot))$ and strictly monotonic in $\psi(\cdot,\cdot)$. By L.3P $\Psi(u, x^0, \lambda x^1) \geqq \Psi(u, x^0, x^1)$, $\lambda \geqq 1$, hence, q must be strictly increasing in

$\psi(\cdot,\cdot).q^{-1}$ is therefore strictly increasing in λ^{-1}, and this implies that for $(\lambda^{-1})' \lesseqgtr (\lambda^{-1}), (\lambda^{-1})'/\omega((\lambda^{-1})'^{-1}x^0) \lesseqgtr (\lambda^{-1})/\omega((\lambda^{-1})^{-1}x^0)$ and hence as $\lambda' \lesseqgtr \lambda$, $\lambda/\lambda' \lesseqgtr \omega(\lambda' x^0)/\omega(\lambda x^0)$. This implies that for $\lambda > 1, \lambda^{-1}\omega(x^0) < \omega(\lambda x^0)$ and $\lambda\omega(x^0) < \omega(\lambda^{-1}x^0)$, or, that $\omega(\cdot)$ is strictly super-homogeneous of degree minus one.

(ii) $\Psi(u, x^0, x^1) = \{\lambda^{-1} : \epsilon(u)\, h(\lambda x^1, \lambda x^0) = 1\}$

$$= \{\lambda^{-1} : \lambda^{-1}/h(x^1/|x^1|, (\lambda^{-1})^{-1}x^0) = \epsilon(u)\,|x^1|\}.$$

Let $\beta^{-1}(\lambda^{-1}, x^0, x^1/|x^1|) := \lambda^{-1}/h(x^1/|x^1|, (\lambda^{-1})^{-1}x^0)$ be strictly monotonic in λ^{-1}. Then $\Psi(u, x^0, x^1) = \lambda^{-1} = \beta(x^0, \epsilon(u)\,|x^1|, x^1/|x^1|)$. β must therefore be strictly increasing or strictly decreasing in $\epsilon(\cdot)\,|\cdot|$. It is the former, since otherwise L.3P would be violated. By an argument similar to that concerned with the super-homogeneity of $\omega(\cdot)$ in (i), it can be shown that $h(x^1/|x^1|, x^0)$ must therefore be strictly super-homogeneous of degree -1 in x^0.

Q.E.D.

Note that our approach has generated no truly separable structures for inputs in the usual sense of the term, though 3.2.4 (i) generates a structure for the output correspondence in which it can be said that inputs $\nu_1, \ldots, \nu_k$ are separable from rays of inputs $\nu_{k+1}, \ldots, \nu_n$. It would be sufficient for separability to hold in (i) if $\omega(x^0, (x^1/|x^1|)) = \omega(x^0)$, and in (ii) and (iii) if $h(x^0, (x^1/|x^1|)) = h(x^0)$. The types of separability involved are asymmetric separability of x^1 from x^0 in (i), and asymmetric homothetic separability of x^1 from x^0 in (ii) and (iii). Formally

3.2.5 Proposition

(i) $\Psi(u, x^1|x^0) = \psi(u, x^1)\,\omega(x^0)$

(ii) $\Psi(u, x^1|x^0) = \phi(u, x^0)\,|x^1|\,h(x^0)$

(iii) $\Psi(u, x^1|x^0) = \epsilon(u)\,|x^1|\,h(x^0)$

with ψ p.l.h. in x^1 and ω and h strictly super-homogeneous of degree -1 in x^0, iff

(i) $P(x^0, x^1) = P^*(\omega(x^0)\,x^1)$

$\Psi(u, x^0, x^1) = q(x^0, \psi(u, x^1))$

(ii) $P(x^0, x^1) = P^{**}(x^0, h(x^0)\,|x^1|)$

$\Psi(u, x^0, x^1) = \gamma(u, x^0, |x^1|)$

(iii) $P(x^0, x^1) = P^{***}(h(x^0)\,|x^1|)$

$\Psi(u, x^0, x^1) = \beta(x^0, \epsilon(u)\,|x^1|)$.

The proof parallels that of Proposition 3.2.4. This result is quite restrictive in (ii) and (iii) of this proposition in that the aggregator for x^1 is the Euclidean norm. However, a more general result obtains if, in

(ii) $\Psi(u, x^1|x^0) = \phi(u, x^0)\,g(x^1)\,h(x^1/g(x^1), x^0)$

(iii) $\Psi(u, x^1|x^0) = \epsilon(u)\,g(x^1)\,h(x^1/g(x^1), x^0)$,

h is independent of $x^1/g(x^1)$ for some linear homogeneous function $g(\cdot)$. Hence, with no loss of generality, $|x^1|$ may be replaced by $g(x1)$ in Proposition 3.2.5.

Using the homogeneity of q, γ, and β in $(x^0, \cdot)$, $(x^0, h(\cdot) g(\cdot))$, and $(x^0, \epsilon(\cdot) g(\cdot))$, respectively, it is simple to put (i) – (iii) of Proposition 3.2.5 in the separable [*Blackorby/ Primont/Russell*] or quasi-separable [*Gorman*] canonical form $\Psi(u, x^0, x^1) = \Psi^*(u, x^0, \psi(u, x^1))$.

4. Concluding Remarks

This has been a study in penetrating the "fine structure" of the *Shephard* [1974] model of a stationary state technology, aimed in this case at discerning the structure of a production model in which a subvector of inputs is held fixed. In section 3, the results suggest that the analyst may have to begin with a set of properties even weaker than Shephard's when specifying a technical model for a particular application, unless he is confident that all inputs are enumerated, or that he will incur negligible error by ignoring omitted inputs. The greater generality permits the use of, for example, translated models in which the translation point is outside R^n_+, with the domain restricted to R^n_+. This is allowed by the weakened first axiom of the partial model, L^0.1E, which admits the possibility that $0 \in L(u|x^0)$, $u \geqslant 0$, when x^1 is inessential. It is not surprising that an attainability axiom L^0.4 fails to hold when fixed inputs are essential and hence weak limitational. In section 3, invariance of the input partial scaling function to fixed inputs and/or variable inputs mix is shown to be allowed when the unrestricted technology exhibits various structures, similar to, but weaker than, separability between fixed and variable inputs. These invariances may be useful when, for example, it is desired to index the change in a subvector of inputs required by a change in output given that the remaining inputs are constant, but have unknown levels.

References

Aczél, J.: Lectures in Functional Equations and Their Applications. New York–San Francisco–London 1970.

Blackorby, C., D. Primont, and *R. Russell*: Duality, Separability, and Functional Structure: Theory an and Applications. New York–Amsterdam 1978.

Färe, R., and *R. Shephard*: Ray-Homothetic Production Functions. Econometrica **45**, 1977, 133–146.

Gorman, W.: Tricks with Utility Functions. Essays in Economic Analysis: Proceedings of the 1975 AU AUTE Conference, Sheffield. Ed. by M. Artis and A. Mobay. Cambridge 1976.

Shephard, R.: Theory of Cost and Production Functions. Princeton 1970.

– : Semi-Homogeneous Production Functions and Scaling of Production. Production Theory. Ed. by W. Eichhorn et al. New York–Heidelberg–Berlin 1974.

Shephard, R., and *R. Färe*: The Law of Diminishing Returns. Zeitschrift für Nationalökonomie **34**, 1974, 69–90.

Part II
Dynamic Structures and Optimization

Quantitative Studies on Production and Prices © Physica-Verlag, Würzburg–Wien, 1983.

Optimal Capital Utilisation in British Manufacturing Industry[1])

Derek L. Bosworth and *Peter J. Dawkins*

1. Introduction

The study of capital utilisation has occupied an increasingly important place in the literature on both the production function and factor demand models, which focus on the relationship between output (itself a per period flow) and the flows of various factor services consumed in the production process. In such models the associated flows are specified for a given period, but the time at which the factor services are consumed in the production process within the period are not considered to be important. To ignore variations in the rate of input flows is to ignore a central technical characteristic of the production process. It may be conceivable that the firm can modify the number of employees required to man a particular machine, at least within certain limits, but it seems unlikely that the vast majority of machines can be left to work unmanned for any substantial period of time. In contrast with the production and employment function literature, the timing of input flows has been a central concern of the capital utilisation literature, but the theories have tended to be simplistic and have not been incorporated into production and employment models.

The research reported in this paper attempts a more realistic explanation of the optimal level of intended capital idleness, linking capital utilisation with the associated patterns of work commonly observed in the real world. In so doing it develops an explanation of the distribution of work patterns and provides a basis on which future research can incorporate this important element of time patterns of work into employment functions. In Section (2) we provide a brief, but critical review of the existing theory relating to optimal capital utilisation and optimal work patterns. Section (3) describes a theoretical framework that attempts to bridge the gap between capital utilisation and the work patterns adopted by firms. This theory depends crucially on the concepts of the least cost labour envelope and the marginal capital savings curve. The data available to test the new theoretical framework are discussed in Section (4). In Section (5) we report on the results of an attempt to establish the least cost labour envelope and the associated average and

[1]) We would like to thank our colleagues at Loughborough University and at Warwick University who have taken the trouble to comment on earlier drafts of this paper. We would also like to express our gratitude to the European Foundation for the Improvement of Living and Working Conditions, which funded some of our early research in this area. Last, and not least, we wish to thank the organizers for allowing us to present the ideas contained in this paper before a distinguished audience.

marginal cost of labour curves. In Section (6) a similar exercise is reported for the attempt to establish the marginal capital savings curve. These two curves are brought together in Section (7) in order to establish the optimal utilisation/work pattern combination for British manufacturing industry, bearing in mind that the analysis is rather aggregate and the results relate to some form of average or modal position. Finally, Section (8) draws a number of conclusions about the approach adopted in this paper, about the difficulties encountered and about associated policy issues.

Before starting on the main body of the paper, one or two further introductory comments seem to be in order. First, while the research reported below has been going on for some time, a great deal remains to be done. For example, work has only just begun to incorporate shiftworking into factor demand models estimated for the British economy. Second, space does not allow a complete discussion of all of the theoretical niceties, data problems, etc., that we would like to have touched upon. Nevertheless, the interested reader can find further discussion reported elsewhere.[2])

2. Review of the Literature

For all that the traditional employment models [e.g. *Ball/St. Cyr*] say about the matter, labour might work during daylight hours, while the capital stock is run at night. Even the factor demand models that purport to explain capital utilisation [e.g. *Nadiri/Rosen*] do not develop any links between the timing of various inputs. If it seems reasonable to assume that a machine that is run for, say, 20 hours per day requires a certain cohort of labour to man it at each and every point in time,[3]) then a new technical link is being introduced that the conventional models cannot handle. Where capital must be manned when it is in operation, then the degree of capital utilisation cannot be independent of the pattern of work adopted by the firm for its employees. The pattern of work chosen has direct implications for the total number of men that the firm will require and the number of hours that each employee will work at any given level of output.

The large and growing literature on capital utilisation appears to fall into two fairly distinct schools. The first has attempted to develop theoretical models of capital utilisation, analysing and explaining[4]) the cessation of productive activities at less than 100 per cent of technical maximum productive capacity caused by rhythmically varying factor prices. While the predictions of such models [*Winston/McCoy*] give important insights about the causes of intended capital idleness, the assumptions that have to be made to ensure mathematical tractability severely restrict the usefulness of the models in context of the real world. More realistic models will need to take into account somewhat more complicated factor price rhythms and, in addition, the fact that the lengths of shift are

---

[2]) A general review of the area (and, in particular, our contribution to the debate) is provided in *Bosworth/Dawkins* [1981]. A more detailed review of data can be found in *Bosworth/Dawkins* [1979].

[3]) This may not, of course, be reasonable in certain processes (particularly where chemical reactions are involved) such as in the production or iron and steel and in certain chemicals industrials.

[4]) We ignore here the work dealing with unintended idleness caused by such events as deficient product demand and input shortages [for a general review, see *Winston*, 1974, p. 1302; for a discussion of some U.K. examples, see *Eels*; and for some practical international examples, see UNIDO].

not perfectly divisible. Existing models are only indirectly and very tenuously linked to particular types of observable work patterns. The theoretical models simply assume a rhythmical wage pattern without investigating the implied shift systems and the underlying supply and demand for labour curves that give rise to the observed premia [*Bosworth/Dawkins/Westaway*, 1981a, 1981b]. Shiftwork data have been used to construct measures of capital utilisation, [*Foss*, p. 16; *Bosworth/Dawkins*, 1981, Chapter 13] and, thereby, as a basis for testing *ad hoc* models explaining machine idleness, using the central variables thrown up by the theoretical exercises, *Winston* [1971, 1974] and *Hughes* et al. [1976].

The second group of models are those dealing with the firm's choice between one-, two- or three-shift systems and have, therefore, developed more intimate links between the choice of work pattern and the degree of capital utilisation [*Winston*, 1974; *Kim/Winston; Heathfield*, 1976; *Robinson*, 1977, 1978]. The models comprising this second group are also unrealistic in certain respects. First, they deal only with one-, two- or three-shift alternatives and not with the large variety of choices of patterns open to firms. Second, the models incorporate no real role for overtime working, in contrast with the short-run factor demand models where overtime tends to act as a buffer against short-term adjustments [*Ball/St. Cyr*] but where shiftworking is not explicitly included. It is of some concern that models of optimal work patterns do not fit naturally into the employment function and factor demand literature.

It is already clear from this discussion that, in both sets of work, the research has not advanced beyond the most rudimentary of connections between capital utilisation and shiftwork. The focus of this paper is the choice of the optimal work pattern (i.e., shift and overtime system) to man a given level of utilisation. The model developed below incorporates the choice between all of the common alternative work patterns open to the firm and is therefore substantially more realistic than the existing discrete models. Because of the nature of the choices open to the firm (and, in particular, the existence of fixed costs per worker) overtime working can be shown to often be a potentially permanent feature of desired factor services and not just the transitory buffer assumed in earlier models. In order to demonstrate this, the concept of a 'least cost labour envelope' is developed which can, in principle, not only be incorporated into a *Nadiri/Rosen* [1969] type model, but can be estimated directly on the basis of available British data. While this means that (at a later date) revised factor demand equations can be estimated, this present paper limits itself to the more modest goal of establishing the existence and nature of the least cost labour envelope for the British manufacturing sector and, in a partial model, estimates the optimal level of capital utilisation and the associated mix of work patterns. The least cost envelope is argued in Section (3) to be the bridging link between the continuous and discrete models described above.

3. A Theoretical Framework Linking Capital Utilisation and Work Patterns

The theory developed in this section relates to production processes used in the manufacturing sector, where machines must be manned when they are operating. Thus, the hours that machines are running must be covered by labour: normal hours (i.e. of about 40 hours per week) can be covered wholly within the normal working week (i.e. of five days length, from, say, 9.00 am to 5.00 pm) with no overtime; higher levels of capital utilisation require the firm to adopt a more intensive sort of work pattern, such as 'normal day plus overtime' or 'normal day plus twilight' working. As more intensive shift patterns are adopted, working hours increasingly spread outside of the 'normal working day' and are associated with higher wage payments. Based on information about shift premia, it is possible to construct a curve that represents the costs of maintaining machine coverage by a single worker at any given point in time during the operating week. This does not mean that it is necessarily the same worker at all points during the operating week, the model allows one worker to replace another on a shift system. The first cost concept therefore is the average cost per hour of ensuring that one worker is available in the plant during all of the hours that the machinery is running.

As far as the analysis of the labour costs of manning plant and machinery are concerned, the normal taxonomy of 'fixed' and 'variable' costs is useful. In this context, fixed costs are those that depend on the number of employees (i.e., a per person payment), while variable costs are established as an hourly rate. The burden of fixed costs per hour can be expected to decline therefore, as they are spread increasingly thinly over larger numbers of hours per worker. The variable costs of labour can be expected to rise as the length of operating day increases, with employers incurring higher and higher overtime rates or shift premia. On this logic, the average labour cost per hour will fall with the length of operating day up to the point where the higher hourly rates associated with overtime just offset the declining fixed costs per hour. A '*U*-shaped' average labour cost curve is expected to characterise each type of system.[5]) The minimum point on the '*U*-shaped' curve can be expected at, or just after, the normal length of working day (i.e., at or just after the point where overtime rates become operative). This will occur around the 40 hour mark for a normal day system, 80 hours for a two-shift system, 120 hours for a three-shift and 160 hours for a four-crew-three-shift system.

On the assumption that the fixed costs per worker on the more intensive shift patterns are at least the same as for normal day workers, then the average cost of labour curve for progressively more intensive systems will lie at successively higher levels. In addition, we might expect that turnover, absenteeism, training, transport and canteen costs will also increase with the intensity of the shift system adopted. The result is the set of labour cost curves shown in Figure 1.[6])

If, in addition, it can be assumed that the curves lie in a fairly regular pattern, the minimum cost or best practice situation can be represented by the dotted line, the 'average labour cost per machine hour envelope', *E*, in Figure 1. Thus, the envelope function shows the minimum average cost per hour of maintaining 'one worker cover' on a particular process during the whole of the operational day. In focusing at such a micro level, the curves ignore the fact that the total number of workers required to man the process at any one point during the operating day will vary with the length of operating day. The total labour cost of running the process at the desired level is therefore the 'average cost

[5]) There may, however, be additional, physical limits laid down by the law or by company policy, concerning the maximum number of hours overtime that it is possible to work in any one day, week or any other stipulated period of time (Health and Safety Executive).

[6]) The notation in Figure 1 is as follows: *ND* – normal day; *T* – twilight shift; *DD* – double days; *PN* – permanent nights; 3*S* – three shifts; 4*C*3*S* – four crew: three shift; *O* – overtime.

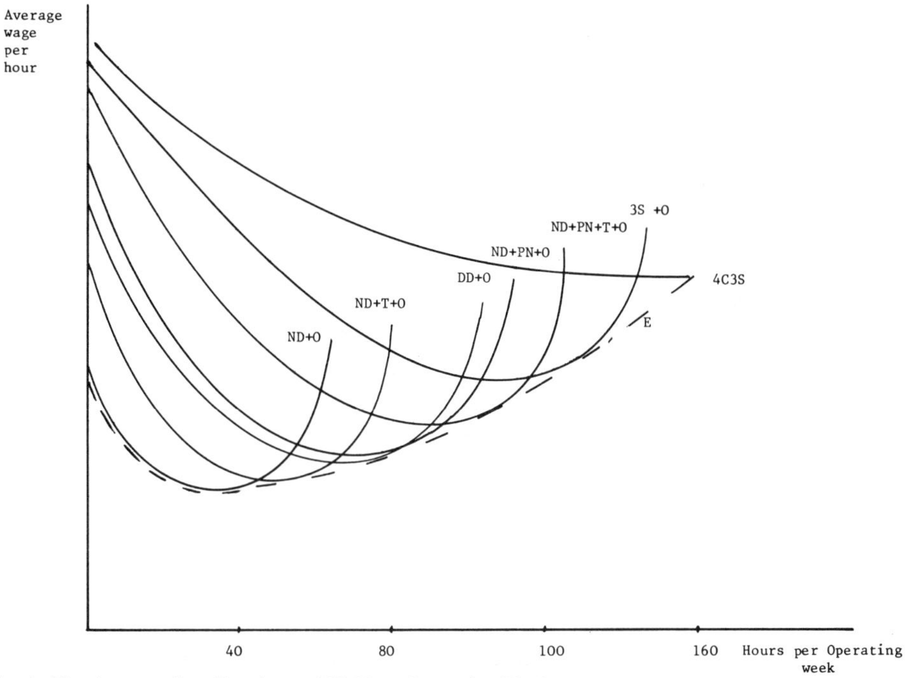

Fig. 1: The Average Cost Envelope: 168 Hour Operating Week

per hour' (as indicated in Figure 1) x the number of operating hours x the number of men employed on that process at any one point in time during the operating day. The average cost per hour at the process level can be obtained by dividing this total labour cost by the length of operating day; the marginal cost of capital utilisation is found by differentiating the total labour cost with respect to the length of operating day. The theoretical forms of the average cost envelope, ACE, and the marginal cost curve, MC, are shown in Figure 2 .

At first sight, the minimum point on the ACE curve in Figure 2 would appear to be the optimal point for the firm. At this point, however, only the labour costs are at a minimum. Only if no other costs varied with the length of operating day would this be the cost minimising solution. The model would collapse to a form almost identical to the hours 'sub model' described by *Ball/St. Cyr* [1966]. It is clear, however, that the length of operating day will also affect the amount of capital required by the firm. While the precise magnitude of capital savings are difficult to measure, it is relatively easy to show the existence and potential importance of the concept. *A priori* expectations would suggest that the physical amount of capital required (i.e., the number of machines of a given type) and the number of hours that the capital works are fairly close substitutes in the production of a given level of output. The precise degree of substitution should be found by specifying and estimating the production relationship. Based on the simplest of approaches, the marginal capital savings curve appears to decline with the length of operating day, as shown in Figure 2. Equilibrium of the firm can therefore be expected to occur at utilisation level U^*, where the marginal labour costs of working an extra hour are exactly off-set by the marginal capital savings.

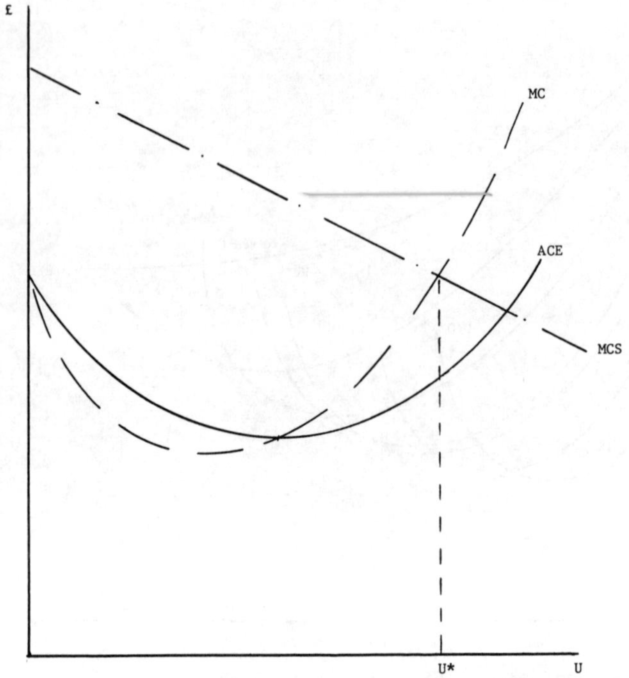

Fig. 2: The Costs and Benefits of Capital Utilisation: The Optimal Level of Capital Utilisation

The existing theories of capital utilisation and the optimal choice of work pattern, including the theory outlined above, assume a single, homogenous output and a single production process. These assumptions simplify the theoretical models, but are clearly untenable at the firm or industry level, where many processes are involved and a mix of work patterns are observable in practice. While the generalisation of the theory to allow for different mixes of processes has been discussed elsewhere [*Bosworth/Dawkins*, 1981], there is insufficient space here, and the analysis proceeds on the assumption that it makes sense to talk in terms of an average or modal position.

4. Data and Sources

Detailed information is required about both labour and capital. Construction of the model requires information about the amounts of the factors used in the production process and the prices that the firm faces in purchasing them. Thus, empirical validation of the theory makes rather unusual data demands that cannot entirely be met. Official sources simply do not collect the sort of information that would allow all aspects of the labour costs and the capital savings to be estimated. Ideally, for example, information is required about the productivity of labour on different work patterns, about the different costs of non-wage payments to labour (such as the provision of transport and canteen facilities), etc. It is hoped that these additional dimensions will be the subject of future firm level survey activity. Nevertheless, the essential numbers and costs necessary to approximate the labour cost envelope and the marginal capital savings curve are available, even if considerable work is needed on them to manipulate them into a useful form.

In order to construct the labour cost curves, information is needed about the numbers of workers employed on the alternative work patterns and about all of the various labour costs by type of system. The five basic dimensions to the wage paid to employees are: (a) guaranteed wage; (b) basic wage per hour; (c) normal length of working week; (d) (d) shift premia; (e) overtime premia. Data on all these aspects of employment and labour costs are taken from *Time Rates of Wages and Hours of Work*, published annually by the Department of Employment. This source has several important problems: it relates to a series of collective agreements for which there is no simple set of weights available to aggregate the data to the level of all manufacturing industry,[7]) in addition, as the data relates to collective agreements, it almost certainly means that actual plant level prices and costs will tend to be minima.[8]) In addition, there is a single, non-wage payment of employer's National Insurance Contributions. Data on NICs are taken from the *Annual Abstract of Financial Statistics*, published by the Central Statistical Office (CSO) [annually].

In order to estimate the marginal capital savings curve, data are required about the amount of plant and machinery utilised by the manufacturing sector, about its life expectancy and about its rate of deterioration as it is used in the production process. Capital stock data are available annually for the manufacturing sector in *National Income and Expenditure*, published by the CSO. Compatible information concerning life expectancies is also available, in this case from *Economic Trends*, published by the CSO. The latter are only available as a single spot observation and it is not possible to estimate the relationship between life expectancy and utilisation from available data, although, again, it is hoped that later survey work will be useful here. While it is impossible to avoid using published data on life expectancies, the use of information about the rate of depreciation of capital (which is probably even less reliable) was circumvented by simulating possible utilisation/life expectancy/depreciation alternatives. While further work is possible using official statistics of capital consumption (relating them to levels of utilisation of capital), this does not appear to be a particularly rewarding avenue to investigate, given the immense problems of measurement associated with the available statistics on the deterioration of capital.

It is hoped that, in time, the model can be constructed for several years during the post-war period. Given the detailed and far-reaching data requirements, however, the present study concentrates on the year 1977–1978. The data, its sources and main problems are discussed in somewhat more detail elsewhere [see *Bosworth/Dawkins*, 1979, Appendix].

---

[7]) Simple averages across agreements are used in the calculations reported in this paper. While we are just about to experiment with weights based on the relative numbers of workers covered by the various collective agreements, we do not think that the end results will be particularly sensitive to these changes.

[8]) In the later simulations, the basic wage is increased from the level shown in the nationally negotiated premia to the average level indicated to exist in other sources as explained below.

5. Labour Cost Envelope and the Marginal Labour Cost Curve

The calculations were carried out for the 168 hours potentially available during the week (although analogous calculations can be undertaken covering the 24 hour day or the potential operating year). For simplicity in the tables, the results are reported as averages or totals for 5 hourly intervals. The first element of pay, the guaranteed wage, was calculated to average £38.72 across collective agreements in the manufacturing sector. The employer's costs per hour are therefore extremely high if a guaranteed wage is in operation and the employees are only working a proportion of the normal hours for that system. The average labour cost per hour on any given system therefore declines as this fixed cost is averaged out over a larger and larger number of hours per day. The second element of pay is the normal hourly wage. For normal day workers this is the basic rate, cumulated over the number of hours actually worked. Where a shift premium is in operation, which is the case on all systems except normal day, earnings are accumulated at the enhanced rate (ranging from about 13 per cent for double day shifts to over 25 per cent for permanent nights). As long as earnings per week are less than the guaranteed wage, then the effective wage rate is the guaranteed weekly wage divided by the number of hours worked (the guaranteed wage of £38.72 compared with a basic wage of £40.68). As soon as earnings achieve this guaranteed level then the basic or the shift enhanced rate becomes operative. Once normal hours have been completed then any further work is paid for at the going overtime rate (ranging from around time-and-a-third for the first few hours of overtime each week, up to approximately double-time for the most expensive hours). These basic labour costs are further augmented by the necessity of paying National Insurance Contributions (at an average rate of 9.25% for the period covered by the study), the lower and upper earnings limits (i.e. of around £14 and £100 respectively) did not affect any of the calculated employer payments as average earnings of all the groups under consideration fell within this range.

Having calculated the total costs of coverage for each system, they are divided by the number of hours covered in order to derive the average labour cost curves (i.e. the costs of maintaining one worker cover over the operating day). These average cost curves appear in Figure 3 and each of them (with perhaps the exception of the four crew: three shift) is '*U*-shaped', intersecting a higher curve in its upward sloping range. The diagram indicates that, other things equal, the employer will alter the choice of system according to the operating week worked by the firm: at a level of 42 hours per week, the firm chooses a normal day system with a small amount of overtime ($ND + O$); at a level of 130 hours per week or more, the firm will choose a four-crew-three-shift system ($4C3S$).[9]) The firm must clearly have some reason why it might choose to pay an extra £0.24 per hour (or around £40.32 per week) on an intensive shift system, rather than employ a larger number of employees on a normal day system.

Figure 3 shows the average cost envelope as the dotted line E. While it is a continuous curve, nevertheless, it is formed from two distinct parts: the main body of the E curve, which lies to the right of its minimum point, is determined by the levels of basic pay, shift premia and overtime rates; the E curve to the left of its minimum point is dominated

[9]) See footnote 6 for a description of the notation used.

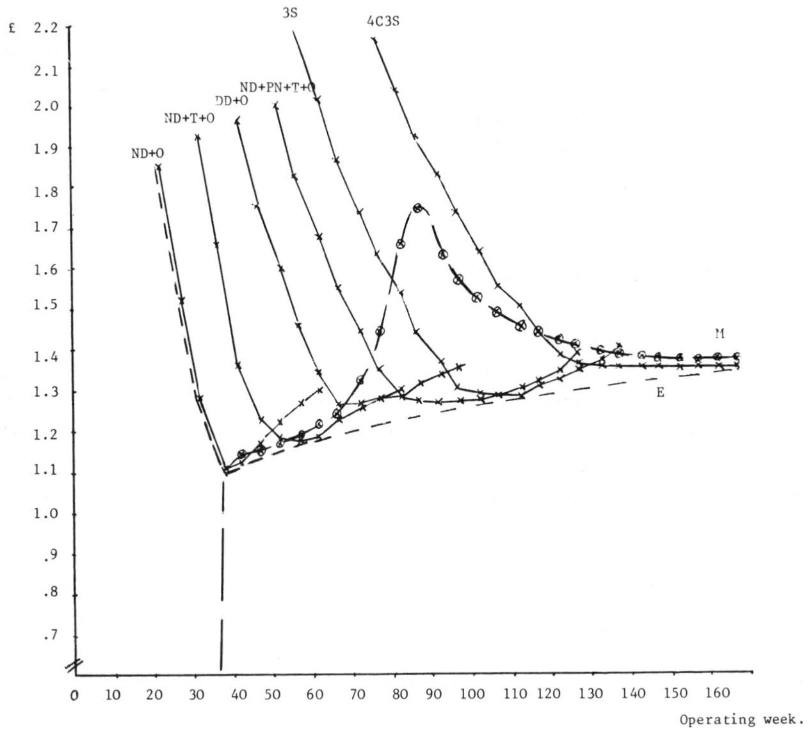

Fig. 3: The Average Labour Cost Curves

by the guaranteed minimum wage. The associated marginal cost of maintaining one worker cover is calculated as the change in the total cost (defined as E x number of hours) brought about by a change in the number of hours worked. The shape of the M curve is determined largely by the two halves of the E curve. The guaranteed wage is a fixed cost and, in the range where the guaranteed wage is operative, the marginal costs of extra hours of work are close to zero. As soon as the guaranteed wage has been covered, the marginal cost curve becomes positive. It continues to rise as longer operating hours call in progressively more and more expensive overtime and shift systems. Above the two shift systems, however, the three-shift and continental systems, although more expensive, do not raise the total costs of labour at the same rate. The result is that the marginal cost curve reaches a maximum and then falls away gradually. It should be remembered, however, that the M curve (even on its downward sloping section) is formed as a locus of points, each of which is drawn from an upward sloping marginal cost curve associated with a particular work pattern.

These curves only relate to the costs of ensuring single worker cover during the operating day. The total labour costs, however, can be calculated as the average labour costs per hour x the number of hours x the number of men. Clearly, therefore, what happens to total labour costs depends crucially on the rate at which men can be substituted for hours. This could be estimated directly in a factor demand model of the Nadiri and Rosen type (although using a more general technology of production). In the work reported in this paper, it is assumed that firms can compensate a one per cent decrease in hours by a one per cent increase in the number of men employed at any point during the operating day. Total costs are therefore a constant multiple of average costs per hour (the multiple chosen is the total number of employee hours consumed by the manufacturing sector, of just under 170 millions).

6. Capital Savings and Capital Utilisation

The value of capital stock for the manufacturing sector is used to calculate a 'rental' or 'user cost' of capital per week. While the gross replacement value of plant and machinery (totalling some £138.13 thousand millions in 1977) is perhaps the most reliable capital concept reported in official statistics, the net value of capital (which allows for past depreciation in deriving a measure of the current stock of capital) is perhaps more appropriate. This suggests a net value of plant and machinery in the order of £86.31 thousand millions for the manufacturing sector. Using this data, it is possible to construct an approximate rental. The calculation assumes: a fixed rate of interest over the life expectancy of the capital; that the firm pays interest on the debt outstanding; and that it repays the cost of capital in equal weekly installments over the expected lifetime of the capital. The rental also takes into account investment allowances, which are assumed to be set against taxes on company profits. Thus, the rental is calculated using the formula,

$$R = \frac{1}{52} \cdot Z \cdot \frac{(1+i)^T - t\sigma Z\,(1+i)^{T-1}}{[(1+i)^{T-1} + (1+i)^{T-2} + \ldots + (1+i)^0}$$

where R is the constant weekly payment or 'rental'; Z is the initial cost of the capital, the 'sunk' cost; T denotes the life expectancy of capital; i is the rate of interest to be paid on the funds used to finance the purchase of machinery or the opportunity cost of those funds used elsewhere; t is the tax rate on company profits; σ is the proportion of the investment allowable against profits.

Data to slot into this formula can only be approximate. Examination of the shiftwork data indicated that plant and machinery in the manufacturing sector were operated for an average of 50.17 hours per week. The life expectancy of capital was around 32.9 years at this time. It was again assumed that a one percent increase in the number of hours capital is utilised results in a one percent reduction in the amount of capital required, other things being equal. While it seems likely that the life expectancy of capital will be related to the degree of utilisation, no data exists to establish the precise relationship. Hence, a number of alternative scenarios are simulated, where a one percent increase in utilisation produces either a zero, one, two or three percent decrease in life expectancy. The rate of interest varied during 1977 and, again, it was decided to simulate alternative rentals based on rates of interest of 6, 8 and 10 per cent. The rate of tax on company profits was assumed to be 52 per cent, with a 100 per cent of the investment allowable against tax.

The resulting estimates of the marginal capital savings curves are shown in Figure 4. The figures in brackets (e.g. (6, 3)) indicate the assumed rate of interest and the assumed

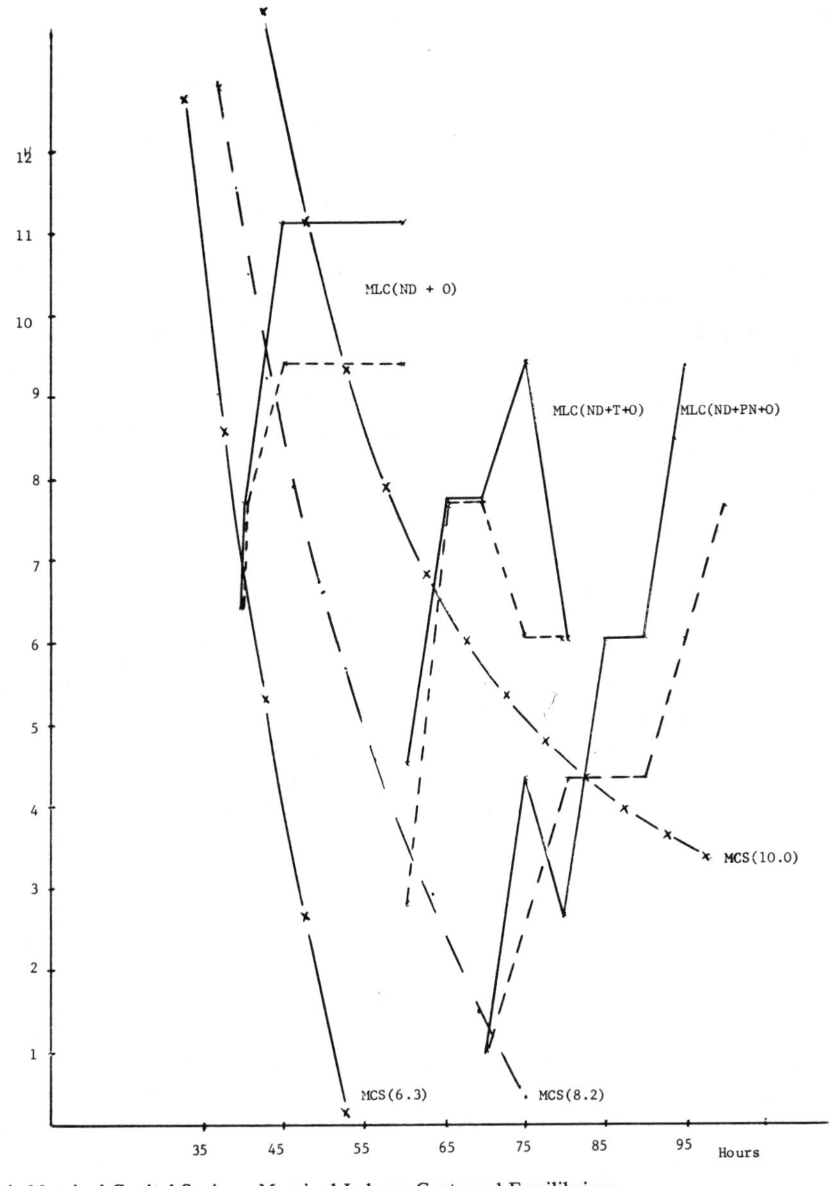

Fig. 4: Marginal Capital Savings, Marginal Labour Costs and Equilibrium

rate of trade-off between utilisation and life expectancy. Thus, the extreme *MCS* curves are shown by *MCS* (6,3) and *MCS* (10,0), while a more likely combination is shown by *M* (8,2). Clearly, the higher the rate of interest to be paid and the lower the effect of utilisation on life expectancy, then the further from the origin the *MCS* curve lies.

7. Optimal Capital Utilisation and Choice of Work Patterns

The results for marginal labour, costs and marginal capital savings are now brought together in order to isolate the optimal average level of capital utilisation in British manufacturing industry. We again turn to Figure 4, which shows both sets of marginal curves under a variety of alternative assumptions. The marginal labour cost curves, *MLC*, for each system come in pairs, associated with the alternative levels of £50 and £60 of basic pay (rather than the £40 of the collective agreements, which refer to minima), on the evidence that the average basic pay of workers was somewhere between these two figures in 1977.[10]) The marginal capital savings curves are associated with the alternative levels of interest of 6, 8 and 10 per cent and the alternative rates of trade-off between utilisation and life expectancy of 0, 1, 2 and 3 per cent. The two extreme curves of *MCS* (6,3) and *MCS* (10,0) lie on either side of the more likely alternative *MCS* (8,2).

Each point of intersection is a marginal capital savings curve and a marginal labour cost curve is associated with a particular level of total cost. These are calculated using the total labour and total capital costs for each system corresponding to the level of capital utilisation picked out in Figure 3. The resulting calculations indicate that the lower boundary *MCS* curve is associated with an optimal utilisation of 40 hours per week, while the upper boundary curve picks out a level of over 60 hours per week. The marginal labour cost and marginal capital savings curves that were thought to be based on the most realistic assumptions in fact picked out an optimal level of utilisation of about 57.5 hours per week. Thus, the curves based on the most realistic assumptions in fact pick out a level of utilisation very close to, although somewhat higher than, the actual level observed in the manufacturing sector at this point in time. Given that a distribution occurs around the curves thought to be most likely, the most frequent observed work patterns can be expected to be 'normal day plus overtime' and some form of 'two-shift' system, which is in fact the case.

8. Conclusions and Policy Issues

The results reported above seem to indicate that it is possible to predict the optimal level of capital utilisation and the associated work patterns. Nevertheless, it should be emphasised that the model, at present, has only been used to estimate the average level of capital utilisation and not the more discerning test of predicting the range of utilisation levels associated with the various processes in a particular industry and thereby the mix of work patterns in the industry. Without doubt, there is a great deal of variation about the average position we have focused upon in this paper. The main hinderance to further progress is the lack of information about various processes used within the industry chosen for study, in particular, about capital intensities, life expectancies and labour costs. It is hoped to begin the detailed survey work that will yield such information in the near future.

---

10) The lower of the two *MLC* curves for each system relates to a level of basic pay of £50, while the higher curve relates to a level of £60.

The existing information, however, still has considerable scope for supporting further research. It is hoped, for example, to further develop the theoretical model that we have briefly sketched out above, in an attempt to explain inter-industry differences in the degree of capital utilisation and the associated variations in the observed mixes of work patterns. This is a tedious and time consuming task, however, as it involves constructing data on overtime and shift premia for each industry group. Some evidence that such research would be rewarded can be gleaned from the results reported above. The sensitivity of the position of the marginal capital savings curve to variations in capital intensity indicate that this may well be a key variable in determining the optimal level of capital utilisation and mix of work patterns. Indeed, the rank correlation between capital per man on the main shift across industries and the average level of utilisation has been calculated to be $r = 0.64$ [see *Bosworth/Dawkins*, 1981, Chapter 13]. Further work along these lines will link up nicely with other research we have been undertaking, explaining the incidence of shiftworking across industries using regression analysis [see *Bosworth/Dawkins/Westaway*, 1981a, 1981b].

Clearly, a more complete understanding of the causes of observed levels of capital utilisation are of considerable interest in their own right. Tracing the implications to the adopted mix of work patterns, however, opens up entirely new and interesting avenues of research. The construction of the average cost envelope was undertaken on the basis of commonly observed work patterns. It could equally be used as a test-bed for economically evaluating less common or new work patterns. It should be possible to evaluate systems specially designed for certain work groups. Multiple part-time shifts, for example, which may be particularly suited to married women. The model could be used to pose the question of what cost changes (i.e. what government subsidies) would be needed to make such a system economically viable and therefore acceptable to employers. The model can also be developed to evaluate the impact of the shorter working week. More immediate, perhaps, is the need to evaluate protective legislation of the type recently proposed by the ILO and EEC, even though this has been put to one side for the moment because of the current economic climate. For the same reasons, there is a need to investigate the implications of the current proposals being placed before the Health and Safety Executive by the Equal Opportunities Commission for altering U.K. legislation protecting women at work.

References

Ball, R.J., and *E.B.A. St. Cyr*: Short-Term Employment Functions in British Manufacturing Industry. Review of Economic Studies **33**, 1966, 179–208.

Bosworth, D.L., and *P.J. Dawkins*: Patterns of Work and Capital Savings: A Model of Capital Utilisation in British Manufacturing Industry. Department of Economics Discussion Paper, Loughborough University of Technology, Loughborough 1979.

– : Work Patterns: An Economic Analysis. Aldershot 1981.

Bosworth, D.L., P.J. Dawkins and *A.J. Westaway*: Explaining the Incidence of Shiftworking in Great Britain. Economic Journal, 1981a (forthcoming).

– : The Causes of the Supply of and Demand for Shiftworkers. Proceedings of the AUTE Conference, 1980. London 1981b.

Central Statistical Office: Economic Trends. London, annually.
– : National Income and Expenditure. London, annually.
– : Annual Abstract of Financial Statistics. London, annually.
Department of Employment: Time Rates of Wages and Hours of Work. London, annually.
Eels, J.R.: The Economics of Shiftworking. Journal of Industrial Economics, 1956, 51–62.
Foss, M.F.: The Utilisation of Capital Equipment: Post-War Compared with Pre-War. Survey of Current Business **43**, 1963, 8–16.
Health and Safety Executive: Hours of Employment of Women and Young Persons. Health and Safety Booklet No. 23. Department of Employment. London, 1973.
Heathfield, D.: The Measurement of Capital Usage Using Electricity Consumption Data for the U.K. Journal of the Royal Statistical Society **135**, 1972, 208–220.
– : Capital Utilisation. Conference on Capital, University of Nantarre, Paris, 1976.
Hughes, H., et al.: Capital Utilisation in Manufacturing in Developing Countries. Bank Staff Working Paper No. 242, International Bank Reconstruction and Development, Washington, September 1976.
Kim, Y.C., and *G.C. Winston*: The Optimal Utilisation of Capital Stock and the Level of Economic Development. Economica, 1974, 377–386.
Nadiri, M.I., and *S. Rosen*: Inter-Related Factor Demand Functions. American Economic Review **59**, 1969, 457–471.
Robinson, C.M.G.F.: Allocation of Time Across the Day: An Analysis of the Demand and Supply of Shiftworkers. Unpublished Ph.D. Thesis, Chicago, Ill., 1977.
– : An Analysis of the Demand and Supply of Shiftworkers. Discussion Paper, Department of Economics, University of Western Ontario Research Report No. 7817, London, Ontario, 1978.
United Nations Industrial Development Organisation UNIDO: Profiles of Manufacturing Establishments. Industrial Planning and Programming Series **1** (4), New York 1967.
Winston, G.C.: Capital Utilisation in Economic Development. Economic Journal **81**, 1971, 36–60.
– : The Theory of Capital Utilisation and Idleness. Journal of Economic Literature, 1974, 1301–1320.
Winston, G.C., and *T.O. McCoy*: Investment and the Optimal Idleness of Capital. Review of Economic Studies **127**, 1974, 419–428.

Quantitative Studies on Production and Prices © Physica-Verlag, Würzburg–Wien, 1983.

The Optimal Investment Ratio for an Economy with Changing Depreciation of Capital, Discounting of Future Consumption, and Exogenous Technical Progress

Wolfgang Eichhorn, Winfried Gleißner, and *Hans Ulrich Buhl*[1])

1. Introduction

In a previous paper [*Buhl/Eichhorn/Gleißner*] we formulated and analysed a macroeconomic model in which we determined optimal new-capital-investment policies under the assumption of finite lifetime of capital. During its lifetime a capital investment was supposed to perform always equally well. In contrast to this the present paper takes changing capital depreciation into account. Using discrete dynamic programming methods similar to those used in *Buhl/Eichhorn/Gleißner* [1982], we derive optimal investment ratios. As in the foregoing model, exogenous technical progress and discounting of future consumption are taken into consideration.

The problem of determining optimal investment ratios for an economy has been attracting widespread interest among economists for a long time. Based on *Ramsey's* [1928] famous paper, considerable research has been done and great advances were made in the late fifties and sixties.

Adding yet some more papers to the extensive literature already existing on the theory of economic growth requires some explanation.

Much has already been done in formulating and analysing continuous models of economic growth. Some outstanding books on the topic are, for instance, *Meade* [1964], *Phelps* [1966], and *Morishima* [1969]. However, most of the publications suffer from some obvious limitations. Some authors worked with very special assumptions on the production function, e.g. assumed constancy over time. Others did introduce technical progress and found that either the analysis of their results became prohibitively difficult or, again, very special assumptions on the effect of technical progress were needed.

But to the best of our knowledge, surprisingly little research has been done on discrete models with relatively general assumptions on the production function and, in particular, the effect of technical progress, that still yield simple and easily interpretable results.

Perhaps the most interesting result is the following.

If the optimal investment policy is implemented in some period t, then the optimal investment ratio in t, say α_t^*, is (in a certain sense to be specified later) *independent* of the future production functions $F_{t+2}, F_{t+3}, \dots$ and even more surprisingly, *independent* of

[1]) We are indebted to Helmut Funke, Wilhelm Gehrig, Murray Kemp, Ulrike Leopold-Wildburger, Hans Schoch, Frank Stehling, Joachim Voeller and Reiner Wolff for valuable remarks and suggestions.

the planning horizon T. Thus in order to implement an optimal investment policy in some period t, we do not need perfect foresight on the behavior of the production function. We conclude that in this model a generation wanting to act best for itself only and having little knowledge about the future necessarily will act best for all following generations, too. Therefore, whenever there is agreement on the value of the future discount rate, the problem of intergenerational justice so often discussed in the literature really does not exist in our model [e.g. *Koopmans; Tobin; Hammond/Mirrlees; Phelps/Riley*]. Thus our optimal investment ratio is actually a bit different from "golden" as characterized, e.g., by *Phelps* [1961, 1966].

Section 2 introduces the assumptions that constitute our model. After stating the problem (Section 3) the main results are presented and proved (Section 4). In Section 5 we consider the simplest case and show that if the production functions, depreciation allowances and discount factors are constant in time, then so are the optimal investment ratios. Moreover, we give examples for the CES production functions, in particular for the Cobb-Douglas production function. The concluding Section 6 is devoted to a refinement of the investment policy. The investment ratios α_t are there assumed to be restricted from above by a positive $\epsilon < 1$ and from below by a positive $\delta < \epsilon$.

2. The Model

Throughout this paper we assume that Y_t, the gross domestic product during period t, is some function F_t: $\mathbf{R}_+ \to \mathbf{R}_+$ ($\mathbf{R}_+$ the nonnegative real numbers) of the capital stock, that is the amount of capital goods, K_{t-1}:

$$Y_t = F_t\,(K_{t-1}). \tag{1}$$

We point out here that the form of the production function depends on the period t. In other words, exogenous technical progress is considered in a very general manner. Note that the dependence of F on t renders it possible, in a sense, to neglect variations of labor and capacity utilization.

Let I_t denote the (gross domestic) investment during period t. Then the investment ratio of period t, α_t say, is

$$\alpha_t = I_t/Y_t \tag{2}$$

and we have

$$I_t = \alpha_t\,F_t\,(K_{t-1}). \tag{3}$$

We assume that the depreciation allowance of the capital stock K_{t-1} depends on t. Thus we take the time dependency of both the technical obsolescence and the production requirements into account, that is, in particular, we do not ignore the effect of technical progress that makes it cheaper to substitute new capital investments for less productive ones. [For a discussion of the reasons for substitution see, e.g., *Johansen; Solow; Solow* et al.; *Gehrig*.] Let m_t denote the depreciation allowance and let us call $1 - m_t =: q_t$ the depreciation factor. With these notations we have

$$K_t = \alpha_t\,F_t\,(K_{t-1}) + q_t\,K_{t-1} \tag{4}$$

or, equivalently,

$$K_t - K_{t-1} = \alpha_t F_t (K_{t-1}) - m_t K_{t-1} = I_t - m_t K_{t-1}, \tag{5}$$

and (1) can be written

$$Y_t = \alpha_t F_t (K_{t-1}) + (1 - \alpha_t) F_t (K_{t-1}) = I_t + C_t, \tag{6}$$

where C_t is the (gross) consumption during period t and $(1 - \alpha_t)$ can be called the consumption ratio during period t. Obviously we are considering a *closed* economy (or an open economy where exports = imports) and we are assuming that there do not exist any problems concerning distribution of supply.

3. The Problem

In this paper we are interested in determining optimal investment ratios. More precisely, given a planning horizon n_t and a capital stock K_t at (the beginning of) period $t + 1$ we want to find investment ratios $\alpha^*_{1t}, \alpha^*_{2t}, \ldots, \alpha^*_{n_t t}$ that maximize the discounted consumption

$$\sum_{k=1}^{n_t} r_t^{(k-1)} (1 - \alpha_{kt}) F_{k+t} (K_{k+t-1}). \tag{7}$$

Here

$$r_t^{(k-1)} := r_{t+2} r_{t+3} \cdots r_{t+k}, \quad r_t^{(0)} := 1, \tag{8}$$

and r_{t+i} is the discount factor during period $t + i$.

4. The Solution

Theorem 1: Let the concave functions F_t: $\mathbf{R}_+ \to \mathbf{R}_+$ be twice differentiable and let the inverses of the derivatives exist in a neighbourhood of the points $1/r_t$ and $(1 - r_t q_t)/r_t$. Let $F_t''(\widetilde{K}_t) < 0$ and $F_t''(\overline{K}_t) < 0$ for

$$\widetilde{K}_t := (F_t')^{-1} \left(\frac{1}{r_t}\right) \text{ and } \overline{K}_t := (F_t')^{-1} \left(\frac{1 - r_t q_t}{r_t}\right). \tag{9}$$

Then the sequence of optimal investment ratios $(\alpha_{kt})_{1 \leqslant k \leqslant n_t}$ is

$$\alpha_{kt} (K_{k-1,t}) = \begin{cases} 0 & \text{for } k = n_t \\ \dfrac{\widetilde{K}_{k+t+1} - q_{k+t} K_{k-1,t}}{F_{k+t} (K_{k-1,t})} & \text{for } k = n_t - 1 \\ \dfrac{\overline{K}_{k+t+1} - q_{k+t} K_{k-1,t}}{F_{k+t} (K_{k-1,t})} & \text{for } 1 \leqslant k < n_t - 1, \end{cases} \tag{10}$$

where $K_{k-1,t} := K_{k+t-1}$, $K_{0,t} = K_{0t} = K_t$. *The present value of consumption during the periods* $t+k$, $1 \leqslant k \leqslant n_t$, *is*

$$C_{kt}(K_{k-1,t}) = \begin{cases} r_t^{(k-1)}(F_{k+t}(K_{k-1,t}) + q_{k+t} K_{k-1,t}) + d_{kt} & \text{for } 1 \leqslant k \leqslant n_t - 1 \\ r_t^{(k-1)} F_{k+t}(K_{k-1,t}) & \text{for } k = n_t, \end{cases}$$

where

$$d_{kt} = \begin{cases} r_t^{(k)}(F_{k+t+1}(\bar{K}_{k+t+1}) + q_{k+t} \bar{K}_{k+t+1}) - r_t^{(k-1)} \bar{K}_{k+t+1} + d_{k+1,t} & \\ & \text{for } 1 \leqslant k < n_t - 1 \\ r_t^{(k)} F_{k+t+1}(\tilde{K}_{t+t+1}) - r_t^{(k-1)} \tilde{K}_{k+t+1} + d_{k+1,t} & \text{for } k = n_t - 1 \\ 0 & \text{for } k = n_t. \end{cases}$$

Proof: We use Bellman's principle of backward dynamic programming [see, e.g., *Neumann* or *Dreyfus/Law*].

Period n_t:

$$C_{n_t t}(K_{n_t-1,t}) = \max_{\alpha_{n_t t} \in \mathbf{R}} [(1 - \alpha_{n_t t}) r_t^{(n_t-1)} F_{n_t+t}(K_{n_t-1,t})]$$

yields

$$\alpha_{n_t t} = 0, \; C_{n_t t}(K_{n_t-1,t}) = r_t^{(n_t-1)} F_{n_t+t}(K_{n_t-1,t}). \tag{11}$$

Period $n_t - 1$:

$$C_{n_t-1,t}(K_{n_t-2,t}) = \max_{\alpha_{n_t-1,t} \in \mathbf{R}} [(1 - \alpha_{n_t-1,t}) r_t^{(n_t-2)} F_{n_t+t-1}(K_{n_t-2,t}) + C_{n_t t}(K_{n_t-1,t})],$$

where the last term satisfies

$$C_{n_t t}(K_{n_t-1,t}) = r_t^{(n_t-1)} F_{n_t+t}(\alpha_{n_t-1,t} F_{n_t+t-1}(K_{n_t-2,t}) + q_{t+n_t-1} K_{n_t-2,t})$$

by (11) and (4), gives as a necessary condition for a maximum:

$$0 = -r_t^{(n_t-2)} F_{n_t+t-1}(K_{n_t-2,t}) + r_t^{(n_t-1)} F_{n_t+t-1}(K_{n_t-2,t})$$
$$+ F'_{n_t+t}(\alpha_{n_t-1,t} F_{n_t+t-1}(K_{n_t-2,t}) + q_{t+n_t-1} K_{n_t-2,t}),$$

that is

$$1 = r_{n_t+t} F'_{n_t+t}(\alpha_{n_t-1,t} F_{n_t+t-1}(K_{n_t-2,t}) + q_{t+n_t-1} K_{n_t-2,t}),$$

whence

$$\alpha_{n_t-1,t}(K_{n_t-2,t}) = \frac{\tilde{K}_{t+n_t} - q_{t+n_t-1} K_{n_t-2,t}}{F_{n_t+t-1}(K_{n_t-2,t})}. \tag{12}$$

As

$$\frac{\partial^2}{\partial \alpha^2_{n_t-1,t}} C_{n_t-1,t}(K_{n_t-2,t}) = r_t^{(n_t-1)} F^2_{n_t+t-1}(K_{n_t-2,t}) F''_{n_t+t}(\tilde{K}_{t+n_t}) < 0,$$

this condition is sufficient. One calculates

$$C_{n_t-1,t}(K_{n_t-2,t}) = F_{n_t+t-1}(K_{n_t-2,t}) r_t^{(n_t-2)} - r_t^{(n_t-2)} (\tilde{K}_{t+n_t} - q_{t+n_t-1} K_{n_t-2,t}) + r_t^{(n_t-1)} F_{n_t+t}(\tilde{K}_{t+n_t}),$$

which proves, together with (12), the assertions of Theorem 1 for $k = n_t - 1$.

Period k: Assume that

$$C_{k+1,t}(K_{k,t}) = r_t^{(k)} (F_{t+k+1}(K_{kt}) + q_{t+k+1} K_{kt}) + d_{k+1,t}.$$

Then

$$\begin{aligned} C_{kt}(K_{k-1,t}) &= \max_{\alpha_{kt}\in \mathbf{R}} [(1-\alpha_{kt}) r_t^{(k-1)} F_{t+k}(K_{k-1,t}) + C_{k+1,t}(K_{k,t})] \\ &= \max_{\alpha_{kt}\in \mathbf{R}} \{(1-\alpha_{kt}) r_t^{(k-1)} F_{t+k}(K_{k-1,t}) \\ &\quad + r_t^{(k)} [F_{t+k+1}(\alpha_{kt} F_{t+k}(K_{k-1,t}) + q_{t+k} K_{k-1,t}) \\ &\quad + q_{t+k+1}(\alpha_{kt} F_{t+k}(K_{k-1,t}) + q_{t+k} K_{k-1,t})] + d_{k+1,t}\}. \end{aligned}$$

This gives as a necessary condition for a maximum:

$$0 = -r_t^{(k-1)} F_{t+k}(K_{k-1,t}) + r_t^{(k)} [F_{t+k}(K_{k-1,t}) F'_{t+k+1}(\alpha_{kt} F_{t+k}(K_{k-1,t}) + q_{t+k} K_{k-1,t}) + q_{t+k+1} F_{t+k}(K_{k-1,t})],$$

that is

$$1 = r_{t+k+1} [F'_{t+k+1}(\alpha_{kt} F_{t+k}(K_{k-1,t}) + q_{t+k} K_{k-1,t}) + q_{t+k+1}],$$

whence

$$\alpha_{kt} F_{t+k}(K_{k-1,t}) + q_{t+k} K_{k-1,t} = (F'_{t+k+1})^{-1} \left(\frac{1 - q_{t+k+1} r_{t+k+1}}{r_{t+k+1}} \right)$$

and eventually

$$\alpha_{kt}(K_{k-1,t}) = \frac{\bar{K}_{t+k+1} - q_{t+k} K_{k-1,t}}{F_{t+k}(K_{k-1,t})}. \tag{13}$$

The inequality

$$\frac{\partial^2 C_{kt}}{\partial \alpha_{kt}^2}(K_{k\text{-}1,t}) = r_t^{(k)} F_{t+k}(K_{k\text{-}1,t})^2 F''_{t+k+1}(\bar{K}_{t+k+1}) < 0$$

shows that this condition is also sufficient. One calculates

$$\begin{aligned} C_{kt}(K_{k\text{-}1,t}) &= r_t^{(k\text{-}1)} F_{t+k}(K_{k\text{-}1,t}) - r_t^{(k\text{-}1)} (\bar{K}_{t+k+1} - q_{t+k} K_{k\text{-}1,t}) \\ &\quad + r_t^{(k)} (F_{t+k+1}(\bar{K}_{t+k+1}) + q_{t+k} \bar{K}_{t+k+1}) + d_{k+1,t} \\ &= r_t^{(k\text{-}1)} (F_{t+k}(K_{k\text{-}1,t}) + q_{t+k} K_{k\text{-}1,t}) + d_{kt}, \end{aligned}$$

where

$$d_{kt} = d_{k+1,t} - r_t^{(k\text{-}1)} \bar{K}_{t+k+1} + r_t^{(k)} (F_{t+k+1}(\bar{K}_{t+k+1}) + q_{t+k} \bar{K}_{t+k+1}).$$

By this and (13) the remaining assertions of Theorem 1 are proved.

Suppose $n_t \geqslant 3$ for all $t = 1, 2, 3, \ldots$ If this is the case we shall recursively describe an investment policy that will be proven to be an optimal one for an infinite number of periods. Beginning with

$$K_0 := K_{00}$$

we define:

$$\alpha_1(K_0) = \alpha_{1,0}(K_{00}) = \frac{\bar{K}_1 - q_1 K_{00}}{F_1(K_{00})} = \frac{\bar{K}_1 - q_1 K_0}{F_1(K_0)},$$

$$K_1 := K_{10} = \bar{K}_1,$$

and

$$C_1 := (1 - \alpha_1(K_0)) F_1(K_0).$$

If the sequences $(\alpha_i)_{1 \leqslant i < k}, (C_i)_{1 \leqslant i < k}, (K_i)_{0 \leqslant i < k}$ are already calculated, we proceed as follows:

$$\alpha_k(K_{k\text{-}1}) = \alpha_{1,k\text{-}1}(K_{0,k\text{-}1}) = \frac{\bar{K}_k - q_k K_{0,k\text{-}1}}{F_k(K_{0,k\text{-}1})} = \frac{\bar{K}_k - q_k K_{k\text{-}1}}{F_k(K_{k\text{-}1})},$$

$$K_k = K_{1,k\text{-}1} = \bar{K}_k,$$

$$C_k = C_{k\text{-}1} + (1 - \alpha_k(K_{k\text{-}1})) r_0^{(k\text{-}1)} F_k(K_{k\text{-}1}).$$

Now the following remarks are noteworthy.

(i) α_k and K_k are functions of the initial capital stock K_0 and the production functions of the past only. They are independent of any future production function. We denote the optimal values of α_k and K_k by α_k^* and K_k^*, respectively.

(ii) Optimal investment ratios and capital stocks in the same column are equal to each other if they are not too close to the end of the planning horizon:

$$\alpha_k^* = \alpha_{1,k\text{-}1}^* = \alpha_{i,k\text{-}i}^*, \bar{K}_k = K_k^* = K_{i,k\text{-}i}^* \qquad \text{for } 1 \leqslant i \leqslant n_{k\text{-}i} - 2;$$

see, in this connection the following figure.

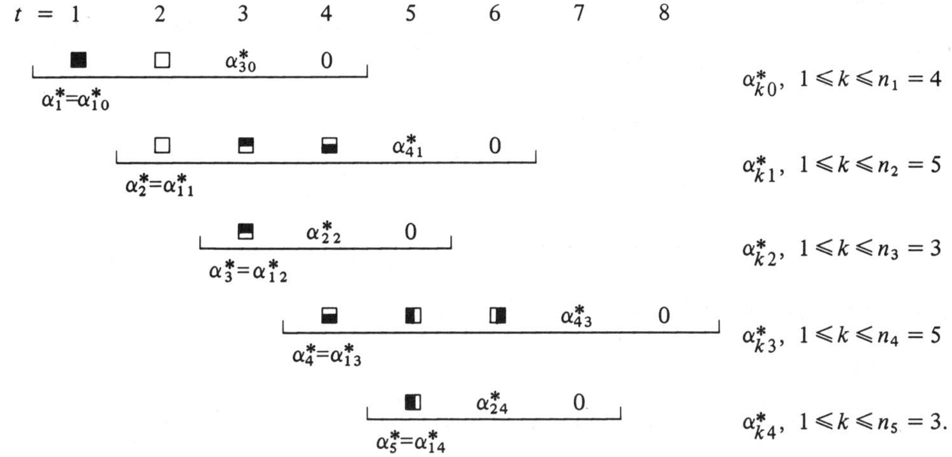

The sequence $(\alpha_k^*)_{k=1,2,3,\ldots}$ is optimal as the following theorem shows.

Theorem 2: Let the assumptions of Theorem 1 be satisfied. Suppose that the optimal discounted consumption during the last two periods of a planning horizon of length $T \geqslant 3$

$$D_T := r_0^{(T-1)} F_T(\widetilde{K}_T) + r_0^{(T-2)} (F_{T-1}(\overline{K}_{T-1}) - \widetilde{K}_T + q_{T-1}\, \overline{K}_{T-1}) \to 0 \qquad \textit{for } T \to \infty.$$

Then $(\alpha_k^*)_{k=1,2,3,\ldots}$ is a sequence of optimal investment ratios in the sense that the total discounted consumption

$$C := \lim_{t\to\infty} \sum_{k=1}^{t} (1-\alpha_k)\, r_0^{(k-1)}\, F_k\,(K_{k-1})$$

attains its maximum for $\alpha_k = \alpha_k^*$ and $K_{k-1} = K_{k-1}^*$, where $K_0^* = K_0$ = initial capital stock and $(K_k^*)_{k=1,2,3,\ldots}$ = sequence of capital stocks belonging to $(\alpha_k^*)_{k=1,2,3,\ldots}$.

Proof: If $C = \infty$ there is nothing to prove. Now let $C < \infty$ and suppose there exists a sequence $(\beta_k)_{k=1,2,3,\ldots}$ with

$$C' := \lim_{t\to\infty} \sum_{k=1}^{t} (1-\beta_k)\, r_0^{(k-1)}\, F_k\,(K_{k-1}) > C.$$

If $C' = \infty$ there exists a natural number n such that

$$\sum_{k=1}^{n+2} (1-\beta_k)\, r_0^{(k-1)}\, F_k\,(K_{k-1}) > C+1 \text{ and } D_{n+2} < 1.$$

This shows that

$$\sum_{k=1}^{n} (1-\alpha_k)\, r_0^{(k-1)}\, F_k\,(K_{k-1}) + D_{n+2} \leqslant C+1 < \sum_{k=1}^{n+2} (1-\beta_k)\, r_0^{(k-1)}\, F_k\,(K_{k-1})$$

contradicting the maximality of the $(\alpha_{k0})_{1 \leq k \leq n+2}$ calculated according to Bellman's method in the case of planning horizon $n+2$ in the first period.

If $C' < \infty$ and $C' > C$, let $\epsilon := C' - C$. Then there exist natural numbers n_1, n_2, n_3 such that for all natural numbers $n > n_1$

$$\sum_{k=n}^{\infty} (1-\beta_k) r_0^{(k-1)} F_k(K_{k-1}) < \frac{\epsilon}{3},$$

for all natural numbers $n > n_2$

$$\sum_{k=n}^{\infty} (1-\alpha_k) r_0^{(k-1)} F_k(K_{k-1}) < \frac{\epsilon}{3},$$

and for all natural numbers $n > n_3$

$$D_{n+2} < \frac{\epsilon}{3}.$$

If in the first period we take a planning horizon $n+2$, where $n \geq \max\{n_1, n_2, n_3\}$, we obtain

$$\sum_{k=1}^{n+2} (1-\beta_k) r_0^{(k-1)} F_k(K_{k-1}) - \sum_{k=1}^{n} (1-\alpha_k) r_0^{(k-1)} F_k(K_{k-1}) - D_{n+2}$$

$$= \sum_{k=1}^{\infty} (1-\beta_k) r_0^{(k-1)} F_k(K_{k-1}) - \sum_{k=n+3}^{\infty} (1-\beta_k) r_0^{(k-1)} F_k(K_{k-1})$$

$$- \sum_{k=1}^{\infty} (1-\alpha_k) r_0^{(k-1)} F_k(K_{k-1}) + \sum_{k=n+1}^{\infty} (1-\alpha_k) r_0^{(k-1)} F_k(K_{k-1}) - D_{n+2}$$

$$\geq C' - \epsilon/3 - C - \epsilon/3 = \epsilon/3$$

which contradicts the maximality of the investment policy $(\alpha_{k0})_{1 \leq k \leq n+2}$. Therefore $C' \leq C$, which proves the assertion.

5. Some Specializations

In order to illustrate our results presented in the last section for a sequence of general concave production functions we will now consider the simple case of time-constant production functions and give examples for the CES (and particularly for the Cobb-Douglas) production functions. This case often appears in the literature, e.g. in *Phelps* [1961] and *v. Weizsäcker* [1962a, 1962b], where in contrast to our discrete model continuous models are treated. It is interesting to compare our results with the ones derived there.

Let the assumptions of Theorems 1 and 2 be valid. For all periods $t = 1, 2, 3, \ldots$ let $r_t = r$, $q_t = q$, $F_t = F$. If the planning horizons n_t are always ≥ 3, then the sequences $(K_0, K_1^*, K_2^*, \ldots)$ and $(\alpha_1^*, \alpha_2^*, \alpha_3^*, \ldots)$ of the optimal capital stocks and the optimal investment ratios have the form $(K_0, K^*, K^*, \ldots)$ and $(\alpha_1^*, \alpha^*, \alpha^*, \ldots)$, respectively. In other words, if in our model both the depreciation allowance and the discount factor are constant and if there is no technical progress, then the optimal investment policy yields a growth rate of zero for the economy.

In the case of the *Cobb-Douglas production function*

$$F(K) = cK^{\gamma} \qquad (c \text{ and } \gamma < 1 \text{ positive real constants})$$

we obtain

$$K^* = (F')^{-1}\left(\frac{1-rq}{r}\right) = \left(\frac{rc\gamma}{1-rq}\right)^{1/(1-\gamma)}, \tag{14}$$

$$\alpha^* = \frac{K^* - qK^*}{cK^{*\gamma}} = \frac{(1-q)\,rc\gamma}{c\,(1-rq)} = \frac{1-q}{1-rq}\,r\gamma. \tag{15}$$

The other *CES production functions*

$$F(K) = (\beta K^{-\rho} + \delta)^{-1/\rho} \quad (\beta > 0, \delta > 0, \rho > -1, \rho \neq 0 \text{ real constants})$$

yield

$$K^* = \left(\frac{(\beta r/(1-rq))^{\rho/(1+\rho)} - \beta}{\delta}\right)^{1/\rho}, \tag{16}$$

$$\alpha^* = (1-q)\left(\frac{\beta r}{1-rq}\right)^{1/(1+\rho)}. \tag{17}$$

The proof is a straightforward application of Theorems 1 and 2.

We learn from (14) and (15) that in the cases of the Cobb-Douglas production function an economy E_1 whose r (valuation of future consumption) is greater than that of an otherwise identical economy E_2 has both a greater optimal capital stock and a greater optimal investment ratio than economy E_2. The same is true for the optimal capital stock when ceteris paribus economy E_1 has a greater q, that is, a lower depreciation than economy E_2. But then the optimal investment ratio of economy E_1 is smaller than that of economy E_2.

Formula (15) states that

$$\alpha^* \leqslant \gamma \qquad (\text{since } 0 \leqslant q \leqslant 1,\ 0 \leqslant r \leqslant 1).$$

If $r = 1$ in (15) we have $\alpha^* = \gamma$ which is the elasticity of production. Note that given any investment ratio $\hat{\alpha}$ satisfying $0.116 \leqslant \hat{\alpha} \leqslant 0.5$ there exists a triple $(\hat{\gamma}, \hat{q}, \hat{r})$ satisfying the quite realistic conditions

$$0.2 \leqslant \hat{\gamma} \leqslant 0.5,\ 0.88 \leqslant \hat{p} \leqslant 0.96,\ 0.92 \leqslant \hat{r} \leqslant 1,$$

which inserted in the right-hand side of (15) provides $\hat{\alpha}$. In other words, depending on γ, q, r the value of the optimal investment ratio varies in a wide interval, at least when we specialize our model as done in the present section. If we let $\hat{\gamma} = 0.3$, $\hat{q} = 0.9$ and $\hat{r} = 0.97$ we obtain $\alpha^* = 0.229$ which was the 1980 investment ratio of the Federal Republic of Germany.

6. A Refinement of the Investment Policy

Until now there was no restriction on our investment policy. The investment ratio α_t was allowed to be any real number. This is quite unrealistic, because α_t is allowed to be greater than one, which means that there is an external capital at the disposal of the economy considered, or less than zero which may be interpreted that in period t consumption is larger than the gross domestic product. To be more realistic one demands $\delta < \alpha_t < \epsilon$ for all $t = 1, 2, \ldots$, where δ and ϵ are constants satisfying $0 < \delta < \epsilon < 1$. To cope with this situation we prove

Theorem 3: Let the assumptions of Theorem 1 be satisfied. For all t = 1, 2, . . . let $0 < \delta < \alpha_t < \epsilon < 1$ *and* $r_t = r$, $q_t = q$, $F_t = F$. *Suppose that for* $K^* > K_0$ *there exists* K' *satisfying* $0 < K' < K_0$ *such that for all K satisfying* $K' < K < K^*$

(i) $\alpha(K) > \alpha(K^*)$ *(α calculated as in Theorem 1)*

and

(ii) $\dfrac{F(K)}{F(K^*)} - \dfrac{K}{K^*} \geqslant 0.$

Then

$$K_t = \begin{cases} \alpha(K_{t-1}) F(K_{t-1}) + qK_{t-1} & \text{for } \delta < \alpha(K_{t-1}) < \epsilon \quad \text{(see (4))} \\ \epsilon F(K_{t-1}) + qK_{t-1} & \text{else} \end{cases}$$

defines a monotonically increasing sequence $(K_t)_{t=0,1,2,\ldots}$ *satisfying* $\lim_{t \to \infty} K_t = K^*$.

If $K^* < K_0$ *suppose that there exists* K' *satisfying* $K_0 < K' < \infty$ *such that for all K satisfying* $K^* < K < K'$

(I) $\alpha(K) < \alpha(K^*)$ *(α calculated as in Theorem 1)*

and

(II) $\dfrac{F(K)}{F(K^*)} - \dfrac{K}{K^*} \leqslant 0.$

Then

$$K_t = \begin{cases} \alpha(K_{t-1}) F(K_{t-1}) + qK_{t-1} & \text{for } \delta < \alpha(K_{t-1}) < \epsilon \quad \text{(see (4))} \\ \delta F(K_{t-1}) + qK_{t-1} & \text{else} \end{cases}$$

defines a monotonically decreasing sequence $(K_t)_{t=0,1,2,\ldots}$ *satisfying* $\lim_{t \to \infty} K_t = K^*$.

Proof: Induction. $\underline{t = 1}$: $K' < K_0 < K^*$ implies $\alpha(K_0) > \alpha(K^*) > \delta$. If $\alpha(K_0)$ satisfies $\delta < \alpha(K_0) < \epsilon$ the process becomes stationary after the first period, that is $K_1 = K^*$, $K_2 = K^*, \ldots$ If $\alpha(K_0)$ does not satisfy $\delta < \alpha(K_0) < \epsilon$ we define

$$K_1 := \epsilon F(K_0) + qK_0 < K^*$$

and obtain

$$\begin{aligned} K_1 - K_0 &= \epsilon F(K_0) + qK_0 - K_0 > \alpha(K^*) F(K_0) + (q-1) K_0 && \text{(by (i))} \\ &= \frac{K^* - qK^*}{F(K^*)} F(K_0) + (q-1) K_0 && \text{(by (4))} \\ &= (1-q) K^* \left(\frac{F(K_0)}{F(K^*)} - \frac{K_0}{K^*} \right) \geqslant 0 && \text{(by (ii)).} \end{aligned}$$

Arbitrary $t > 1$: For $K_t \leqslant K^*$ we have to show $K_{t+1} \leqslant K^*$ and $K_{t+1} \geqslant K_t$. If $\alpha(K_t)$ satisfies $\delta < \alpha(K_t) < \epsilon$ the process becomes stationary after the t-th period, that is $K_{t+1} = K^*$, $K_{t+2} = K^*$, . . . If $\alpha(K_t)$ does not satisfy $\delta < \alpha(K_t) < \epsilon$ we have

$$\alpha(K_t) \geqslant \epsilon > \alpha(K^*)$$

and

$$K_{t+1} = \epsilon F(K_t) + qK_t \leqslant \alpha(K_t) F(K_t) + qK_t = K^*,$$

$$K_{t+1} - K_t = \epsilon F(K_t) + qK_t - K_t > \alpha(K^*) F(K_t) + (q-1) K_t \qquad \text{(by (i))}$$

$$= \frac{K^* - qK^*}{F(K^*)} F(K_t) + (q-1) K_t \qquad \text{(by (4))}$$

$$= (1-q) K^* \left(\frac{F(K_t)}{F(K^*)} - \frac{K_t}{K^*} \right) \geqslant 0 \qquad \text{(by (ii))}.$$

This shows that the sequence $(K_t)_{t=0,1,2,\dots}$ is monotonically increasing and bounded from above by K^*. Therefore it has a limit point K^{**} which is calculated as

$$K^{**} = \alpha(K^{**}) + qK^{**} = K^*.$$

In the case $K_0 > K^*$ the argument runs along analogous lines.

Corollary 1: The proof shows that the process actually is finite.

Corollary 2: From Bellman's method of backward dynamic programming [see, e.g. *Neumann* or *Dreyfus/Law*] it follows that the sequence $(\alpha_t)_{t=1,2,3,\dots}$ as defined in Theorem 3 is an optimal one for the boundary condition $\delta < \alpha_t < \epsilon$.

References

Buhl, H.U., W. Eichhorn and *W. Gleißner*: Optimal New-Capital-Investment Policies for Economies with Finite Capital Longevity and Technical Progress. Optimal Control Theory and Economic Analysis. Ed. by G. Feichtinger. Amsterdam 1982, 169–183.

Dreyfus, S., and *A. Law*: The Art and Theory of Dynamic Programming. New York 1977.

Gehrig, W.: Technischer Fortschritt. Handwörterbuch der Volkswirtschaft. Ed. by W. Glastetter et al. Wiesbaden 1980, 1263–1287.

Hammond, P., and *J.A. Mirrlees*: Agreeable Plans. Models of Economic Growth. Ed. by J.A. Mirrlees and N.H. Stern. London 1973, 283–305.

Johansen, L.: Substitution versus Fixed Production Coefficients in the Theory of Economic Growth: A Synthesis. Econometrica, 1959, 157–176.

Koopmans, T.: Intertemporal Distribution and Optimal Aggregate Growth. Ten Economic Studies in the Tradition of Irving Fisher. Ed. by W. Fellner et al. New York 1967, 95–126.

Meade, J.: A Neo-Classical Theory of Economic Growth. London 1964.

Morishima, M.: Theory of Economic Growth. Oxford 1969.

Neumann, K.: Dynamische Optimierung. Mannheim 1969.

Phelps, E.: The Golden Rule of Accumulation. American Economic Review, 1961, 638–642.

– : The Golden Rules of Economic Growth. New York 1966.

Phelps, E., and *J. Riley*: Rawlsian Growth: Dynamic Programming of Capital and Wealth for Intergenerational Maximin Justice. Review of Economic Studies, 1978, 103–120.

Ramsey, F.: A Mathematical Theory of Savings. Economic Journal, 1928, 543–559.
Solow, R.: Investment and Technical Progress. Mathematical Methods in the Social Sciences. Ed. by K.J. Arrow et al. Stanford 1960, 89–104.
Solow, R., et al.: Neoclassical Growth with Fixed Factor Proportions. Review of Economic Studies, 1966, 79–115.
Tobin, J.: Live Cycle Saving and Balanced Growth. Ten Economic Studies in the Tradition of Irving Fisher. Ed. by W. Fellner et al. New York 1967.
Weizsäcker, C.v.: Wachstum, Zins und Optimale Investitionsquote. Basel 1962a.
– : Das Investitionsoptimum in einer wachsenden Wirtschaft. Optimales Wachstum und Optimale Standortverteilung. Ed. by R. Henn et al. Berlin 1962b, 60–76.

Quantitative Studies on Production and Prices © Physica-Verlag, Würzburg–Wien, 1983.

On Invariance and Periodicity Properties in Set-Valued Processes

Peter Kischka

Set-valued mappings (correspondences) arise in economic theory in quite different fields. They were used for instance by John v. Neumann in order to investigate the equilibria in input-output models and they are a main instrument of production theory since the early fifties. More recently correspondences are used to describe the dynamic behaviour of an economy [see e.g. *Champsaur/Drèze/Henry; Cherene*]. In these cases a set-valued process is considered, which determines (in the discrete case) the *set* of all possible states at time $t + 1$ given the state at time t; in the continuous case the set valued process is given by a set-valued differential equation (Set-valued differential equations or generalized dynamical systems are described in *Roxin.*

These processes are used e.g. in the theory of optimal growth if no assumptions can be made to ensure that given an initial state the whole time path (which maximizes utility) is uniquely determined [see *Cherene*]. Other examples are tâtonnement processes [see *Champsaur/Drèze/Henry*], barter processes or models of resource allocation [see *Aubin/Day*].

We will use an example of a firm producing with myopic prediction of prices to illustrate the definitions and some of the results. It is shown that according to the structure of the set of accumulation points of a time path certain recurrency properties of these points can be proved. For this some invariance properties of sets (which partly agree in the case a single-valued system is given) are investigated and a single valued process associated with the given set-valued one is introduced, which allows for the application of some results of the "single-valued theory" from [*Bhatia/Chow*]. We will restrict to discrete models in this paper.

Now we will give the example mentioned above. We consider the production of a firm using a production set $Q \subset \mathbf{R}^n$. In period 0 the firm produces according to some $q^0 \in Q$; let p^0 denote the prevailing price system in period 0. We assume that the price p^1 in period 1 is a function of p^0 and q^0:

$$p^1 = g(q^0, p^0).$$

(g is the "environmental selection" introduced by *Cherene* [1978].) In our example the lag of one period with respect to q^0 and p^1 can be thought of as the fact that the firm sells the production of period 0 in period 1 or more generally: current production is sold next period.

We assume that the firm predicts next period's prices to equal this period's prices (the price mechanism is not known to the firm). If there is no technological progress therefore in period 1 a solution of

$$\max_{q \in Q} q \cdot p^1 \qquad (*)$$

is to be found. In general the solution of this maximization – if it exists – will not be unique. We denote the set of all solutions of (*) by $\phi(p^1)$. The price in period 2 is given by the environmental selection g and depends on p^1 and on the vector $q^1 \in \phi(p^1)$ the firm selects:

$$p^2 = g(q^1, p^1).$$

Each $q^1 \in \phi(p^1)$ in general implies a different price system $p^2 = g(q^1, p^1)$; since the set of possible productions in period 2 which maximize profit with respect to p^2, is given by $\phi(p^2) = \phi(g(q^1, p^1))$, the selection $q^1 \in \phi(p^1)$ determines this set of optimal productions. In this way a dynamical process is defined which in general will be set-valued. Denoting by $\phi(p^t)$ the set of solutions of (*) with respect to p^t this dynamical process is described by the time paths (q_t), $q_t \in Q$:

$$q^{t+1} \in \phi(g(q^t, p^t)), p^{t+1} = g(q^t, p^t), p^0, q^0 \text{ given.}$$

This example is a special case of the general concept of a set-valued process as introduced in *Cherene* [1978]. We will now make some further assumptions; by these we get a numerical example which we will use to illustrate the following concepts. Especially the environmental selection g will be specified. Assume that the firm produces two goods with a fixed input vector and denote by Q the set of possible productions for this vector given by a system of linear inequalities

$$Q = \left\{ (q_1, q_2) \,\middle|\, \begin{pmatrix} 2 & 1 \\ 2 & 2 \\ 5 & 1 \end{pmatrix} \begin{pmatrix} q_1 \\ q_2 \end{pmatrix} \leqslant \begin{pmatrix} 10 \\ 18 \\ 20 \end{pmatrix}, \begin{pmatrix} q_1 \\ q_2 \end{pmatrix} \geqslant \begin{pmatrix} 0 \\ 0 \end{pmatrix} \right\}.$$

Further we assume that there is a demand function $f = (f_1, f_2)$ for the two goods and the firm has to accept the price that clears the market in each period. Let f be given by

$$f(p_1, p_2) = (f_1(p_1), f_2(p_2)) = (10 - p_1, 12 - 2p_2)$$

(i.e. the demand can be separately expressed).

The environmental selection g is given by

$$g(q^{t-1}, p^{t-1}) = f^{-1}(q^{t-1}) = (f_1^{-1}(q_1^{t-1}), f_2^{-1}(q_2^{t-1}))$$

and is independent of previous price systems.

Starting with the initial production $q^0 = (q_1^0, q_2^0)$ in period 1 the price $p^1 = (p_1^1, p_2^1) = (f_1^{-1}(q_1^0), f_2^{-1}(q_2^0)) = (10 - q_1^0, 6 - (1/2)\, q_2^0)$ in period 1 prevails. By assumption the firm assumes that p^1 is the price in period 2, too, and therefore produces some $q^1 = (q_1^1, q_2^1)$ s.t.

$$p^1 \cdot q^1 \geqslant p^1 \cdot q \qquad \text{for all } q \in Q.$$

Denote the set of all productions maximizing profit by $\hat{\phi}(p^1)$ or $\hat{\phi}(p^t)$ more generally. Any time path (q^t) with

$$q^t = (q_1^t, q_2^t) \in \hat{\phi}(p_1^t, p_2^t) = \hat{\phi}(f_1^{-1}(q_1^{t-1}), f_2^{-1}(q_2^{t-1}))$$
$$= \hat{\phi}\left(10 - q_1^{t-1}, 6 - \frac{1}{2} q_2^{t-1}\right)$$

is an optimal path – depending on q^0 – for the firm with respect to the above assumptions. E.g. if the initial value is $(1/2, 17/2) = (q_1^0, q_2^0)$, the price in period 1 will be $(19/2, 7/4) = (p_1^1, p_2^1)$. According to the myopic foresight assumption the firm produces in period 1 (q_1^1, q_2^1) maximizing profits with respect to (p_1^1, p_2^1). This production in uniquely determined as $(4, 0)$. But in period 2 the price will be $(6, 6)$ and each production $(q_1^2, q_2^2) \in \{(q, 9-q) \mid 0 \leqslant q \leqslant 1\}$ maximizes profit with respect to $(6, 6) = (p_1^2, p_2^2)$.

By the Kakutani fixpoint theorem there must be an equilibrium of $\hat{\phi}$, i.e. a production $(\bar{q}_1, \bar{q}_2)$ with $(\bar{q}_1, \bar{q}_2) \in \hat{\phi}((\bar{q}_1, \bar{q}_2))$. We have $(\bar{q}_1, \bar{q}_2) = (8/3, 14/3)$; this equilibrium is totally unstable since in every neighbourhood of $(8/3, 14/3)$ there are points of the form $(q, 10 - 2q)$ which in the next period lead to productions necessarily being in $\{(10/3, 10/3), (1, 8)\}$. Later we will consider this example again.

Let X be a closed subset of $\mathbf{R}^n$; by 2^X we denote the set of all subsets of X.

Definition 1: Let $\phi: X \to 2^X$ be given. A (discrete) ϕ-process starting at $x_0 \in X$ is a function $x: \mathbf{N} \to X$ s.t. $x(0) = x_0$, $x(t+1) \in \phi(x(t))$.

The set of all ϕ-processes starting in x_0 is denoted by $C(x_0)$. Instead of $x(t)$ we will write x_t; a ϕ-process is given by $(x_t)_{t \in \mathbf{N}}$.

Most ϕ-processes are defined with an upper semicontinuous (USC) ϕ.[1]) This is the case with our introductory example, too. USC correspondences often arise because of the maximum theorem of C. Berge [see *Takayama*], which roughly speaking states, that the set of optimal actions which maximizes a continuous function with respect to continuous constraints is given by an USC correspondence. If ϕ in Definition 1 is a single-valued function a ϕ-process reduces to a dynamical discrete model (difference equation system).

Definition 2: Let $\phi: X \to 2^X$ define a ϕ-process and let $A \subset X$. A is called
a) weakly invariant, if for every $a \in A$ there is some $(x_t) \in C(a)$ s.t. $x_t \in A$ $(t \in \mathbf{N})$,
b) strongly invariant, if $\phi(A) \subset A$,
c) quasiinvariant, if $A \subset \phi(A)$.

A set A is weakly invariant, if for each $a \in A$ there exists a ϕ-process (x_t) starting in a, which remains in A for all t. It is strongly invariant, if every ϕ-process remains in A whenever it starts in A. Quasiinvariance means that for every $a \in A$ and every t_0 there is some $a' \in A$ s.t. $a \in \phi^{t_0}(a')$.

In the single-valued case a) and b) agree. If $A = \{x\}$ then weak- and quasiinvariance imply: x is a fixpoint of ϕ, i.e. $x \in \phi(x)$; strong invariance implies that x is an endpoint:

---

[1]) $\phi: X \to 2^X$ is USC, if $\phi(x) \neq \emptyset$, compact for every $x \in X$ and if for every $y \in X$ and every open set U containing $\phi(y)$ there exists an open set V containing y s.t. $\phi(v) \subset U$ $(v \in V)$.

$x = \phi(x)$. We introduce the following notions for various limit sets; let $\phi: X \to 2^X$ be given and $(x_t) \in C(x_0)$ for some x_0.

$$l((x_t)) := \{y \mid \text{there exists a sequence } t_k \to \infty \text{ with } x_{t_k} \to y\}$$

$$L(x_0) := \bigcup_{(x_t) \in C(x_0)} l((x_t))$$

$$\Lambda(x_0) := \{y \mid \text{there are } (x_t^n) \in C(x_0) \ (n \in \mathbf{N}) \text{ and } t_n \to \infty \text{ s.t. } x_{t_n}^n \to y\}$$

$L(x_0)$ is the set of all accumulation points of all ϕ-processes in x_0 (limit set in the sense of *Champsaur/Drèze/Henry* [1977]); $\Lambda(x_0)$ allows diagonalization (limit set in the sense of *Cherene* [1978]).

We illustrate these concepts by the introductory example. For the initial value (1/2, 17/2) a possible $\hat{\phi}$-process is

$$(q_1^t, q_2^t) := \left(\left(\frac{1}{2}, \frac{17}{2}\right), (4, 0), (0, 9), (4, 0), (1, 8), \left(\frac{10}{3}, \frac{10}{3}\right), (1, 8), \left(\frac{10}{3}, \frac{10}{3}\right), \ldots\right)$$

with

$$l((q_1^t, q_2^t)) = \left\{\left(\frac{10}{3}, \frac{10}{3}\right), (1, 8)\right\}.$$

One easily determines

$$L\left(\left(\frac{1}{2}, \frac{17}{2}\right)\right) = \left\{(q, 9-q) \mid 0 \leqslant q \leqslant \frac{5}{7}\right\} \cup \left\{(4, 0), \left(\frac{10}{3}, \frac{10}{3}\right), (1, 8)\right\}.$$

For determining $\Lambda((1/2, 17/2))$ one has to consider that it is possible to reach e.g. the state (6/7, 57/7) at any time t starting from (1/2, 17/2) and therefore

$$\Lambda\left(\left(\frac{1}{2}, \frac{17}{2}\right)\right) = \{(q, 9-q) \mid 0 \leqslant q \leqslant 1\} \cup \left\{(q, 20-5q) \mid \frac{10}{3} \leqslant q \leqslant 4\right\}.$$

The Λ-set is the same for any initial value $(q_1^0, 9 - q_1^0)$ with $0 \leqslant q_1^0 \leqslant 5/7$.
Starting in (6/7, 57/7) the L-and the Λ-set agree and are given by

$$L\left(\left(\frac{6}{7}, \frac{57}{7}\right)\right) = \Lambda\left(\left(\frac{6}{7}, \frac{57}{7}\right)\right) = \left\{\left(\frac{10}{3}, \frac{10}{3}\right), (1, 8)\right\}.$$

The following result shows some invariance properties of limit sets.

Proposition 1: Let ϕ be an USC correspondence on X and let $x_0 \in X$. If there is some $(x_t) \in C(x_0)$ with $l((x_t)) \neq \emptyset$ then $l((x_t))$, $L(x_0)$, $\Lambda(x_0)$ are weakly invariant. If X is compact these sets are quasiinvariant, too.

Proof: We prove proposition 1 for $\Lambda(x_0)$; the other cases can be proved in an analogue way.

Let $y \in \Lambda(x_0)$, $y = \lim_k x_{t_k}^k$ with $t_k \to \infty$ and $(x_t^k) \in C(x_0)$ for all k.

Let V be a compact neighbourhood of $\phi(y)$; because of USC there is a neighbourhood W of y s.t.:

$$x \in W \Rightarrow \phi(x) \subset V.$$

For some k_0 we have $x^k_{t_k} \in W \ (k \geqslant k_0)$ and therefore:

$$\phi(x^k_{t_k}) \subset V \quad (k \geqslant k_0).$$

Since $x^k_{t_k+1} \in \phi(x^k_{t_k})$ and by the compactness of V we can assume

$$x^k_{t_k+1} \to z \qquad \text{for } k \to \infty.$$

Therefore $z \in \Lambda(x_0)$ and by USC $z \in \phi(y)$, too. This proves $\Lambda(x_0)$ to be weakly invariant.

Now let X be compact[2]) and $y \in \Lambda(x_0)$, $y = \lim x^k_{t_k}$.

By compactness we can assume $x^k_{t_k-1} \to v \in \Lambda(x_0)$. Let R be any neighbourhood of $\phi(v)$ and let S be a neighbourhood of v, s.t.: $x \in S \Rightarrow \phi(x) \subset R$; For some k_1 we have: $x^k_{t_k-1} \in S \ (k \geqslant k_1)$ implying

$$x^k_{t_k} \in \phi(x^k_{t_k-1}) \subset R.$$

Therefore $y \in R$; since R was an arbitrary neighbourhood of $\phi(v)$ this implies $y \in \phi(v)$ proving the quasiinvariance of $\Lambda(x_0)$.

In our introductory example we have

$$L\left(\left(\frac{8}{3}, \frac{14}{3}\right)\right) = \left\{\left(\frac{8}{3}, \frac{14}{3}\right), \left(\frac{10}{3}, \frac{10}{3}\right), (1, 8)\right\}$$

and this set is weakly invariant; e.g. starting in (8/3, 14/3) one can choose (10/3, 10/3) in period 2 and afterwards change between (1, 8) and (10/3, 10/3). Since

$$\hat{\phi}\left(L\left(\left(\frac{8}{3}, \frac{14}{3}\right)\right)\right) = \left\{(q, 10 - 2q) \mid 1 \leqslant q \leqslant \frac{10}{3}\right\}$$

L is not strongly invariant. $\Lambda((8/3, 14/3)) = \hat{\phi}(L((8/3, 14/3)))$ happens to be strongly invariant in this case.

This is not true for USC correspondences in general; consider the correspondence ϕ: $[0, 1] \to 2^{[0,1]}$ defined by

$$\phi(x) = \begin{cases} \{\sqrt{x}\} & 0 \leqslant x < 1 \\ [0, 1] & x = 1 \end{cases}$$

We have $\Lambda(1/2) = \{1\} \not\supset \phi(\Lambda(1/2)) = [0, 1]$.

---

[2]) It suffices to assume that $C(x_0)$ is bounded.

Proposition 2: Let $\phi : X \to 2^X$ be USC and let (x_t) be a ϕ-process.

i) If $l((x_t)) = \{y\}$, then $y \in \phi(y)$.

ii) If $l((x_t)) = \{y_1, \ldots, y_k\}$, then there are $(x_t^i) \in C(y_i)$ and $t_i \in \{1, \ldots, k\}$ s.t.:

$$x_t^i = x_{t+t_i}^i \qquad \text{for all } t \text{ and } i \in \{1, \ldots, k\}$$

iii) If $l((x_t)) \neq \emptyset$ is bounded, then there is some subset $A \subset l((x_t))$, $A \neq 0$ s.t. for each $a \in A$ there is some $(x_t) \in C(a)$ s.t. for each neighbourhood U of a there is some t_0 with

$$\{x_t, \ldots, x_{t+t_0}\} \cap U \neq 0 \qquad \text{for all } t. \qquad (*)$$

Proof:

i) Since $l((x_t)) = \{y\}$ is weakly invariant we have $\{y\} \cap \phi(y) \neq \emptyset$.

ii) This is proved in *Meyer* [1979] using the fact that

$$l((x_t)) \subset \bigcup_{j=0}^{k-1} \phi^j(y_i) \qquad \text{for every } i \in \{1, \ldots, k\}.$$

iii) This is a consequence of the following result since $l((x_t))$ is closed (and therefore compact) and weakly invariant by proposition 1.

Proposition 3: Let $\phi: X \to 2^X$ be USC and let $B \subset X$ be a compact weakly invariant set. There is a subset $A \subset B$, $A \neq \emptyset$ s.t. for each $a \in A$ (*) holds.

Proof:

$$C_B := \{(x_t) \mid x_{t+1} \in \phi(x_t), x_t \in B, (t \in \mathbf{N})\}; \text{ by assumption } C_B \neq \emptyset.$$

Because of ϕ is USC C_B is a closed (and therefore compact) subset of $B^{\mathbf{N}}$ provided with the topology of pointwise convergence. Consider the mapping

$$S : X^{\mathbf{N}} \to X^{\mathbf{N}}$$
$$(x_t)_{t \in \mathbf{N}} \to (x_{t+1})_{t \in \mathbf{N}}$$

S maps C_B into C_B and is continuous. Let $\mathcal{K}$ denote the set of all (with respect to S) invariant closed subsets $K \subset C_B$ (i.e. $S(K) \subset K$); by compactness there is a minimal element $K_0 \in \mathcal{K}$, $K_0 \neq \emptyset$. Applying theorem 3.10. of *Bhatia/Chow* [1972] to (C_B, S): For each $k = (k_t) \in K_0$ and each neighbourhood W of k there is some t_0 s.t.

$$\{S^l(k), \ldots, S^{l+t_0}(k)\} \cap W \neq \emptyset \qquad \text{for all } l. \qquad (+)^{3)}.$$

Let A be the projection of K_0 onto the first coordinate. Then A is a closed subset of B and for each $a \in A$ there is a ϕ-process of K_0 starting in a. Let $a \in A$ and a neighbourhood U of a be given. Let $k = (k_t) \in K_0$ be a ϕ-process s.t. $k_0 = a$. Then $U \times B \times B \times \ldots \cap C_B$

---

3) $S^l(k) = S^l((k_t)) = (k_{t+l})$.

is a neighbourhood of k in C_B. From (+) it follows that

$$\{k_l, \ldots, k_{l+t_0}\} \cap U \neq \emptyset \qquad \text{for all } l \text{ and some } t_0.$$

Remark: The proposition can be applied to the set $\Lambda(x_0) \neq \emptyset$, too, since this set is closed and weakly invariant.

It should be pointed out that the results only hold if the set valued process is autonomous, i.e. the set of possible states in period $t + 1$ only depends on the state in period t and not on the special time t. A nonautonomous process is described by

$$x_{t+1} \in \phi(x_t, t).$$

Some authors suggest to transform this process into the following autonomous one. Replace X by $X \times \mathbf{N}$ and define $\tilde{\phi}$: $X \times \mathbf{N} \rightarrow 2^{(X \times \mathbf{N})}$ by

$$\tilde{\phi}(y, t) = \phi(y, t) \times \{t + 1\}.$$

A $\tilde{\phi}$-process starting at $x = (y, 0)$ is given by $(x_t) = (y_t, t)$

$$x_{t+1} \in \tilde{\phi}(x_t) = \phi(x_t) \times \{t + 1\}.$$

But this process has very unpleasant properties, e.g. there are no bounded $\tilde{\phi}$-processes and for each $\tilde{\phi}$-process (x_t) we have $l((x_t)) = \emptyset$.

References

Aubin, J.-P., and *R.H. Day*: Trajectories for a Class of Adapting Economic Systems. Journal of Economic Dynamics and Control **2**, 1980, 185–203.

Bhatia, N.P., and *S.-N. Chow*: Weak Attraction, Minimality, Recurrence and Almost Periodicity in Semi-Systems. Funkicialaj Ekvaciaj **15**, 1972.

Champsaur, P., J. Drèze and *C. Henry*: Stability Theory with Economic Applications. Econometrica **45**, 1977, 273–295.

Cherene, L.J.: Set Valued Dynamical Systems and Economic Flow. Lecture Notes in Economics and Mathematical Systems 158, 1978.

Meyer, G.G.L.: Asymptotic Properties of Sequences Iteratively Generated by Point-to-Set Maps. Point-to-Set Maps and Mathematical Programming. Ed. by P. Huard. 1979, 115–127.

Roxin, E.: On Generalized Dynamical Systems Defined by Contingent Equations. Journal of Differential Equation **I**, 1965, 188–205.

Takayama, A.: Mathematical Economics. Hinsdale 1974.

Quantitative Studies on Production and Prices © Physica-Verlag, Würzburg–Wien, 1983.

Dynamical Systems Without Closed Integral Curves

Diethard Pallaschke

1. Introduction

Starting point of this paper is an article of *Medvedev* [1970]. In this article Medvedev states sufficient conditions for a dynamical system on an n-dimensional simply connected manifold to have no closed integral curves. The special case $n = 2$ has been treated by *Poincaré/Bendixson* (see [1955]), the case $n = 3$ has been studied by *Demidowitsch* [1966]. For applications to economics we refer to the paper of *Rose* [1967], where this theory is used for the study of the employment cycle.

2. Notations and Basic Results

We will now give a short survey on the results of *Medvedev* [1970] for the special case where the dynamical system is defined on an open simply connected subset of the euclidean n-spaces $\mathbf{R}^n$.

Let $n \geqslant 2$, $G \subseteq \mathbf{R}^n$ be an open simply connected subset of $\mathbf{R}^n$ and let

$$\frac{dx_i}{dt} = f_i(x_1, \ldots, x_n), \qquad i \in \{1, \ldots, n\}$$

be a system of differential equations, where

$$f_i: G \longrightarrow \mathbf{R}, \qquad i \in \{1, \ldots, n\}$$

is a continuously differentiable function.

Then we have the following result [see *Medvedev*, Theorem 2].

Theorem 1: Let $n \geqslant 2$ and let the dynamical system

$$\frac{dx_i}{dt} = f_i(x_1, \ldots, x_n), \qquad i \in \{1, \ldots, n\}$$

be given as above. Furthermore, let us assume that there exist $(n - 2)$ continuously differentiable functions

$$\mu_i : G \longrightarrow \mathbf{R}^n$$
$$\mu_i := (\mu_i^1, \ldots, \mu_i^n)$$

and let us denote for $i<j,\ i,j\in\{1,\dots,n\}$

$$\mu_{ij} := (-1)^{i+j+1} \det \begin{pmatrix} \mu_1^1, \dots, \hat{\mu}_1^i, \dots, \hat{\mu}_1^j, \dots, \mu_1^n \\ \vdots \\ \mu_{n-2}^1, \dots, \hat{\mu}_{n-2}^i, \dots, \hat{\mu}_{n-2}^j, \dots, \mu_{n-2}^n \end{pmatrix}, \tag{2.1}$$

where the indices i, j are dropped in the determinant.

Now, if for all $i<j,\ i,j\in\{1,\dots,n\}$ the conditions

$$\begin{aligned} &\frac{\partial f_j}{\partial x_i} - \frac{\partial f_i}{\partial x_j} + \sum_{k=1}^{j-1} \frac{\partial}{\partial x_i}(\mu_{kj}\cdot f_k) - \sum_{k=j+1}^{n} \frac{\partial}{\partial x_i}(\mu_{jk} f_k) - \\ &\qquad - \sum_{k=1}^{i-1} \frac{\partial}{\partial x_j}(\mu_{ki} f_k) + \sum_{k=i+1}^{n} \frac{\partial}{\partial x_j}(\mu_{ik} f_k) = 0 \end{aligned} \tag{2.2}$$

are satisfied, then there exists no closed 1-dimensional solution manifold.

The proof of this Theorem uses only elementary facts of exterior differential forms and the Theorem of Stokes.

Now we will state condition (2.2) in a slightly different way. Let us set for abbreviation

$$\varphi_j := \sum_{k=1}^{j-1} \mu_{kj} f_k - \sum_{k=j+1}^{n} \mu_{jk} f_k.$$

Then (2.2) is nothing else but:

$$\frac{\partial}{\partial x_i}(f_j + \varphi_j) = \frac{\partial}{\partial x_j}(f_i + \varphi_i), \qquad i<j,\ i,j\in\{1,\dots,n\}. \tag{2.2'}$$

If we set

$$\Phi_j := f_j + \varphi_j$$

then the functions μ_{ij} satisfy the following linear equation:

$$\begin{pmatrix} -f_2 & -f_3 & \cdots & -f_n & 0 & & & & & & 0 \\ f_1 & & & & -f_3 & -f_4 & \cdots & -f_n & & & \vdots \\ & \ddots & & & f_2 & & & & -f_4 \cdots -f_n & & 0 \\ & & \ddots & & \vdots & \ddots & & & f_3 & \ddots & \vdots \\ & & & f_1 & \vdots & & f_2 & & \vdots & & 0 \\ & & & & \vdots & & & \ddots & 0 & & -f_{n-1},\ -f_n \\ & & & & 0 & & & & \vdots & \ddots & f_{n-2},\ 0\ -f_n \\ & & & & f_1 & & & & f_2 & \cdots & \end{pmatrix} \begin{pmatrix} \mu_{12} \\ \mu_{13} \\ \vdots \\ \mu_{1n} \\ \mu_{23} \\ \vdots \\ \mu_{n-1,n} \end{pmatrix} = \begin{pmatrix} \Phi_1 - f_1 \\ \vdots \\ \Phi_n - f_n \end{pmatrix} \tag{2.3}$$

Let us furthermore assume that the function $f_1 : G \longrightarrow \mathbf{R}$ does not vanish in any point of G. Then the matrix of coefficients of (2.3) has rank $(n-1)$. By an easy calculation we see that (2.3) has a solution if and only if

$$\sum_{i=1}^{n} \Phi_i f_i = \sum_{i=1}^{n} f_i^2 .$$

Thus if condition (2.2) is satisfied, then there exist n continuously differentiable functions

$$\Phi_i : G \longrightarrow \mathbf{R}, \qquad i \in \{1, \ldots, n\}$$

such that

i) $$\frac{\partial \Phi_i}{\partial x_j} = \frac{\partial \Phi_j}{\partial x_i}, \qquad i<j, \; i, j \in \{1, \ldots, n\}$$

ii) $$\sum_{i=1}^{n} \Phi_i f_i = \sum_{i=1}^{n} f_i^2 .$$

3. Dynamical Systems Without Integral Cycles

We will now state two sufficient conditions for a dynamical system on an open simply connected subset of $\mathbf{R}^n$ to have no closed 1-dimensional solution manifolds. These conditions are slightly stronger than condition (2.2).

Theorem 2: Let $n \geqslant 2$ and let the dynamical system

$$\frac{dx_i}{dt} = f_i(x_1, \ldots, x_n), \qquad i \in \{1, \ldots, n\}$$

be given as above on an open simply connected subset $G \subseteq \mathbf{R}^n$. Furthermore let us assume that f_1 does not vanish at any point of G and that there exist continuously differentiable functions

$$\Phi_i \longrightarrow \mathbf{R}$$

which satisfy the following conditions:

i) for all $i, j \in \{1, \ldots, n\}$ with $i<j$

$$\frac{\partial \Phi_i}{\partial x_j} = \frac{\partial \Phi_j}{\partial x_i}$$

ii) $$\sum_{i=1}^{n} \Phi_i f_i = \sum_{i=1}^{n} f_i^2$$

iii) for $i \in \{n-1, n\}$ the functions

$$\Phi_i - f_i : G \longrightarrow \mathbf{R}$$

do not vanish at any point of G.

Then there exists no closed 1-dimensional solution manifold.

Proof: We will show that the assumptions of Theorem 1 are satisfied. First observe that from condition ii) follows that the linear system (2.3) has a solution. In particular, if we set

$$s_{1j} := \frac{\Phi_j - f_j}{f_1}, \qquad j \in \{2, \ldots, n\}$$

then for $i < j$

$$\mu_{ij} := \begin{cases} s_{1j} & \text{if } i = 1 \\ 0 & \text{if } i \neq 1 \end{cases}$$

is a solution of (2.3). From i) follows now that condition (2.2) of Theorem 1 is satisfied.

It remains to show that there exist $(n-2)$ continuously differentiable functions

$$\mu_i : G \rightarrow \mathbf{R}^n, \qquad i \in \{1, \ldots, n-2\}$$

such that for every μ_{ij} formula (2.1) holds.

From the Laplace Theorem for calculating determinants, we see that the required functions μ_i are given by:

α) if i is odd and $i \leqslant n-3$:

$$\mu_i := \Big(0, \ldots, 0, \underset{\substack{\text{at position}\\ i+1}}{1}, 0, \ldots \quad 0, 0, \ldots, \underset{\substack{\text{at position}\\ n}}{-\frac{s_{1i+n}}{s_{1n}}}\Big)$$

β) if i is even and $i \leqslant n-3$

$$\mu_i := \Big(0, \ldots, 0, \underset{\substack{\text{at position}\\ i+1}}{1}, \ldots \quad 0, \ldots, \underset{\substack{\text{at position}\\ n-1}}{-\frac{s_{1i+1}}{s_{1n-1}}}, 0\Big)$$

γ) for $i := n-2$

$$\mu_{n-2} = (0, \ldots, 0, \ldots\ 0, (-1)^n s_{1n}, (-1)^{n-1} s_{1n-1})$$

□

Next we state:

Theorem 3: Let $n \geqslant 2$ and let the dynamical system

$$\frac{dx_i}{dt} = f_i(x_1, \ldots, x_n), \qquad i \in \{1, \ldots, n\}$$

be given as above on an open simply connected subset $G \subseteq \mathbf{R}^n$. Furthermore let us assume that for all $i < j,\ i, j \in \{1, \ldots, n\}$

$$\frac{\partial f_i}{\partial x_j} = \frac{\partial f_j}{\partial x_i}.$$

Then there exists no closed 1-dimensional solution manifold.

Proof: Again we will show that the assumptions of Theorem 1 are satisfied. We set $\Phi_i = f_i$.

Observe that now the system (2.3) of linear equations is homogeneous and that

$$\mu := (\mu_{ij})_{i<j}$$

with

$$\mu_{n-1,n} := f_{n-2}$$

$$\mu_{n-2,n-1} := f_n$$

$$\mu_{n-2,n} := -f_{n-1}$$

and all other components μ_{ij} are zero is a solution of (2.3). Since for all $i<j$

$$\frac{\partial f_i}{\partial x_j} = \frac{\partial f_j}{\partial x_i},$$

condition (2.2) of Theorem 1 is satisfied.

It remains to show that there exist $(n-2)$ continuously differentiable functions

$$\mu_i : G \rightarrow \mathbf{R}^n, \qquad i \in \{1, \ldots, n-2\}$$

such that for μ_{ij} formula (2.1) holds.

In an analogous way as in the proof of the last theorem we set:

α) for $i \leqslant n-3$:

$$\mu_i := (0, \ldots, 0, 1, \ldots, 0)$$

at position i

and

β) for $i = n-2$:

$$\mu_{n-2} := (0, \ldots, 0, +f_{n-2}, -f_{n-1}, +f_n).$$

□

References

Demidowitsch, W.B.: Eine Verallgemeinerung des Kriteriums von Bendixson. ZAMM **46**, 1966, 145–146.

Medvedev, V.S.: Sufficient Conditions for Dynamical Systems to Have no Integral Cycles. Differentsial'nye Uravneniya **6**, 1970, 454–466.

Poincaré, A., and *J. Bendixson*: Theory of Ordinary Differential Equations. E.A. Coddington and N. Levinson. Chapter 16, 389–403. New York 1955.

Rose, H.: On the Non-Linear Theory of the Employment Cycle. Review of Economic Studies **34**, 1967, 153–173.

Quantitative Studies on Production and Prices © Physica-Verlag, Würzburg–Wien, 1983.

Dynamic Production Networks

Ronald W. Shephard †

1. Introduction

Production systems are typically an interacting collection of production activities the outputs of which may be intermediate products serving as inputs for some activities of the system or final products, or both. The flows of intermediate products may be represented as arcs of a linear graph with activities represented by nodes. In such terms production may be modeled by a directed network connecting activities along which system exogenous inputs, intermediate and final products flow dynamically. The developments to follow are addressed to this structure of a dynamic production correspondence. See *Shephard/Färe* [1980] for the abstract model of a dynamic production correspondence relating histories of exogenous inputs to histories of net outputs without consideration of the network structure and intermediate products.

In the development of the abstract structure of a production network as a dynamic production correspondence, certain network axioms are needed to characterize the role of intermediate products, and to verify that the correspondence between dynamic flows of network system exogenous inputs and final outputs obeys the axioms taken for such systems and used for the network activities in treating intermediate products as activity exogenous inputs.

With this theoretical foundation one may progressively develop „*Activity Analysis*" dynamic models from abstract to computational forms. The computational dynamics for production networks is an interesting departure from the superficial practice of indexing variables by time and writing down the Hamilton-Jacobi differential equations for minimizing or maximizing some statement for an unstructured production model. It would seem that representing production dynamics economically by mechanical analogies is an idle practice, despite the mathematical artistry of the coordinate and variable substitutions involved in so representing the equations of motion of an arbitrary point mass system subject to forces, inertia and equations of form restricting motion.

In the discussion of computational dynamics for production networks, discrete time points will be used with step functions for histories. This approach enables use of the techniques of mathematical programming for practical purposes.

---

[1]) Here the input rate histories exogenous to an activity may span both system exogenous inputs and intermediate product transfers.

[2]) The sign $\geqslant$ means that at least one component is "greater than" on a subset of $\mathbf{R}_+$ of positive measure.

For acyclic production networks a dynamic computation of a feasible output trajectory will be outlined to illustrate the evolutionary character of "motion" for production networks, and to show possibilities for Time as well as Factor Substitution in production, an added dimension for dynamic economics.

2. Abstract Structure of Dynamic Production Networks

Consider a production system with N elementary activities and a final activity $(N+1)$ for recording final output rate histories. All histories are taken as time rates. As notation, the source of exogenous input rate histories is denoted by A_0. Thus the production system consists of elementary activities $A_0, A_1, A_2, \ldots, A_N, A_{N+1}$.

The primitive elements of the goods and services related to this network of production activities are time rate histories of system exogenous inputs, activity outputs, intermediate product transfers and final outputs, each defined on the nonnegative real line $\mathbf{R}_+$. Each history is an element of $(L_\infty)_+$, i.e., the nonnegative domain of equivalence classes of bounded and measurable real functions defined on $\mathbf{R}_+$. (Two functions are equivalent if they differ only on a subset of measure zero.) The norm $\| f \|$ of a function $f \in (L_\infty)_+$ is taken as the essential supremum. Addition, and multiplication of histories by a positive real number, are taken pointwise in time.

As notation: $x = (x_1, x_2, \ldots, x_n) \in (L_\infty)_+^n$ is a vector of input rate histories for n system exogenous inputs (factors).

$V_i = (V_i^1, V_i^2, \ldots, V_i^m) \in (L_\infty)_+^m$, $i = 1, 2, \ldots, N$, are vectors of net output rate histories for the N activities of the network.

$V_{ij} = (V_{ij}^1, V_{ij}^2, \ldots, V_{ij}^m) \in (L_\infty)_+^m$, $i = 1, 2, \ldots, N$, are vectors of transfer rate histories from A_i to A_j as intermediate and final outputs for $j = 1, 2, \ldots, N$, and $j = N+1$ respectively.

$u = (u_1, u_2, \ldots, u_m) \in (L_\infty)_+^m$ is a vector of net output rate histories for the production system.

A common space $(L_\infty)_+^m$ is taken for all activity output rate histories, transfers of the same and network output rate histories. Not all component histories of V_i, V_{ij}, u need be positive on subsets of $\mathbf{R}_+$ of positive measure.

$$\| x \| = \operatorname*{Max}_i \| x_i \|, \quad \| v_i \| = \operatorname*{Max}_k \| V_i^k \|,$$

$$\| V_{ij} \| = \operatorname*{Max}_k \| V_{ij}^k \|, \quad \| u \| = \operatorname*{Max}_i \| u_i \|.$$

By defining the distance $\rho(f, g)$ between two histories to be the essential supremum of $| f - g |$, i.e., $\rho(f, g) = \| (| f - g |) \|$, the model of production is defined by primitive elements in metric spaces. Notions of closure, convergence and limits for these elements follow naturally.

The activities of the production network each follow net output and net input dynamic production correspondences defined respectively by:

$$(x_{0i}, \sum_{j=1}^{N}{}' V_{ji}) \in (L_\infty)_+^n \times (L_\infty)_+^m \to \mathbf{P}_i (x_{0i}, \sum_{j=1}^{N}{}' V_{ji}) \in 2^{(L_\infty)_+^{2m}}$$

$$(V_{i,N+1}, \sum_{j=1}^{N}{}' V_{ij}) \in (L_\infty)_+^{2m} \to \mathbf{L}_i (V_{i,N+1}, \sum_{j=1}^{N}{}' V_{ij}) \in 2^{(L_\infty)_+^n \times (L_\infty)_+^m}$$

where x_{0i}, $i = 1, 2, \ldots, N$, is an allocation to A_i from the vector x, subject to

$$\sum_{i=1}^{N} x_{0i} \leqq x,$$

and Σ' denotes a summation with the term for $j = i$ omitted.

The axioms governing the activity dynamic correspondences may be found in *Shephard/Färe* [1980] and will not be repeated here. Since the activities of the production network are primitive production elements for the system, they are taken to relate only exogenous input rate histories[1]) to net output rate histories. They may range from elementary processes to factories, depending upon the extent of aggregation for the production system studied.

The production network dynamic output correspondence is expressed by:

$$x \in (L_\infty)_+^n \to \mathbf{PN}(x) \in 2^{(L_\infty)_+^m},$$

$$\mathbf{PN}(x) = \{u \in (L_\infty)_+^m : u \leqq \sum_{i=1}^{N} V_{i,N+1}, \sum_{i=1}^{N} x_{0i} \leqq x,$$

$$(V_{i,N+1}, \sum_{j=1}^{N}{}' V_{ij}) \in \mathbf{P}_i (x_{0i}, \sum_{j=1}^{N}{}' V_{ji}), i = 1, 2, \ldots, N\}.$$

The production network dynamic input correspondence is expressed by:

$$u \in (L_\infty)_+^m \to \mathbf{LN}(u) = \{x \in (L_\infty)_+^n : u \in \mathbf{PN}(x)\} \in 2^{(L_\infty)_+^n},$$

$$\mathbf{LN}(u) = \{x \in (L_\infty)_+^n : x \geqq \sum_{i=1}^{N} x_{0i}, \sum_{i=1}^{N} V_{i,N+1} \geqq u$$

$$(x_{0i}, \sum_{j=1}^{N}{}' V_{ji}) \in \mathbf{L}_i (V_{i,N+1}, \sum_{j=1}^{N}{}' V_{ij}), i = 1, 2, \ldots, N\}.$$

In these expressions, the output vector of each activity is taken net of the use by the activity of its own products. The allocation of the total vector x to activities is taken freely disposable, without loss of generality. Free disposability of activity final products is not likely to be generally applicable, but is taken so here for simplicity of presentation. See *Shephard* [1981] for such complications. However, input and output histories are not taken freely disposable for the activity dynamic production correspondences. More on this in the next section.

3. Network Axioms

It is important to investigate whether the production network correspondences **PN** and **LN** obey the properties (axioms) taken for the dynamic production correspondences of the activities of the network. The properties taken for $\mathbf{P}_i$, $\mathbf{L}_i$ do not propagate for **PN** and **LN** without some properties (axioms) postulated for production networks, since intermediate products are involved. The network axioms are:

PN.1 For each component history $u_i \in (L_\infty)_+$ of $u \in (L_\infty)_+^m$ which is not entirely intermediate product, there exists a vector $x \in (L_\infty)_+^n$ such that $u \in \mathbf{PN}(x)$ with $\| u_i \| > 0$.

PN.2 For each activity A_i there exists a subset $\{i_1, i_2, \ldots, i_k\}$, $1 \leqq k \leqq n$, of the n exogenous input histories x_{0i} which is *globally essential* and *strong limitational* for the output vector V_i, i.e., x_{0i_j} has to be essentially positive, $j = 1, 2, \ldots, k$, for $\| V_i \| > 0$, and, if $\| x_{0i_1}, x_{0i_2}, \ldots, x_{0i_k} \| \leqq B \in \mathbf{R}_{++}$, there exists for each V_i^0 a positive scalar θ depending upon B and V_i^0 such that $V_i \ngeqq \theta V_i^0$ (θ_j such that $(V_i)_j \ngeqq \theta_j (V_i^0)_j$, $j = 1, 2, \ldots, m$) for all $V_i \in \mathbf{P}_i (x_{0i}, \sum_{j=1}^{N}{}' V_{ji})$.

PN.2S For each activity A_i, $\{i_1, i_2, \ldots, i_k\}$ is taken *globally totally essential* and *strong norm limitational*, i.e., x_{0i_j} has to be essentially positive, $j = 1, 2, \ldots, k$, for any subset of V_i to be essentially positive, and there exists a scalar A depending on B and V_i such that $\| V_i \| \ngeqq A$ when $\| x_{0i_1}, \ldots, x_{0i_k} \| < B$, for all V_i.

PN.3 If $u \in (L_\infty)_+^m$ is summable in each component on $\mathbf{R}_+$ there exist x_{0i}, V_i, $i = 1, 2, \ldots, N$, summable in each component with $(x_{0i}, \sum_{j=1}^{N}{}' V_{ji}) \in \mathbf{L}_i (V_{i,N+1}, \sum_{j=1}^{N}{}' V_{ij})$, $V_i = \sum_{j=1}^{(N+1)}{}' V_{ij}$ and $\sum_{i=1}^{N}{}' V_{i,N+1} \geqq u$.

PN.4 If $\bar{t}_u := \operatorname{Max}_i (\operatorname{Ess\,Sup} \{t \in \mathbf{R}_+ : u_i(t) > 0\}) < \infty$ and x, V_{ij} ($i = 1, 2, \ldots, N$, $j = 1, 2, \ldots, N, N+1$) yield u, then

$$\left.\begin{aligned} y_i(t) &= x_i(t), \ t \in [0, \bar{t}_u) \\ y_i(t) &= 0, \ t \in [\bar{t}_u, +\infty) \end{aligned}\right. \quad (i = 1, 2, \ldots, n)$$

$$\left.\begin{aligned} w_{ij}(t) &= V_{ij}(t), \ t \in [0, \bar{t}_u) \\ w_{ij}(t) &= 0, \ t \in [\bar{t}_u, +\infty) \end{aligned}\right. \quad \begin{pmatrix} i = 1, 2, \ldots, N \\ j = 1, 2, \ldots, N, N+1 \end{pmatrix}.$$

PN.5 For each activity A_i, $V_{i,N+1}$ and $\sum_{j=1}^{N}{}' V_{ij}$ are weakly disposable subvectors of V_i, i.e., if $(V_{i,N+1}, \sum_{j=1}^{N}{}' V_{ij}) \in \mathbf{P}_i (x_{0i}, \sum_{j=1}^{N}{}' V_{ji})$ then $(\theta_1 \cdot V_{i,N+1}, \theta_2 \cdot \sum_{j=1}^{N}{}' V_{ij}) \in \mathbf{P}_i (x_{0i}, \sum_{j=1}^{N}{}' V_{ji})$ for $\theta_1 \in [0, 1]$, $\theta_2 \in [0, 1]$.

PN.6 For each activity A_i, if $(x_{0i}, \sum_{j=1}^{N\prime} V_{ij}) \in \mathbf{L}_i (V_{i,N+1}, \sum_{j=1}^{N\prime} V_{ij})$, $(\lambda x_{0i}, \mu \sum_{j=1}^{N\prime} V_{ji}) \in \mathbf{L}_i (V_{i,N+1}, \sum_{j=1}^{N\prime} V_{ij})$, $\lambda \in [1, +\infty)$, $\mu \in [1, +\infty)$, i.e., x_{0i} and $\sum_{j=1}^{N\prime} V_{ji}$ are weakly disposable vectors of input rate histories.

PN.7 For each activity A_i if $(V_{i,N+1}, \sum_{j=1}^{N\prime} V_{ij}) \in \mathbf{P}_i (x_{0i}, \sum_{j=1}^{N\prime} V_{ji})$ and $\| V_{i,N+1}, \sum_{j=1}^{N\prime} V_{ij} \| > 0$, there exists for $\theta \in \mathbf{R}_{++}$ a positive scalar $\lambda_\theta^{(i)}$ such that $\theta \cdot (V_{i,N+1}, \sum_{j=1}^{N\prime} V_{ij}) \in \mathbf{P}_i (\lambda_\theta^{(i)} x_{0i}, \theta \cdot \sum_{j=1}^{N\prime} V_{ji})$.

EN.1 For all vectors $V = (V_1, V_2, \ldots, V_N)$ such that u is obtainable from the related production network, the efficient subsets

$$\mathbf{E}_i (V_i) = \{(x_{0i}, \sum_{j=1}^{N\prime} V_{ji}) : (x_{0i}, \sum_{j=1}^{N\prime} V_{ji}) \in \mathbf{L}_i (V_i), (y_{0i}, \sum_{j=1}^{N\prime} w_{ji}) \notin \mathbf{L}_i (V_i)$$
$$\text{for } (y_{0i}, \sum_{j=1}^{N\prime} w_{ji}) \geqslant (x_{0i}, \sum_{j=1}^{N\prime} V_j)\} \;{}^{2})$$

are uniformly bounded.

Concerning the first of these network axioms, since $(L_\infty)_+^m$ is taken to span all intermediate and final output histories, some component histories of u may be essentially null. Hence the need for this network axiom.

Axiom **PN**.2 states that the activities of the network cannot produce net output without some system exogenous inputs, and if the vector of essential system exogenous input histories is bounded in the norm, the scaling of each possible vector of output histories is bounded. The stronger version **PN**.2S replaces global essential by global totally essential, and strong limitational by strong norm limitational. See *Shephard/Färe* [1980] for definitions.

Axiom **PN**.3 is a statement for the network correspondence similar to **L**.T.1 taken for the activity correspondences.

Axiom **PN**.4 is a statement for the network correspondence like axiom **L**.T.2 assumed for the activity correspondences.

Axiom **PN**.5 permits scaling of activity distributions to final output independently of the scaling of vectors of intermediate product transfer histories. A similar assumption is made in **PN**.6 for vectors of exogenous input histories and vectors of intermediate product input histories to an activity.

Axiom **PN**.7 postulates that the scaling of a vector of output histories for an activity may be obtained by the same scaling of intermediate product input histories while the scaling of exogenous inputs may exhibit decreasing, constant or increasing returns to scale.

The axioms for dynamic production correspondences require that the subsets $\mathbf{E}_i (V_i)$ be bounded, and the network axiom **EN**.1 results in this same property for the production network as a whole.

Two topologies are considered for the metric spaces $(L_\infty)_+^n, (L_\infty)_+^m, (L_\infty)_+^{n+m}$, $(L_\infty)^{2m}$. The norm topology under the essential supremum norm, and a weak* topology for those spaces by price histories taken in L_1.

With the foregoing network axioms, the axioms for the activity dynamic production correspondences propagate for the network correspondences **PN** and **LN**. See *Shephard* [1981]. The closure property **P**.5 is the only property with complications for showing propagation. Two alternatives arise:

P.2S, **P**.5 (NORM TOPOLOGY) and **P**.5 B1S for the activities, with **PN**.2 and **PN**.5,

P.2, **P**.5 (WEAK* TOPOLOGY) and **P**.5 B1S for the activities, with **PN**.2 and **PN**.5.

Regarding the production network efficient subset

$$\mathbf{EN}(u) = \{x \in (L_\infty)_+^n : x \in \mathbf{LN}(u), y \notin \mathbf{LN}(u) \text{ for } y \leqslant x\},$$

EN.1 implies **EN** (u) is bounded. **EN**.1 is required because there are an unbounded number of ways in which the outputs V_i $(i = 1, 2, \ldots, N)$ may be composed to yield u.

4. An Abstract Activity Analysis Model for Dynamic Production Networks

In some physical units or dimensionless terms, let $z = (z_1, z_2, \ldots, z_N) \in (L_\infty)_+^N$ denote a vector of intensity functions, stating for each activity the intensity of operation. These intensity functions are bounded by a vector $\bar{z} \in (L_\infty)_+^N$ of nonnegative intensity-bound-functions expressing the inherent limitations arising from physical limitations not otherwise reflected by the exogenous service inputs of facilities, equipment, and also by product design.

Technical coefficients are:

$$\mathbb{A} := \| \mathbb{A}^1 \mathbb{A}^2 \ldots \mathbb{A}^N \|^{TR},$$

$$\mathbb{A}^i := \| a_{i1}\, a_{i2} \ldots a_{in} \|, \qquad i = 1, 2, \ldots, N, \; a_{ij} \in (L_\infty)_+$$

$$\bar{\mathbb{A}} := \| \mathbb{A}^1 \mathbb{A}^2 \ldots \mathbb{A}^N \|^{TR},$$

$$\bar{\mathbb{A}}^i := \| \bar{a}_{i1}\, \bar{a}_{i2} \ldots \bar{a}_{im} \|, \qquad i = 1, 2, \ldots, m, \; \bar{a}_{ij} \in (L_\infty)_+$$

$$\mathbb{C} := \| \mathbb{C}^1 \mathbb{C}^2 \ldots \mathbb{C}^N \|^{TR},$$

$$\mathbb{C}^i := \| c_{i1}\, c_{i2} \ldots c_{im} \|, \qquad i = 1, 2, \ldots, m, \; c_{ij} \in (L_\infty)_+$$

in some units such that $z_i \mathbb{A}^i$, $z_i \bar{\mathbb{A}}^i$ and $z_i \mathbb{C}^i$ are time rate histories of exogenous and intermediate product inputs, and time rate histories of outputs respectively. Then the production network dynamic output and input correspondences are:

$$\mathbf{PN}(x) = \{u \in (L_\infty)_+^m : 0 \leqq z \leqq \bar{z}, z\mathbb{A} \leqq x, z(\mathbb{C} - \bar{\mathbb{A}}) \geqq 0, u \leqq z(\mathbb{C} - \bar{\mathbb{A}})\}$$

$$\mathbf{LN}(u) = \{x \in (L_\infty)_+^n : 0 \leqq z \leqq \bar{z}, z(\mathbb{C} - \mathbb{A}) \geqq u, x \geqq z\mathbb{A}\}.$$

For these formulations certain assumptions are made concerning the technical coefficients:

For each activity some exogenous input is required during $[0, +\infty)$ except on subsets of measure zero.
Each exogenous input is required by some activity during $[0, +\infty)$ on subsets of positive measure.
Each activity can produce some output on a subset of $[0, +\infty)$ of positive measure.
Each output is produced by some activity on a subset of $[0, +\infty)$ of positive measure.

The technical coefficients $\bar{a}_{ij}$ are merely taken as nonnegative as stated.

The input and output histories have been taken freely disposable for simplicity of expression. Extensions for limited disposability will be given in *Shephard* [1981].

As abstract statements these two dynamic production correspondences do not provide one with computational systems, but point the way toward such dynamic structures for production theory, expressing the inherent structure of production dynamics.

5. A Computational Dynamics for Leontief-Like Production Networks

Partition the nonnegative real line into half open intervals

$$[t-1, t), \qquad t = 1, 2, 3, \ldots$$

Take the intensity functions $z = (z_1, z_2, \ldots, z_N)$ constant on each interval. Thus among the functions $(L_\infty)_+$ only step function intensity histories are considered. This restriction is natural for a computational system. The unit of time is arbitrary. In the same way, histories of system exogenous inputs available will be taken as step functions.

At this juncture it is convenient to introduce more detail than previously considered. Exogenous inputs may be storable as well as nonstorable, but not both. In order to accommodate this fact the notation for exogenous input histories is expanded to

$$x \in (L_\infty)^s \quad \text{STORAGE}$$
$$y \in (L_\infty)^{n-s} \quad \text{NONSTORAGE.}$$

Initial inventories of storable exogenous inputs are included in the system exogenous input histories

$$x_i(0), \qquad i = 1, 2, \ldots, s.$$

Concerning intermediate products, initial inventories of the same are denoted by

$$v_k^0, \qquad k = 1, 2, \ldots, m$$

shared by all activities of the network, and capacities for storage of intermediate products are denoted by

$$\sigma_k(t) \qquad k = 1, 2, \ldots, m, \qquad t = 1, 2, 3, \ldots$$

independent of activity producing. Intermediate and final outputs for production during $[t-1, t)$ are taken to be realized at t. The intensity functions $z_i(t)$ and intermediate product inputs are applied at $(t-1)$ for $[(t-1), t)$.

Since some activities may yield outputs which are both intermediate product and final product, the intensity functions $z \in (L_\infty)_+^N$ are bifurcated as

$Iz_i \in (L_\infty)_+$, intermediate product production

$Fz_i \in (L_\infty)_+$, final product production.

In these terms the computational dynamics of the production network is subject to the following constraints: [See *Shephard* et al., 1977]

$$z_i(t) = Iz_i(t) + Fz_i(t), z_i(t) \leqq \bar{z}_i(t), Iz_i(t) \geqq 0, Fz_i(t) \geqq 0, \quad (i = 1, 2, \ldots, N), (t = 0, 1, 2, \ldots) \tag{1}$$

$$\sum_{\tau=0}^{t} \sum_{i=1}^{N} a_{ij}(\tau) z_i(\tau) \leqq \sum_{\tau=0}^{t} x_j(\tau), \quad (j = 1, 2, \ldots, s), (t = 0, 1, 2, \ldots) \tag{2}$$

$$\sum_{i=1}^{N} a_{ij}(t) z_i(t) \leqq y_j(t), \quad (j = s+1, s+2, \ldots, n), (t = 0, 1, 2, \ldots) \tag{3}$$

$$\sum_{i=1}^{N} \sum_{\tau=0}^{t} \bar{a}_{ik}(\tau) z_i(\tau) \leqq v_k^0 + \sum_{i=1}^{N} \sum_{\tau=0}^{t-1} c_{ik}(\tau+1) Iz_i(\tau), \sum_{i=1}^{N} \bar{a}_{ik}(0) z_i(0) \leqq v_k^0, \quad (k = 1, 2, \ldots, m), (t = 1, 2, 3, \ldots) \tag{4}$$

$$v_k^0 + \sum_{i=1}^{N} \sum_{\tau=0}^{t-1} c_{ik}(\tau+1) Iz_i(\tau) - \sum_{i=1}^{N} \sum_{\tau=0}^{t} \bar{a}_{ik}(\tau) z_i(\tau) \leqq \sigma_k(t), \tag{5}$$

$$v_k^0 - \sum_{i=1}^{N} \bar{a}_{ik}(0) z_i(0) \leqq \sigma_k(0), \quad (k = 1, 2, \ldots, m), (t = 1, 2, 3, \ldots).$$

The constraints (1) limit the intensities of operation of the activities of the production network to be nonnegative and not to exceed certain physical limitations not otherwise expressed by the service components of the exogenous input histories.

The constraints (2) and (3) limit exogenous inputs to available resources as given by the time histories $x \in (L_\infty)_+^s$ and $y \in (L_\infty)_+^{n-s}$. The constraints (4) require that inputs of intermediate products by the network activities do not exceed the supply available from the outputs of the activities and initial inventories. The last set of constraints does not allow accumulation of inventories of intermediate products beyond capacities for the same. All these constraints are limitations on network activity intensities.

The foregoing constraint system does not in any way predetermine the allocation of resources. However, it is a general basis for a computational dynamics of Leontief-like production networks. But since nothing has been specified concerning final outputs the dynamic evolution of the production network is not directed. The intensity functions Fz_i, $(i = 1, 2, \ldots, N)$ are so to speak free elements.

Since the output set **PN** (x, y) in general may be taken to exhibit weak disposability for vectors $u \in (L_\infty)_+^m$ of output histories, one may generate for various feasible output mixes of output histories the maximal scalar extension in **PN** (x, y), i.e., determine the dynamic evolution of the system to find points on the frontier of **PN** (x, y). Also for some price histories of the various outputs and inputs, one may seek to control the dynamics of the system to maximize (Revenue-Cost of Resources). In either case it is convenient to make these generations of the dynamics of the system with respect to a finite planning horizon T.

Now suppose there are $1 \leqq P \leqq m$ net products possible for the system. Let

$$\bar{a}_{N+1,p} \in \mathbf{R}_+$$

be coefficients related to an index

$$z_{N+1} \in \mathbf{R}_+$$

such that

$$\bar{a}_{N+1,p} \cdot z_{N+1}, \quad p = 1, 2, \ldots, P$$

defines the total amount of the p-th final product accumulated over the planning interval $[0, T]$. The coefficients $\bar{a}_{N+1,p}$ may be chosen to determine a specified output mix.

Then, in order to direct the system this way one adds the constraint

$$\bar{a}_{N+1,p} \cdot z_{N+1} \leqq \sum_{i=1}^{N} \sum_{t=1}^{T} c_{ip}(t)\, Fz_i(t-1), \qquad (p = 1, 2, \ldots, P) \tag{6}$$

and determines the dynamic evolution of the system by the following linear program:

$$\begin{cases} \text{Max} & z_{N+1} \\ \text{Subject to} & z_{N+1} \geqq 0, \ (1), (2), (3), \ldots, (5), (6) \text{ on } [0, T]. \end{cases}$$

A calculation of this type has been outlined by *Leachman* [1980] for the case of a network with each activity producing a single output, possibly with cycles in the network, i.e., for a Leontief-like network. Also similar calculations were outlined for this particular network to minimize the cost of obtaining a given program of output histories.

It is clear from the foregoing that productivity of a production system is a complicated concept. For any given output mix one may determine the maximal throughput for the mix, but this will vary with output mix. The resource inputs likewise condition the throughput. How is one then to determine properly the maximal productivity potential of a system unless resources and output mix are balanced for this purpose? Obviously a good deal of study is needed for such questions. With declining energy resources it would be of interest to know how the maximal throughput of various output mixes would retrogress.

In the general terms of the formulation of production networks used here, real capital is expressed in terms of service input rates, and for those components of (x, y) which are fully utilized in the dynamic solution of the linear program and reflect real capital, one may make marginal analyzes (linear programs) for incremental changes in such inputs. Indeed for energy supply decreases one may seek to estimate the consequences for economic sectors by the dynamic Leontief model detailed by Leachman, using "constant dollar values" for measures of aggregate output.

In order to drive the dynamics of the system by maximizing total revenue minus cost of resources (x, y) applied, one need merely define for given price histories $r_p(t), q_j(t)$ the objective function

$$\Pi(T) = \sum_{i=1}^{N} \left(\sum_{t=0}^{T-1} r_p (t+1)\, c_{ip} (t+1)\, Fz(t) \right)$$

$$- \sum_{\tau=0}^{T-1} \left(\sum_{j=1}^{s} q_j(\tau)\, x_j(\tau) - \sum_{j=s+1}^{n} q_j(\tau)\, y_j(\tau) \right)$$

and determine the dynamic evolution of the system by the linear program:

$$\begin{cases} \text{Max} & \Pi(T) \\ \text{Subject to} & (1), (2), (3), \ldots, (5) \text{ on } [0, T]. \end{cases}$$

Here $x_j(\tau)$, $y_j(\tau)$ are also variables in the linear program. Obviously refinements can be made in this kind of generation of the dynamics of the production network by discounting and adding other costs to complicate the definition of profit. For the purposes of this paper, interest is mainly in structure, and not management practice.

6. Acyclic Production Networks

In a production network without cycles the activities of the network may be ordered so that the outputs of an activity A_i can serve as intermediate product only for A_{i+1}, $A_{i+2}, \ldots, A_N$, or what is the same, intermediate product inputs to A_i can arise only from $A_1, A_2, \ldots, A_{i-1}$. Then, for preassignment of (1) resources, (2) preallocation of distributing intermediate products and (3) preallocation of activity outputs to final product, dynamic trajectories may be calculated (evolved) for the intensity functions of the activities and thereby determine the time histories of intermediate and final products. See *Shephard* et al. [1977] for such calculations for shipbuilding.

For the general model of computational dynamics for production networks, let

$$x_{0i} = (x_{0i1}, x_{0i2}, \ldots, x_{0is}) \qquad i = 1, 2, \ldots, N$$

$$y_{0i} = (y_{0i1}, y_{0i2}, \ldots, y_{0i(n-s)}) \qquad i = 1, 2, \ldots, N$$

denote a preallocation of exogenous input histories to the activities, with

$$\sum_{i=1}^{N} x_{0i} \leqq x, \quad \sum_{i=1}^{N} y_{0i} \leqq y .$$

Further, the ordering taken for the network is such that $\bar{A}_i$ takes the form

$$\| \bar{a}_{i1}\ \bar{a}_{i2} \ldots \bar{a}_{i,i-1}, 0 \ldots 0 \| \qquad i = 1, 2, \ldots, N.$$

Let

$$\delta_{j,k}^{N+1}(t), \quad (j = 1, 2, \ldots, N), \ (k = 1, 2, 3, \ldots, m), \ (t = 1, 2, 3, \ldots)$$

denote the fraction of the k-th output rate history of A_j going to net output at the time t. These preassignments satisfy

$$0 \leqq \delta_{j,k}^{N+1}(t) \leqq 1, \quad (t = 1, 2, 3, \ldots), \ (k = 1, 2, \ldots, m), \ (j = 1, 2, \ldots, N)$$

$$\sum_{j=1}^{N} \delta_{j,k}^{N+1}(t) > 0, \quad \text{for some } k \in \{1, 2, \ldots, m\}, \; t \in \{1, 2, 3, \ldots\}$$

and the net output histories $u \in (L_\infty)_+^m$ are given by

$$u_k(t) = \sum_{j=1}^{N} \delta_{j,k}^{N+1}(t)\, Z_j(t-1)\, c_{j,k}(t), \quad (t = 1, 2, 3, \ldots), \; (k = 1, 2, \ldots, m).$$

Let

$$1 \geqq \Delta_{ijk}(t) \geqq 0, \quad (k = 1, 2, \ldots, m), \; (j = 1, 2, \ldots, N-1),$$
$$(i = (j+1), (j+2), \ldots, N)$$

denote a preallocation of the k-th output rate history of A_j at time t to the activities A_i, $(i = (j+1), (j+2), \ldots, N)$ as intermediate product. These coefficients satisfy

$$\sum_{i=j+1}^{N} \Delta_{ijk}(t) = 1 - \delta_{j,k}^{N+1}(t), \qquad (k = 1, 2, \ldots, m), \; (t = 1, 2, 3, \ldots)$$
$$(j = 1, 2, \ldots, (N-1)).$$

Since intermediate product time histories are preallocated, initial inventories and capacities for storing intermediate products are now distinguished by activity as:

$$v_{ik}^0 \qquad (i = 1, 2, \ldots, N), \; (k = 1, 2, \ldots, m)$$

$$\sigma_{ik}(t) \qquad (i = 1, 2, \ldots, N), \; (k = 1, 2, \ldots, m), \; (t = 0, 1, 2, 3, \ldots).$$

Note that

$$v_{ik}^0 \leqq \sigma_{ik}(0).$$

Certain simplifying assumptions may be taken for the coefficients $\bar{a}_{ik}(\tau)$, $c_{jk}(\tau)$:
either $\bar{a}_{ik}(\tau) > 0$ for all $\tau \in [0, \infty)$ or $\bar{a}_{ik}(\tau) = 0$ for all $\tau \in [0, \infty)$, $(i = 1, 2, \ldots, N)$
either $c_{jk}(\tau) > 0$ for all $\tau \in [0, +\infty)$ or $c_{jk}(\tau) = 0$ for all $\tau \in [0, +\infty)$, $(j = 1, 2, \ldots, N)$.

In other words, an activity is consistent in the use of intermediate products and production of outputs. This does not preclude alternative activities with different intermediate product inputs and different output commodities. If an activity cannot satisfy the two assumptions it may be subdivided until it does.

Also, with little if any loss of generality one may assume

$$\sigma_{ik}(t) \geqq \sigma_{ik}(t-1), \quad (t = 1, 2, \ldots), \; (i = 1, 2, \ldots, N), \; (k = 1, 2, \ldots, m).$$

By definition

$$\Delta_{ijk}(\tau) = 0 \quad \text{if } \bar{a}_{ik}(\tau) = 0.$$

One does not transfer intermediate product output to an activity not using it.

Then the previous constraints for the dynamic system take the following form:

$$0 \leqq z_i(t)\, \bar{z}_i(t), \qquad (t = 0, 1, 2, 3, \ldots), \; (i = 1, 2, \ldots, N) \qquad (1)^*$$

$$\sum_{\tau=0}^{t} a_{ik}(\tau)\, z_i(\tau) \leqq \sum_{\tau=0}^{t} x_{0ik}(\tau), \quad (k = 1, 2, \ldots, s), \; (i = 1, 2, \ldots, N), \qquad (2)^*$$
$$(t = 0, 1, 2, \ldots)$$

$$a_{ik}(t)\, z_i(t) \leqq y_{0ik}(t), \qquad (k = (s+1), (s+2), \ldots, n), \quad (i = 1, 2, \ldots, N), \ (t = 0, 1, 2, \ldots) \tag{3*}$$

$$\sum_{\tau=0}^{t} \bar{a}_{ik}(\tau)\, z_i(\tau) \leqq v_{ik}^0 + \sum_{\tau=1}^{t} \sum_{j=1}^{(i-1)} \Delta_{ijk}(\tau)\, c_{j,k}(\tau)\, z_j(\tau-1)\, \bar{a}_{ik}(0)\, z_i(0) \leqq v_{ik}^0, \tag{4*}$$

$$(t = 1, 2, 3, \ldots), \ (i = 2, 3, 4, \ldots, N), \ (k = 1, 2, 3, \ldots, m)$$

$$v_{ik}^0 + \sum_{\tau=1}^{t} \sum_{j=1}^{(i-1)} \Delta_{ijk}(\tau)\, c_{jk}(\tau)\, z_j(\tau-1) - \sum_{\tau=0}^{t} \bar{a}_{ik}(\tau)\, z_i(\tau) \leqq \sigma_{ik}(\tau) \tag{5*}$$

$$(i = 1, 2, \ldots, N), \ (k = 1, 2, \ldots, m), \ (t = 1, 2, 3, \ldots).$$

Notice now that the intensity functions need not be separated into *Iz, Fz* due to the coefficients $\delta_{j,k}^{N+1}(t)$, $(t = 1, 2, \ldots)$.

It is of some interest to consider the dynamic development of the trajectories for final outputs from given preallocations. The inequality system (1)*, (2)*, . . . , (5)* may be used to develop trajectories for the intensity functions $z_i(t)$, $t = 0, 1, 2, \ldots$ which generates the histories of all outputs, both intermediate and final. A policy of applying feasible intensities $z_i(t)$ is needed in order to get a specific trajectory. It is convenient to seek to take this policy as: "utilize the maximal value of $z_i(t)$ possible for each $t = 0, 1, 2, \ldots$," i.e., a Greedy Policy. This policy ignores the problem of "variable loading." However, it will enable one to observe that dynamic systems of production involve Time Substitution as an additional dimension beyond those for static or steady state systems.

The Greedy policy for this system is generated as follows.

Define:

$$S^{(i)}(t) = \{k \in \{1, 2, \ldots, s\} : a_{ik}(t) > 0\}$$

$$\tilde{S}^{(i)}(t) = \{k \in \{s+1, s+2, \ldots, n\} : a_{ik}(t) > 0\}$$

$$\Sigma^{(i)}(t) = \{k \in \{1, 2, \ldots, m\} : \bar{a}_{ik}(t) > 0\}.$$

Define:

$$R^{(i)}(0) = \min_{k \in S^{(i)}(0)} \left\{ \frac{x_{0ik}(0)}{a_{ik}(0)} \right\} \quad \text{if } S^{(i)}(0) \neq \emptyset$$

$$= +\infty \quad \text{if } S^{(i)}(0) = \emptyset$$

$$R^{(i)}(t) = \min_{k \in S^{(i)}(t)} \left\{ \frac{\sum_{\tau=0}^{t} x_{0ik}(\tau) - \sum_{\tau=0}^{t-1} a_{ik}(\tau)\, z_i(\tau)}{a_{ik}(t)} \right\} \quad \text{if } S^{(i)}(t) \neq \emptyset$$

$$= +\infty \quad \text{if } S^{(i)}(t) = \emptyset$$

$$\tilde{R}^{(i)}(t) = \min_{k \in \tilde{S}^{(i)}(t)} \left\{ \frac{y_{0ik}(t)}{a_{ik}(t)} \right\} \quad \text{if } \tilde{S}^{(i)}(t) \neq \emptyset$$

$$= +\infty \quad \text{if } \tilde{S}^{(i)}(t) = \emptyset$$

$$W^{(i)}(t) = \underset{k \in \Sigma^{(i)}(t)}{\text{Min}} \left\{ \frac{v_{ik}^0 + \sum_{\tau=1}^{t} \sum_{j=1}^{(i-1)} \Delta_{ijk}(\tau)\, c_{jk}(\tau)\, z_j(\tau-1) - \sum_{\tau=1}^{t-1} \bar{a}_{ik}(\tau)\, z_i(\tau)}{\bar{a}_{ik}(t)} \right\} \quad \text{if } \Sigma^{(i)}(t) \neq \emptyset$$

$$= +\infty \qquad \text{if } \Sigma^{(i)}(t) = \emptyset .$$

Define:

$$Q_i(t) = \text{Min } \{R^{(i)}(t), \widetilde{R}^{(i)}(t), W^{(i)}(t), \bar{Z}_i(t)\}.$$

Then the Greedy Policy is

$$Z_i(t) = Q_i(t) \qquad (i = 1, 2, \ldots, N), \ (t = 1, 2, 3, \ldots)$$

if constraint (5)* is satisfied. However, (5)* may not be satisfied at some time $t_0 > 0$ for one or more commodities k and activity i. Let k_0 yield the maximal value

$$v_{ik_0}^0 + \sum_{\tau=1}^{t_0} \sum_{j=1}^{(i-1)} \Delta_{ijk_0}(\tau)\, c_{jk_0}(\tau)\, z_j(\tau-1) - \sum_{\tau=0}^{t_0} \bar{a}_{ik_0}(\tau)\, z_i(\tau) - \sigma_{ik_0}(t_0) > 0.$$

Presumably (5)* is satisfied at $(t_0 - 1)$ for i and k_0, which implies

$$\sum_{j=1}^{(i-1)} \Delta_{ijk_0}(t_0)\, c_{jk}(t_0)\, z_j(t_0 - 1) - \bar{a}_{ik_0}(t_0)\, z_i(t_0) > 0.$$

Evidently, (5)* may be satisfied at t_0 if $z_j(\tau) = 0$ for $\tau = (t_0 - 1)$, $(j = 1, 2, \ldots, (i-1))$. As an approximation to a Greedy Policy one may take these values for $z_j(t_0 - 1)$ for $(j = 1, 2, \ldots, (i-1))$. The solutions for $z_j(\tau)$, $(j = 1, 2, \ldots, (i-1)$, $(\tau = t_0, (t_0 + 1), (t_0 + 2), \ldots)$ need to be updated. Then one may proceed t with the calculation for $z_i(t_0)$, $z_i(t_0 + 1)$, etc.

The inventory capacity bounds $\sigma_{ik}(t)$ may require considerable recalculation. However, the routine suggested is a simple one and does provide a ready policy.

The evolutionary character of the trajectory for a greedy type solution is evident. In the order $(i = 1, 2, 3, \ldots, N)$ one calculates $z_i(t)$ for $(t = 0, 1, 2, 3, \ldots)$ corresponding to the given preassignments of activity outputs to other activities and final output. The net output histories for the production network are given by

$$u_k(t) = \sum_{j=1}^{N} \delta_{jk}^{(N+1)}(t)\, c_{jk}(t)\, z_j(t-1) \qquad \begin{pmatrix} k = 1, 2, \ldots, m \\ t = 1, 2, 3, \ldots \end{pmatrix}.$$

Now, insofar as the modified Greedy Policy implies for some activity intensities that periods of zero intensity occur, one may seek to smooth load such production intensities by operating them at less than maximal intensity without altering the output histories obtained over some planning period, i.e., there may be possibilities for Time Substitution.

Time substitution for the activity intensity trajectories, and through them the application of exogenous input and intermediate product histories is an added dimension for dynamic production networks over that of static or steady state models of production. The related problems of smooth loading are the gist of dynamic production planning. See

Leachman [1980] for some mathematical programming methods to smooth load for shipbuilding.

Maximizing throughput as discussed in the previous section and the one to follow, and other optimizations, are not always meaningful, because preassignments of exogenous inputs and intermediate and final outputs may be required for the facilities (activities) of a large production network. Also a compounding of the complexity of an optimization may be involved to assure a reasonable smooth loading. There is some advantage to simulate a dynamic trajectory, in the face of uncertainty of information, for policy formation which can be updated from time to time.

7. A Computational Dynamics for Generalized Production Networks

In Sections 4, 5 and 6 above, the activities of the network were driven by intensity functions $z_i \in (L_\infty)_+$ operating on fixed technical coefficients for system exogenous inputs, intermediate product inputs and activity outputs, independently of the intended distribution of activity outputs.

Now instead of a single intensity function $z_i \in (L_\infty)_+$ for A_i, let

$$z_i := (z_{i1}, z_{i2}, \ldots, z_{iN}, z_{i,N+1}) \in (L_\infty)_+^{N+1}$$

denote an intensity vector with $z_{ij} \in (L_\infty)_+$ denoting the intensity of operating A_i for output to go to A_j, $(j = 1, 2, \ldots, N, N+1)$. The system exogenous input histories implied by z_i are $z_i \mathcal{A}_i$ where

$$\mathcal{A}_i := \text{TRANSPOSE} \parallel \mathcal{A}_{i1}\ \mathcal{A}_{i2} \ldots \mathcal{A}_{iN}, \mathcal{A}_{i(N+1)} \parallel, \qquad (i = 1, 2, \ldots, N)$$

$$\mathcal{A}_{ij} := \parallel a_{ij1}\ a_{ij2} \ldots a_{ijn} \parallel, \qquad (j = 1, 2, \ldots, N, N+1).$$

Similarly, intermediate product inputs are given by $z_i \bar{\mathcal{A}}_i$ where

$$\mathcal{A}_i := \text{TRANSPOSE} \parallel \bar{\mathcal{A}}_{i1}\ \bar{\mathcal{A}}_{i2} \ldots \bar{\mathcal{A}}_{iN}\ \bar{\mathcal{A}}_{i(N+1)} \parallel, \qquad (i = 1, 2, \ldots, N)$$

$$\bar{\mathcal{A}}_{ij} := \parallel \bar{a}_{ij1}\ \bar{a}_{ij2} \ldots \bar{a}_{ijn} \parallel, \qquad (j = 1, 2, \ldots, N, N+1)$$

and activity outputs are given by $z_i \mathcal{C}_i$ $(i = 1, 2, \ldots, N)$ where

$$\mathcal{C}_i := \text{TRANSPOSE} \parallel \mathcal{C}_{i1}\ \mathcal{C}_{i2} \ldots \mathcal{C}_{iN}\ \mathcal{C}_{i(N+1)} \parallel, \qquad (i = 1, 2, \ldots, N)$$

$$\mathcal{C}_{ij} := \parallel C_{ij1}, C_{ij2} \ldots C_{ijn} \parallel, \qquad (j = 1, 2, \ldots, N, N+1).$$

The constraints for the production network are:

$$0 \leqq \sum_{j=1}^{N+1} z_{ij}(t) \leqq \bar{z}_i(t) \in (L_\infty)_+, \qquad \begin{pmatrix} i = 1, 2, \ldots, N \\ t = 0, 1, 2, \ldots \end{pmatrix} \qquad (1)^{**}$$

$$\sum_{i=1}^{N} \sum_{j=1}^{N+1} \sum_{\tau=0}^{t} a_{ijk}(\tau) z_{ij}(\tau) \leqq \sum_{\tau=0}^{t} x_k(\tau), \quad \begin{pmatrix} k = 1, 2, \ldots, s \\ t = 0, 1, 2, \ldots \end{pmatrix} \tag{2**}$$

$$\sum_{i=1}^{N} \sum_{j=1}^{N+1} a_{ijk}(t) z_{ij}(t) \leqq y_k(t), \quad \begin{pmatrix} k = (s+1), \ldots, n \\ t = 0, 1, 2, \ldots \end{pmatrix} \tag{3**}$$

$$\sum_{j=1}^{N+1} \sum_{\tau=0}^{t} \bar{a}_{ijk}(\tau) z_{ij}(\tau) \leqq v_{ik}^{0} + \sum_{j=1}^{N} \sum_{\tau=1}^{t} c_{jik}(\tau) z_{ji}(\tau - 1) \tag{4**}$$

$$\sum_{j=1}^{N+1} \bar{a}_{ijk}(0) z_{ij}(0) \leqq v_{ik}^{0}, \quad (i = 1, 2, 3, \ldots, N),$$
$$(k = 1, 2, \ldots, m), (t = 1, 2, 3, \ldots)$$

$$v_{ik}^{0} + \sum_{j=1}^{N} \sum_{\tau=1}^{t} c_{jik}(\tau) z_{ji}(\tau - 1) - \sum_{j=1}^{N+1} \sum_{\tau=0}^{t} \bar{a}_{ijk}(\tau) z_{ij}(\tau) \leqq \sigma_{ik}(t) \tag{5**}$$
$$(i = 1, 2, 3, \ldots, N), \; (k = 1, 2, \ldots, m), \; (t = 1, 2, 3, \ldots).$$

The "motion" of this system for a production plan needs direction by optimizing some objective. Maximum throughput of a given output mix over a planning period T can be used to direct this production system by the following linear program

Max $\quad Z_{N+1}$

Subject to: $\quad Z_{N+1} \geqq 0$, (1)**, (2)**, (3)**, (4)**, (5)**, (6)** on $[0, T]$

where

$$\bar{a}_{N+1,k}\, z_{N+1} \leqq \sum_{i=1}^{N} \sum_{t=1}^{T} c_{i,N+1,k}(\tau) z_{i,N+1}(\tau - 1), \quad (k = 1, 2, \ldots, P). \tag{6**}$$

The conventions of Section 5 are used in this formulation.

The minimal time horizon for a production plan to yield given accumulations

$$w_k, \quad (k = 1, 2, \ldots, P)$$

of the final products can be found by replacing (6)** by

$$w_k \leqq \sum_{i=1}^{N} \sum_{\tau=1}^{T} c_{i,N+1,k}(\tau) z_{i,N+1}(\tau - 1) \quad (k = 1, 2, \ldots, P) \tag{7}$$

and consecutively seeking a feasible solution to (1)**, (2)**, (3)**, (4)**, (5)**, (7) for increasing $T = 1, 2, 3, \ldots$ until feasibility is first attained. See *Leachman* [1980] for this computation for production networks with activities each of which produce a single output.

Other optimizations are possible to drive the "motion" of the production system; and additional constraints may be significant. For example, large changes of service inputs may involve learning and shift the system retrogressively to higher amounts required per unit intensity.

References

Leachman, R.C.: Production Planning for Multi-Resource Network Systems. ORC 80–18, Operations Research Center, University of California, Berkeley 1980.
Also appeared in Naval Research Logistics Quarterly **29** (1), 1982.

Shephard, R.W.: Dynamic Theory of Production Networks. Operations Research Center, University of California, Berkeley 1981 forthcoming.

Shephard, R.W., and *R. Färe*: Dynamic Theory of Production Correspondences. Mathematical Systems in Economics **50**, Meisenheim 1980.

Shephard, R.W., et al.: Shipbuilding Production Functions. Quantitative Wirtschaftsforschung, Wilhelm Krelle zum 60. Geburtstag. Ed. by H. Albach, E. Helmstädter und R. Henn. Tübingen 1977.

Part III
Measurement and Aggregation

Quantitative Studies on Production and Prices © Physica-Verlag, Würzburg–Wien, 1983.

Linear Programming Tests of Regularity Conditions for Production Functions[1])

W. Erwin Diewert and *Celik Parkan*

1. Introduction

The main purpose of this paper is to extend the nonparametric tests of regularity conditions on production functions and the related tests for the consistency of a data set with the hypothesis of productive efficiency or with the hypotheses of cost minimizing or profit maximizing behavior suggested by *Afriat* [1972] and *Hanoch/Rothschild* [1972]. The tests suggested by these authors can be regarded as extensions of some tests due to *Farrell* [1957] and *Farrell/Fieldhouse* [1962]. Typically these tests involve the solution of a number of linear programming problems where the objective functions and the constraint functions are known functions of the given data; hence the title of the present paper.

We consider three different sets of regularity conditions on the technology: the first set of conditions assumes that the underlying production function f is quasiconcave and nondecreasing, the second set of conditions assumes that f is concave and nondecreasing, and the third set of regularity conditions assumes that f is concave, nondecreasing and linearly homogeneous (so that production is subject to constant returns to scale).

The tests that we suggest are nonparametric in the sense that we do not assume that the underlying production function belongs to a certain class of functions of a specific functional form which depends on a finite number of parameters, such as the well known Cobb-Douglas functional form.

We see two main uses for the tests we suggest: (i) they can be used to construct efficient frontiers and measure the efficiency of individual firms, or the same firm over different time periods, (see the original contributions of *Farrell* [1957] and *Farrell/Fieldhouse* [1962]) and (ii) they may be used to "screen" data before the data are used in order to estimate the parameters of a specific parametric functional form for the production function. With the growth of "flexible" functional forms [see the literature surveyed by *Diewert*, 1978], this second use is an important one, since econometrically estimated "flexible" production, cost or profit functions frequently fail to satisfy the appropriate regularity conditions. Hence it becomes important to know whether the failure is due to an inappropriate functional form or whether the given data are simply inconsistent with any functional form satisfying the appropriate regularity conditions.

---

[1]) The authors are indebted to C. Blackorby for helpful comments and to the Social Sciences and Humanities Research Council of Canada for financial support.

It should be noted that our proposed tests are not statistical tests with type 1 and type 2 errors. It seems clear that if one of our tests "fails" and the associated measures of violation are all extremely small, then the test has not failed in a statistically significant sense. However, to go beyond this rather obvious observation is a difficult problem. For some suggestions on how to approach this problem, the reader is referred to the very astute observations of *Hanoch/Rothschild* [1972; 263–264] and the literature which is nicely summarized and extended by *Aigner/Lovell/Schmidt* [1977].

In section 2 below, we present tests for the consistency of a given set of data on inputs and a single output with a production function *f* satisfying each of our three sets of regularity conditions. Test 3a, which tests for the existence of a concave, linearly homogeneous, nondecreasing production function which is consistent with a given body of data on the production of a single output with multiple inputs, is due to *Afriat* [1972] but it is a straightforward modification of the pioneering work of *Farrell* [1957]. Test 3a involves solving a certain linear program. Test 3b, due to *Hanoch/Rothschild* [1972], is the same test except that we solve the dual to the original linear program. Similarly, Test 2a [due to *Afriat*, 1972] which tests for the existence of a concave, nondecreasing production function involves solving another linear program while Test 2b [due to *Hanoch/Rothschild*] involves solving the dual linear program. Our contribution in this section is to present the Farrell-Afriat-Hanoch-Rothschild results in a unified manner, providing "economic" interpretations for the primal and dual problems.

In section 3, we generalize the tests presented in section 2 to the multiple output, multiple input case. Our tests 4a, 4b, 5a and 6a do not appear explicitly in the literature but the dual tests to 5a and 6a, tests 5b and 6b, are due to *Hanoch/Rothschild* [1972].

In section 4, we consider tests for the existence of a production function satisfying various regularity conditions which is consistent with a given body of data on prices rather than quantities (although our tests for quasiconcavity assume that quantity data for at least one input or output are available). Our tests 7b and 8b are generalizations of tests due to *Hanoch/Rothschild* [1972]. The dual tests, 7a and 8a, do not appear in the literature but Test 8a is a straightforward generalization to the multiple output case of a test due to *Afriat* [1972] (a similar remark applies to our Test 9a). As in the previous sections, we attempt to present unified "economic" interpretations for both the primal of "a" tests (which are mainly due to Afriat) as well as the dual or "b" tests (which are mainly due to Hanoch and Rothschild).

In section 5, we assume that we have both price and quantity data. The tests presented here are the production theory counterparts to the revealed preference theory relations which occur in consumer theory. Our Tests 10, 11 and 12 generalize tests due to *Hanoch/Rothschild* [1972] (we have much weaker maintained regularity conditions). Test 11 also generalizes (to the multiple output case) a test due to *Afriat* [1972]. The tests presented in this section do not involve the solution of a linear program, and hence there are no "a" and "b" tests.

In section 6, we indicate how all of the above tests can be extended to make allowance for the possibility of technological progress. These new tests should prove to be very useful in the context of examining time series data for its consistency with the economic theory of production.

Section 7 notes some further possible applications of the various tests; in particular, we suggest how some of the tests could be modified in order to interpolate data.

The tests presented in section 2 and 3 can be interpreted as tests of the *efficiency hypothesis*; i.e., given data on inputs and outputs, do the given data lie on the *frontier* of a set of technologically feasible inputs and outputs S say, where S satisfied various regularity conditions? If the test passes, then we say that the data are consistent with the efficiency hypothesis under consideration (there are different efficiency hypotheses for different assumptions about S), while if the test fails, then we construct an index of its failure or a violation index. Our measures of violation are based on a measure of inefficiency due originally to *Debreu* [1951] and later utilized by *Farrell* [1957]: the reader is referred to the recent papers by *Färe/Lovell* [1978] and *Färe/Lovell/Zieschang* [1982] for an excellent discussion of the problems associated with measures of inefficiency.

The tests presented in sections 4 and 5 can also be interpreted as tests of the efficiency hypothesis, but in addition, they are also tests of the hypothesis of *cost minimizing* or *profit maximizing* behavior. It turns out that this is why the tests presented in sections 4 and 5 below require much weaker maintained regularity conditions than the tests presented in sections 2 and 3.

This brief overview should help to explain why a given body of data can "pass" one test but yet "fail" another test. This is because: (i) different tests maintain different assumptions about the technology set S and (ii) some tests assume cost minimizing or profit maximizing behavior while other tests do not.

2. Quantity Data: The Single Output Case

Let $x \equiv (x_1, x_2, \ldots, x_N) \geqslant 0_N$ denote a nonnegative N dimensional vector of inputs and let $y \equiv f(x) \geqslant 0$ denote the maximum amount of output that a firm (or industry) can produce given the vector of inputs x. Suppose that we are given J observations on inputs and output, $\{x_1^j, x_2^j, \ldots, x_N^j; y^j\}, j = 1, 2, \ldots, J$. In this section, we ask the following question: are the observed data consistent with a production function f (satisfying various regularity conditions)? In other words, we ask if the observed data are consistent with the *efficiency hypothesis*; i.e., does there exist a production function f such that y^j is the maximal amount of output which is producible from the vector of inputs x^j for $j = 1, 2, \ldots, J$?

The first set of regularity conditions that we place on f are the following *Conditions I:* f is a nonnegative real valued function of N variables defined over the nonnegative orthant $\Omega \equiv \{x : x \geqslant 0_N\}$ and is: (i) continuous from above, (ii) nondecreasing and (iii) quasiconcave. Part (i) simply means that the level set $L(y) \equiv \{x : f(x) \geqslant y\}$ is a closed set for each $y \geqslant 0$, (ii) means that greater amounts of inputs do not lead to decreased outputs, and (iii) means that each level set $L(y)$ is a convex set.[2])

---

[2]) A set S is convex iff for every $x' \in S$, $x'' \in S$ and scalar λ such that $0 \leqslant \lambda \leqslant 1$, we have $\lambda x' + (1 - \lambda) x'' \in S$.

For our first test in this section, we assume that the observed outputs are all distinct[3]) so that we can reorder the observations in the following way:

$$0 \leqslant y^1 < y^2 < \ldots < y^J. \tag{1}$$

Now consider the following linear programming problem in the variables $\mu^i, \lambda^{i+1}, \lambda^{i+2}, \ldots, \lambda^J$:

$$\min_{\mu^i \geqslant 0, \lambda^{i+1} \geqslant 0, \ldots, \lambda^J \geqslant 0} \{\mu^i : \sum_{j=i+1}^{J} \lambda^j x^j \leqslant \mu^i x^i, \sum_{j=i+1}^{J} \lambda^j = 1\} \tag{2}$$

Note that if $x^i \gg 0_N$ (each component of x^i is positive), then a feasible solution to (2) exists.[4]) Moreover, since each $x^j \geqslant 0_N$, it can be seen that the objective function for (2) is bounded from below by 0. Thus a finite optimal solution to (2) will exist and we denote the optimal value of the objective function for (2) as μ^{i*}. Note that (2) depends on i; in fact, (2) can be solved for $i = 1, 2, \ldots, J-1$. We can now state our first test.

Test 1a:[5]) If $\mu^{i*} > 1$ for $i = 1, 2, \ldots, J-1$ where μ^{i*} is the optimal μ^i for (2), then the data $\{(x^j, y^j) : j = 1, 2, \ldots, J\}$ are consistent with the efficiency hypothesis for some production function f satisfying Conditions I. On the other hand, if any $\mu^{i*} \leqslant 1$, then the given data are not consistent for any production function satisfying Conditions I.

A geometric interpretation of Test 1a can be obtained as follows. If the efficiency hypothesis is true for some f satisfying Conditions I, then we have $f(x^i) = y^i < y^{i+1} < y^{i+2} < \ldots < y^J$ by assumption (1). Since f is quasiconcave, for all $\lambda^{i+1} \geqslant 0, \ldots, \lambda^J \geqslant 0$ such that $\sum_{j=i+1}^{J} \lambda^j = 1$, we have $y^i < f(\sum_{j=i+1}^{J} \lambda^j x^j) \leqslant f(x^i) = y^i$ if $\sum_{j=i+1}^{J} \lambda^j x^j \leqslant x^i$ (using the nondecreasing property of f), and we have obtained a contradiction. Thus if $\sum_{j=i+1}^{J} \lambda^j x^j \leqslant \mu^i x^i$, we must have $\mu^i > 1$ in order to eliminate this contradiction. Thus if $\mu^{i*} \leqslant 1$ for any i, then the efficiency hypothesis fails for the given data.

On the other hand if $\mu^{i*} > 1$ for all $i = 1, 2, \ldots, J-1$, then it can be shown [cf. *Hanoch/Rothschild*, p. 260] that f^* defined below is consistent with the efficiency hypothesis for the given data:

$$f^*(x) \equiv \max_k \{y^k : k = 0, 1, \ldots, J \text{ and } k \text{ is such that } x \geqslant \sum_{j=k}^{J} \lambda^j x^j,$$
$$\lambda^k \geqslant 0, \lambda^{k+1} \geqslant 0, \ldots, \lambda^J \geqslant 0, \sum_{j=k}^{J} \lambda^j = 1\} \tag{3}$$

where $(y^0, x^0) \equiv (0, 0_N)$.

---

[3]) This assumption is not necessary [cf. *Hanoch/Rothschild*, Theorem 2] but it simplifies the algebra considerably. Moreover, it is not restrictive from an empirical point of view.

[4]) If some components of x^i are zero, then we transform all of the input vectors x^j into $\tilde{x}^j \equiv x^j + \epsilon 1_N, j = 1, \ldots, J$ where $\epsilon > 0$ and 1_N is a vector of ones. The original x^j in (2) are then replaced by the $\tilde{x}^j$ and then a feasible solution to (2) will exist.

[5]) This test is due to *Hanoch/Rothschild* [1972, 259–261]. Our LP problem (2) is essentially the dual to their LP problem (8).

The dual[6]) to the linear programming problem (2) is the following linear programming problem in the unrestricted scalar variable α^i and the vector of nonnegative variables w^i.

$$\max_{\alpha^i, w^i \geqslant 0_N} \{\alpha^i : w^{iT} x^i \leqslant 1, \alpha^i \leqslant w^{iT} x^j, j = i+1, \ldots, J\} \equiv \alpha^{i*} \tag{4}$$

where

$$w^{iT} x^i \equiv \sum_{n=1}^{N} w_n^i x_n^i .$$

Since the primal problem (2) has a finite optimal solution, so will the dual problem (4), and, we will have $\mu^{i*} = \alpha^{i*}$. Thus *Test 1b*[7]) is simply Test 1a, except that μ^{i*} is replaced by α^{i*} for $i = 1, 2, \ldots, J-1$; i.e., we solve the dual problems (4) in place of the primal problems (2).

Geometrically, Test 1b can be interpreted as follows. If the data are consistent with the efficiency hypothesis for some f satisfying Conditions I, then for $i = 1, 2, \ldots, J-1$, x^i is on the boundary of the closed convex set $L(y^i) \equiv \{x : f(x) \geqslant y^i\}$ and a hyperlane supporting $L(y^i)$ through the point x^i will exist; i.e., for each i, there exists $w^i \neq 0_N$ such that $x \in L(y^i)$ implies $w^{iT} x \geqslant w^{iT} x^i$. We can normalize w^i so that $w^{iT} x^i = 1$ and the nondecreasing property of f implies that $w^i \geqslant 0_N$. If production is efficient, then if $y^j > y^i$, x^j must be in the interior of $L(y^i)$ and thus $1 = w^{iT} x^i < w^{iT} x^j$ for $j = i+1$, $i+2, \ldots, J$, and $\alpha^{i*} > 1$. Thus if $\alpha^{i*} < 1$ for any i, then the efficiency hypothesis is not consistent with the given data for any f satisfying Conditions I.

Suppose $0 < \mu^{i*} = \alpha^{i*} < 1$ for some i, so that the efficiency hypothesis fails for observation i. Inspection of the programming problem (2) shows that if we replaced the input vector x^i by the "shrunken" input vector $(\mu^{i*} - \epsilon) x^i$ for any ϵ such that $0 < \epsilon < \mu^{i*}$, then the optimal solution of the resulting programming problem would be greater than one; i.e., the efficiency hypothesis would no longer fail for observation i. Thus if $\mu^{i*} < 1$ for the i-th linear program (2), then $\delta^i \equiv 1 - \mu^{i*}$ is the proportional reduction in each component of the i-th input vector x^i required in order to make the i-th programming problem in (2) virtually consistent with the efficiency hypothesis; i.e., if $\mu^{i*} < 1$, then $\delta^i \equiv 1 - \mu^{i*} > 0$ is a natural measure of violation of the efficiency hypothesis for x^i, the i-th input vector.[8])

A final observation on Test 1a and Test 1b: the tests do not require complete knowledge about the magnitude of the output y^j in each period: all we require is an ordinal ordering of the outputs so that the observations can be reordered in accordance with (1). The actual y^j do not appear in either (2) or (4).

---

[6]) See *Dantzig* [1963, p. 126] for a description of the formal rules for forming the dual to a linear programming problem.

[7]) This test is due to *Hanoch/Rothschild* [1972, p. 262] except that they use the normalization $w^{iT} x^i = 1$ in place of $w^{iT} x^i \leqslant 1$. This difference does not matter since if w^{i*} is a solution to (4), we will have $w^{i*T} x^i = 1$.

[8]) Alternatively, if $\mu^{i*} < 1$, then μ^{i*} can be interpreted as *Debreu's* [1951, p. 285] *coefficient of resource utilization* and $\delta^i \equiv 1 - \mu^{i*}$ is *Debreu's* [1951, p. 286] measure of economic loss due to the inefficient utilization of resources. See *Färe/Lovell* [1977] for a discussion of various measures of loss and their merits.

The second set of regularity conditions that we place on f are *Conditions II: f* is: (i) continuous, (ii) nondecreasing and (iii) concave.[9]) If f is defined over a convex set S, then concavity of f is equivalent to convexity of the production possibilities set $G \equiv \{(x, y) : y \leqslant f(x), x \in S\}$; [cf. *Rockafellar*, p. 23].

Given a set of J observations on inputs and outputs $\{(x^j, y^j) : j = 1, 2, \ldots, J\}$, define the free disposal convex hull of the set of inputs as the set $S(x^1, \ldots, x^J) \equiv \{x : x \geqslant \sum_{j=1}^{J} \lambda^j x^j, \lambda^1 \geqslant 0, \ldots, \lambda^J \geqslant 0, \sum_{j=1}^{J} \lambda^j = 1\}$ and for any $x \in S(x^1, \ldots, x^J)$, define $\check{f}(x)$ as the solution to the following linear programming problem:[10])

$$\check{f}(x) \equiv \max_{\lambda^1 \geqslant 0, \ldots, \lambda^J \geqslant 0} \{\sum_{j=1}^{J} \lambda^j y^j : \sum_{j=1}^{J} \lambda^j x^j \leqslant x, \sum_{j=1}^{J} \lambda^j = 1\}. \tag{5}$$

Note that in order to calculate $\check{f}(x^i)$ for $i = 1, 2, \ldots, J$, we have to solve J linear programming problems of the form (5). We assume that $x^j > 0_N$ (i.e., $x^j \geqslant 0_N$ but $x^j \neq 0_N$) for each j. In this case, it is easy to verify that $y^i \leqslant \check{f}(x^i) < +\infty$ for each i.

Test 2a:[11]) If $y^i = \check{f}(x^i)$ for $i = 1, 2, \ldots, J$, then the data $\{(x^j, y^j) : j = 1, \ldots, J\}$ are consistent with the efficiency hypothesis for some production function f satisfying Conditions II where f is defined over $S(x^1, \ldots, x^J)$, the free disposal convex hull of the x^j. On the other hand, if $y^i < \check{f}(x^i)$ for any i, then the given data are not consistent for any f satisfying Conditions II over $S(x^1, \ldots, x^J)$.

It is easy to verify that $\check{f}$ defined by (5) is continuous, nondecreasing and concave over $S(x^1, \ldots, x^J)$. Thus if $y^i = \check{f}(x^i)$ for all i, then the given data are consistent with the efficiency hypothesis for the production function $\check{f}$. On the other hand, suppose $y^i < \check{f}(x^i)$ for some i. Then there exist $\lambda^{1*} \geqslant 0, \ldots, \lambda^{J*} \geqslant 0$ such that $\sum_{j=1}^{J} \lambda^{j*} = 1$, $\sum_{j=1}^{J} \lambda^{j*} x^j \leqslant x^i$ and $y^i < \sum_{j=1}^{J} \lambda^{j*} y^j$. If the efficiency hypothesis were true for some f satisfying Conditions II, then we must have $y^j = f(x^j)$ for all j. Thus $f(x^i) \equiv y^i < \sum_{j=1}^{J} \lambda^{j*} y^j \equiv \sum_{j=1}^{J} \lambda^{j*} f(x^j) \leqslant f(\sum_{j=1}^{J} \lambda^{j*} x^j)$ (since f is concave) $\leqslant f(x^i)$ (since $\sum \lambda^{j*} x^j \leqslant x^i$ and f is nondecreasing), which is a contradiction and thus the efficiency hypothesis cannot be true.

---

[9]) A function f defined over a convex set S is concave iff for every $x' \in S$, $x'' \in S$, $0 \leqslant \lambda \leqslant 1$, we have $f(\lambda x' + (1 - \lambda) x'') \geqslant \lambda f(x') + (1 - \lambda) f(x'')$.

[10]) The function $\check{f}$ was defined by *Afriat* [1972, p. 571] although Afriat did not observe that $\check{f}(x)$ is undefined if x does not belong to the free disposal convex hull of $\{x^1, \ldots, x^J\}$. Afriat's definition can be viewed as a generalization of a construction due to *Farrell* [1957, p. 258].

[11]) This test is due to *Afriat* [1972, p. 571]. If we add the following condition to Conditions II: (iv) $f(0_N) = 0$, then Test 2a can be changed to deal with the modified Conditions II in the following manner: simply add the point $(x^0, y^0) \equiv (0_N, 0)$ to the data points, add an additional variable $\lambda^0 \geqslant 0$ to (5), and let $j = 0, 1, \ldots, J$ in (5). In this case, $S(x^0, x^1, \ldots, x^J) = \Omega$, the nonnegative orthant.

Geometrically, Test 2a forms the free disposal convex hull in $N+1$ space of the data points (x^j, y^j) and then checks whether each point (x^i, y^i) is on or below the frontier of this set. If $y^i < \check{f}(x^i)$, then (x^i, y^i) is below the frontier and if $y^i > 0$, then $\Delta^i \equiv (\check{f}(x^i) - y^i)/y^i > 0$ is the proportion by which y^i must be increased in order to put (x^i, y^i) on the "efficient" frontier. Thus if $0 < y^i < \check{f}(x^i)$, then Δ^i is a natural measure of violation of the efficiency hypothesis for the i-th observed data point (x^i, y^i).

The dual to the linear programming problem (5) when $x = x^i$ is the following linear programming problem:

$$\check{f}(x^i) \equiv \min_{w^i \geqslant 0_N, \alpha^i} \{w^{iT}x^i + \alpha^i : w^{iT}x^j + \alpha^i \geqslant y^j, j = 1, 2, \ldots, J\}. \tag{6}$$

The dual linear programming problems (6) for $i = 1, 2, \ldots, J$ can be used to calculate $\check{f}(x^i)$ in place of the corresponding primal problems (5). Thus *Test 2b*[12]) is simply Test 2a except that the dual problems (6) are used to calculate the $\check{f}(x^i)$ in place of the corresponding primal problems (5).

In order to geometrically interpret Test 2b, suppose that the efficiency hypothesis were true for some f satisfying Conditions II. Then the hypograph of f, $G(f) \equiv \{(x, y): y \leqslant f(x), x \in S(x^1, \ldots, x^J)\}$ is a closed convex set and (x^i, y^i) belongs to the frontier of this set for each i. Thus there exists a supporting hyperplane to $G(f)$ through (x^i, y^i); i.e., there exists (w^{i*}, α^{i*}) such that $(x, y) \in G(f)$ implies $y - w^{i*T}x \leqslant \alpha^{i*} = y^i - w^{i*T}x^i$. Since $(x^j, y^j) \in G(f)$, $y^j - w^{i*T}x^j \leqslant \alpha^{i*}$ for $j = 1, 2, \ldots, J$. Since f is nonincreasing, $w^{i*} \geqslant 0_N$. Thus $y^i = \check{f}(x^i)$ where $\check{f}(x^i)$ is defined by (6). On the other hand, suppose that for $i = 1, 2, \ldots, J$, $y^i = \min_{w^i \geqslant 0_N, \alpha^i} \{w^{iT}x^i + \alpha^i : w^{iT}x^j + \alpha^i \geqslant y^j, j = 1, \ldots, J\} =$ $w^{i*T}x^i + \alpha^{i*}$ where $w^{i*} \geqslant 0_N$ and α^{i*} solve the linear programming problem. Then define the function $\hat{f}(x)$ as the minimum of the J linear functions $w^{i*T}x + \alpha^{i*}$; i.e., for $x \geqslant 0_N$,

$$\hat{f}(x) \equiv \min \{w^{j*T}x + \alpha^{j*} : j = 1, 2, \ldots, J\}. \tag{7}$$

It is easy to verify that $\hat{f}$ defined by (7) is continuous, nondecreasing and concave over Ω. Moreover, since

$$w^{i*T}x^j + \alpha^{i*} \geqslant y^j \quad \text{and} \quad w^{i*T}x^i + \alpha^{i*} = y^i; \qquad i, j = 1, 2, \ldots, J, \tag{8}$$

it can be seen that $\hat{f}(x^i) = y^i$ for $i = 1, 2, \ldots, J$ and thus $\hat{f}$ satisfies the efficiency hypothesis for the given data.

In summary: if Test 2a passes, then the given data $\{(x^j, y^j) : j = 1, 2, \ldots, J\}$ are consistent with the efficiency hypothesis for at least one f satisfying Conditions II and $\check{f}$ defined by (5) is one such f; if Test 2b passes, then the given data are consistent for at least

---

[12]) This test is essentially a specialization of a more general test due to *Hanoch/Rothschild* [1972, p. 268] (their normalizations are slightly different).

one f and $\hat{f}$ defined by (7) is one such f. Moreover, it can be shown that [cf. *Afriat*, 1972, p. 596] for every $x \in S(x^1, \ldots, x^J)$, $\check{f}(x) \leqslant \hat{f}(x)$ with $\check{f}(x^j) = \hat{f}(x^j)$ for $j = 1, 2, \ldots, J$. Thus $\check{f}$ and $\hat{f}$ can be interpreted as inner and outer approximations to a true f which is consistent with the data.[13])

The third set of regularity conditions that we place on f are *Conditions III:* f is defined over Ω and is: (i) continuous, (ii) nondecreasing, (iii) concave and (iv) (positively) linearly homogeneous; i.e., for every $x \in \Omega$, $\lambda \geqslant 0$, $f(\lambda x) = \lambda f(x)$.

Given a set of J observations on inputs and outputs $\{(x^j, y^j) : x^i > 0_N, j = 1, 2, \ldots, J\}$. Define $f^*(x)$ for $x \geqslant 0_N$ as the solution to the following linear programming problem:

$$f^*(x) \equiv \max_{\lambda^1 \geqslant 0, \ldots, \lambda^J \geqslant 0} \{\sum_{j=1}^{J} \lambda^j y^j : \sum_{j=1}^{J} \lambda^j x^j \leqslant x\}. \tag{9}$$

Test 3a:[14]) if $y^i = f^*(x^i)$ for $i = 1, \ldots, J$, then the given data $\{(x^j, y^j) : j = 1, \ldots, J\}$ are consistent with the efficiency hypothesis for some production function f satisfying Conditions III. If $y^i < f^*(x^i)$ for any i, then the data are not consistent for any f satisfying Conditions III.

It is easy to verify that f^* defined by (9) satisfies Conditions III. Thus if $y^i = f^*(x^i)$ for all i, then the data are consistent with the efficiency hypothesis for the production function f^*. On the other hand, suppose $0 \leqslant y^i < f^*(x^i)$ for some i. Then by definition (9), we have $\lambda^{1*} \geqslant 0, \ldots, \lambda^{J*} \geqslant 0$ such that $\sum_{j=1}^{J} \lambda^{j*} x^j \leqslant x^i$ and $y^i < \sum_{j=1}^{J} \lambda^{j*} y^j$ where at least one $\lambda^{j*} > 0$. If the efficiency hypothesis were true for some f satisfying Conditions III, then $y^j = f(x^j)$ for all j. Define $\mu \equiv \sum_{j=1}^{J} \lambda^{j*} > 0$. Then by linear homogeneity of f, $\mu^{-1} f(x^i) = f(\mu^{-1} x^i) = \mu^{-1} y^i < \mu^{-1} \sum_{j=1}^{J} \lambda^{j*} y^j \equiv \sum_{j=1}^{J} \mu^{-1} \lambda^{j*} f(x^j) =$ $\sum_{j=1}^{J} f(\mu^{-1} \lambda^{j*} x^j)$ (by linear homogeneity) $\leqslant f(\sum_{j=1}^{J} \mu^{-1} \lambda^{j*} x^j)$ (by concavity of f) $= \mu^{-1} f(\sum_{j=1}^{J} \lambda^{j*} x^j)$ (by linear homogeneity) $\leqslant \mu^{-1} f(x^i)$ (since $\sum_j \lambda^{j*} x^j \leqslant x^i$ and f is nondecreasing), which is a contradiction. Thus if $y^i < f^*(x^i)$ for some i, then the efficiency hypothesis cannot be true for any f satisfying Conditions III.

The dual to the linear programming problem (9) when $x = x^i$ is

$$f^*(x^i) \equiv \min_{w^i \geqslant 0_N} \{w^{iT} x^i : w^{iT} x^j \geqslant y^j, j = 1, 2, \ldots, J\} \tag{10}$$

---

[13]) However different w^{i*}, α^{i*} solutions to (6) will generate different outer approximations and in general, there will not exist a greatest outer approximation. On the other hand, the inner approximation is unique.

[14]) This test is due to *Afriat* [1972, p. 573] and (in a somewhat different form) to *Farrell* [1957, p. 258] and *Farrell/Fieldhouse* [1962, p. 264].

Test 3b[15]) is simply Test 3a, except that the dual programs (10) are used to calculate $f^*(x^i)$ for $i = 1, 2, \ldots, J$ in place of the corresponding primal problems (9) with x replaced by x^i.

If $w^{i*} \geqslant 0_N$ is a solution to (10) for $i = 1, \ldots, J$, then define

$$\hat{f}^*(x) \equiv \min \{w^{j*T}x : j = 1, 2, \ldots, J\}. \tag{11}$$

Again, it is easy to verify that $\hat{f}^*$ defined by (11) satisfies Conditions III. Moreover if Test 3b passes (i.e., if $f^*(x^i) = y^i$ for $i = 1, \ldots, J$ where $f^*(x^i)$ is defined by (10)), then $y^i = \hat{f}^*(x^i)$ and the given data are consistent with the efficiency hypothesis for $\hat{f}^*$ defined by (11).

The geometric interpretations of the above tests are similar to the interpretations of Tests 2a and 2b: the main difference is that if f satisfied Conditions III, the hypograph of f, $G(f) \equiv \{(x, y) : y \leqslant f(x), x \geqslant 0_N\}$, is a closed convex cone, and thus the supporting hyperplanes to $G(f)$ through (x^i, y^i) now pass through the origin (i.e., $\alpha^{i*} = 0$ now). As before, f^* can be interpreted as the inner approximation to the "true" f and $\hat{f}^*$ can be interpreted as an outer approximation.

As was the case with Test 2, if $0 < y^i < f^*(x^i)$, then (x^i, y^i) is below the efficiency frontier generated by the given data, and again $\Delta^{*i} \equiv (f^*(x^i) - y^i)/y^i > 0$ is the natural measure of the violation of the efficiency hypothesis for the i-th data point (x^i, y^i). Note that this measure is invariant to scale changes in the units of measurement for the input and output.

3. Quantity Data: The Multiple Output Case

Let $x \equiv (x_1, \ldots, x_N) \geqslant 0_N$ denote a nonnegative vector of inputs and $y \equiv (y_1, \ldots, y_M) \geqslant 0_M$ denote a nonnegative vector of outputs. A firm's production function can again be denoted by f and $y_1 \equiv f(-\hat{y}, x)$ denotes the maximal amount of the first output that the firm can produce given that it can utilize the vector of inputs $x \geqslant 0_N$ and that it must produce the vector of "other" outputs $\hat{y} \equiv (y_2, y_3, \ldots, y_M) \geqslant 0_{M\text{-}1}$. As in the previous section, it is natural to assume that f is nondecreasing in its arguments; i.e., if $x' \geqslant x'' \geqslant 0_N$ and $0_{M\text{-}1} \geqslant -\hat{y}' \geqslant -\hat{y}''$, then $f(-\hat{y}', x') \geqslant f(-\hat{y}'', x'')$ since greater amounts of inputs $(x' \geqslant x'')$ and lesser amounts of other outputs $(\hat{y}' \leqslant \hat{y}'')$ will not lead to a decrease in the production of y_1.[16]) We can also assume that f is continuous, concave or linearly homogeneous, as in the previous section. However, in the present section, we cannot assume that $f(-\hat{y}, x)$ will be well defined for all $\hat{y} \geqslant 0_{M\text{-}1}$ and $x \geqslant 0_N$. If the components of $\hat{y}$ are large relative to the components of the input vector x, then it may not be technologically feasible to produce the vector of other outputs $\hat{y}$. In this case, we could assume that $f(-\hat{y}, x) \equiv -\infty$ or we could simply restrict the domain of definition of f to exclude such infeasible $(-\hat{y}, x)$ points. We shall take the latter alternative.

---

[15]) This test is essentially a specialization of a *Hanoch/Rothschild* [1972, p. 270] test.

[16]) If the firm could utilize the vector of other outputs $\hat{y}$ as a vector of inputs, then in this case, $\hat{y} \leqslant 0_{M\text{-}1}$, and the nonnegativity constraints on $\hat{y}$ $(\hat{y} \geqslant 0_{M\text{-}1})$ could be dropped.

We are used to thinking of a production function as a mapping which gives the maximum amount of output which is producible, given that a vector of other outputs must be produced and given that a vector of inputs is available to the firm. However, the firm's technology can also be described by means of a *factor requirements function g* [cf. *Diewert*, 1974], which gives the minimal amount of an input, ($x_1 \geqslant 0$ say, which is required to produce a vector of outputs $y \geqslant 0_M$ given a vector of other inputs $\hat{x} \equiv (x_2, \ldots, x_N) \geqslant 0_{N-1}$ that is available to the firm; i.e., $x_1 = g(y, -\hat{x})$. It is natural to assume that g is nondecreasing in its arguments; i.e., $g(y, -\hat{x})$ will generally increase as the components of y increase (more input is required to produce more output) and $g(y, -\hat{x})$ will generally decrease as the components of $\hat{x}$ increase (less of input 1 is required as the other inputs increase).

It is convenient to be able to use the same tests in order to test for the existence of either a valid production function or a factor requirements function which is consistent with a given data set. This can be done if we transform a given factor requirements function g into a production function as follows: if $x_1 = g(y, -\hat{x})$, then define $f(-y, \hat{x}) \equiv -g(y, -\hat{x}) = -x_1$. The resulting f will be nondecreasing in its arguments, and the output $f(-y, \hat{x})$ is now the negative of the minimal amount of input 1 required to produce $y \geqslant 0_M$ given $\hat{x} \geqslant 0_{N-1}$.

The above two cases can be combined using a uniform scheme of notation in the following manner: for the original production function model, define $z_0 \equiv y_1$, $z \equiv (z_1, z_2, \ldots, z_K) \equiv (-\hat{y}, x)$, $K \equiv M - 1 + N$ and $z_0 = f(z)$; for the factor requirements model, define $z_0 \equiv -x_1$, $z \equiv (z_1, z_2, \ldots, z_K) \equiv (-y, \hat{x})$, $K \equiv M + N - 1$ and $z_0 = f(z)$. Thus $z_0 > 0$ (< 0) corresponds to the first good being produced (used as an input), while $z_k > 0$ (< 0) for $k = 1, \ldots, K$ corresponds to the corresponding good being used as an input (produced as an output). We shall adhere to this more general notational scheme for the remainder of this section. We shall call z_0 net output and $z \equiv (z_1, \ldots, z_K)$ a vector of net inputs.

The first set of regularity conditions that we place on f are *Conditions I'*: f is a real valued function of K variables which is defined over a nonempty, closed convex set S[17]) and is: (i) continuous from above, (ii) nondecreasing and (iii) quasiconcave.

Suppose that J observations on net output and net inputs $\{(z_0^j, z^j) : j = 1, 2, \ldots, J\}$ are given. Assume that the z_0^j are all distinct, so that for Test 4 in this section, we can reorder the observations so that $z_0^1 < z_0^2 < \ldots < z_0^J$. For $k = 1, 2, \ldots, K$, define $\bar{z}_k \equiv \min \{z_k^j : j = 1, 2, \ldots, J\} \tilde{z}_k^j \equiv \{z_k^j \text{ if } \bar{z}_k \geqslant 0; z_k^j - \bar{z}_k \text{ if } \bar{z}_k < 0\}$ for $j = 1, 2, \ldots, J$. Thus the translated net input vectors $\tilde{z}^j \equiv (\tilde{z}_1^j, \tilde{z}_2^j, \ldots, \tilde{z}_k^j)$ are nonnegative and Test 1 in the previous section can be applied to the translated data virtually word for word: in the primal problems (2) and the dual problems (4), the vectors x^j are replaced by the z^j and $w^i \geqslant 0_N$ in (4) becomes $w^i \geqslant 0_K$. Summarizing, we have:

Test 4a: If $\mu^{i*} > 1$ for $i = 1, 2, \ldots, J-1$ where μ^{i*} is the optimal μ^i for (2) (with the $\tilde{z}^j$ replacing the x^j),[18]) then the given data $\{(z_0^j, z^j) = j = 1, 2, \ldots, J\}$ are consistent

---

[17]) S is also assumed to be unbounded from above; i.e., if $z' \in S$ and $z' \leqslant z''$, then $z'' \in S$.

[18]) If no feasible solution to the modified problem (2) exists, then it is necessary to resort to the same construction that was described in footnote 4.

with the efficiency hypothesis for some production function f satisfying Conditions I. On the other hand, if any $\mu^{i*} \leqslant 1$, then the data are not consistent for any function satisfying Conditions I′, where z_0 is singled out to play the role of net output.

If $\mu^{i*} > 1$ for $i = 1, 2, \ldots, J-1$, then define the nonempty, closed convex set

$S^* \equiv \{z : z \geqslant \sum_{j=1}^{J} \lambda^j z^j, \sum_{j=i}^{J} \lambda^j = 1, \lambda^1 \geqslant 0, \ldots, \lambda^J \geqslant 0\}$ and define f^* over S^* by

$$f^*(z) \equiv \max \{z_0^i : i = 1, 2, \ldots, J \text{ and } i \text{ is such that } \sum_{j=i}^{J} \lambda^j z^j \leqslant z$$

$$\text{for some } \lambda^i \geqslant 0, \lambda^{i+1} \geqslant 0, \ldots, \lambda^J \geqslant 0 \text{ such that } \sum_{j=i}^{J} \lambda^j = 1\}. \qquad 12)$$

If $\mu^{i*} > 1$ for $i = 1, 2, \ldots, J-1$, it can be shown that f^* defined by (12) satisfies Conditions I′ and that $z_0^j = f^*(z^j)$ for $j = 1, 2, \ldots, J$.

Test 4b is the same as Test 4a except that α^{i*}, the optimal α^i for the modified linear programming problem (4), replaces μ^{i*}.

If the test fails at observation i (i.e., if $\mu^{i*} \leqslant 1$), then we could report the violation measure $\delta^i \equiv 1 - \mu^{i*} \equiv 1 - \alpha^{i*} \geqslant 0$ as in the previous section. Thus once we translate our input and output data into the nonnegative orthant in the manner explained above, Test 4 can be interpreted in the same manner as Test 1 in the previous section.

However, there is one essential difference between Test 1 and Test 4. In the single output case, we tested for the existence of a quasiconcave production function f; i.e., we tested for the convexity of the level sets $L(y) \equiv \{x : f(x) \geqslant y, x \geqslant 0_N\}$. This test is a natural one, particularly if the data were generated by a competitive cost minimizing producer, since in this case we cannot detect nonconvex level sets [see *Afriat*, 1972, 592–593; *Diewert*, 1978, references 24–25]. However, in the multiple output case, which output case, which output should be asymmetrically singled out in forming the family of level sets $\{z : f(z) \geqslant z_0, z \in S\} \equiv L(z_0)$? The answer to this question will depend on the particular economic application under consideration. In empirical applications, the investigator may wish to run Test 4 several times, perhaps singling out each output and input in turn to play the role of the asymmetrically singled out good z_0.

Tests 2 and 3 explained in the previous section can also be extended in a straightforward manner to deal with the multiple output case.

Thus Conditions II′ are: f is a real valued function of K variables z defined over a nonempty closed, convex set S which is unbounded from above and f is (i) continuous, (ii) nondecreasing and (iii) concave over S.

Tests 5a and *5b* are simply Tests 2a and 2b in the previous section, except that z^j, z_0^j and $w^i \geqslant 0_K$ replace x^j, y^j and $w^i \geqslant 0_N$ respectively, for $i, j = 1, 2, \ldots, J$. In order to

ensure that $\check{f}(z^i) \equiv \max_{\lambda^1 \geqslant 0, \ldots, \lambda^J \geqslant 0} \{\sum_{j=1}^{J} \lambda^j z_0^j : \sum_{j=1}^{J} \lambda^j z^j \leqslant z^i, \sum_{j=1}^{J} \lambda^j = 1\} < +\infty$ for $i = 1, 2, \ldots, J$, we assume that at least one component of z^j is positive (and hence represents a quantity of an input) for $j = 1, 2, \ldots, J$.

Conditions III′ are: f is a real valued function of K variables z defined over a nonempty, closed, convex cone S and is: (i) continuous, (ii) nondecreasing, (iii) concave and (iv) (positively) linearly homogeneous over S. *Tests 6a* and *6b* [essentially due to *Hanoch/Rothschild*, 268–270] are simply Tests 3a and 3b with x^j, y^j and N replaced by z^j, z_0^j and K respectively, and of course Conditions III are replaced by Conditions III′.

Assuming that $z_0^i \neq 0$, $\Delta^i \equiv (\check{f}(z^i) - z_0^i)/z_0^i \geqslant 0$ and $\Delta^{*i} \equiv (\check{f}^*(z^i) - z_0^i)/z_0^i \geqslant 0$ are again natural measures of the violation of the efficiency hypothesis for the i-th data point (z_0^i, z^i).

It can be shown that the validity of Tests 5 and 6 does not depend on which good is asymmetrically singled out to play the role of z_0 (although the measures of violation Δ^i and Δ^{i*} are not invariant to changes in the ordering of the goods). This is because Tests 5 and 6 test whether the observed data points lie on the frontier of the free disposed convex hull of the data points in $1 + K$ dimensional space and this frontier is invariant to changes in the ordering of the goods.

4. Price, Cost and Profit Data

As in the previous section, let $x \geqslant 0_N$, $y \equiv (y_1, \hat{y}) \geqslant 0_M$ and f denote a vector of inputs, a vector of outputs and the firm's production function respectively, so that $y_1 = f(-\hat{y}, x)$ denotes the maximum amount of the first output which can be produced by the vector of inputs $x \geqslant 0_N$ given that the vector of other outputs $\hat{y} \geqslant 0_{M-1}$ has to be produced. As before, f may not be defined for all $\hat{y} \geqslant 0_{M-1}$, $x \geqslant 0_N$. We assume that $M \geqslant 1$ and $N \geqslant 1$ so that there is at least one output and one input.

For our first test in this section, we assume that data on the first output $y_1^j > 0$ are given along with data on input prices $w^j \geqslant 0_N$, other output prices $\hat{p}^j \geqslant 0_{M-1}$, and the net cost of producing y_1^j, $C^j > 0$, for $j = 1, 2, \ldots, J$. We assume that the outputs y_1^j are all distinct and reorder the observations so that

$$y_1^1 < y_1^2 < \ldots < y_1^J. \tag{13}$$

Consider the following *Conditions I″* on the production function f: f is a continuous from above function of $M - 1 + N$ variables which is such that at least one solution $(-\hat{y}^{j*}, x^{j*})$ exists for the (net) cost minimization problem

$$\min_{\hat{y} \geqslant 0_{M-1}, x \geqslant 0_N} \{w^{jT}x - \hat{p}^{jT}\hat{y} : f(-\hat{y}, x) \geqslant y_1^j\} \equiv C(y_1^j, \hat{p}^j, w^j) \tag{14}$$

for $j = 1, 2, \ldots, J$. Note that C is the (net) cost function that corresponds to the production function f.[19])

---

[19]) Using the techniques outlined in *Diewert* [1978, section 1], we can show that if f satisfies Conditions I″, then C is well defined and finite for $(y_1, \hat{p}, w)$ such that $y_1^1 \leqslant y_1 \leqslant y_1^J$ and $w \geqslant \sum_{j=1}^{J} \lambda^j w^j$, $p \leqslant \sum_{j=1}^{J} \lambda^j p^j$ where $\lambda^1 \geqslant 0, \ldots, \lambda^J \geqslant 0$. Over this domain, $C(y_1, \hat{p}, w)$ is nondecreasing and left continuous in y_1 for fixed $\hat{p}$, w and is linearly homogeneous and concave in $(\hat{p}, w)$ for fixed y_1. Also C is nondecreasing in w for fixed $(y_1, \hat{p})$ and nonincreasing in $\hat{p}$ for fixed (y_1, w) over the above domain. Alternatively, the above properties of C can be deduced by modifying the techniques used in the literature on gross, restricted or variable profit functions [see *Gorman; McFadden*, 1966, 1978; *Diewert*, 1973a; *Lau*].

Define the J linear programming problems

$$\min_{\hat{y}\geqslant 0_{M-1}, x\geqslant 0_N} \{w^{iT}x - \hat{p}^{iT}\hat{y} : C^j \leqslant w^{jT}x - \hat{p}^{jT}\hat{y}, j = 1, 2, \ldots, i\} \equiv C^{i*} \tag{15}$$

for $i = 1, 2, \ldots, J$. Note that a feasible solution to (15) exists and that the objective function is bounded below by C^i. Thus $C^i \leqslant C^{i*}$.

Test 7b:[20]) If $C^i = C^{i*}$ for $i = 1, 2, \ldots, J$, then the data $\{(C^j, y_1^j, \hat{p}^j, w^j) : j = 1, 2, \ldots, J\}$ are consistent with competitive cost minimizing behavior for some f satisfying Conditions I″ and the additional properties of quasiconcavity and nondecreasingness. On the other hand, if $C^i < C^{i*}$ for any i, then the given data are not consistent with competitive cost minimizing behavior for any production function f satisfying Conditions I″.

Note that type b tests involve inner products of the data points in the constraints while type a tests involve linear combinations of the data points in the constraints of the relevant linear programming problem.

Suppose that the data $(C^j, y_1^j, \hat{p}^j, w^j)$ were consistent with competitive cost minimizing behavior for some f satisfying Conditions I″. Thus there exist solutions $\hat{y}^{j*} \geqslant 0_{M-1}, x^{j*} \geqslant 0_N$ to the cost minimization problem (14) for $j = 1, 2, \ldots, J$. Since $f(-\hat{y}^{i*}, x^{i*}) \geqslant y_1^i > y_1^{i-1} > \ldots > y_1^1$ using (13), it can be seen that $\hat{y}^{i*}, x^{i*}$ is a feasible (but not necessarily optimal) solution for the cost minimization problem associated with observations $1, 2, \ldots, i-1$. Thus

$$C^j \leqslant w^{jT}x^{i*} - \hat{p}^{jT}\hat{y}^{i*}, \qquad j = 1, 2, \ldots, i-1. \tag{16}$$

Moreover, since $\hat{y}^{i*}, x^{i*}$ is a solution to the cost minimization problem (14) when $j = i$, $C^i = w^{iT}x^{i*} - \hat{p}^{iT}\hat{y}^{i*}$. This last equality along with the inequalities (16) imply that the i-th linear programming problem in (15) has $\hat{y}^{i*}, x^{i*}$ as an optimal solution with $C^{i*} = C^i$. The same analysis can be repeated for $i = 1, 2, \ldots, J$. Thus if $C^{i*} > C^i$ for any i, the given data cannot be consistent with the cost minimization hypothesis.

On the other hand, suppose that the data $(C^j, y_1^j, \hat{p}^j, w^j)$ are such that $C^{i*} = C^i$ for $i = 1, 2, \ldots, J$ where the C^{i*} are defined as the optimal values of the objective functions for the linear programming problems (15). For $i = 1, 2, \ldots, J$, define the level sets

$$L(y_1^i) \equiv \{(-\hat{y}, x) : x \geqslant 0_N, \hat{y} \geqslant 0_{M-1}, w^{jT}x - \hat{p}^{jT}\hat{y} \geqslant C^j, j = 1, 2, \ldots, i\}. \tag{17}$$

Note that the sets $L(y_1^1)$ become smaller (or at least do not become larger) as i increases. Note also that (13) implies that $y_1^i < y_1^j$ if $i < j$. We may now define the "plateau" production function $\hat{f}$ in terms of the level sets $L(y_1^i)$: for $(-\hat{y}, x) \in L(y_1^1)$,

$$\hat{f}(-\hat{y}, x) \equiv \{\max y_1^j : j = 1, 2, \ldots, J \text{ and } j \text{ is such that } (-\hat{y}, x) \in L(y_1^j)\}. \tag{18}$$

It is straightforward to verify that $\hat{f}$ satisfies Conditions I″ and is nondecreasing and quasi-

---

[20]) This test generalizes a test due to *Hanoch/Rothschild* [1972, p. 266].

concave over the set $L(y_1^1)$. Moreover, if we let $\hat{C}$ denote the (net) cost function which corresponds to $\hat{f}$, then

$$\begin{aligned}\hat{C}(y_1^i, \hat{p}^i, w^i) &\equiv \min_{\hat{y},x} \{w^{iT}x - \hat{p}^{iT}\hat{y} : \hat{f}(-\hat{y}, x) \geq y_1^i, (-\hat{y}, x) \in L(y_1^1)\} \\ &= \min_{\hat{y},x} \{w^{iT}x - \hat{p}^{iT}y : (-\hat{y}, x) \in L(y_1^i)\} \\ &\qquad \text{using (13), (17) and (18)} \\ &\equiv \min_{\hat{y} \geq 0_{M-1}, x \geq 0_N} \{w^{iT}x - \hat{p}^{iT}y : C^j \leq w^{jT}x - \hat{p}^{jT}\hat{y}, j = 1, 2, \ldots, i\} \\ &\qquad \text{using (17)} \\ &\equiv C^{i*} \quad \text{using (15)} \\ &= C^i \quad \text{by assumption.}\end{aligned}$$

Thus $\hat{C}(y_1^i, \hat{p}^i, w^i) = C^i$ for $i = 1, 2, \ldots, J$ and the given data are consistent with the cost minimization hypothesis for the f defined by (18).[21])

The geometry of Test 7b should be clear: the level set $L(y_1^i)$ defined by (15) should be an outer approximation to the "true" production possibility set $\{(-\hat{y}, x) : f(-\hat{y}, x) \geq y_1^i\}$ where f is the producer's "true" production function f. The isocost line $\{(-\hat{y}, x) : w^{iT}x - \hat{p}^{iT}\hat{y} = C^i\}$ should be tangent to $L(y_1^i)$ if there is competitive cost minimizing behavior. If $C^{i*} > C^i$, the isocost line passes below $L(y_1^i)$ and thus there cannot be competitive cost minimizing behavior.

The dual to the linear programming problem (15) is

$$\max_{\lambda^1 \geq 0, \ldots, \lambda^i \geq 0} \{\sum_{j=1}^{i} \lambda^j C^j : \sum_{j=1}^{i} \lambda^j w^j \leq w^i, \sum_{j=1}^{i} \lambda^j \hat{p}^j \geq \hat{p}^i\} \equiv C^{i*} \tag{19}$$

for $i = 1, 2, \ldots, J$. Since (15) has a finite optimal solution, (19) also has a finite optimal solution and the optimal values of the objective functions for (15) and (19) both equal C^{i*}. Note that $\lambda^1 = 0, \lambda^2 = 0, \ldots, \lambda^{i-1} = 0$ and $\lambda^i = 1$ is feasible for (19) and thus $C^{i*} \geq C^i$ (as before). *Test 7a* is simply Test 7b, except that (19) instead of (15) is used in order to compute the C^{i*}.

What is an interpretation of the dual problems (19)? Suppose that Test 7a fails; i.e., $C^{i*} > C^i$ for some i. Then there exists some nonzero λ^{j*} such that

---

21) If $C^{i*} = C^i$ and $x^{i*} \geq 0_N$, $\hat{y}^{i*} \geq 0_{M-1}$ denote an optimal solution to the LP (15) for $i = 1, 2, \ldots, J$, then another production function satisfying Conditions I″ plus quasiconcavity and nondecreasingness which is consistent with the data may be defined as $\check{f}(-\hat{y}, x) \equiv \max \{y_1^i : i = 1, 2, \ldots, J$ and i is such that $\sum_{j=i}^{J} \lambda^j x^{j*} \leq x$ and $\sum_{j=i}^{J} \lambda^j \hat{y}^{j*} \geq \hat{y}$ for some $\lambda^i \geq 0, \ldots, \lambda^J \geq 0$ such that $\sum_{j=i}^{J} \lambda^j = 1\}$. We may think of $\check{f}$ as an inner approximation to the true f while $\hat{f}$ is an outer approximation. The inner approximations will be unique only if all J programming problems (15) have unique solutions.

$$\sum_{j=1}^{i} \lambda^{j*} C^j > C^i, \sum_{j=1}^{i} \lambda^{j*} x^j \leqslant w^i, \sum_{j=1}^{i} \lambda^{j*} \hat{p}^j \geqslant \hat{p}^i, \lambda^{1*} \geqslant 0, \ldots, \lambda^{i*} \geqslant 0. \tag{20}$$

If the cost minimization hypothesis were true, then we have

$$\begin{aligned}
C^i &< \sum_{j=1}^{i} \lambda^{j*} C^j && \text{by (20)} \\
&= \sum_{j=1}^{i} \lambda^{j*} C(y_1^j, \hat{p}^j, w^j) && \text{by the cost minimization hypothesis} \\
&\leqslant \sum_{j=1}^{i} \lambda^{j*} C(y_1^i, \hat{p}^j, w^j) && \text{by (13) and nondecreasingness of } C \text{ in } y_1 \\
&\leqslant C(y_1^i, \sum_{j=1}^{i} \lambda^{j*} p^j, \sum_{j=1}^{i} \lambda^{j*} w^j) && \text{by linear homogeneity and concavity of } C \\
&\leqslant C(y_1^i, \hat{p}^i, w^i) && \text{by (20) and the monotonicity properties of } C \text{ in } \hat{p} \text{ and } w \\
&= C^i && \text{by the cost minimization hypothesis}
\end{aligned}$$

which is a contradiction. Thus if (20) were true, the cost minimization hypothesis could not hold.

At this point, we should mention the fact that the cost minimization hypothesis does not necessarily imply the efficiency hypothesis of the previous sections; i.e., if Test 7 passes, it is not necessarily the case that production is on the efficient frontier of the production possibility set. This case can occur if two or more of the level sets $L(y_1^i)$ defined by (17) coincide. Note that the production function is discontinuous in this case. This will occur if $C^i = C^{i+1}$, $p^i = p^{i+1}$, $w^i = w^{i+1}$ but $y_1^i < y_1^{i+1}$ for some i. In this case, although the producer may be producing output y_1^i using minimal inputs, he is not producing maximal output for given inputs [see *Färe/Lovell* for a further discussion of the two concepts of efficiency]. However, we can check for the validity of the efficiency hypothesis in addition to the cost minimization hypothesis by letting the index j in (15) run to $i-1$ instead of i: if $C^i > C^{i*}$ for $i = 2, 3, \ldots, J$, then the data are consistent with efficiency and cost minimizing behavior; if $C^i \geqslant C^{i*}$ for $i = 2, \ldots, J$ with at least one equality, then the data are consistent with cost minimizing behavior but not efficiency; finally if $C^i < C^{i*}$ for any i, then the data are not consistent with either efficiency or cost minimizing behavior.

If $C^i < C^{i*}$ (and $C^i > 0$), then a natural measure of violation of the cost minimization hypothesis is $\delta^i \equiv (C^{i*}/C^i) - 1 > 0$. Thus δ^i is the proportion by which we must increase C^i in order to make the given data pass Test 7 at observation i. It can be shown that δ^i is invariant to scale changes in the units of measurement (which preserve values).

For our second test in this section, we assume that data on input prices $w^j \gg 0_N$, output prices $p^j \gg 0_M$ and profits Π^j $(\equiv p^{jT} y^j - w^{jT} x^j)$ are given for $j = 1, 2, \ldots, J$. Instead of phrasing our regularity conditions on the firm's production function f where

$y_1 = f(-\hat{y}, x)$, it proves to be slightly more convenient to place regularity conditions on the firm's production possibility set $S \equiv \{y_1, \hat{y}, -x) : y_1 \leqslant f(-\hat{y}, x)\}$.[22])

Consider the following *Conditions II″*: S is a closed set such that at least one solution $(y^{j^*}, -x^{j^*})$ exists for the profit maximization problem

$$\max_{y \geqslant 0_M, x \geqslant 0_N} \{p^{jT}y - w^{jT}x : (y, -x) \in S\} \equiv \Pi(p^j, w^j) \tag{21}$$

for $j = 1, 2, \ldots, J$. Define the J linear programming problems

$$\max_{y \geqslant 0_M, x \geqslant 0_N} \{p^{iT}y - w^{iT}x : p^{jT}y - w^{jT}x \leqslant \Pi^j, j = 1, 2, \ldots, J\} \equiv \Pi^{i^*} \tag{22}$$

for $i = 1, 2, \ldots, J$. Since we are assuming that $w^j \gg 0_N$ for every j, feasible solutions to (22) always exist. Moreover, for the i-th problem in (22), the objective function is bounded from above by $\Pi^{i^*} \leqslant \Pi^i$ for $i = 1, 2, \ldots, J$.

Test 8b:[23]) If $\Pi^i = \Pi^{i^*}$ for $i = 1, 2, \ldots, J$, then the data $\{(\Pi^j, p^j, w^j) : j = 1, 2, \ldots, J\}$ are consistent with competitive profit maximizing behavior for some production possibility set S satisfying Conditions II″ plus the additional properties of convexity and free disposal. On the other hand, if $\Pi^{i^*} < \Pi^i$ for any i, then the given data are not consistent with competitive profit maximizing behavior for any S satisfying Conditions II″.

Thus if Test 8b passes (i.e., $\Pi^i = \Pi^{i^*}$ for all i), then the data are consistent with profit maximizing behavior subject to a production function constraint and moreover, the production function can satisfy Conditions II′ listed in the previous section. To see this, suppose that $\Pi^i = \Pi^{i^*}$ for $i = 1, 2, \ldots, J$. Then define $\hat{S}$, an outer approximation to the true technology set S,[24]) as

$$\hat{S} \equiv \{(y, -x) : y \geqslant 0_M, x \geqslant 0_N, p^{jT}y - w^{jT}x \leqslant \Pi^j, j = 1, 2, \ldots, J\}. \tag{23}$$

It is trivial to verify using (22) that $\Pi^i = \Pi^{i^*}$ implies that $\Pi^i = \max_{y \geqslant 0_M, x \geqslant 0_N} \{p^{iT}y - w^{iT}x : (y, -x) \in \hat{S}\}$ for $i = 1, 2, \ldots, J$ and thus the given data are consistent with the profit maximization hypothesis for the production possibilities set $\hat{S}$ defined by (23). It is also easy to verify that the production function which corresponds to $\hat{S}$ when we single out the first component of y as the output, $\hat{f}$ say, satisfies Conditions II′.

---

22) Note that S is the hypograph of f. It is of course straightforward to reinterpret conditions on S as conditions on f.

23) This test is due to *Hanoch/Rothschild* [1972, p. 269]; however, their regularity conditions on S are stronger – they assume that S is a closed, convex set that exhibits free disposal, whereas we assume only closure. Free disposal means: if $z' \in S$ and $z'' \leqslant z'$, then $z'' \in S$ also.

24) An inner approximation to the true S can be defined as $\check{S} \equiv \{(y, -x) : y \geqslant 0_M, x \geqslant 0_N, y \leqslant \sum_{j=1}^{J} \lambda^j y^{j^*}, x \geqslant \sum_{j=1}^{J} \lambda^j x^{j^*}, \lambda^1 \geqslant 0, \ldots, \lambda^J \geqslant 0$ and $\sum_{j=1}^{J} \lambda^j = 1\}$ where (y^{i^*}, x^{i^*}) is any solution to the linear program (22) for $i = 1, 2, \ldots, J$. Thus $\check{S}$ will not generally be uniquely defined.

On the other hand, suppose that we have profit maximizing behavior for an S satisfying Conditions II″. Then for $j = 1, 2, \ldots, J$, we have the existence of $(y^{j*}, -x^{j*}) \in S$ such that $y^{j*} \geqslant 0_M$, $x^{j*} \geqslant 0_N$ and $\Pi(p^j, w^j)$ defined by (21) equals $p^{jT}y^{j*} - w^{jT}x^{j*} \equiv \Pi^j$. Therefore, since $(y^{i*}, -x^{i*})$ is feasible for the $\Pi(p^j, w^j)$ profit maximization problem but is not necessarily optimal, we have

$$\Pi^j = p^{jT}y^{j*} - w^{jT}x^{j*} \geqslant p^{jT}y^{i*} - w^{jT}x^{i*}, \; i, j = 1, 2, \ldots, J. \tag{24}$$

From (24), it follows that $(y^{i*}, -x^{i*})$ is an optimal solution to (22) with $\Pi^i = \Pi^{i*}$ for $i = 1, 2, \ldots, J$. Thus profit maximizing behavior implies that Test 8b will pass. Hence if $\Pi^{i*} < \Pi^i$ for any i, then the given data cannot be consistent with competitive profit maximizing behavior for any S satisfying Conditions II″.

The dual to (22) is

$$\min_{\lambda^1 \geqslant 0, \ldots, \lambda^J \geqslant 0} \{\sum_{j=1}^{J} \lambda^j \Pi^j : \sum_{j=1}^{J} \lambda^j p^j \geqslant p^i, \sum_{j=1}^{J} \lambda^j w^j \leqslant w^i\} \equiv \Pi^{i*} \tag{25}$$

for $i = 1, 2, \ldots, J$. *Test 8(a)*[25]) is the same as Test 8(b) above except that the numbers Π^{i*} are calculated by solving the dual problems (25) instead of (22).

By inspecting (25), we see that $\Pi^{i*} \leqslant \Pi^i$ for all i. As before, if $\Pi^{i*} < \Pi^i$ for some i, then we cannot have profit maximizing behavior. To see this in the context of (25) instead of (22), assume profit maximizing behavior and assume that there exist $\lambda^{1*} \geqslant 0, \ldots, \lambda^{J*} \geqslant 0$ such that

$$\Pi^i > \Pi^{i*} \equiv \sum_{j=1}^{J} \lambda^{j*} \Pi^j; \; \sum_{j=1}^{J} \lambda^{j*} p^j \geqslant p^i; \; \sum_{j=1}^{J} \lambda^{j*} w^j \leqslant w^i. \tag{26}$$

$\therefore \; \Pi^i > \sum_{j=1}^{J} \lambda^{j*} \Pi^j$	using (26)
$= \sum_{j=1}^{J} \lambda^{j*} \Pi(p^j, w^j)$	by the profit maximization hypothesis
$\geqslant \Pi(\sum_{J=1}^{J} \lambda^{j*} p^J, \sum_{j=1}^{J} \lambda^{j*} w^j)$	since the profit function Π must be linearly homogeneous and convex in prices [see *Hanoch/Rothschild*, 1972, p. 266]
$\geqslant \Pi(p^i, w^i)$	by (26) since Π is nondecreasing in p and nonincreasing in w
$= \Pi^i$	by the profit maximization hypothesis.

We have obtained a contradiction. Thus if $\Pi^{i*} < \Pi^i$, then the profit maximization hypothesis cannot hold for the given data.

---

[25]) This is a modified generalization of a test due to *Afriat* [1972, p. 593]. Afriat deals only with the single output case and he also adds the constraint $\sum_{j=1}^{J} \lambda^j = 1$ to (25).

It is worth noting that if Test 8 passes so that the given data are consistent with the profit maximization hypothesis, then the data are also consistent with the efficiency hypothesis; i.e., we cannot distinguish between the two hypotheses as we could in Test 7.

Natural violation measures for observation i for Test 8 are $\Delta^i \equiv \Pi^i - \Pi^{i*} \geqslant 0$ (there is no violation if $\Delta^i = 0$ at observation i) and $\delta^i \equiv \Delta^i/\Pi^i \geqslant 0$ provided that $\Pi^i \neq 0$. Thus δ^i is the proportion by which the observed profit during period i, Π^i, must be reduced in order to make the i-th profit-price vector (Π^i, p^i, w^i) consistent with the profit maximization hypothesis.

For our final test in this section, we assume that data on input prices $w^j \gg 0_N$ and output prices $p^j \gg 0_M$ are given and that production is subject to constant returns to scale. In this case, it is well known that profits Π^j must either equal 0 or plus infinity. We assume that $\Pi^j = 0$ for $j = 1, 2, \ldots, J$. As in the previous test, we place regularity conditions on the firm's production possibility set S.

Consider the following Conditions III″: S is a closed cone such that at least one *non-zero* finite solution $(y^{j*}, -x^{j*})$ exists for the profit maximization problem

$$\max_{y \geqslant 0_M, x \geqslant 0_N} \{p^{jT}y - w^{jT}x : (y, -x) \in S\} \equiv \Pi(p^j, w^j) \tag{27}$$

for $j = 1, 2, \ldots, J$. Since we assume that the solution $(y^{j*}, -x^{j*})$ is finite, we cannot have $\Pi(p^j, w^j) = +\infty$. Since S is assumed to be a cone, if $\Pi(p^j, w^j) = p^{jT}y^{j*} - w^{jT}x^{j*} > 0$, then since $(y^{j*}, -x^{j*})$ is also feasible for the maximization problem (27) for any $\lambda \geqslant 0$, we would have for $\lambda > 1$, $\Pi(p^j, w^j) < p^{jT}\lambda y^{j*} - w^{jT}\lambda x^{j*}$, a contradiction. Thus we must have $\Pi(p^j, w^j) = 0$.

Given the price data $\{(p^j, w^j) : p^j \gg 0_M, w^j \gg 0_N, j = 1, 2, \ldots, J\}$, if S satisfies Conditions III″, then we say that the data are consistent with *nontrivial* (competitive) profit maximizing behavior; if we allowed *zero* solutions $(y^{j*}, -x^{j*}) = (0_M, 0_N)$ in the definition of Conditions III″ and if the price data and S satisfied this modification of Conditions III″, then we would say that the data are consistent with (competitive) profit maximizing behavior.

Define the J linear programming problems:

$$\max_{y \geqslant 0_M, x \geqslant 0_N} \{p^{iT}y - w^{iT}x : p^{jT}y - w^{jT}x \leqslant 0, j = 1, \ldots, J, w^{iT}x = 1\} \equiv \Pi^{i*} \tag{28}$$

for $i = i, 2, \ldots, J$. Note that $\Pi^{i*} \leqslant 0$.

Test 9b:[26]) If $\Pi^{i*} = 0$ for $i = 1, 2, \ldots, J$, then the price data $\{(p^j, w^j) : j = 1, 2, \ldots, J\}$ are consistent with nontrivial competitive profit maximizing behavior for some production possibility set S satisfying Conditions III″ plus the additional properties of convexity

---

[26]) *Hanoch/Rothschild* [1972, p. 270] suggest a similar test except they omit the constraint $w^{iT}x = 1$ from their version of (28). As a result, $y = 0_M$ and $x = 0_N$ are always feasible and optimal for their modification of (28) and thus their test *always* passes. However, our test for *nontrivial* profit maximizing behavior does not suffer from this defect.

and free disposal. On the other hand, if $\Pi^{i*} < 0$ for any i, then the given data are not consistent with nontrivial competitive profit maximizing behavior for any S satisfying Conditions III″.

Suppose we have nontrivial profit maximizing behavior for some S satisfying Conditions III″. Then there exists nonzero $(y^{j*}, -x^{j*}) \in S$ such that $\Pi(p^j, w^j) = p^{jT}y^{j*} - w^{jT}x^{j*} = 0$ for $j = 1, 2, \ldots, J$. Since at least one of the vectors y^{j*} and x^{j*} is nonzero, this fact along with $y^{j*} \geqslant 0_M$, $x^{j*} \geqslant 0_N$, $p^j \gg 0_M$, $w^j \gg 0_N$ and $p^{jT}y^{j*} = w^{jT}x^{j*}$ imply that $y^{j*} > 0_M$ and $x^{j*} > 0$ for $j = 1, 2, \ldots, J$. Define $\lambda^j \equiv 1/w^{jT}x^{j*} > 0$ and $(y^{j**}, -x^{j**}) \equiv (\lambda^j y^{j*}, -\lambda^j x^{j*})$ for $j = 1, 2, \ldots, J$. Since S is a cone, it can be seen that $(y^{j**}, -x^{j**})$ is also a solution to the profit maximization problem (26) and thus we have $p^{iT}y^{j**} - w^{iT}x^{j**} \leqslant 0 = p^{iT}y^{i**} - w^{iT}x^{i**}$ for $i, j = 1, 2, \ldots, J$ with $y^{i*} \geqslant 0_M$, $x^{i*} \geqslant 0_N$ and $w^{iT}x^{i**} = 1$ for $i = 1, 2, \ldots, J$. These inequalities and equalities imply that $\Pi^{i*} = 0$ for $i = 1, 2, \ldots, J$ where Π^{i*} is defined by (27).

On the other hand, suppose $\Pi^{i*} = 0$ for $i = 1, 2, \ldots, J$. Then define $\hat{S}$, the outer approximation to the true technology, by (23) (except that now $\Pi^j \equiv 0$ for $j = 1, 2, \ldots, J$). It can readily be shown that $0 = \max_{y \geqslant 0_M, x \geqslant 0_N} \{p^{iT}y - w^{iT}x : (y, -x) \in \hat{S}\} = p^{iT}y^{i*} - w^{iT}x^{i*}$ for $i = 1, 2, \ldots, J$ where (y^{i*}, x^{i*}) is a solution to the LP (28).[27]) Since $x^{i*} \geqslant 0_N$ and $w^{iT}x^{i*} = 1$, it can be seen that the given price data $\{(p^j, w^j) : j = 1, 2, \ldots, J\}$ are consistent with nontrivial profit maximizing behavior for $\hat{S}$, which satisfies Conditions III″ plus the additional properties of convexity and free disposal. It also can be verified that the production function which corresponds to $\hat{S}$, $\hat{f}$ say, satisfies Conditions III′ listed in the previous section.

The dual to (27) is

$$\min_{\alpha^i, \lambda^1 \geqslant 0, \ldots, \lambda^J \geqslant 0} \{\alpha^i : \sum_{j=1}^{J} \lambda^j p^j \geqslant p^i, \sum_{j=1}^{J} \lambda^j w^j + \alpha^i w^i \geqslant -w^i\} \equiv \alpha^{i*}. \tag{29}$$

Note that $\alpha^i \equiv 0$, $\lambda^i \equiv 0$, $\lambda^j \equiv 0$ for all $j \neq i$ is a feasible solution for (29). Thus $\Pi^{i*} = \alpha^{i*} \leqslant 0$. *Test 9a* is the same as Test 9b above except that the numbers Π^{i*} are replaced by the numbers α^{i*} defined by (29) for $i = 1, 2, \ldots, J$.

If $\alpha^{i*} < 0$, then there exist $\lambda^{1*} \geqslant 0, \ldots, \lambda^{J*}$ such that $\sum_{j=1}^{J} \lambda^{j*} p^j \geqslant p^i$ and $-\sum_{j=1}^{J} \lambda^{j*} w^j \gg -w^i$. If these inequalities hold, then the given data $\{(p^j, w^j) : j = 1, 2, \ldots, J\}$ cannot be consistent with nontrivial profit maximizing behavior. For example, if there is only one output ($M = 1$) and one input ($N = 1$), it can be seen that the given price vectors (p^j, w^j) must all be proportional (i.e., $(p^j, w^j) = \lambda^j (p, w)$ for some

---

[27]) These solutions can be used to define an inner approximation to the true S, $\check{S} \equiv \{(y, -x) : y \geqslant 0_M, x \geqslant 0_N, y \leqslant \sum_{j=1}^{J} \lambda^j y^{j*}, x \geqslant \sum_{j=1}^{J} \lambda^j x^{j*}, \lambda^1 \geqslant 0, \lambda^2 \geqslant 0, \ldots, \lambda^J \geqslant 0\}$.

$\lambda^j > 0, p > 0, w > 0, j = 1, 2, \ldots, J$) in order for the price data to be consistent with nontrivial profit maximizing behavior.

A violation measure for observation i is $-\alpha^{i*} \geqslant 0$: if $\alpha^{i*} < 0$ then $-\alpha^{i*} > 0$ represents the proportional reduction in the i-th input price vector $w^i \gg 0_N$ that would be required in order to make the test pass at observation i.

5. Price and Quantity Tests

For our first test in this section, we assume that complete price and quantity data are available with the possible exception of price data on the first output. Thus we assume that we have data on the first output $y_1^j > 0$ (the observations j are reordered so that (13) is satisfied) along with data on inputs $x^j \geqslant 0_N$ and input prices $w^j \gg 0_N$, and on other outputs $\hat{y}^j \geqslant 0_{M-1}$ and other output prices $\hat{p}^j \gg 0_{M-1}$ for $j = 1, 2, \ldots, J$. Given this information, we can calculate the net cost of producing y_1^j as $C^j \equiv -\hat{p}^{jT}\hat{y}^j + w^{jT}x^j$ for $j = 1, \ldots, J$.

Suppose that the data $\{(y_1^j, \hat{y}^j, \hat{p}^j, x^j, w^j) : j = 1, \ldots, J\}$ are consistent with competitive cost minimizing behavior for some production function f satisfying Conditions I″ listed in the previous section. Then $(\hat{y}^j, x^j)$ is a solution to the cost minimization problem (14), and since $f(-y^i, x^i) \geqslant y_1^i > y_1^{i-1} > \ldots > y_1^1$ by (13), it can be seen that $\hat{y}^i, x^i$ is a feasible solution for the cost minimization problems associated with observations $1, 2, \ldots, i-1$. Thus

$$C^j \equiv -\hat{p}^{jT}\hat{y}^j + w^{jT}x^j \leqslant -\hat{p}^{jT}\hat{y}^i + w^{jT}x^i;\ j = 1, 2, \ldots, i. \tag{30}$$

Moreover, the inequalities (30) must hold for $i = 1, 2, \ldots, J$. This establishes the second part of the following test.

Test 10:[28]) If the inequalities (30) hold for $i = 1, 2, \ldots, J$, then the data $\{(y_1^j, \hat{y}^j, \hat{p}^j, x^j, w^j) : j = 1, \ldots, J\}$ are consistent with competitive cost minimizing behavior for some f satisfying Conditions I″ and the additional properties of quasiconcavity and nondecreasingness. On the other hand, if any one of the inequalities (30) is not satisfied for any i, then the given data are not consistent with competitive cost minimizing behavior for any production function f satisfying Conditions I″.

The first part of the above test can readily be established if we define the level sets $L(y_1^i)$ by (17) and the plateau production function $\hat{f}$ by (18). Then it is straightforward to show that the inequalities (30) imply that the given data are consistent with competitive cost minimizing behavior for the $\hat{f}$ defined by (18).[29])

---

[28]) This test is a slight generalization of a test due to *Hanoch/Rothschild* [1972, p. 266]: we have generalized their test to the multiple output case and our test does not require that f be quasiconcave and nondecreasing as a maintained hypothesis. Hanoch and Rothschild also note that this test essentially determines whether the data satisfy the production function counterpart to the *Konüs* [1939, p. 15] – *Samuelson* [1947, p. 110] revealed preference conditions in consumer theory.

[29]) Just rework the cost equations below (18) using (30) in place of (15).

As in the previous section, it should be mentioned that the cost minimization hypothesis does not necessarily imply the efficiency hypothesis. Also, the modification of Test 10 to test for (variable) profit maximizing behavior should be obvious.

For our second and third tests in this section, we assume that data on inputs $x^j \geqslant 0_N$, input prices $w^j \gg 0_N$, outputs $y^j \geqslant 0_M$ and output prices $p^j \gg 0_M$ are given for observations $j = 1, 2, \ldots, J$. Given this information, we calculate profits in period j as $\Pi^j \equiv p^{jT}y^j - w^{jT}x^j$. As in the previous section, it proves to be more convenient to place regularity conditions on the firm's production possibility set S rather than the firm's production function f.

Suppose that the data $\{(y^j, p^j, x^j, w^j) : j = 1, 2, \ldots, J\}$ are consistent with competitive profit maximizing behavior for some S satisfying Conditions II″ listed in the previous section. Then (y^j, x^j) is a solution to the profit maximization problem (21). Since $(y^j, -x^j) \in S$, it can be seen that y^j, x^j is a feasible (but not necessarily optimal) solution for the profit maximization problem associated with observation i. Thus

$$\Pi^i \equiv p^{iT}y^i - w^{iT}x^i \geqslant p^{iT}y^j - w^{iT}x^j, \qquad j = 1, 2, \ldots, J. \tag{31}$$

Moreover, the inequalities (31) must hold for all observations i. This establishes the second part of the following test.

Test 11:[30]) If the inequalities (31) are satisfied for $i = 1, 2, \ldots, J$, then the data $\{(y^j, p^j, x^j, w^j) : j = 1, 2, \ldots, J\}$ are consistent with competitive profit maximizing behavior for some production possibility set S satisfying Conditions II″ plus the additional properties of convexity and free disposal. On the other hand, if any one of the inequalities (31) is not satisfied for any i, then the given data are not consistent with competitive profit maximizing behavior for any S satisfying Conditions II″.

The first part of the above test can readily be established if we define the (outer approximation) production possibility set $\hat{S}$ by (23) and show that the inequalities (31) for all i imply that $\max_{y \geqslant 0_M, x \geqslant 0_N} \{p^{iT}y - w^{iT}x : (y, -x) \in \hat{S}\} = p^{iT}y^i - w^{iT}x^i$ for all i, which implies that the given data are consistent with the profit maximization hypothesis for $\hat{S}$.

For our final test, again assume that data on inputs $x^j > 0_N$, input prices $p^j \gg 0_N$, outputs $y^j > 0_M$, and output prices $p^j \gg 0_M$ are given and define $\Pi^j \equiv p^{jT}y^j - w^{jT}x^j$ for $j = 1, 2, \ldots, J$. We wish to test for nontrivial profit maximizing behavior[31]) assuming that the technology exhibits constant returns to scale.

[30]) This test generalizes slightly tests due to *Hanoch/Rothschild* [1972, 268–270] (our test does not require that S be convex and exhibit free disposal as a maintained hypothesis) and *Afriat* [1972, p. 594] (Afriat deals only with the single output case). Afriat also notes the relationship of the inequalities (31) to the inequalities of revealed preference theory.

[31]) Nontrivial profit maximizing behavior takes place at observation J iff a nonzero, noninfinite solution (y^j, x^j) exists for the profit maximization problem (26).

Suppose that the data $\{(y^j, p^j, x^j, w^j) : j = 1, 2, \ldots, J\}$ are consistent with nontrivial competitive profit maximizing behavior for some S satisfying Conditions III″ listed in the previous section. Then (y^j, x^j) is a solution to the profit maximization problem (26) and we can again show that the inequalities (31) must hold for $i = 1, 2, \ldots, J$. However, since S is a closed cone, $(0_M, 0_N)$ is a feasible solution for (26) and thus

$\Pi^j \equiv p^{jT} y^j - w^{jT} x^j = \Pi(p^j, w^j) \equiv \max_{y \geqslant 0_M, x \geqslant 0_N} \{p^{jT} y - w^{jT} x : (y, -x) \in S\} \geqslant$

$p^{jT} 0_M - w^{jT} 0_N = 0$. *Suppose* $\Pi^j \equiv p^{jT} y^j - w^{jT} x^j > 0$, then since S is a cone $(\lambda y^j, -\lambda x^j) \in S$ and for $\lambda > 1$, we find that $p^{jT} \lambda x^j - w^{jT} \lambda x^j > \Pi^j \equiv \Pi(p^j, w^j)$ which contradicts our assumption that (y^j, x^j) is a solution to (26). Thus our supposition cannot be true and we must have

$$\Pi^j \equiv p^{jT} y^j - w^{jT} x^j = 0, \qquad j = 1, 2, \ldots, J. \tag{32}$$

This establishes the second part of the following test.

Test 12:[32]) If the inequalities (31) are satisfied for $i = 1, 2, \ldots, J$ as well as the equalities (32), then the data $\{(y^j, p^j, x^j, w^j) : j = 1, 2, \ldots, J\}$ are consistent with nontrivial competitive profit maximizing behavior for some production possibility set S satisfying Conditions III″ plus the additional properties of convexity and free disposal. On the other hand if any of the inequalities (31) for $i = 1, \ldots, J$ or if any of the equalities (32) are not satisfied, then the given data are not consistent with nontrivial competitive profit maximizing behavior for any S satisfying Conditions III″.

The first part of the above test follows readily if we define $\hat{S}$ by (23) and show that the inequalities (31) for all i and the equalities (32) imply that

$\max_{y \geqslant 0_M, x \geqslant 0_N} \{p^{iT} y - w^{iT} x : (y, -x) \in \hat{S}\} = p^{iT} y^i - w^{iT} x^i$ for all i, which implies that the given data are consistent with the (nontrivial) profit maximization hypothesis for $\hat{S}$.

If any of the tests described in this section fail, so that the given data are not consistent with cost minimizing or profit maximizing behavior, then we can define violation measures which are analogous to the violation measures defined in the previous section. Note that none of these tests involve solving linear programming problems: the tests only involve checking certain inequalities (and equalities in the case of Test 12).

If all price and quantity data are available for both inputs and outputs so that we can run any of the tests in sections 3–5, then there are certain relationships between the tests. If Tests 4 or 7 fail, then the corresponding Test 10 must fail; if Tests 5 or 8 (6 or 9) fail, then Test 11 (12) must fail. On the other hand, Tests 4 and 7 could both pass and the corresponding Test 10 could still fail; Tests 5 and 8 (6 and 9) could pass while Test 11 (12) failed. Finally, if Test 10 passes, then the corresponding Tests 4 and 7 must pass; if Test 11 (12) passes then Tests 5 and 8 (6 and 9) must pass.

---

[32]) This test is due to *Hanoch/Rothschild* [1972, p. 270] except that they required the additional maintained hypothesis that S be convex and exhibit free disposal.

If the test involving both price and quantity data fails (e.g. Test 12 fails) and the test involving quantity data alone fails (e.g. Test 6 also fails) but the test involving price data alone passes (e.g. Test 9 passes), then we could assume that our given price data are consistent with the relevant maximization hypothesis but the given quantity data are not consistent. In this case, we might check for errors in the quantity data.

6. Technical Progress

The tests presented above are natural ones to apply in the context of cross section data. However, it would be useful to apply the above tests in the context of time series data where the assumption that the production possibilities set or production function remains the same from period to period becomes suspect; i.e., technical progress could expand the production possibility set from one period to the next.

There are at least three different methods for dealing with the problem of technical progress.

The first method is to ignore it; i.e., we could follow the example set by *Jorgenson/ Griliches* [1967] and assert that if we calculate the correct (rental) prices for all inputs, then unaccounted for technical progress should be negligible.

A second method would be to assume that technical progress is Hicks neutral, use an index number formula in order to calculate the between period shift in the technology (for the details using a superlative index number formula see *Diewert* [1976, 124–129]), and then deflate the observed data so that the resulting deflated data is (approximately) consistent with a nonshifting technology. The tests of the previous sections could be applied to the deflated data. However, this method requires complete data on input and output prices and quantities as well as the dubious hypothesis of Hicks neutrality and moreover, the deflation is only approximately valid for an arbitrary technology.

The third and perhaps most satisfactory methods for dealing with the technological progress problem is to modify our previous tests to take the possibility of technical progress into account. We sketch below how this can be done for a few of the above tests, leaving to the reader the task of extending all of the tests.

Let the observation index j now correspond to time, so $j = 1$ corresponds to the first period and $j = J$ is the last period. Suppose that for each period j, the firm's production function f^j satisfies Conditions II listed in section 2 above. If we assume that there is no technical regress, then we mean that the period specific production functions f^j are such that $f^j(x) \geqslant f^i(x)$ for all $x \geqslant 0_N$ belonging to the domain of definition of f^i and all periods $j \geqslant i$; i.e., the maximal output produced by the input vector x during period i, $f^i(x)$, does not decrease for periods $j \geqslant i$.

Given a set of J observations on inputs and outputs, $\{(x^j, y^j) : j = 1, 2, \ldots, J\}$ where $x^j \geqslant 0_N$ and $y^j \geqslant 0$, define the free disposal convex hull of the set of inputs $S(x^1, \ldots, x^j)$ as in section 2 and for $i = 1, 2, \ldots, J$, define $\check{f}^i(x)$ as the solution to the following LP:

$$\check{f}^i(x) \equiv \max_{\lambda^1 \geqslant 0, \ldots, \lambda^i \geqslant 0} \{\sum_{j=1}^{i} \lambda^j y^j : \sum_{j=1}^{i} \lambda^j x^j \leqslant x, \sum_{j=1}^{i} \lambda^j = 1\}. \tag{33}$$

Then using the same techniques that were used in section 2, we can derive the following modification of Test 2a which makes allowance for the possibility of technical progress:

*Test 2a**: If $y^i = \check{f}^i(x^i)$ for $i = 1, 2, \ldots, J$, then the data $\{(x^j, y^j) : j = 1, 2, \ldots, J\}$ are consistent with the efficiency hypothesis (assuming no technological regress) for some family of production functions $\{f^j : j = 1, \ldots, J\}$, where each f^j satisfies Conditions II over $S(x^1, x^2, \ldots, x^j)$. On the other hand, if $y^i < \check{f}^i(x^i)$ for any i, then the given data are not consistent for any family $\{f^j\}$ satisfying the no technological regress assumption, where f^j satisfies Conditions II over $S(x^1, x^2, \ldots, x^j)$ for $j = 1, 2, \ldots, J$.

Geometrically, Test 2a* at step i forms the free disposal convex hull in $N+1$ space of the first i data points $\{(x^j, y^j) : j = 1, 2, \ldots, i\}$ and then checks whether (x^i, y^i) is on or below the frontier of this set. Since we are assuming no technological regress, each of the first i data points (x^j, y^j) should belong to the production possibility set for period i, $S^i \equiv \{(x, y) : y \geqslant 0, x \in S(x^1, x^2, \ldots, x^i), y \leqslant f^i(x)\}$ and since f^i satisfies Conditions II, the free disposal convex hull in $N+1$ space of the first i data points should form an inner approximation to the true set S^i. If the efficiency hypothesis is satisfied, then (x^i, y^i) should be on the boundary of both S^i and the inner approximation to S^i and thus we should have $y^i = \check{f}^i(x^i)$.

Tests 3, 5 and 6 can be modified to allow for the possibility of technical progress in an analogous manner.

We now consider how Test 1b can be modified. Again let j index time so that $j = 1$ is the first period and $j = J$ is the last period (we make this convention for the remainder of this section) but now we suppose that for each period j, the firm's production function f^j satisfies Conditions I. We say that the family of period production functions f^j satisfies the no technological regress assumption if

$$f^i(x) \leqslant f^j(x) \text{ for every } x \geqslant 0_N, \qquad 1 \leqslant i < j \leqslant J. \tag{34}$$

We assume that the J outputs $\{y^j : j = 1, 2, \ldots, J\}$ are all distinct nonnegative numbers. For $i \geqslant 2$, if there is no index $j < i$ such that $y^j > y^i$, define α^{i*} to be any number greater than one; otherwise define α^{i*} as the optimal value of the following LP:

$$\max_{\alpha^i, w^i \geqslant 0_N} \{\alpha^i : w^{iT} x^i \leqslant 1; \alpha^i \leqslant w^{iT} x^j \text{ for all } j = 1, 2, \ldots, i-1 \text{ such that } y^j > y^i\} \equiv \alpha^{i*}. \tag{35}$$

*Test 1b**: If $\alpha^{i*} > 1$ for $i = 2, 3, \ldots, J$, then the data $\{(x^j, y^j) : j = 1, 2, \ldots, J\}$ are consistent with the efficiency hypothesis for some family of production functions $\{f^j : j = 1, 2, \ldots, J\}$ satisfying the no technological regress assumption (34), where each period production function f^j satisfies Conditions I. On the other hand, if any $\alpha^{i*} \leqslant 1$, then the given data are not consistent with the efficiency hypothesis for any family of production functions $\{f^j\}$ satisfying (34) where each f^j satisfies Conditions I.

Test 1b* can be interpreted as follows. If the data are consistent with the efficiency hypothesis, then for $i \geqslant 2$, x^i is on the boundary of the closed convex set

$L^i(y^i) \equiv \{x : f^i(x) \geqslant y^i\}$ and there exists $w^i > 0_N$ such that $w^{iT}x^i = 1$ and $x \in L^i(y^i)$ implies $w^{iT}x \geqslant w^{iT}x^i$. If $j < i$ and $y^j > y^i$, then $y^i < y^j = f^j(x^j) \leqslant f^i(x^j)$ by (34) and thus x^j belongs to the interior of $L^i(y^i)$ which implies that $1 = w^{iT}x^i < w^{iT}x^j$. Now inspect (35) and it can be seen that α^{i*} must be greater than one. Thus if $\alpha^{i*} \leqslant 1$ for any $i \geqslant 2$, then our efficiency hypothesis with no technological regress cannot be consistent with the given data.

Note that it is impossible to reject Test 1b* if the output of the firm *grows* as time increases (the usual case in time series analysis). However, a nonvacuous test will generally result when we modify Tests 4a or 4b to deal with technical progress. The resulting modified tests will be vacuous when an input is singled out to play the role of the z_0 good only if the amount of that input used by the firm *diminishes* as time increases (i.e., only if the negative of the input quantity grows over time). On the other hand, if the singled out input grows steadily over time, then the corresponding no technological regress modified Tests 4a and 4b will equivalent to Tests 4a and 4b in section 3.

We now consider how the tests in section 4 can be modified to deal with technical progress. Consider Test 7. We assume that the y_1^j are all distinct, but we can no longer reorder our observations so that (13) is satisfied since the observations are now ordered by time (i.e., $j = 1$ is the first period, etc.). Suppose that the period j production function f^j has the following properties: f^j is defined over a closed set S^j such that if $(-\hat{y}, x) \in S^j$, then $y \geqslant 0_{M-1}$ and $x \geqslant 0_N$, f^j is continuous from above and at least one solution $(-\hat{y}^{j*}, x^{j*}) \in S^j$ exists for the following cost minimization problem where $p^j \gg 0_{M-1}$ and $w^j \gg 0_N$:

$$\min_{\hat{y}, x} \{w^{jT}x - \hat{p}^{jT}\hat{y} : f^j(-\hat{y}, x) \geqslant y_1^j, (-\hat{y}, x) \in S^j\}. \tag{36}$$

The family of production functions $\{f^j : j = 1, 2, \ldots, J\}$ satisfies the *no technological regress* assumption if for every $i < j$, then $S^i \subset S^j$ and $(-\hat{y}, x) \in S^i$ implies

$$f^i(-\hat{y}, x) \leqslant f^j(-\hat{y}, x). \tag{37}$$

If $\{f^j : j = 1, 2, \ldots, J\}$ satisfies (37) and each f^j satisfies (36), then we say that the family of production functions $\{f^j : j = 1, 2, \ldots, J\}$ satisfies *Conditions I'''*. Given the data $\{(C^j, y^j, \hat{p}^j, w^j) : j = 1, 2, \ldots, J\}$, define C^{i*} as the optimal value of the objective function of the following LP:

$$\min_{\hat{y} \geqslant 0_{M-1}, x \geqslant 0_N} \{w^{iT}x - \hat{p}^{iT}\hat{y} : C^i \leqslant w^{iT}x - \hat{p}^{iT}y \text{ and } C^j \leqslant w^{jT}x - \hat{p}^{jT}\hat{y} \text{ for all } j > i \text{ such that } y_1^j < y_1^i\} \equiv C^{i*}. \tag{38}$$

Test 7b:* If $C^i = C^{i*}$ for $i = 1, 2, \ldots, J$, then the data $\{(C^j, y_1^j, \hat{p}^j, w^j) : j = 1, \ldots, J\}$ are consistent with competitive cost minimizing behavior for some family of production functions $\{f^j : j = 1, \ldots, J\}$ satisfying Conditions I''' where in addition, each f^j can be taken to be quasiconcave and nondecreasing. On the other hand, if C^i $C^i < C^{i*}$ for any i, then the given data are not consistent with competitive cost minimizing behavior for any family f^j satisfying Conditions I'''.

To see why Test 7b* holds, suppose that the data are consistent and let $(-\hat{y}^{i*}, x^{i*})$ be a solution to the cost minimization problem (36) where $j = i$. Then $C^i = w^{iT}x^{i*} - \hat{p}^{iT}\hat{y}^{i*}$ and $y_1^i \leqslant f^i(-\hat{y}^{i*}, x^{i*})$. If $i < j$ and $y_1^j < y_1^i$, then $y_1^j < y_1^i \leqslant f^i(-\hat{y}^{i*}, x^{i*}) \leqslant f^j(-\hat{y}^{i*}, x^{i*})$ and thus $(-\hat{y}^{i*}, x^{i*})$ is feasible for the period j cost minimization problem (36) which implies that $C^j \leqslant w^{jT}x^{i*} - \hat{p}^{jT}\hat{y}^{i*}$. Thus y^{i*}, x^{i*} solves (38) and $C^{i*} = C^i$. This establishes the second half of Test 7b*. To establish the first part, the reader need only modify our discussion of Test 7b appropriately.

It should be noted that it is impossible to reject Test 7b* if (13) holds; i.e., if y_1 *grows* as time increases. Similarly, if we single out an input instead of an output, the resulting Test 7b* cannot be rejected if the singled out input *diminishes* as time increases. However, if the singled out input *grows* as time increases, then Test 7b* becomes equivalent to the corresponding Test 7b. Similar comments apply to Test 10* (which changes (30) to: $C^j \equiv -\hat{p}^{jT}\hat{y}^j + w^{jT}x^j \leqslant -\hat{p}^{jT}\hat{y}^i + w^{jT}x^i; j = i$ and $j > i$ such that $y_1^j < y_1^i$) which becomes identical to Test 10 (except for a relabelling of the time periods) if y_1 diminishes as time increases, etc.

As a final example of how our earlier tests can be modified to deal with technical progress, consider Test 8. We now assume that the production possibility set for period j, S^j, is a closed set such that at least one solution $(y^{j*}, -x^{j*})$ exists for the period j profit maximization problem:

$$\max_{y \geqslant 0_M, x \geqslant 0_N} \{p^{jT}y - w^{jT}x : (y, -x) \in S^j\} \equiv \Pi^j(p^j, w^j) \tag{39}$$

for $j = 1, 2, \ldots, J$. We say that the technology is not subject to technological regress if the period technologies satisfy

$$S^i \subset S^j \qquad \text{if } 1 \leqslant i < j \leqslant J. \tag{40}$$

If the family of production possibility sets $\{S^j : j = 1, 2, \ldots, J\}$ satisfies (40) where each S^j satisfies (39), then we say that the family satisfies *Conditions II‴*. Given the data $\{(\Pi^j, p^j, w^j) = j = 1, 2, \ldots, J\}$ define Π^{i*} as the optimal objective function of the following linear program:

$$\max_{y \geqslant 0_M, x \geqslant 0_N} \{p^{iT}y - w^{iT}x : p^{jT}y - w^{jT}x \leqslant \Pi^j, j = i, i+1, \ldots, J\} \equiv \Pi^{i*}. \tag{41}$$

*Test 8**: If $\Pi^i = \Pi^{i*}$ for $i = 1, 2, \ldots, J$, then the data $\{(\Pi^j, p^j, w^j) : j = 1, 2, \ldots, J\}$ are consistent with competitive profit maximizing behavior for some family of production possibility sets $\{S^j : j = 1, \ldots, J\}$ satisfying Conditions II‴ where in addition each S^j can have the additional properties of convexity and free disposal. On the other hand, if $\Pi^{i*} < \Pi^i$ for any i, then the given data are not consistent with competitive profit maximizing behavior for any family $\{S^j\}$ satisfying Conditions II‴.

To see why Test 8b* holds, suppose that the data are consistent and let $(y^{i*}, -x^{i*}) \in S^i$ be a solution to the period i profit maximization problem (39) where $j = i$. Then $\Pi^i = p^{iT}y^{i*} - w^{iT}x^{i*}$. Moreover, since $S^i \subset S^j$ for $i < j$ by (40), then $(y^{i*}, -x^{i*})$ is a feasible (but not necessarily optimal) solution for the period j profit maximization problem (39) so we have $p^{jT}y^{i*} - w^{jT}x^{i*} \leqslant \Pi^j$ for $j > i$. Thus y^{i*}, x^{i*} solves (41) and $\Pi^i = \Pi^{i*}$. This establishes the second part of Test 8b*, etc.

Test 9 can be modified to allow for the possibility of technological progress in a manner analogous to the above modification of Test 8. Rests 11 and 12 are modified by changing the inequalities (31) to: $\Pi^i \equiv p^{iT}y^i - w^{iT}x^i \geqslant p^{iT}y^j - w^{iT}x^j$ for $j = 1, 2, \ldots, i$.

Thus all of our tests can be modified to allow for the possibility of technological progress. The general effect of the modification is to increase the chances of accepting the hypothesis of efficiency or of optimizing behavior for the given data set (since the number of constraints that the data set must satisfy in order to pass the appropriate test is approximately divided by two when we modify the original test).

7. Conclusion

The tests proposed in the previous sections can be modified or extended in a number of directions. For example, the tests described in section 4 presume that we know precisely which goods are outputs and which goods are inputs (this information is reflected in the nonnegativity constraints $\hat{y} \geqslant 0_{M-1}$, $x \geqslant 0_N$ in (15) and the constraints $y \geqslant 0_M$, $x \geqslant 0_N$ in (22) and (28)). If we do not know whether a particular good is an input or an output, then the corresponding quantity variable in (15), (22) or (28), x_1 say, should be unrestricted in sign. This leads to a slight modification in Tests 7, 8 or 9 and we leave the details to the reader.

The above tests can be modified in yet another direction. For example, suppose we were given price data for a firm or industry $\{(p^j, w^j) : j = 1, \ldots, J\}$ and we were willing to assume that the production possibility set S for the firm or industry satisfied Conditions III″. Then we could run Test 9 and see whether the given price data is consistent with profit maximizing behavior. If Test 9b passes, then we could take the solutions (y^{i*}, x^{i*}) to the linear programs (28) for $i = 1, 2, \ldots, J$ to represent quantity data which are consistent with the given price data and profit maximizing behavior. Usually, the solutions (y^{i*}, x^{i*}) will have zero components and thus will not look "normal". However, suppose we could observe the actual firm or industry quantity data occassionally, say for periods 1 and J. Then we could drop the constraint $w^{iT}x = 1$ in (– 7) and replace it with $\bar{x}^i \leqslant x \leqslant \bar{\bar{x}}^i$ and $\bar{y}^i \leqslant y \leqslant \bar{\bar{y}}^i$ where the bounding vectors $\bar{x}^i$, $\bar{\bar{x}}^i$, $\bar{y}^i$ and $\bar{\bar{y}}^i$ depend on the time period i and the quantity vectors that we observe in periods 1 and J. Now solve the resulting modified LP (28). If $\Pi^{i*} < 0$, then widen the bounds on x and y until the resulting $\Pi^{i*} = 0$. In this case, the resulting solution $x^i \geqslant 0_N$, $y^i \geqslant 0_M$ to the modified LP (28) could represent reasonable *interpolated* period i quantity vectors for our firm or industry. Thus Test 9b could be modified into a procedure for interpolating quantity data given price data and similar modifications are possible for Tests 7b and 8b. Similarly, Tests 2b, 3b, 5b and 6b could be modified in procedures for interpolating price data given quantity data. The strength of these suggested interpolation procedures over traditional procedures is that our suggested procedures will yield interpolated data which are consistent with the appropriate efficiency or optimizing hypothesis under consideration (if such data exist at all).

The tests suggested above by no means exhaust the potential of the nonparametric approach to testing for the consistency of a data set with various regularity conditions on an underlying production or utility function: there are also nonparametric tests for homotheticity [*Hanoch/Rothschild*, 1972, p. 273; *Diewert*, 1973b, p. 424] and for separability [*Afriat*, 1967]. Also, nonparametric tests are not restricted to situations where production is subject to constant or diminishing returns to scale: *Farrell/Fieldhouse* [1962, p. 259] present an example where an increasing returns to scale production function is subjected to a transformation which makes the resulting production possibility set convex (recall also the above tests involving Conditions I where the production function can exhibit increasing returns to scale).

References

Afriat, S.N.: The Construction of Separable Utility Functions from Expenditure Data. Mimeographed, Purdue University, Lafayette 1967.

– : Efficiency Estimation of Production Functions. International Economic Review **13**, 1972, 568–598.

Aigner, D., C.A.K. Lovell and *P. Schmidt*: Formulation and Estimation of Stochastic Frontier Production Function Models. Journal of Econometrics **6**, 1977, 21–38.

Dantzig, G.B.: Linear Programming and Extensions. Princeton, N.J., 1963.

Debreu, G.: The Coefficient of Resource Utilization. Econometrica **19**, 1951, 273–292.

Diewert, W.E.: Functional Forms for Profit and Transformation Functions. Journal of Economic Theory **6**, 1973a, 284–316.

– : Afriat and Revealed Preference Theory. Review of Economic Studies **40**, 1973b, 419–425.

– : Functional Forms Revenue and Factor Requirements Functions. International Economic Review **15**, 1974, 119–130.

– : Exact and Superlative Index Numbers. Journal of Econometrics **4**, 1976, 115–145.

– : Duality Approaches to Microeconomic Theory. Discussion Paper 78–09, University of British Columbia, Vancouver, March 1978.

Färe, R., and *C.A.K. Lovell*: Measuring the Technical Efficiency of Production. Journal of Economic Theory **19**, 1978, 150–162.

Färe, R., C.A.K. Lovell and *K. Zieschang*: Measuring the Technical Efficiency of Multiple Output Production Technologies. Quantitative Studies on Production and Prices. Ed. by W. Eichhorn et al. Würzburg–Wien 1982 (this volume).

Farrell, M.J.: The Measurement of Productive Efficiency. Journal of the Royal Statistical Society, Series A **120**, 1957, 251–281.

Farrell, M.J., and *M. Fieldhouse*: Estimating Efficient Production Functions under Increasing Returns to Scale. Journal of the Royal Statistical Society, Series A **125**, 1962, 252–267.

Gorman, W.M.: Measuring the Quantities of Fixed Factors. In Value, Capital and Growth: Papers in honour of Sir John Hicks. Ed. by J.N. Wolfe. Chicago 1967.

Hanoch, G., and *M. Rothschild*: Testing the Assumptions of Production Theory: A Nonparametric Approach. Journal of Political Economy **80**, 1972, 256, 275.

Jorgenson, D.W., and *Z. Griliches*: The Explanation of Productivity Change. Review of Economic Studies **34**, 1967, 240–283.

Konüs, A.A.: The Problem of the True Index of the Cost of Living. Econometrica **7**, 1939, 10–29.

Lau, L.J.: A Characterization of the Normalized Restricted Profit Function. Journal of Economic Theory **12**, 1976, 131–163.

McFadden, D.: Cost, Revenue and Profit Functions: A Cursory Review. Working Paper No. 86, IBER, University of California, Berkeley 1966.

– : Cost, Revenue and Profit Functions. Production Economics: A Dual Approach to Theory and Applications, Vol. 1. Ed. by M. Fuss and D. McFadden. Amsterdam 1978, 3–109.

Rockafellar, R.T.: Convex Analysis. Princeton, N.J., 1970.

Samuelson, P.A.: Foundations of Economic Analysis. Cambridge, MA, 1947.

Quantitative Studies on Production and Prices © Physica-Verlag, Würzburg–Wien, 1983.

Measuring the Technical Efficiency of Multiple Output Production Technologies

Rolf Färe, C.A. Knox Lovell and *Kimberly Zieschang*[1])

1. Introduction

In this paper we consider a production unit employing many inputs to produce many outputs, subject to the constraints imposed by given technology. Our purpose is to present and analyze various measures of the effectiveness with which inputs are transformed into outputs. Early efforts in this direction were made by *Koopmans* [1951] and *Debreu* [1951]. Koopmans defined a feasible input-output vector to be efficient if it is technologically impossible to increase any output and/or to reduce any input without simultaneously reducing other outputs and/or increasing other inputs. Using this definition, he was able to prove that a vector is efficient if, and only if, it possesses a positive normal to the production possibilities set. While Koopmans offered a definition and a characterization of efficiency, Debreu provided a measure of efficiency with his "coefficient of resource utilization." This coefficient is computed as one minus the maximum equiproportionate reduction in all inputs consistent with continued production of existing outputs, and from it Debreu obtained a measure of the cost of inefficiency. More recently *Vincze* [1960] and *Eichhorn* [1972, 1978a, 1978b] have considered a production process involving many variable inputs, one fixed input, many outputs and a time dimension. In this context he defined the price-dependent notions of technical and economic "effectiveness" in terms of families of functional equations, and derived closed-form parametric indexes of technical and economic effectiveness as solutions to the respective families of functional equations.

Despite this common theme these studies have little else in common. They consider different production technologies and investigate different notions of efficiency, leaving us without a unified treatment of efficiency in a multiple output production unit. This paper is a first step toward filling that gap. We consider a fairly standard multiple input, multiple output production unit having technological characteristics similar to those of *Shephard* [1970], and we derive and analyze a variety of price-independent measures of technical efficiency. The multiplicity of possible efficiency measures stems from three sources. First, there exists a number of reference sets against which to measure the efficiency of a given input-output vector, and each reference set has its own family of efficiency measures. Second, none of the reference sets is likely to be a singleton, leaving room for choice among various elements of each reference set as the appropriate refer-

---

[1]) We are indebted to W. Erwin Diewert and Wolfgang Eichhorn for their helpful comments.

ence vector. Third, different assumptions on the structure of technology suggest different efficiency measures, a point recently made by *Färe/Lovell* [1978] in a single output context. Thus a major theme of this paper is that there is no such thing as "the" measure of efficiency.

The plan of the paper is as follows. In section 2 we describe the technology by which inputs are transformed into outputs. In section 3 we define what we mean by efficiency, and we propose a list of properties that a measure of efficiency should satisfy. In sections 4–6 we propose and analyze three different types of input-based efficiency measure. Section 7 concludes the paper.

2. Production Technology

We consider a production unit using input vector $x \equiv (x_1, \ldots, x_n) \in R^n_+$ to produce output vector $u \equiv (u_1, \ldots, u_m) \in R^m_+$. Production technology is represented by an input correspondence $u \to L(u) \subset R^n_+$ mapping outputs into subsets of inputs. The input possibilities set $L(u)$ contains all input vectors $x \in R^n_+$ capable of producing at least output vector $u \in R^m_+$. The input correspondence is assumed to satisfy the following properties: [*Shephard*, 1970, 1974]:

L.1 $L(0) = R^n_+$ and $0 \notin L(u)$ for $u \geqslant 0$. [2]

L.2 For $\{|u^r|\} \to +\infty$, $\bigcap\limits_{r=1}^{\infty} L(u^r)$ is empty.

L.3 If $x \in L(u)$, $\lambda x \in L(u)$ for $\lambda \in [1, +\infty)$.

L.4 If $x \geqslant 0$ and $\bar{\lambda} x \in L(\bar{u})$, $\bar{u} \geqslant 0$, for some $\bar{\lambda} \in (0, +\infty)$, the ray $\{\lambda x : \lambda \in [0, +\infty)\}$ intersects all input sets $L(\theta \bar{u})$ for $\theta \in [0, +\infty)$.

L.5 $u \to L(u)$ is a closed correspondence.

L.6 $L(\theta u) \subset L(u)$ for $\theta \in [1, +\infty)$.

Two additional properties are occasionally assumed, namely

L.3.S If $x' \geqq x$ and $x \in L(u)$ then $x' \in L(u)$.

L.6.S $L(u') \subset L(u)$ for $u' \geqq u$.

Production technology also can be represented by an output correspondence $x \to P(x) \subset R^m_+$, mapping inputs into subsets of outputs. $P(x)$ denotes all output vectors obtainable from x and satisfies properties (P.1–P.6) inversely related to (L.1–L.6). The reciprocal relationship between the input correspondence and the output correspondence characterizing production technology is $x \in L(u) \Leftrightarrow u \in P(x)$, and we have $P(x) = \{u \in R^m_+ : x \in L(u)\}$ and inversely $L(u) = \{x \in R^n_+ : u \in P(x)\}$. Thus for a multiple input, multiple output production unit one may use either $u \to L(u)$ or $x \to P(x)$ as production functions with properties (L.1–L.6) $\Leftrightarrow$ (P.1–P.6). It is also possible to add either or both of L.3.S $\Leftrightarrow$ P.3.S and L.6.S $\Leftrightarrow$ P.6.S.

---

[2]) $\geqslant$ means $\geqq$ but not $=$.

For any given output vector the input isoquant is defined as:

$$\operatorname{Isoq} L(u) := \begin{cases} \{x \in R^n_+ : x \in L(u), \lambda x \notin L(u) \text{ if } \lambda \in [0, 1)\}, u \geqslant 0 \\ \text{and} \\ \{0\}, u = 0 \end{cases}$$

and the input efficient subset is defined as:

$$\operatorname{Eff} L(u) := \begin{cases} \{x \in R^n_+ : x \in L(u), y \leqslant x \Rightarrow y \notin L(u)\}, u \geqslant 0 \\ \text{and} \\ \{0\}, u = 0 \end{cases}$$

For any given input vector the output isoquant is defined as:

$$\operatorname{Isoq} P(x) := \begin{cases} \{u \in R^m_+ : u \in P(x), \theta u \notin P(x) \text{ if } \theta > 1\}, u \geqslant 0 \\ \text{and} \\ \{0\}, u = 0 \end{cases}$$

and the output efficient subset is defined as:

$$\operatorname{Eff} P(x) := \begin{cases} \{u \in R^m_+ : u \in P(x), v \geqslant u \Rightarrow v \notin P(x)\}, u \geqslant 0 \\ \text{and} \\ \{0\}, u = 0. \end{cases}$$

We also make use of the input distance function

$$\Psi(u, x) := [\min\{\lambda : \lambda x \in L(u), \lambda \in [0, +\infty)\}]^{-1}$$

and the output distance function

$$\Omega(x, u) := [\max\{\theta : \theta u \in P(x), \theta \in [0, +\infty)\}]^{-1}.$$

3. Requirements on Price-Independent Efficiency Measures

Consider a production unit transforming inputs into outputs in a technically inefficient manner. An input measure of technical efficiency compares the observed input vector to the set of smaller input vectors that are capable of producing the observed output vector. Since this involves a point-to-set comparison, a number of different input measures is possible. In addition, each different measure can be given a direct and an implicit characterization.

Definition 3.1: An *input measure* of technical efficiency is a function[3]) I: $\bar{R}^m_+ \times \bar{R}^n_+ \to R_+ \cup \{+\infty\}$ that compares the observed input vector $x \in \bar{R}^n_+$ with smaller

---

[3]) $\bar{R}^m_+ := R^m_+ / \{0\}$ and likewise for $\bar{R}^n_+$.

feasible input vector for fixed observed output vector $u \in \bar{R}^m_+$, and that satisfies the following properties:

$\mathcal{I}.1$ If $x \in L(u)$, then $\mathcal{I}(u, x) = 1 \Leftrightarrow x \in \text{Eff}\, L(u)$.

$\mathcal{I}.2$ If $x \in L(u)$ and if $x \notin \text{Eff}\, L(u)$, then $\mathcal{I}(u, x)$ should compare x to some $x^* \in \text{Eff}\, L(u)$.

$\mathcal{I}.3$ If $x \in L(u)$ and $\lambda \geqq 1$, then $\mathcal{I}(u, \lambda x) \leqq \lambda^{-1}\, \mathcal{I}(u, x)$.

$\mathcal{I}.4$ If $x \in L(u)$, and if $x' \geqslant x$, then $\mathcal{I}(u, x) > \mathcal{I}(u, x')$.

Property $\mathcal{I}.1$ requires an input measure to call (u, x) technically efficient if, and only if, x belongs to the input efficient subset of $L(u)$. Property $\mathcal{I}.2$ is an attempt to narrow somewhat the set of smaller input vectors with which x is to be compared by an input efficiency measure. It states that x should be compared with some x^* belonging to the input efficient subset of $L(u)$, although it does not specify the location of $x^* \in \text{Eff}\, L(u)$. Property $\mathcal{I}.3$ is a homogeneity property, and requires a feasible scaling of an input vector to lead to a less than or equal inverse scaling of the input efficiency measure. Property $\mathcal{I}.4$ is a sensitivity property requiring input efficiency to vary inversely with input usage. For production technology satisfying (L.1–L.6) $\Leftrightarrow$ (P.1–P.6) the conjunction of these properties guarantees that the input efficiency measure $\mathcal{I}(u, x)$ attains a maximum value of unity for all $x \in \text{Eff}\, L(u)$, declines with any increase in input usage, and declines equiproportionately with any proportionate increase in input usage.

4. Radial Measures of Efficiency

In this section we consider a pair of radial measures of efficiency, due originally to *Debreu* [1951], popularized in a single-output context by *Farrell* [1957], and utilized in a number of empirical studies.[4]) Despite their popularity, their simplicity renders them deficient in a number of respects.

Definition 4.1: The function $\mathcal{F}_d: \bar{R}^m_+ \times \bar{R}^n_+ \to R_+ \cup \{+\infty\}$ defined by $\mathcal{F}_d(u, x) := \min\{\lambda : \lambda x \in L(u)\}$ for $x \in L(u)$ and by $\mathcal{F}_d(u, x) := +\infty$ for $x \notin L(u)$ is called the *direct radial* measure of technical efficiency.

Definition 4.2: The function $\mathcal{F}_i: \bar{R}^m_+ \times \bar{R}^n_+ \to R_+ \cup \{+\infty\}$ defined by $\mathcal{F}_i(u, x) := \min\{\theta : x \in L(u/\theta)\}$ for $x \in L(u)$ and by $\mathcal{F}_i(u, x) := +\infty$ for $x \notin L(u)$ is called the *implicit radial* measure of technical efficiency.

The direct radial measure $\mathcal{F}_d(u, x)$ gives the maximum amount by which an observed input vector can be proportionately decreased and still remain capable of producing the observed output vector. It corresponds to Debreu's "coefficient of resource utilization," and in the single output case to Farrell's input-based measure of technical efficiency. The implicit radial measure $\mathcal{F}_i(u, x)$ gives the maximum amount by which an observed output vector can be proportionately increased and still remain producible with the observed input vector. It corresponds in the single product case to Farrell's output-based measure of

---

[4]) References to much of the empirical literature are available in *Försund/Lovell/Schmidt* [1980].

technical efficiency. It is clear that for $x \in L(u)$, $F_d(u, x) = [\Psi(u, x)]^{-1}$ and $F_i(u, x) = [\Omega(u, x)]^{-1}$, so that the properties of the two radial efficiency measures are inherited from those of the corresponding distance functions. This enables us to provide the following convenient characterization of input and output possibilities sets.

Proposition 4.1:
(a) for $u \in \bar{R}^m_+$, $L(u) = \{x \in R^n_+ : 0 < F_d(u, x) \leqq 1\}$.
(b) for $x \in \bar{R}^n_+$, $P(x) = \{u \in R^m_+ : 0 < F_i(u, x) \leqq 1\}$.

Proof: For part (a), let $x \in L(u)$, $u \in \bar{R}^m_+$, so that $\lambda \in [0, 1]$. Since $0 \notin L(u)$ for $u \in \bar{R}^m_+$, $\lambda > 0$. If $x \notin L(u)$, $u \in \bar{R}^m_+$, $F_d = +\infty$. Part (b) is proved in a similar manner. □

Proposition 4.2:
(a) $F_d(u, x)$ satisfies $I.3$ but does not satisfy $I.1$, $I.2$, $I.4$.
(b) If Eff $L(u) =$ Isoq $L(u)$ and $x \geqq y \in L(u) \Rightarrow x \in L(u)$, $u \in \bar{R}^m_+$, then $F_d(u, x)$ satisfies $I.1$–$I.4$.
(c) If $F_d(u, x)$ satisfies $I.1$, then Eff $L(u) =$ Isoq $L(u)$.

Proof: (a) It follows trivially from Definition 4.1 that $F_d(u, x)$ satisfies $I.3$. To show that $F_d(u, x)$ does not satisfy $\{I.1, I.2, I.4\}$ consider the following example: $L(u) = \{x \in R^2_+ : \min(x_1, x_2) \geqq u\}$. This input correspondence satisfies L.1–L.6. To show that $F_d(u, x)$ does not satisfy $I.1$ let $x_1 = 2, x_2 = u = 1$. Then $F_d(1, 2, 1) = 1$ even though $(2, 1) \notin$ Eff $L(1)$. To show that $F_d(u, x)$ does not satisfy $I.2$, let $x_1 = 4$, $x_2 = 2$ and $u = 1$. Then $(4, 2)$ is compared with $(2, 1)$, even though $(2, 1) \notin$ Eff $L(1)$. To show that $F_d(u, x)$ does not satisfy $I.4$, let $x_1 = 3, x_2 = u = 1$. Then $(3, 1) \geqslant (2, 1)$ even though $F_d(1, 3, 1) = F_d(1, 2, 1)$. This completes the proof of part (a).

The proof of part (b) is obvious. Part (c) follows directly from Definition 4.1 and the definitions of Eff $L(u)$ and Isoq $L(u)$, since Isoq $L(u) = \{x \in R^n_+ : \Psi(u, x) = 1\} = \{x \in R^n_+ : F_d(u, x) = 1\}$. □

It follows that the direct radial measure can distinguish efficient from inefficient input-output vectors only under fairly restrictive technological conditions, conditions that are unlikely to be known in advance of computation. This makes use of $F_d(u, x)$ risky despite its appealing simplicity. Before proceeding to $F_i(u, x)$, we first examine more closely these technological conditions.

Definition 4.3: For all $(u, x) \in \bar{R}^m_+ \times \bar{R}^n_+$ such that $P(x) \neq \{0\}$ and $L(u) \neq \emptyset$, consider

I:1 Isoq $L(\theta u) \cap$ Isoq $L(u)$ empty for $\theta \neq 1$
I:2 Isoq $P(\lambda x) \cap$ Isoq $P(x)$ empty for $\lambda \neq 1$

II:1 $x \in$ Isoq $L(u) \Rightarrow u \in$ Isoq $P(x)$
II:2 $u \in$ Isoq $P(x) \Rightarrow x \in$ Isoq $L(u)$

III:1 $u \geqslant v \geqslant 0 \Rightarrow$ Isoq $L(u) \cap$ Isoq $L(v)$ empty
III:2 $x \geqslant y \geqslant 0 \Rightarrow$ Isoq $P(x) \cap$ Isoq $P(y)$ empty

IV:1 Eff $L(u) =$ Isoq $L(u)$
IV:2 Eff $P(x) =$ Isoq $P(x)$.

Lemma 4.1: I:1 ⇔ II:1 and I:2 ⇔ II:2.

Proof: *Al-Ayat/Färe* [1979, p. 628].

Lemma 4.2: III:1 ⇒ I:1 and III:2 ⇒ I:2.

The proof is trivial and is omitted.

Lemma 4.3:

(a) III:1 and III:2 ⇒ IV:1
(b) III:1 and III:2 ⇒ IV:2
(c) II:2 and IV:1 ⇒ III:2
(d) II:1 and IV:2 ⇒ III:1.

Proof: *Färe* [1982].

Proposition 4.3:

(a) $F_i(u, x)$ does not satisfy $\{I.1 - I.4\}$.
(b) $F_i(u, x)$ satisfies $I.1$ if I:1, I:2, IV:1 hold.
(c) $F_i(u, x)$ satisfies $I.2$ if IV:1 holds.
(d) $F_i(u, x)$ satisfies $I.3$ with equality if, and only if, $L(\lambda u) = \lambda L(u)$.
(e) $F_i(u, x)$ satisfies $I.4$ if I:2 and L.3.S hold.
(f) $F_i(u, x)$ satisfies $\{I.1 - I.4\}$ if $L(\lambda u) = \lambda L(u)$, IV:1, L.3.S hold.

Proof:

(a) Let $L(u) := \{x \in R^2_+ : (\min\{x_1, x_2\})^2 \geqq u\}$. It follows from the proof of part (a) of Proposition 4.2 that $F_i(u, x)$ does not satisfy $I.1$, $I.2$, $I.4$. It is trivial to see that $F_i(u, x)$ does not satisfy $I.3$ for this $L(u)$.

(b) Suppose $F_i(u, x) = 1$. Then $u \in \text{Isoq}\, P(x)$. If I:2 holds, $u \in \text{Isoq}\, P(x)$ implies $x \in \text{Isoq}\, L(u)$. By IV:1 $\text{Eff}\, L(u) = \text{Isoq}\, L(u)$ and so $F_i(u, x) = 1$ is sufficient for $x \in \text{Eff}\, L(u)$. Suppose $x \in \text{Eff}\, L(u) \subset \text{Isoq}\, L(u)$. By I:1 $x \in \text{Isoq}\, L(u)$ implies $u \in \text{Isoq}\, P(x)$. If $u \in \text{Isoq}\, P(x)$ then $F_i(u, x) = 1$. Hence $x \in \text{Eff}\, L(u)$ is sufficient for $F_i(u, x) = 1$.

(c) Proof trivial.

(d) $F_i(u, x) = [\Omega(u, x)]^{-1}$ and $\Omega(u, \lambda x) = \lambda^{-1}\Omega(u, x)$ iff $P(\lambda x) = \lambda P(x)$ iff $L(\lambda u) = \lambda L(u)$.

(e) Suppose $x' \geqslant x$. From P.3.S $\Omega(u, x') \leqq \Omega(u, x)$ and $F_i(u, x') \geqq F_i(u, x)$. From I:2 and P.3.S, if $x' \geqslant x$, $F_i(u, x') > F_i(u, x)$ and $I.4$ holds.

(f) $L(\lambda u) = \lambda L(u)$ implies I:1 and I:2. Given L.3.S and IV:1, the result follows from parts (b)–(e).

□

Comparing Proposition 4.2 with Proposition 4.3 reveals that the technological conditions under which $F_i(u, x)$ satisfies $\{I.1 - I.4\}$ are even more restrictive than those under which $F_d(u, x)$ satisfies $\{I.1 - I.4\}$. In addition to $\text{Eff}\, L(u) = \text{Isoq}\, L(u)$, it is required that $L(\lambda u) = \lambda L(u)$ and that inputs be freely disposable. We next examine the relationship between $F_d(u, x)$ and $F_i(u, x)$.

Lemma 4.4: For $(u, x) \in \bar{R}^m_+ \times \bar{R}^n_+$, $P(x) \neq \{0\}$, and $L(u) \neq \emptyset$, $L(\theta u) \subseteq\!\!\equiv\!\!\supseteq \theta L(u) \Leftrightarrow \frac{1}{\theta} P(x) \subseteq\!\!\equiv\!\!\supseteq P(x/\theta)$.

Proof: Assume $L(\theta u) \subset \theta L(u)$, and let $x \in L(\theta u)$. Then, and only then, $u \in (1/\theta) P(x)$ and $u \in P(x/\theta)$. Now assume that there is a $v \in (1/\theta) P(x)$ such that $v \notin P(x/\theta)$. Then $x \in L(\theta v)$ but $x \notin \theta L(v)$, which contradicts $L(\theta u) \subset \theta L(u)$ and proves one implication. The others follow similarly. □

It is a direct consequence of Lemma 4.4 that the following two propositions hold. Single-output analogues to these propositions are proved in *Färe/Lovell* [1978, p. 156].

Proposition 4.4: $F_i(u, x) = F_d(u, x)$ if, and only if, $L(\lambda u) = \lambda L(u)$.

Proposition 4.5: $F_i(u, x) \gtreqless F_d(u, x)$ if, and only if, $L(\theta u) \subseteq\!\!\equiv\!\!\supseteq \theta L(u)$.

Finally we present two results showing conditions under which $F_d(u, x)$ and $F_i(u, x)$ decompose, enabling one to infer $F_d(u, x)$ from $F_d(1, x)$ or $F_i(u, x)$ from $F_i(u, 1)$. These two propositions follow directly from the facts that $F_d(u, x) = [\Psi(u, x)]^{-1}$ and $F_i(u, x) = [\Omega(u, x)]^{-1}$ and from similar results of *Shephard* [1970] on $\Psi(u, x)$ and $\Omega(u, x)$.

Proposition 4.6: $F_d(u, x) = f(u) \cdot F_d(1, x)$ if, and only if, $L(u) = f(u) \cdot L(1)$ (i.e. input homotheticity). Here $1 = (1, 1, \ldots, 1)$, m-times.

Proposition 4.7: $F_i(u, x) = g(x) \cdot F_i(u, 1)$ if, and only if, $P(x) = g(x) \cdot P(1)$ (i.e. output homotheticity). Here $1 = (1, 1, \ldots, 1)$, n-times

5. Asymmetric Measures of Efficiency

Mainly for econometric convenience *Samuelson* [1966] and *Diewert* [1973] among others have suggested an asymmetric representation of production technology, singling out one output, or one input, as a function of the remaining $m + n - 1$ variables. This in turn suggests an asymmetric input measure of technical efficiency. In this section we consider four such measures, two of which have been proposed by *Färe* [1975] and discussed by *Kopp* [1980] in a single output context.

Definition 5.1: The functions $A^j_d: \bar{R}^m_+ \times \bar{R}^n_+ \to R_+ \cup \{+\infty\}$ defined by $A^j_d(u, x) :=$ $\min \{\lambda_j \in [0, 1]: (x_1, \ldots, \lambda_j x_j, \ldots, x_n) \in L(u)\}$ for $x_j > 0$ and $(x_1, \ldots, \lambda_j x_j, \ldots, x_n) \in L(u)$ for some $\lambda_j \in [0, 1]$, by $A^j_d(u, x) = 1$ for $x_j = 0$ and $(x_1, \ldots, 0, \ldots, x_n) \in L(u)$, and by $A^j_d(u, x) = +\infty$ for $(x_1, \ldots, \lambda_j x_j, \ldots, x_n) \notin L(u)$ for all $\lambda_j \in [0, 1]$, $j = 1, 2, \ldots, n$, are called the *direct asymmetric* measures of technical efficiency.

Definition 5.2: The functions $A_i^j: \bar{R}_+^m \times \bar{R}_+^n \rightarrow R_+ \cup \{+\infty\}$ defined by $A_i^j(u, x) := \min\{\theta_j \in [0, 1]: x \in L(u_1, \ldots, u_j/\theta_j, \ldots, u_m)\}$ for $u_j > 0$ and $(u_1, \ldots, u_j/\theta_j, \ldots, u_m) \in P(x)$ for some $\theta_j \in [0, 1]$, by $A_i^j(u, x) = 1$ for $u_j = 0$ and $(u_1, \ldots, 0, \ldots, u_m) \in P(x)$, and by $A_i^j(u, x) = +\infty$ for $(u_1, \ldots, u_j/\theta_j, \ldots, u_m) \notin P(x)$ for all $\theta_j \in [0, 1]$, $j = 1, 2, \ldots, m$, are called the *implicit asymmetric* measures of technical efficiency.

For $x \in L(u)$, $u \geqslant 0$, $A_d^j(u, x)$ compares the observed input vector x to the smallest feasible input vector formed from x by shrinking its j-th element and holding all other elements fixed. It measures the maximum proportionate shrinkage in x_j consistent with continued production of $u \geqslant 0$. Unfortunately under {L.1–L.6} the reference set of the direct asymmetric measures is the boundary of $L(u)$, which may be larger than Isoq $L(u)$, which may be larger than Eff $L(u)$. For reasons even stronger than those previously noted with reference to the direct radial measure, this fact makes the direct asymmetric measures unacceptable measures of technical efficiency. A similar argument holds for the implicit asymmetric measures. Since neither $A_d^j(u, x)$ nor $A_i^j(u, x)$ satisfies {I.1–I.4} we proceed directly to a pair of measures derived from $A_d^j(u, x)$ and $A_i^j(u, x)$.

Definition 5.3: The function $A_d: \bar{R}_+^m \times \bar{R}_+^n \rightarrow R_+ \cup \{+\infty\}$ defined by $A_d(u, x) := \min\{A_d^j(u, x)\}$, $j = 1, 2, \ldots, n$, is called the *overall direct asymmetric* measure of technical efficiency.

Definition 5.4: The function $A_i: \bar{R}_+^m \times \bar{R}_+^n \rightarrow R_+ \cup \{+\infty\}$ defined by $A_i(u, x) := \min\{A_i^j(u, x)\}$, $j = 1, 2, \ldots, m$, is called the *overall implicit asymmetric* measure of technical efficiency.

Proposition 5.1:
(a) $A_d(u, x)$ satisfies I.1 and I.3.
(b) $A_d(u, x)$ does not satisfy I.2 and I.4.

Proof:
(a) That $A_d(u, x)$ satisfies I.1 is proved in *Färe* [1975, p. 322]. To see that $A_d(u, x)$ satisfies I.3, let $\delta \geqq 1$ and consider

$$\begin{aligned} A_d^j(u, \delta x) &= \min\{\lambda_j \in [0, 1]: (\delta x_1, \ldots, \lambda_j, \delta x_j, \ldots, \delta x_n) \in L(u)\} \\ &\leqq \delta^{-1} A_d^j(u, \delta x_1, \ldots, x_j, \ldots, \delta x_n) \\ &= \delta^{-1} A_d^j(u, x) \end{aligned}$$

from which it follows that $A_d(u, \delta x) \leqq \delta^{-1} A_d(u, x)$.

(b) To see that $A_d(u, x)$ does not satisfy I.2 and I.4 consider $L(u) = \{(x_1, x_2) \in R_+^2: \min\{x_1, x_2\} \geqq u\}$. For $u = 1, x_1 = 4, x_2 = 2$ we have $A_d(1, 4, 2) = 0.25$ with reference vector $x^* = (1, 2) \notin \text{Eff}\, L\,(1)$. Thus $A_d\,(u, x)$ does not satisfy I.2. Next let $u = 1, y_1 = 4, y_2 = 3$, so that $A_d\,(1, 4, 3) = 0.25 = A_d\,(1, 4, 2)$ even though $y \geqslant x$. Thus $A_d\,(u, x)$ does not satisfy I.4. □

Proposition 5.2: If inputs are freely disposable (L.3.S holds), $L\,(u) = \{x \in R^n_+ : 0 < A_d\,(u, x) \leqq 1\}, u \geqslant 0$.

Proof: Färe [1975, p. 322].

Proposition 5.3: For all $(u, x) \in \bar{R}^m_+ \times \bar{R}^n_+$, $A_d\,(u, x) \leqq F_d\,(u, x)$.

The proof is trivial and is omitted.

Proposition 5.4: $A_i\,(u, x)$ does not satisfy $\{I.1 - I.4\}$.

Proof: The proof for I.2 and I.4 parallels that for Proposition 5.1. The proof for I.1 and I.3 is trivial. □

Proposition 5.5: $\text{Eff}\, P\,(x) = \{u \in R^m_+ : A_i\,(u, x) = 1\}$. If outputs are freely disposable (L.6.S holds), then $P\,(x) = \{u \in R^m_+ : 0 < A_i\,(u, x) \leqq 1\}$.

The proof follows those of Propositions 5.1 (a) and 5.2, and is omitted.

Our conclusions regarding $A_d\,(u, x)$ and $A_i\,(u, x)$ are similar to our conclusions regarding $F_d\,(u, x)$ and $F_i\,(u, x)$. The overall direct asymmetric measure, which is preferred to the overall implicit asymmetric measure, remains an unsatisfactory measure of technical efficiency. The shortcomings of the asymmetric measures are traceable to the fact that they, like the radial measures, impose overly severe restrictions on the set of vectors with which to compare an observed vector. These restrictions can easily prevent the reference vector from belonging to the appropriate efficient subset.

6. Nonradial Measures of Efficiency

We now consider a pair of nonradial measures that contain the radial and asymmetric measures as special cases and whose greater flexibility enhances their performance as efficiency measures. Whereas the radial measures scale all inputs (or outputs) equiproportionately, and the asymmetric measures scale only one input (or output), the nonradial measures can scale each input (or output) in different proportions. The benefits of this flexibility for the direct nonradial measure are revealed in Proposition 6.1.

Definition 6.1: The function $R_d : \bar{R}^m_+ \times \bar{R}^n_+ \to R_+ \cup \{+\infty\}$ defined by

$R_d\,(u, x) := \min\, \{(\sum_{i=1}^{k} \lambda_{r_i}/k) : (\lambda_{r_1} x_{r_1}, \ldots, \lambda_{r_k} x_{r_k}; \ldots) \in L\,(u), \lambda_{r_i} \in (0, 1],$
$i = 1, \ldots, k\}, k \in \{1, \ldots, n\}$ for $\{y : 0 \leqq y \leqq x\} \cap L\,(u)$ not empty, and by $R_d\,(u, x) := +\infty$ for $\{y : 0 \leqq y \leqq x\} \cap L\,(u)$ empty, is called the *direct Russell* measure of technical efficiency.

Definition 6.2: The function $R_i: \bar{R}^m_+ \times \bar{R}^n_+ \to R_+ \cup \{+\infty\}$ defined by $R_i(u, x) := \min \{(\sum_{j=1}^{l} \theta_{r_j}/l): x \in L(u_{r_1}/\theta_{r_1}, \ldots, u_{r_l}/\theta_{r_l}; \ldots), \theta_{r_j} \in (0, 1]$, $j = 1, \ldots, l\}, l \in \{1, \ldots, m\}$ for $\{v: v \geqq u\} \cap P(x)$ not empty, and by $R_i(u, x) := +\infty$ for $\{v: v \geqq u\} \cap P(x)$ empty, is called the *implicit Russell* measure of technical efficiency.

Since each element of $x \in L(u)$ can be weighted by a different scalar, $R_d(u, x)$ can be a nonradial measure. It contains $F_d(u, x)$ as a special case ($\lambda_{r_i} = \lambda$ for $i = 1, \ldots, n$) and the $A^j_d(u, x)$ as other special cases ($\lambda_{r_i} = 1$ for all $i \neq j$). Although in $R_d(u, x)$ the unweighted arithmetic mean of the scalars $\lambda_{r_i} \in (0, 1], i = 1, \ldots, k$, is minimized, other mean functions (such as the unweighted geometric or harmonic means) could be used as mimimands and would merely lead to different indexes which would preserve the efficiency ranking of inputs assigned by $R_d(u, x)$. Each of these observations applies with equal force to $R_i(u, x)$.

Proposition 6.1: $R_d(u, x)$ satisfies $\{I.1 - I.4\}$.

The proof follows that of *Färe/Lovell* [1978; p. 158].

Proposition 6.2: If inputs are freely disposable (L.3.S holds), $L(u) = \{x \in R^n_+: 0 < R_d(u, x) \leqq 1\}, u \geqslant 0$.

The proof follows that of *Färe/Lovell* [1978; p. 159].

Proposition 6.1 demonstrates that the direct Russell measure meets all of the requirements for an efficiency measure for any production technology satisfying only properties {L.1–L.6}. It meets these requirements because its flexibility enables it to use Eff $L(u)$ as its reference set, an ability not shared by the less flexible direct radial and direct asymmetric measures. Proposition 6.2 demonstrates that the direct Russell measure completely characterizes production technology under {L.1–L.6, L.3.S}.

Proposition 6.3:

(a) $R_i(u, x)$ does not satisfy $\{I.1 - I.4\}$.

(b) $R_i(u, x)$ satisfies $I.1$ if I:1, I:2, IV:1, and IV:2 hold.

(c) $R_i(u, x)$ satisfies $I.2$ if I:2 and IV:1 hold.

(d) $R_i(u, x)$ satisfies $I.3$ if $L(\lambda u) = \lambda L(u)$.

(e) $R_i(u, x)$ satisfies $I.4$ if I:2, IV:1, and L.3.S hold.

(f) $R_i(u, x)$ satisfies $I.1$, $I.2$, $I.3$, and $I.4$ if $L(\lambda u) = \lambda L(u)$, IV:1, IV:2 and L.3.S hold.

Proof:

(a) Let $L(u) = \{x \in R^2_+: (\min\{x_1, x_2\})^2 \geqq u\}$. The proof follows that of Proposition 4.2 (a) for $I.1$, $I.2$, $I.4$. Trivially, $L(u)$ above does not satisfy $I.3$.

(b) Suppose $R_i(u, x) = 1$. Then $u \in \text{Eff}\, P(x) \subset \text{Isoq}\, P(u)$. If I:2 holds, $u \in \text{Isoq}\, P(x)$

implies $x \in \text{Isoq}\, L(u)$. By IV:1, $\text{Eff}\, L(u) = \text{Isoq}\, L(u)$, and $R_i(u, x) = 1$ is sufficient for $x \in \text{Eff}\, L(u)$. Suppose $x \in \text{Eff}\, L(u) \subset \text{Isoq}\, L(u)$. If I:1 holds, then $x \in \text{Isoq}\, L(u)$ implies $u \in \text{Isoq}\, P(x)$. By IV:2, $\text{Isoq}\, P(x) = \text{Eff}\, P(x)$. $u \in \text{Eff}\, P(x)$ iff $R_i(u, x) = 1$, hence if $x \in \text{Eff}\, L(u)$, $R_i(u, x) = 1$, establishing necessity.

(c) Proof trivial.

(d)
$$\begin{aligned} R_i(u, \lambda x) &= \min \{(\sum_{i=1}^{k} \theta_{r_i}/k) \colon \lambda x \in L(\theta_{r_1}^{-1} \cdot u_{r_1}, \dots, \theta_{r_k}^{-1} \cdot u_{r_k}; \dots, 0), \\ &\quad \theta_{r_i} \in (0, 1]\} \\ &= \min \{(\sum_{i=1}^{k} \theta_{r_i}/k \colon x \in L((\lambda\theta_{r_1})^{-1} \cdot u_{r_1}, \dots, (\lambda\theta_{r_k})^{-1} u_{r_k}; \dots, 0), \\ &\quad \theta_{r_i} \in (0, 1]\} \\ &= \frac{1}{\lambda} \min \{(\sum_{i=1}^{k} (\theta_{r_i}\lambda)/k) \colon x \in L((\lambda\theta_{r_i})^{-1} u_{r_1}, \dots, (\lambda\theta_{r_k})^{-1} \\ &\quad u_{r_k}; \dots, 0), \lambda \cdot \theta_{r_i} \in (0, \lambda]\} \\ &\leqq \frac{1}{\lambda} \min \{\sum_{i=1}^{k} (\mu_{r_i}/k) \colon x \in L(\mu_{r_1}^{-1} u_{r_1}, \dots, \mu_{r_k}^{-1} u_{r_k}; \dots, 0), \\ &\quad \mu_{r_i} \in (0, 1]\} \end{aligned}$$

since $\lambda \geqq 1$.

(e) From Lemma 4.1, I:2 iff II:2. From Proposition 4.4, II:2 and IV:1 implies III:2. From free input disposal L.3.S, for $x \geqslant y \geqslant 0$, $P(x) \supset P(y)$, and from III:2, $x \geqslant y \geqslant 0$ implies $\text{Isoq}\, P(x) \cap \text{Isoq}\, P(y) = \emptyset$. Hence, if $(\theta_{r_1}^*, \dots, \theta_{r_K}^*)$ is such that $(\sum_{i=1}^{k} \theta_{r_i}^*/k) = R_i(u, x)$, and if $(\theta_{r_1}^{**}, \dots, \theta_{r_k}^{**})$ is such that $(\sum_{i=1}^{k} \theta_{r_i}^{**}/k) = R_i(u, y)$ for $x \geqslant y \geqslant 0$, then $(\theta_{r_1}^{**}, \dots, \theta_{r_k}^{**}) \leqslant (\theta_{r_1}^*, \dots, \theta_{r_k}^*)$ and $R_i(u, y) < R_i(u, x)$. Hence $R_i(u, x)$ satisfies $I.4$.

(f) If $L(\lambda u) = \lambda L(u)$, then trivially, I:1 and I:2 hold. Given L.3.S, IV:1, and IV:2 the result follows from (b) – (e). □

Proposition 6.4: If outputs are freely disposable (L.6.S holds), $P(x) = \{u \in R_+^m \colon 0 < R_i(u, x) \leqq 1\}$.

The proof follows that of Proposition 6.2.

Proposition 6.3 states that under {L.1–L.6}, $R_i(u, x)$ satisfies none of the properties $\{I.1–I.4\}$ of an efficiency measure, although various additions to {L.1–L.6} enable $R_i(u, x)$ to satisfy any or all of $\{I.1–I.4\}$. Proposition 6.4 is interpreted in the same way as Proposition 6.2. We now state a proposition relating the direct and implicit Russell measures to the direct and implicit radial measures.

Proposition 6.5:

(a) $F_d(u, x) \geqq R_d(u, x)$.

(b) $F_i(u, x) \geqq R_i(u, x)$.

Proof:

(a) Let $(\lambda^0_{r_1}, \ldots, \lambda^0_{r_k})$ yield the minimum for $R_d(u, x)$ and λ' yield the minimum for $F_d(u, x)$, $(u, x) \in \bar{R}^m_+ \times \bar{R}^n_+$. Assume $\sum_{i=1}^{k} (\lambda^0_{r_i}/k) > \lambda' = \sum_{i=1}^{k} (\lambda'/k)$. Then chose $\lambda^0_{r_i} = \lambda'$, $i = 1, \ldots, k$ (this is possible since $\lambda' x^0 \in L(u)$), so that $\sum_{i=1}^{k} (\lambda^0_{r_i}/k)$ is not the minimum for $R_d(u, x)$, a contradiction. Thus $\sum_{i=1}^{k} (\lambda^0_{r_i}/k) \leqq \lambda'$.

Part (b) is proved in a similar manner. □

7. Summary and Conclusions

In this paper we have proposed three types of technical efficiency measures, and evaluated each in terms of a set of properties that any measure of technical efficiency should satisfy. The direct Russell measure is the only candidate that satisfies all four properties; the overall direct asymmetric measure satisfies two of four properties, the direct radial measure satisfies only one of four properties, and all other candidates fail all four properties. The main source of their failure is the fact that they do not force a comparison between an observed input-output vector and the appropriate reference set, the efficient subset of the input possibilities set for the observed output vector. Their performance could be improved simply by placing restrictions on production technology sufficient to force equality among the efficient subset, the isoquant, and the boundary of the input possibilities set. Such restrictions would enable the direct radial measure to meet all four properties, but would be insufficient for the remaining measures. In any event, we are unwilling to impose such restrictions on production technology, in the belief that they should be tested empirically rather than imposed in advance. Finally, even if these restrictions are valid, different efficiency measures will still assign different magnitudes to measured inefficiency because they use different reference vectors within the same reference set.

There remain several ways in which this research can be extended. We have analyzed only three types of measure, and others can be developed. Output-based measures, in which the reference set is the efficient subset of the output possibilities set, can be formulated and compared with our input-based measures. Graph measures, which compare an observed input-output vector to the set of all smaller feasible input vectors and larger feasible output vectors, can be developed as generalizations of both input-based measures and output-based measures. Price-dependent measures can also be developed to reflect both technical and economic efficiency; such measures can of course vary with the behavioral goal of the production unit.

References

Al-Ayat, R., and *R. Färe*: On the Existence of Joint Production Functions. Naval Research Logistics Quarterly **26** (4), 1979, 627–630.

Debreu, G.: The Coefficient of Resource Utilization. Econometrica **19** (3), 1951, 273–292.

Diewert, W.E.: Functional Forms for Profit and Transformation Functions. Journal of Economic Theory **6** (3), 1973, 284–316.

Eichhorn, W.: Effektivität von Produktionsverfahren. Operations Research-Verfahren **12**, 1972, 98–98–115.

– : What Is an Economic Index? An Attempt of an Answer. Theory and Applications of Economic Indexes. Ed. by W. Eichhorn et al. Würzburg–Wien 1978a.

– : Functional Equations in Economics. Reading, Mass., 1978b.

Färe, R.: Efficiency and the Production Function. Zeitschrift für Nationalökonomie **35**, 1975, 317–324.

– : On Strictly Monotonic Production Correspondences. Quantitative Studies on Production and Prices. Ed. by W. Eichhorn et al. Würzburg-Wien 1982 (this volume).

Färe, R., and *C.A.K. Lovell*: Measuring the Technical Efficiency of Production. Journal of Economic Theory **19** (1), 1978, 150–162.

Farrell, M.J.: The Measurement of Productive Efficiency. Journal of the Royal Statistical Society, Series A General, **120** (3), 1957, 253–281.

Försund, F.R., C.A.K. Lovell and *P. Schmidt*: A Survey of Frontier Production Functions and of Their Relationship to Efficiency Measurement. Journal of Econometrics **13** (1), 1980, 5–26.

Koopmans, T.C.: Analysis of Production as an Efficient Combination of Activities. Activity Analysis of Production and Allocation. Cowles Commission for Research in Economics Monograph No. 13. Ed. by T.C. Koopmans. New York 1951.

Kopp, R.: The Measurement of Productive Efficiency: A Reconsideration. Resources for the Future. Washington, D.C., 1980.

Samuelson, P.S.: The Fundamental Singularity Theorem for Non-Joint Production. International Economic Review 7 (1), 1966, 34–41.

Shephard, R.W.: The Theory of Cost and Production Functions. Princeton 1970.

– : Semi-Homogeneous Production Functions and Scaling of Production. Lecture Notes in Economics and Mathematical Systems **99**. Berlin 1974.

Vincze, E.: Über das Problem der Berechnung der Wirtschaftlichkeit. Acta Technica Academiae Scientiarum Hungarieae **28**, 1960, 33–41.

Quantitative Studies on Production and Prices © Physica-Verlag, Würzburg–Wien, 1983.

Numerical Computation of Short-Run-Production Functions

Kurt Hildenbrand

1. Introduction

In empirical analysis of production functions, the standard approach is to choose *ad hoc* a parameterized family of functions (e.g., Cobb-Douglas- or CES-production functions) and then to fit the parameters according to a given set of observed data. This means that assumptions on the functional relationships are made, e.g. constant elasticity of substitution. In contrast to this approach we describe some numerical methods for a parameter-free approach which is based on the technical information on the micro-level.

2. The Short-Run ex post Technology

We consider a *production sector* consisting of *N production units*. Each production unit uses n goods as inputs and produces 1 homogenous output. The j-th production unit is described by a *capacitated process vector* [*Koopmans*, 1977, p. 147]

$$a_j := (a_{0j}, a_{1j}, \ldots, a_{nj}) \in R_+^{n+1}, \qquad j = 1, \ldots, N.$$

The interpretation is as follows: working on full capacity level, the j-th production unit can produce a_{0j} units of output by using $a_{1j}, \ldots, a_{nj}$ units of the input goods $1, \ldots, n$. The production unit can not work on a higher level than on full capacity. Below the full capacity level, we assume constant returns to scale. We emphasize that this linearity assumption on the micro-level does not imply constant returns to scale for the whole production sector. With this interpretation the technology of the production sector is given by

$$Y = \sum_{j=1}^{N} \lambda_j a_j, \qquad 0 \leqslant \lambda_j \leqslant 1.$$

This is the *short-run ex post technology* of the sector. We have just collected the technical data a_j of the already existing production units, therefore Y is the *ex post* technology. We do not consider any time process for the production units, therefore Y is the *short-run* technology. We have not asked (i) whether these production units have been actually used in the proceeding periods, (ii) why these production units have been built, and (iii) which potential production units one should try to construct. We only have collected the technical data.

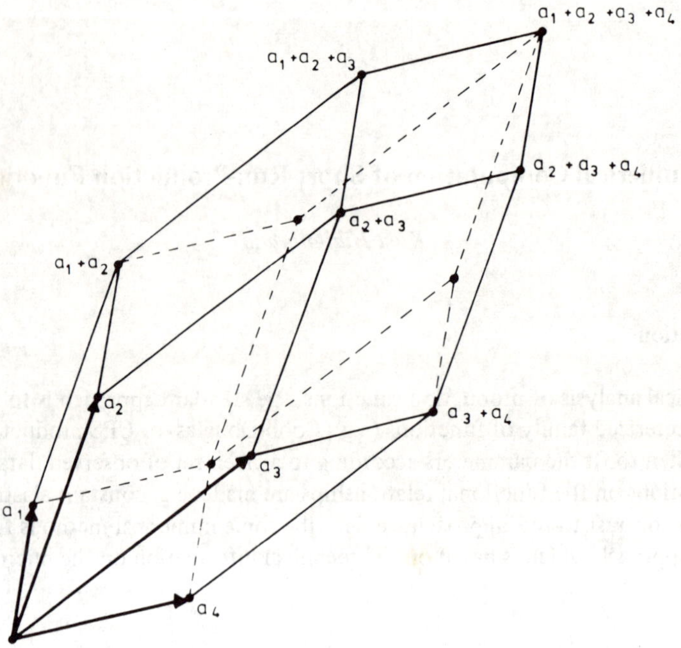

Fig. 1: As an example, the technology Y in case of 2 inputs and 4 production units

3. The Efficient Production Function

Given the technology Y, the *efficient production function* F is defined by

$$F(v_1, \ldots, v_n) := \max \{y \mid (y, v_1, \ldots, v_n) \in Y\}.$$

We emphasize that we have not assumed free disposal for the inputs. Therefore the range of definition

$$D := \{(v_1, \ldots, v_n) \mid \text{there exists a } y \text{ with } (y, v_1, \ldots, v_n) \in Y\}$$

of F is some proper subset of the positive input-space.

In case one wants to include free disposal for the i-th input, this can be done, within this model, only by adding the appropriate (artificial) production unit. This would mean that there is a capacity bound also for the disposal activity.

Denote by pr_{rs} the projection on the plane generated by the r-th and s-th input. The following proposition is an immediate consequence of the geometry of the model.

Proposition 1: Assume that the production units are renumbered such that

$$a_{r1}/a_{s1} \underset{(\geqslant)}{\leqslant} a_{r2}/a_{s2} \underset{(\geqslant)}{\leqslant} \ldots, \underset{(\geqslant)}{\leqslant} a_{rN}/a_{sN}.$$

Then the polygon defined by the edge-points

$$A_k := \sum_{j=1}^{k} (a_{rj}, a_{sj}), \qquad k = 0, 1, \ldots, N$$

is the lower (upper) bound of the projection pr_{rs} (D) of D in the (r, s)-plane.

Note, for an input-vector v to lie in D it is a necessary condition – but only in the case of two inputs also a sufficient condition – that $pr_{rs}(v) \in pr_{rs}(D)$ for all input pairs r and s.

If one is merely interested in computing the value of F for given input quantities then the Simplexalgorithm is an appropriate tool. Instead doing this, we will show in the next sections how to compute characteristics of F – like expansion paths, iso-outputlines, elasticities.

4. Computation of an Expansion Path

Given a pricevector $p \in R^n$, $p \neq 0$, for the inputs, the associated expansion path is

$$E(p) := \left\{ (y, v_1, \ldots, v_n) \;\middle|\; \begin{array}{l} \text{with respect to the input prices } p \text{, the input bundle} \\ (v_1, \ldots, v_n) \text{ is a costminimizer for the production} \\ \text{of } y \text{ units of output} \end{array} \right\}.$$

In other words, $E(p)$ is the set of those boundary points of Y for which the vector of shadow-prices is proportional to p.

We give the following geometric interpretation: To choose the (relative) input-prices means that we have still one degree of freedom – the price for the output. Increasing the outputprice means that we are running on the surface of the technology from the origin to the top. There is nothing different if an inputprice is negative; eventually we are not running on the "upper" but on the "lower" surface of Y (note: we have not assumed free disposal).

We remark that for some pricevectors p the set $E(p)$ contains facets of Y, i.e. for some p the expansion path is not a "line". On the other hand, for some boundary points of Y the shadow-prices are not uniquely defined. The reason for these facts is that Y is the sum of finitely many segments $[0, a_j]$, i.e. is a zonotope. In order to simplify the exposition we will neglect these facts – if the number N of production units is large then the technology Y is "almost smooth" (see figures 3, 4, and 5).

The following proposition shows how to compute an expansion path:

Proposition 2: Given $p \in R^n$, $p \neq 0$. Assume after renumbering of the production units, with $a'_j := (a_{1j}, \ldots, a_{nj})$,

$$p \cdot a'_1/a_{01} \leqslant p \cdot a'_2/a_{02} \leqslant \ldots \leqslant p \cdot a'_N/a_{0N}$$

(i.e. costs per unit output are increasing). *Then the polygon defined by the edge-points*

$$E_k := \sum_{j=1}^{k} a_j, \qquad k = 0, 1, \ldots, N$$

is the expansion path $E(p)$. Moreover, E_k lies on the upper surface of Y (i.e. $E_k \in$ graph (F)) *if $p \cdot a_k' \geqslant 0$ and E_k lies on the lower surface of Y* (i.e. output is minimized) *if $p \cdot a_k' \leqslant 0$.*

Proof: The claimed result is an immediate consequence of Koopmans Efficiencyprice Theorem [e.g. *Koopmans*, 1951]. Consider the linear program

$$\max \sum_{j=1}^{N} x_j a_{0j} \text{ such that } 0 \leqslant x_j \leqslant 1, \qquad j = 1, \ldots, N$$

$$\sum_{j=1}^{N} x_j a_{hj} = \sum_{j=1}^{k} a_{hj}, \qquad h = 1, \ldots, n.$$

In the case $p_0 := p \cdot a_k' / a_{0k} > 0$ the proposition is proved if we show that $\bar{x} \in R^N$, with $\bar{x}_j = 1$ for $j = 1, \ldots, k$ and $\bar{x}_j = 0$ for $j > k$, is a optimal solution of the above linear program. Define the shadow-prices q_j corresponding to the j-th capacity restriction $x_j \leqslant 1$ by $q_j = p_0 a_{0j} - p \cdot a_j'$ for $j = 1, \ldots, k$ and $q_j = 0$ for $j > k$. One easily shows that $q_j \geqslant 0$ for $j = 1, \ldots, k$ and one obtains for the profitability of the j-th activity-vector $\bar{a}_j = (a_j, e_j)$, where e_j denotes the j-th unitvector in R^N,

$$p_0 a_{0j} - p \cdot a_j' - q_j \begin{cases} = 0 & \text{for } j \leqslant k \\ \leqslant 0 & \text{for } j > k \end{cases}.$$

Hence, the pricevector (p_0, p, q) and the intensity vector $\bar{x}$ fulfill the conditions of Koopmans Efficiencyprice Theorem, i.e. in the case $p_0 > 0$ the proposition is proven. In case $p_0 < 0$ the proof is identical to the above one after substitution of $-a_{0j}$ for a_{0j}, $j = 1, \ldots, N$.

5. Computation of Elasticities and Iso-Outputsurfaces

In the following we assume that each production unit needs for production some positive amount of all inputs, i.e. $a_j \gg 0, j = 1, \ldots, N$. Then the expansion path $E(p)$ is the graph of a strictly increasing function. Since $E(p)$ is a polygon, one can easily numerically compute the *input demand*, given the output quantity y and the inputprices p:

$$v_h = V_h(y) \text{ with } (V_1(y), \ldots, V_n(y)) \in E(p).$$

Again the functions V_h are polygons. Hence, we can compute the *elasticities of input demand*

$$\frac{dV_h}{dy} \Big/ \frac{V_h(y)}{y} \qquad h = 1, \ldots, n$$

and the *elasticity of costs*

$$\frac{d(p \cdot (V_1(y), \ldots, V_n(y))}{dy} \Big/ \frac{p \cdot (V_1(y), \ldots, V_n(y))}{y}.$$

When computing these elasticities one has to be a little bit careful since the derivatives do not exist in the edge points of the polygons and the numerical procedure may enforce some numerical fluctuation of the results.

Next we want to compute an *iso-outputsurface*, given the outputquantity y,

$$I(y) := \{(v_1, \ldots, v_n) \mid (y, v_1, \ldots, v_n) \in \text{boundary}(Y)\}.$$

As we have seen, the computation of an expansion path $E(p)$ consists only of an easy renumbering of the production units and a summation. Since $E(p)$ is a strictly monotone polygon, the intersection $I(y) \cap E(p)$, i.e. points on the iso-outputsurface, can be computed. The vector p is proportional to the marginal rates of substitution in the point $I(y) \cap E(p)$. Hence, varying p in a systematical way, let's say equally distanced on the unit sphere, the obtained points on $I(y)$ lie "close" together if in that region the curvature of $I(y)$ is high, and the obtained points on $I(y)$ have a "large" distance from each other if in that region $I(y)$ tends to be linear.

We remember that we have not assumed free disposal and therefore $I(y)$ is a closed surface. Let us consider the case of 2 inputs. Then $I(y)$ is a closed curve in the 2-dimensional input-plane. Moreover,

$$I_{\text{eff}}(y) := \{(v_1, v_2) \mid y = F(v_1, v_2)\},$$

the part of $I(y)$ lying on the upper surface of Y, is not a monotone decreasing curve – there are points on the upper surface of Y where there are negative shadow-prices.

The iso-outputline $I(y)$ is a polygon and therefore the *elasticity of substitution*

$$\sigma = -\frac{d(V_2/V_1)}{d(p_2/p_1)} \bigg/ \frac{V_2/V_1}{p_2/p_1}$$

is not well defined – in the edgepoints σ is infinite, in the segments between the edgepoints σ is zero. In order to obtain numerical approximations one can substitute the differential quotient by the difference quotient. In the case of a smooth iso-outputline the elasticity of substitution σ is well defined. However, neither the absolute value of σ nor the sign of σ is constant. Figure 2 shows the typical shape of an iso-outputline and the sign of σ. The broken line lies on the lower surface of Y. There are 4 points where the sign of σ changes. In these points (thickly drawn in figure 2) σ is zero. These facts illustrate the difference between the approach given above and the approach by Cobb-Douglas- or CES-production functions.

6. A Numerical Example

As a numerical example I have used the Norwegian tanker fleet in 1967 consisting of 377 ships (of more than 15.000 deadweight tons). These were tankers of different types (e.g., 320 motor and 57 turbine tankers) and of different vintages (from 1950 until 1966). Output of tankers is defined as ton-miles transported per period. Only two variable inputs are considered: fuel and labor. They are measured in values at prices and wages in a given year. The basic data are taken from the Norwegian ship register. For a detailed

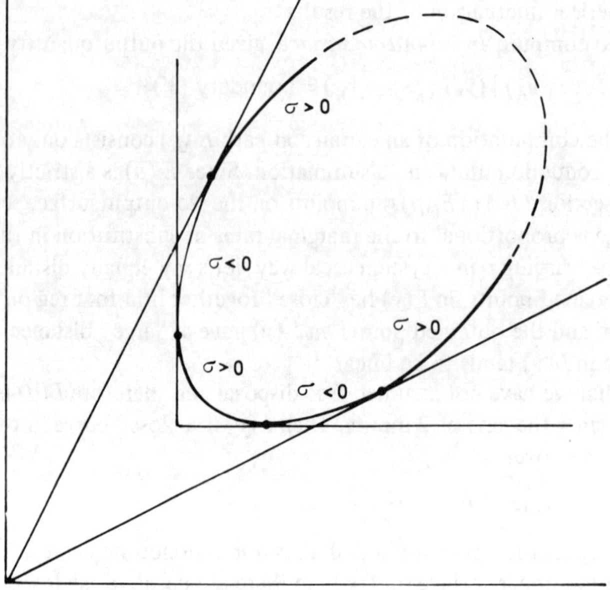

Fig. 2: The typical shape of an iso-outputline and the sign of the elasticity of substitution

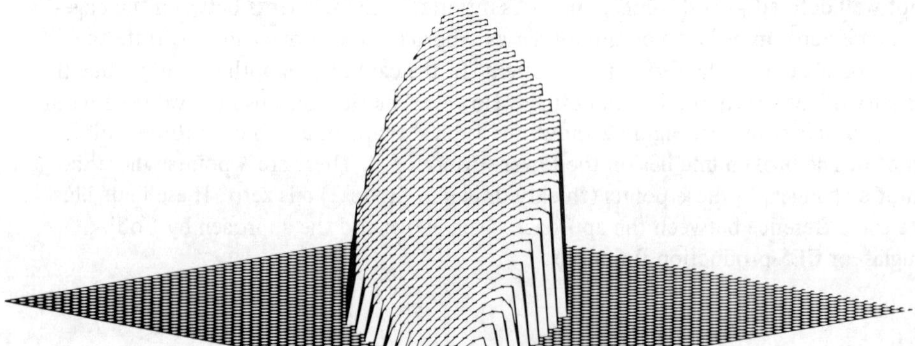

Fig. 3

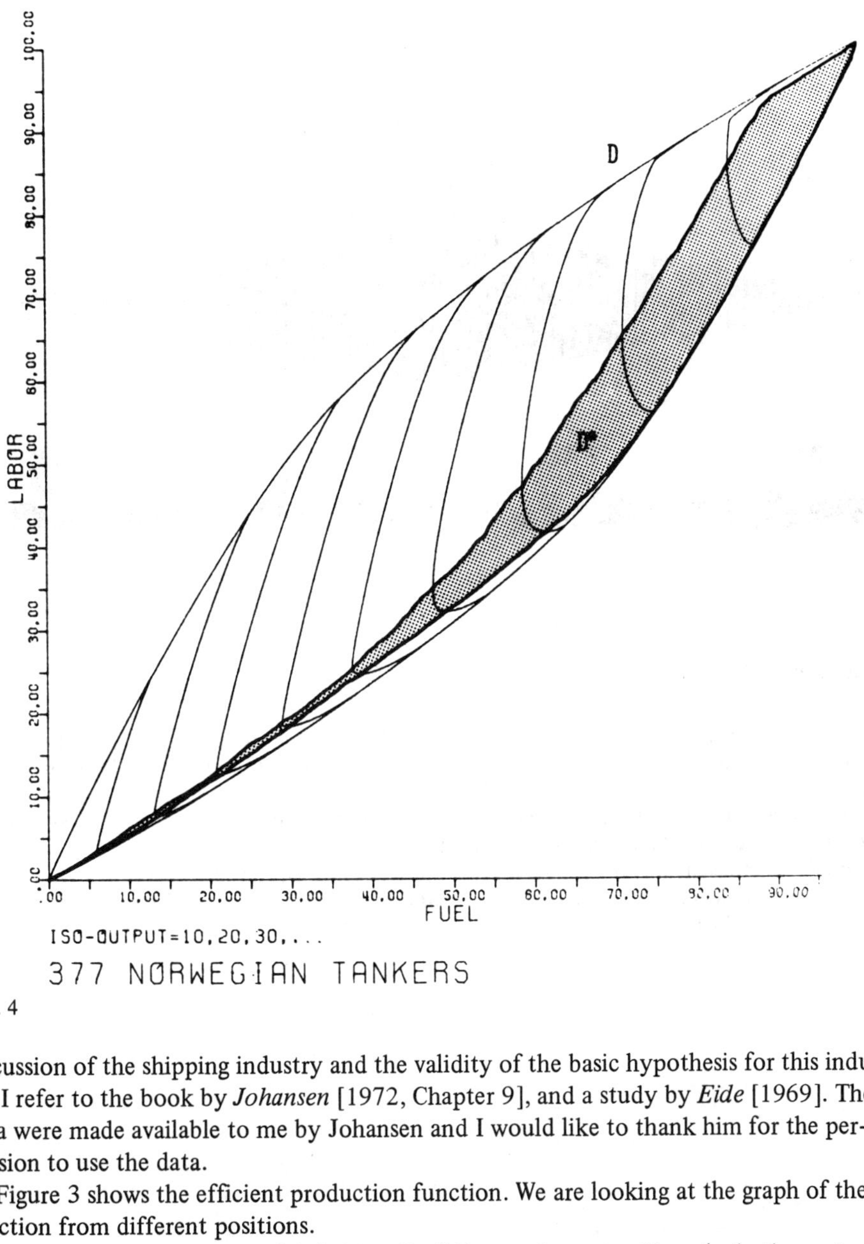

Fig. 4

discussion of the shipping industry and the validity of the basic hypothesis for this industry I refer to the book by *Johansen* [1972, Chapter 9], and a study by *Eide* [1969]. The data were made available to me by Johansen and I would like to thank him for the permission to use the data.

Figure 3 shows the efficient production function. We are looking at the graph of the function from different positions.

Figure 4 shows the range of definition D of F, some iso-outputlines (only the part on the upper surface of Y is drawn), and the part D^* of D where the iso-outputlines have a negative slope. We have made a transformation of the input-output-measuring such that

$$\sum_{j=1}^{377} a_j = (100 \mid 100 \mid 100).$$

Figure 5 shows the graph of F restricted to D^*.

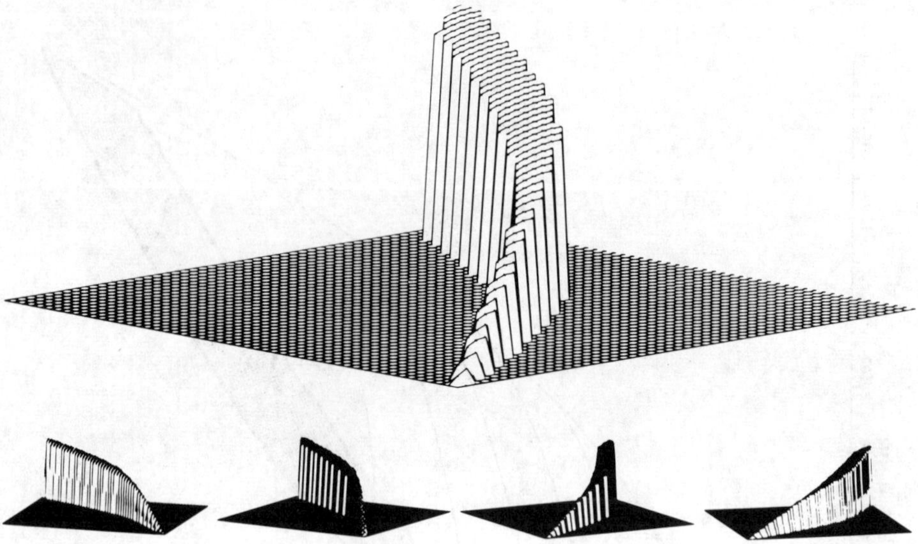

Fig. 5

References

Eide, E.: En metode for konstruksjon av aggregerte korttids produktfunksjoner illustrert med data for den Norske tankflåte. Memorandum from the Institut of Economics, University of Oslo, Oslo 1969.

Hildenbrand, W.: Short-Run Production Functions Based on Microdata. Econometrica **48**, 1981.

Johansen, L.: Production Functions. Amsterdam 1972.

Koopmans, T.: Efficient Allocation of Ressources. Econometrica **19**, 1951, 455–465.

– : Examples of Production Relations Based on Microdata. The Microeconomic Foundation of Macroeconomics. Ed. by G.C. Harcourt. London 1977, 144–171.

Quantitative Studies on Production and Prices © Physica-Verlag, Würzburg–Wien, 1983.

Aggregation of Input Price Subindexes

Daniel Primont

1. Introduction and Summary

Suppose we are given a set of inputs, denoted by N, for which a complete input price index is defined. The index is complete in the sense that N includes all inputs which enter into the production function. An input price subindex, if defined, is an index for a subset of inputs, $N^r \subset N$.

This general notion of a subindex was first proposed by *Pollak* [1975] who defined several types of subindexes in the context of consumer theory. One is the "conditional subindex" which places no restrictions on the underlying production function. However, it depends on quantities of goods outside the group as well as prices within the group. Another is the "partial subindex." It is independent of prices and quantities outside the group but is only defined when the group is separable in the production function. *Blackorby/Russell* [1978] proposed what is called here the "implicit subindex." It is also independent of prices and quantities outside the group; however, it is only defined when the group is separable in the cost function.

The present paper is an investigation of the conditions under which either the partial or the implicit subindex may be aggregated into a complete index. Specifically, for each of the two subindexes, conditions are sought for which the value of the complete index is a function of the value of the group subindex and of prices outside the group. As will be seen in each case, aggregability requires that the group of commodity prices be separable in the cost function. In addition, the convention that the complete index be computed as a ratio imposes further restrictions on the cost function. The results are then easily extended to cases where there is more than one subindex.

Suppose there are only two groups, group c and group r. A Blackorby-Russell "implicit" subindex for group r is aggregable if and only if (a) the cost function can be written as the product of a function of group c prices and a function of group r prices and (b) there exists an aggregable implicit subindex for group c. The condition in (a) is not too surprising given the discussion in *Pollak* [1975]. The multiplicative form of the cost function is a modified version of the "generalized Cobb-Douglas form" in *Pollak* [1975, p. 139] and is a special case of the "implicit CES form" in *Blackorby/Russell* [1978, p. 233, eq. (17)]. Condition (b) is perhaps more surprising, but as will be seen it is a simple consequence of the fact that the multiplicative form of condition (a) is symmetric.

Similar results hold for the Pollak partial subindex with one important addition. While aggregability implies separability in the cost function, the definition of the partial subindex requires separability in the production function. Together, these imply homothetic separability and a more restrictive form of the cost function. Moreover, when all groups of commodities possess an aggregable partial subindex the production function must be homothetic.

2. Definitions and Notation

It is assumed that the technology is represented by a continuous, nondecreasing, locally nonsatiated, quasiconcave, real-valued production function U. U is defined for nonnegative input vectors, $X = (x_1, \ldots, x_n)$, and the image of U is denoted by $u = U(X)$. The cost function is defined by $C(u, P) = \underset{X}{\text{Min}} \{P \cdot X \mid U(X) \geqslant u, X \geqq 0\}$, where $P = (p_1, \ldots, p_n)$ is a vector of positive prices and $P \cdot X = \sum_{i=1}^{n} p_i x_i$. Given the assumed properties of the production function, C is increasing in u, nondecreasing, concave, and homogeneous of degree one in P, and jointly continuous in u and P. In addition, assume C is twice continuously differentiable.

Let $P(a)$ and $P(b)$ represent n-dimensional price vectors in situations a and b respectively. The input price index defined by:

$$\pi = I(u, P(a), P(b)) = \frac{C(u, P(a))}{C(u, P(b))},$$

is an index of comparison prices in situation a relative to reference prices in situation b.

Let $N(t)$ be the set of n variable subscripts of the vector $P(t)$, $t = a, b$, and let $N^* = N(a) \cup N(b)$. Loosely, $N(t)$ is the set of prices that prevail in situation t. Each of these sets of prices may be partitioned into m categories:

$$\hat{N}(t) = \{N^1(t), \ldots, N^r(t), \ldots, N^m(t)\}, \; t = a, b.$$

In much of what follows we shall be interested in examining an input price subindex for group r alone. Let

$$N^c(t) = \bigcup_{s \neq r} N^s(t), \quad t = a, b.$$

A quaternary partition of N^* is:

$$\hat{N}_4^* = \{N^c(a), N^r(a), N^c(b), N^r(b)\},$$

with a corresponding price vector,

$$(P(a), P(b)) = (P^c(a), P^r(a), P^c(b), P^r(b)).$$

Finally, let $N = \{1, \ldots, n\}$ be the set of n prices (or inputs) whenever they are not distinguished by situation. The production function is strictly separable in the partition $\hat{N} = \{N^1, \ldots, N^m\}$ if and only if it can be written as:

$$U(X) = \hat{U}(U^1(X^1), \ldots, U^m(X^m)) \tag{2.1}$$

where X^r, $r = 1, \ldots, m$, is a vector of inputs in group r and $\hat{U}$ is increasing in its m arguments. The cost function is strictly separable in the partition $\hat{N}$ if and only if it can be written as:

$$C(u, P) = \hat{C}(u, C^1(u, P^1), \ldots, C^m(u, P^m)), \tag{2.2}$$

where P^r, $r = 1, \ldots, m$, is a vector of prices in group r and $\hat{C}$ is increasing in its last m arguments.

3. The Implicit Input Price Subindex

The subindex proposed by *Blackorby/Russell* [1978] is defined only when the cost function is separable as in (2.2). Given this structure, the implicit input price subindex for group r is defined as:

$$\overset{*}{\pi}_r = \frac{C^r(u, P^r(a))}{C^r(u, P^r(b))}, \qquad r = 1, \ldots, m.$$

The implicit subindex possesses two relevant properties: (i) $\overset{*}{\pi}_r$ depends only on overall output u and on sector r prices in situations a and b and (ii) $\overset{*}{\pi}_r$ is a ratio of values of C^r evaluated at prices in situations a and b respectively. By retaining the first property and dropping the second property one might define a generalized implicit subindex as:

$$\pi_r = \Pi^r(u, P^r(a), P^r(b)).$$

As it turns out, aggregability of π_r implies that $\pi_r = \overset{*}{\pi}_r$. Thus, aggregability is defined below in terms of π_r, $r = 1, \ldots, m$.

An implicit subindex for sector r is *aggregable* if and only if there exists a function $\bar{\Pi}$ such that for all positive prices,

$$\begin{aligned} \pi &= I(u, P^c(a), P^r(a), P^c(b), P^r(b)) \qquad (3.1)\\ &= \bar{\Pi}(u, P^c(a), P^c(b), \Pi^r(u, P^r(a), P^r(b))), \end{aligned}$$

where $\bar{\Pi}$ is increasing in $\pi_r = \Pi^r(u, P^r(a), P^r(b))$.

Thus, by definition, aggregability of an implicit subindex for sector r implies that sector r prices are strictly separable from prices outside sector r in the overall cost of living index. As shown below, this implies (but is not implied by!) strict separability of sector r prices in the cost function.

Theorem 1: There exists $m - 1$ aggregable implicit input price subindexes of the form:

$$\pi_r = \Pi^r(u, P^r(a), P^r(b)), \qquad r = 2, \ldots, m,$$

and a function $\hat{\Pi}$ such that for all positive prices,

$$I(u, P(a), P(b)) = \hat{\Pi}(u, P^1(a), P^1(b), \pi_2, \ldots, \pi_m),$$

where $\hat{\Pi}$ is increasing in $\pi_2, \ldots, \pi_m$ if and only if the cost function has the form:

$$C(u, P) = \phi(u) \prod_{r=1}^{m} C^r(u, P^r)^{\alpha_r}, \tag{3.2}$$

where each C^r is nondecreasing, concave and homogeneous of degree one in P^r, $\sum_{r=1}^{m} \alpha_r = 1$, and $\alpha_r > 0, r = 1, \ldots, m$. In this case there will be an m-th aggregable subindex of the form:

$$\pi_1 = \pi^1(u, P^1(a), P^1(b)) = \frac{C^1(u, P^1(a))}{C^1(u, P^1(b))}. \tag{3.3}$$

4. The Partial Input Price Subindex

Pollak defined the partial subindex for sector r by first assuming that sector r is strictly separable from its complement in N. Thus, the production function may be written in the form:

$$U(X) = \bar{U}(X^c, U^r(X^r)).$$

The partial cost function for sector r is

$$E^r(u_r, P^r) = \min_{X^r} \{P^r \cdot X^r \mid U^r(X^r) \geqq u_r\},$$

and the partial subindex I^r is defined by

$$I^r(u_r, P^r(a), P^r(b)) = \frac{E^r(u_r, P^r(a))}{E^r(u_r, P^r(b))}. \tag{4.1}$$

In the above definition of the partial subindex, sector output u_r may take on any value in the range of the function U^r. Suppose $X^r(a)$ and $X^r(b)$ represent cost minimizing input vectors of sector r commodities at prices $P(a)$ and $P(b)$ respectively. Obviously, u_r cannot be set equal to both $U^r(X^r(a))$ and $U^r(X^r(b))$ simultaneously since the latter two values are not, in general, equal. Nevertheless, aggregability of I^r may depend on the values of u_r selected. Rather than require that aggregability holds for all possible values of u_r, the definition given below requires only that there exist at least one value of u_r for which aggregability holds.

Let $(\bar{X}^c, \bar{X}^r)$ be an input bundle on a base isoquant. This reference vector determines two values, $u_r = U^r(\bar{X}^r)$, and $u = \bar{U}(\bar{X}^c, u_r)$. The partial subindex I^r is *aggregable* if there exists a function $\bar{I}$ such that

$$\begin{aligned}\pi &= I(u, P^c(a), P^r(a), P^c(b), P^r(b)) \\ &= \bar{I}(u, P^c(a), P^c(b), I^r(u_r, P^r(a), P^r(b)))\end{aligned}$$

for all prices and for the values of u and u_r satisfying (a) $u = \bar{U}(\bar{X}^c, u_r)$ and (b) $u_r = U^r(\bar{X}^r)$ for some $(\bar{X}^c, \bar{X}^r)$ in the domain of U.

Aggregability of partial subindexes $I^2, \ldots, I^m$ may be defined in a similar way by letting $(\bar{X}^1, \ldots, \bar{X}^m)$ denote some reference vector, setting $u_r = U^r(\bar{X}^r)$ and requiring that $u = \hat{U}(\bar{X}^1, u_2, \ldots, u_m)$.

Theorem 2: There exist $m - 1$ aggregable partial input price subindexes of the form:

$$\pi_r = I^r(u_r, P^r(a), P^r(b)) = \frac{E^r(u_r, P^r(a))}{E^r(u_r, P^r(b))}, \qquad r = 2, \ldots, m,$$

and a function $\hat{I}$ such that:

$$I(u, P(a), P(b)) = \hat{I}(u, P^1(a), P^1(b), \pi_2, \ldots, \pi_m),$$

where $\hat{I}$ is increasing in $\pi_2, \ldots, \pi_m$, for all positive prices and for the values of u, $u_2, \ldots, u_m$ satisfying (a) $u_r = U^r(\bar{X}^r)$, $r = 2, \ldots, m$ and (b) $u = \hat{U}(\bar{X}^1, u_2, \ldots, u_m)$, if and only if the cost function has the form:

$$C(u, P) = \psi(u)\, C^1(u, P^1)^{\beta_1} \prod_{r=2}^{m} \hat{C}^r(P^r)^{\beta_r}, \tag{4.2}$$

where each C^r is nondecreasing, concave and homogeneous of degree on in P^r, $\sum_{r=1}^{m} \beta_r = 1$, and $\beta_r > 0$, $r = 1, \ldots, m$. In this case there exists an m-th aggregable implicit input price subindex of the form:

$$\pi_1 = I^1(u, P^1(a), P^1(b)) = \frac{C^1(u, P^1(a))}{C^1(u, P^1(b))}.$$

Corollary: There exists m aggregable partial input price subindexes in the above sense if and only if the cost function has the form:

$$C(u, P) = \psi(u) \prod_{r=1}^{m} \hat{C}^r(P^r)^{\beta_r}, \beta_r > 0, r = 1, \ldots, m, \Sigma\, \beta_r = 1 \tag{4.3}$$

where each C^r is nondecreasing, concave, and homogeneous of degree one in P^r. In this case the production function is homothetic.

5. Concluding Remarks

In his discussion of aggregability, *Pollak* [1975] considered a special case in which each of the m groups consists of only one good. He showed that the complete cost of living index can be written as a function of the m subindexes if and only if the underlying technology is representable by an indirect production function implicitly defined by

$$\sum_i \beta_i(u) \ln p_i - \sum_i \beta_i(u) \ln y = 1. \tag{5.1}$$

Solving (5.1) for y yields the corresponding cost function,

$$y = e^{-1/\beta(u)} \prod_{i=1}^{m} p_i^{\alpha_i(u)}, \tag{5.2}$$

where $\beta(u) = \sum_k \beta_k(u)$ and $\alpha_i(u) = \beta_i(u)/\beta(u)$.

The form in (5.2), a "generalized Cobb-Douglas," is a special case of the forms in (A.11) and (A.13) in the proofs of theorems 1 and 2 given in the Appendix. It is shown there that cost functions of this form are not increasing in u for all positive prices unless the exponents are independent of u. In this case, (5.2) reduces to the Cobb-Douglas function.

However, in some applications one may only need a cost function which satisfies the regularity conditions locally, i.e. for a subset of price space. In this case one can rely on the local duality results of *Blackorby/Diewert* [1979], and cost functions such as (5.2), (A.11) or (A.13) can be admissible. Hence the restrictive forms given in theorems 1 and 2 can be somewhat generalized if these theorems are restated as local results.

Appendix

The proofs of the theorems involve the notion of strict independence which is characterized below. Let $\Omega_+^n = \{P = (p_1, \ldots, p_n) \in \mathbf{R}^n \mid p_i > 0, i = 1, \ldots, n\}$ and let S be a subset of the reals. Suppose a function $F : S \times \Omega_+^n \to \mathbf{R}$ is real valued and twice continuously differentiable. Let $\bar{N} = \{N^c, N^r\}$ be a binary partition of $N = \{1, \ldots, n\}$. Then $y = F(u, P) = F(u, P^c, P^r)$ where $u \in S$ and $(P^c, P^r) \in \Omega_+^n$. The set of variables N^r is strictly independent of N^c in F if

$$\frac{\partial \log F(u, P^c, P^r)}{\partial p_i} = f^i(u, P^r),$$

for all $i \in N^r$. A necessary and sufficient condition for strict independence [*Blackorby/Lovell/Thursby; Blackorby/Primont/Russell*, Theorem 4.15] is that there exist functions F^c and F^r such that $F(u, P^c, P^r) = F^c(u, P^c) F^r(u, P^r)$.

Proof of Theorem 1: Aggregability of the r-th subindex implies that,

$$\pi = \frac{C(u, P^c(a), P^r(a))}{C(u, P^c(b), P^r(b))} = \bar{\Pi}(u, P^c(a), P^c(b), \Pi^r(u, P^r(a), P^r(b))). \tag{A.1}$$

It is evident that each of the following subsets of variables, $N^c(a) \cup N^r(a)$, $N^c(b) \cup N^r(b)$, and $N^r(a) \cup N^r(b)$, is separable from its complement in N^*. *Gorman's* [1968] theorem on overlapping separable sets implies that $N^c(a)$, $N^r(a)$, $N^c(b)$, and $N^r(b)$ are each strictly separable from their complements in N^*. Thus, the complete index may be written as,

$$\pi = I(u, P(a), P(b)) = \tilde{\Pi}(u, z_{ca}, z_{ra}, z_{cb}, z_{rb}) \tag{A.2}$$

where $z_{st} = \Pi^{st}(u, P^s(t))$, $s = c, r$, and $t = a, b$. But since $N^c(a) \cup N^r(a)$ and $N^c(b) \cup N^r(b)$ are strictly independent and $N^r(a) \cup N^r(b)$ is separable, then there exist functions h^a, h^b, $\bar{g}$ and g such that

$$\pi = \tilde{\Pi}(u, z_{ca}, z_{ra}, z_{cb}, z_{rb}) \tag{A.3}$$

$$= \frac{h^a(u, z_{ca}, z_{ra})}{h^b(u, z_{cb}, z_{rb})}$$

$$= \bar{g}(u, z_{ca}, z_{cb}, g(u, z_{ra}, z_{rb})).$$

This implies that

$$\frac{\partial \log \pi / \partial z_{ra}}{\partial \log \pi / \partial z_{rb}} = \frac{\partial \log h^a(u, z_{ca}, z_{ra}) / \partial z_{ra}}{-\partial \log h^b(u, z_{cb}, z_{rb}) / \partial z_{rb}}$$

$$= \frac{\partial g(u, z_{ra}, z_{rb}) / \partial z_{ra}}{\partial g(u, z_{ra}, z_{rb}) / \partial z_{rb}}.$$

Rearranging the latter identity,

$$\frac{\partial \log h^a(u, z_{ca}, z_{ra})}{\partial z_{ra}} = \frac{-\partial \log h^b(u, z_{cb}, z_{rb})}{\partial z_{rb}} \frac{\partial g(u, z_{ra}, z_{rb}) / \partial z_{ra}}{\partial g(u, z_{ra}, z_{rb}) / \partial z_{rb}}. \quad \text{(A.4)}$$

As the right hand side of (A.4) is independent of z_{ca}, then so is the left hand side. This implies that z_{ra} is strictly independent of z_{ca} in h^a. A similar argument implies that z_{rb} is strictly independent of z_{cb} in h^b. Thus there exist functions, h^{ca}, h^{ra}, h^{cb}, and h^{rb} such that

$$h^a(u, z_{ca}, z_{ra}) = h^{ca}(u, z_{ca})\, h^{ra}(u, z_{ra}), \quad \text{(A.5)}$$

and

$$h^b(u, z_{cb}, z_{rb}) = h^{cb}(u, z_{cb})\, h^{rb}(u, z_{rb}). \quad \text{(A.6)}$$

Let $C^{st}(u, P^s(t)) \equiv h^{st}(u, \Pi^{st}(u, P^s(t)))$, $s = c, r$ and $t = a, b$. Then from (A.1), (A.3), (A.5), and (A.6),

$$\pi = \frac{C(u, P^c(a), P^r(a))}{C(u, P^c(b), P^r(b))} = \frac{C^{ca}(u, P^c(a))\, C^{ra}(u, P^r(a))}{C^{cb}(u, P^c(b))\, C^{rb}(u, P^r(b))}$$

or rearranging,

$$\frac{C^{ca}(u, P^c(a))\, C^{ra}(u, P^r(a))}{C(u, P^c(a), P^r(a))} = \frac{C^{cb}(u, P^c(b))\, C^{rb}(u, P^r(b))}{C(u, P^c(b), P^r(b))}. \quad \text{(A.7)}$$

Since the left hand side of (A.7) is independent of situation b prices and the right hand side is independent of situation a prices, each side is equal to some function of u alone. Moreover, from (A.1), $\pi = 1$ when $(P^c(a), P^r(a)) = (P^c(b), P^r(b))$. Thus we may, without loss of generality, let $C^{ca} = C^{cb} = \tilde{C}^c$ and $C^{ra} = C^{rb} = \tilde{C}^r$. Then the cost function has the form,

$$C(u, P^c, P^r) = \phi(u)\, \tilde{C}^c(u, P^c)\, \tilde{C}^r(u, P^r). \quad \text{(A.8)}$$

Since the cost function is homogeneous of degree one in prices, we have, by Euler's

Theorem:

$$\phi(u)\,\tilde{C}^c(u, P^c)\,\nabla_r\,\tilde{C}^r(u, P^r)\cdot P^r \qquad \text{(A.9)}$$
$$+\,\phi(u)\,\tilde{C}^r(u, P^r)\,\nabla_c\,\tilde{C}^c(u, P^c)\cdot P^c$$
$$=\phi(u)\,\tilde{C}^c(u, P^c)\,\tilde{C}^r(u, P^r),$$

where

$$\nabla_s\,\tilde{C}^s(u, P^s)\cdot P^s = \sum_{i\in N^s} \frac{\partial\,\tilde{C}^s(u, P^s)}{\partial\,p_i}\cdot p_i\,, \qquad s = c, r.$$

Dividing both sides of (A.9) by its right hand side and rearranging yields:

$$\tilde{C}^r(u, P^r)^{-1}\,\nabla_r\,\tilde{C}^r(u, P^r)\cdot P^r \qquad \text{(A.10)}$$
$$= 1 - \tilde{C}^c(u, P^c)^{-1}\,\nabla_c\,\tilde{C}^c(u, P^c)\cdot P^c.$$

Since the right hand side of (A.10) is independent of P^r, the left hand side can only depend on u. Let

$$\alpha_r(u) = \tilde{C}^r(u, P^r)^{-1}\,\nabla_r\,\tilde{C}^r(u, P^r)\cdot P^r.$$

Hence

$$\nabla_r\,\tilde{C}^r(u, P^r)\cdot P^r = \alpha_r(u)\,\tilde{C}^r(u, P^r),$$

which implies, by Euler's Theorem, that $\tilde{C}^r$ is homogeneous of degree $\alpha_r(u)$. A similar argument establishes that $\tilde{C}^c$ is homogeneous of degree $\alpha_c(u)$, where $\alpha_c(u) = 1 - \alpha_r(u)$.

Letting

$$C^c(u, P^c) = \tilde{C}^c(u, P^c)^{1/\alpha_c(u)}$$

and

$$C^r(u, P^r) = \tilde{C}^r(u, P^r)^{1/\alpha_r(u)}$$

and substituting into (A.8) yields

$$C(u, P^c, P^r) = \phi(u)\,C^c(u, P^c)^{\alpha_c(u)}\,C^r(u, P^r)^{\alpha_r(u)} \qquad \text{(A.11)}$$

where C^c and C^r are each homogeneous of degree one in P^c and P^r respectively and $\alpha_c(u) + \alpha_r(u) = 1$.

To be a valid cost function C must be increasing in u for all positive prices, i.e. if $u' > u''$ then $C(u', P^c, P^r) > C(u'', P^c, P^r)$. For this to be so requires that:

$$\phi(u')\,C^c(u', P^c)^{\alpha_c(u')}\,C^r(u', P^r)^{\alpha_r(u')} >$$
$$\phi(u'')\,C^c(u'', P^c)^{\alpha_c(u'')}\,C^r(u'', P^r)^{\alpha_r(u'')}$$

for all P in Ω_+^n. Rearranging,

$$\frac{\phi(u')\,C^c(u', P^c)^{\alpha_c(u')}}{\phi(u'')\,C^c(u'', P^c)^{\alpha_c(u'')}} > \frac{C^r(u'', P^r)^{\alpha_r(u'')}}{C^r(u', P^r)^{\alpha_r(u')}}$$

for all P in Ω^n_+. In particular this implies that

$$\frac{\phi(u')\,C^c(u',P^c)^{\alpha_c(u')}}{\phi(u'')\,C^c(u'',P^c)^{\alpha_c(u'')}} > \frac{C^r(u'',\lambda P^r)^{\alpha_r(u'')}}{C^r(u',\lambda P^r)^{\alpha_r(u')}} =$$

$$= \lambda^{\alpha_r(u'')-\alpha_r(u')} \frac{C^r(u'',P^r)^{\alpha_r(u'')}}{C^r(u',P^r)^{\alpha_r(u')}}$$

for all $\lambda > 0$ (since C^r is homogeneous of degree one in prices). But if $\alpha_r(u'')-\alpha_r(u')>0$ then there is a sufficiently large λ that will violate this condition and if $\alpha_r(u'')-\alpha_r(u')<0$, then there is a sufficiently small λ that will violate this condition. Thus if the cost function is to be increasing in u for all positive prices then $\alpha_r(u'')=\alpha_r(u')=\alpha_r$ for all $u'>u''$. Moreover, $\alpha_c(u)=1-\alpha_r(u)=1-\alpha_r=\alpha_c$. Thus the exponents cannot depend on u.

Now it is shown that C^r must be concave. Since C^c is homogeneous of degree one in P^c, there exists a price vector, $\bar{P}^c$, such that $C^c(u,\bar{P}^c)=1$. (If $C^c(u,P^c)=\lambda$, then $\bar{P}^c=P^c/\lambda$.) Let

$$P_i=(P_i^c,P_i^r)=(\bar{P}^c,P_i^r), \qquad i=1,\ldots,k.$$

Concavity of C implies that

$$\phi(u)\,C^c(u,\sum_i\theta_iP_i^c)\,C^r(u,\sum_i\theta_iP_i^r) \geqq \sum_i\theta_i\,\phi(u)\,C^c(u,P_i^c)\,C^r(u,P_i^r),$$

for $0\leqq\theta_i\leqq 1$ and $\sum_i\theta_i=1$. By construction this reduces to

$$C^r(u,\sum_i\theta_iP_i^r)\geqq\sum_i\theta_i\,C^r(u,P_i^r),$$

implying concavity of C^r.

It is obvious that C^r is nondecreasing in prices since C is.

The above argument may be reapplied to each group, $r=2,\ldots,m$, to arrive at the form (3.2). Equation (3.2), in turn, clearly implies the existence of the m-th subindex given in (3.3).

The converse of the theorem is obvious. Given (3.2), the m aggregable subindexes have the form

$$\pi_r=\frac{C^r(u,P^r(a))}{C^r(u,P^r(b))}, \qquad r=1,\ldots,m,$$

and the overall index has the form

$$\pi=\prod_{r=1}^{m}\pi_r^{\alpha_r}.$$

Proof of Theorem 2: Sufficiency is immediate. The proof of necessity resembles the proof of theorem 1 in parts. Aggregability of the r-th subindex implies that

$$\frac{C(u, P^c(a), P^r(a))}{C(u, P^c(b), P^r(b))} = \bar{I}(u, P^c(a), P^c(b), I^r(u_r, P^r(a), P^r(b))). \tag{A.12}$$

Thus, $N^c(a) \cup N^r(a)$, $N^c(b) \cup N^r(b)$, and $N^r(a) \cup N^r(b)$ are separable from their complements in N^*. By *Gorman's* [1968] theorem on overlapping separable sets this implies that $N^c(a)$, $N^r(a)$, $N^c(b)$ and $N^r(b)$ are each strictly separable from their complements in N^*. In particular, sector r prices are separable in the cost function. Since sector r inputs are separable in the production function this implies that the sector function U^r is homothetic [*Blackorby/Primont/Russell*, Theorem 3.9].

Homotheticity of U^r implies that the partial cost function may be written as:

$$E^r(u_r, P^r) = \psi^r(u_r)\hat{E}^r(P^r)$$

and therefore the partial subindex may be written as:

$$I^r(u_r, P^r(a), P^r(b)) = \hat{I}^r(P^r(a), P^r(b)) = \frac{\hat{E}^r(P^r(a))}{\hat{E}^r(P^r(b))}.$$

Thus (A.12) becomes

$$\frac{C(u, P^c(a), P^r(a))}{C(u, P^c(b), P^r(b))} = \bar{I}(u, P^c(a), P^c(b), \hat{I}^r(P^r(a), P^r(b))).$$

Again, Gorman's theorem on overlapping separable sets implies that $N^c(a)$, $N^c(b)$, $N^r(a)$ and $N^r(b)$ are each strictly separable from their complements in N^*. In addition, $N^r(a)$ and $N^r(b)$ are each separable from the output variable u. Thus, we may write the complete index as,

$$I(u, P(a), P(b)) = \tilde{I}(u, z_{ca}, z_{ra}, z_{cb}, z_{rb})$$

where

$$z_{ct} = I^{ct}(u, P^c(t)) \text{ and } z_{rt} = \hat{I}^{rt}(P^r(t)) \text{ for } t = a, b.$$

This is essentially the same form as equation (A.2) in the proof of Theorem 1 except that I^{ra} and I^{rb} do not depend on u. Taking into account this difference, reapplication of the argument in the proof of theorem 1 through the steps that led to (A.11) yields the following form of the cost function:

$$C(u, P^c, P^r) = \psi(u)\, C^c(u, P^c)^{\beta_c(u)}\, \hat{C}^r(P^r)^{\beta_r(u)}, \tag{A.13}$$

where C^c and C^r are nondecreasing, concave and homogeneous of degree one in P^c and P^r respectively, and $\beta_c(u) + \beta_r(u) = 1$.

If (A.13) is to be a valid cost function for all positive prices the exponents cannot depend on u. This can be shown by reapplying the argument in the proof of Theorem 1 to the somewhat less general case of (A.13). Thus (A.13) becomes

$$C(u, P^c, P^r) = \psi(u)\, C^c(u, P^c)^{\beta_c}\, \hat{C}^r(P^r)^{\beta_r}. \tag{A.14}$$

Reapplication of this argument for each group, $r = 2, \ldots, m$, yields the form in (4.2).

To prove Corollary 2.1 note that if all m groups have aggregable partial input price subindexes, the form in (4.3) results. Moreover, (4.3) implies that the set of all prices is separable from u. Thus U is homothetic [see *Blackorby/Primont/Russell*, Lemma 3.4].

References

Blackorby, C., and *W.E. Diewert*: Expenditure Functions, Local Duality, and Second Order Approximations. Econometrica **47**, 1979, 579–601.

Blackorby, C., C.A.K. Lovell and *M.C. Thursby*: Extended Hicks Neutral Technical Change. Economic Journal **86**, 1976, 845–852.

Blackorby, C., D. Primont and *R.R. Russell*: Duality, Separability, and Functional Structure; Theory and Economic Applications. New York 1978.

Blackorby, C., and *R.R. Russell*: Indices and Subindices of the Cost of Living and the Standard of Living. International Economic Review **19**, 1978, 229–240.

Gorman, W.M.: The Structure of Utility Functions. Review of Economic Studies **35**, 1968, 369–390.

Pollak, R.A.: Subindexes of the Cost of Living. International Economic Review **16**, 1975, 135–150.

Part IV
Econometric Models

Quantitative Studies on Production and Prices

Dynamic Adjustment of Internal Prices to External Price Changes, Federal Republic of Germany, 1958–1979 An Application of Rank-Reduced Distributed-Lag Estimation by Spline Functions

John S. Chipman[1])

1. Introduction

This paper presents a method for estimating lag distributions in a large-scale dynamic model in which import and export prices are treated as the explanatory variables explaining internal prices. The model is applied to monthly data on import prices, export prices, and domestic producer prices of industrial products in the Federal Republic of Germany, covering the 22-year period 1958–1979. The basic data set consists of monthly price indices (multiplied by their weights) for 34 import categories, 32 export categories, and 34 domestic categories of commodities, as indicated in Table 1.

The theoretical justification for the model has been presented in detail in *Chipman* [1980]. The underlying model is an extension of Samuelson's model of international trade [*Samuelson*, 1953], allowing for the presence of nontradable domestic goods the production of which competes with the production of importables and exportables for the same set of factors of production, which are fixed in aggregate supply within the country but perfectly mobile among industries. The main substantive assumption is that the number of tradable commodities produced in the country is greater than or equal to the number of primary factors of production. This enables one to solve the system of minimum-unit-cost functions [cf. *Samuelson; Shephard*] uniquely for the factor rentals, which then (in conjunction with prices of imported or exported products used as intermediate inputs) uniquely determines the prices of the nontradables – again via the minimum-unit-cost functions. In the special case of fixed-coefficient production functions, the cost functions are linear; because of its great simplicity, as well as the flexibility it

[1]) Research was supported by National Science Foundation grant SOC77-27561, and in its initial stages by grants from the Graduate School and the Office of International Programs at the University of Minnesota. I am greatly indebted to George McCandless and Ronald Sands for their expert computational assistance, and to Barbara Craig, Kristine McFeaters, and Marie Fellbaum for their work in preparing the data set. I wish also to express my sincere thanks to Friedrich Marx and Dietrich Gralla of the Statistisches Bundesamt, Wiesbaden, for their cooperation in furnishing me with supplementary unpublished data on international and domestic prices used in this study. Finally I wish to thank the many people who have furnished valuable criticisms in numerous seminar presentations, among whom I wish particularly to mention John Helliwell of the University of British Columbia; the useful criticisms and comments of a referee are also gratefully acknowledged.

WI Code	Name of commodity category	Import price index G00	58	62	70
000000	Total	000058	1000.000[7]	1000.000	1000.000
100000	Agricultural, forestry, fishery products	100005	312.640	258.157	142.580
210000	Mining products	210000	134.480	102.193	98.700
211000	Coal & lignite	211000	42.270	11.152	6.230
216000	Crude petroleum & natural gas	216000	34.730	50.942	60.630
213000	Iron ore	213100	37.740	27.053	18.260
214000	Nonferrous metal ores	213200	17.040	10.320	11.240
210700[1]	Salts, other nonmetallic minerals, peat	210700	3.060	2.726	2.340
211000	Coal & lignite				
215000	Salts				
210406[2]	Other mining products				
000101	Electricity				
000103	City gas				
000107	Water				
220000	Petroleum products	220000	28.300	28.994	25.290
250000	Quarrying products	250000	13.380	15.278	14.380
270000	Iron & steel	270000	55.720	55.057	56.290
280000	Nonferrous metals	280000	65.200	63.147	79.090
290000	Foundry products	290000	2.290	1.936	1.690
300000	Products of drawing plants & cold rolling mills & steel shaping	300000	2.470	4.424	8.680
310000	Structural-steel engineering products	310000	2.220	3.073	3.870
320500[3]	Machinery including office machines & data-processing equipment	320005	39.800	67.472	81.770
360000	Electrical goods	360000	15.420	29.144	55.220
320501[4]	Machinery including office machines				
360505[5]	Electrical goods including data-processing equipment				
330000	Road vehicles	330000	15.890	21.709	46.980
370000	Precision & optical goods	370000	5.180	6.001	11.040
380000	Iron, steel, sheet & metal goods	380000	3.750	7.619	16.130
390000	Musical instruments, toys, athletic & sporting goods, jewelry, etc.	390000	3.300	7.855	9.030
400000	Chemicals	400000	55.680	56.709	78.220
510000	Pottery	510000	1.370	1.963	3.220
520000	Glass & glassware	520000	1.880	2.666	5.930
530000	Sawn wood, plywood, other worked wood	530005	27.300	22.615	15.090
540000	Wood products	540000	3.300	5.474	6.170
550000	Wood-pulp, cellulose, paper & paperboard	550000	27.690	30.041	28.820
560000	Paper & paperboard products	560000	0.850	1.484	3,060
570000	Printed products	570000	3.170	3,422	3.650
580000	Plastic products	580000	0.910	3.307	9.210
590000	Rubber & asbestos	590000	3.360	6.041	10.090
610000	Leather	610000	4.570	5.560	3.890
620000	Leather products & footwear	620000	3.380	6.250	9.930
630000	Textiles	630000	65.650	71.876	62.920
640000	Clothing	640000	12.500	13.566	21.540
680690[6]	Food, beverages & tobacco	202400	78.420	96.967	87.520

[1] Consists of 215, 217, and 218
[2] Consists of 213, 214, 216, 217, and 218
[3] Consists of 32 and 50
[4] Consists of 32 and 501
[5] Consists of 36 and 505
[6] Consists of 68 and 69

Export price index				Producer price index			
G10	58	62	70	G30	58	62	70
000058	1000.000[7]	1000.000	1000.000	000000	1000.000	1000.000	1000.000
100000	8.910	9.268	13.960				
211000	66.630	48.993	23.550	210000	43.841	32.595	25.474
211000	60.140	43.997	20.340	211000	43.841	32.595	19.758
215000	5.100	4.049	2.060	215000	2.082	1.568	1.271
210406	1.390	0.947	1.150	210406	6.526	4.394	8.172
				101000	29,229	32.790	46.393
				103000	8.262	7.026	5.393
				107000	4.427	3.712	5.326
220000	10.460	12.081	9.360	220000	22.519	34.868	40.707
250000	8.940	8.217	7.580	250000	30.291	33.653	29.094
270000	92.210	80.726	59.640	270000	62.196	49.406	48.133
280000	24.700	20.133	22.740	280000	16.499	14.506	18.494
290000	3.820	3.176	2.960	290000	18.069	16.626	15.068
300000	21.770	23.345	20.990	300000	32.758	29.429	30.630
310000	20.610	11.948	8.500	310000	19.241	21.883	17.671
320005	198.010	229.402	217.640				
360000	83.080	91.905	98.900				
				320005	74.269	83.904	83.953
				360005	63.741	74.108	90.691
330000	109.540	131.730	150.010	330000	41.371	52.348	55.404
370000	26.140	25.647	23.380	370000	7.411	7.661	8.390
380000	51.110	44.084	43.040	380000	36.123	38.036	39.697
390000	11.060	11.141	8.090	390000	3.698	3.872	3.616
400000	119.310	120.522	143.310	400000	77.460	74.074	77.738
510000	8.080	8.491	6.990	510000	5.330	4.851	3.950
520000	8.000	8.387	7.350	520000	7.557	7.527	4.731
530000	2.940	3.392	3.300	530000	11.782	10.600	9.484
540000	5.200	5.710	8.210	540000	22.746	22.752	24.592
550000	4.930	5.676	6.670	550000	15.237	11.818	9.591
560000	2.470	2.913	4,270	560000	14,588	14.571	15.796
570000	5.460	6.296	7.500	570000	17.176	18.397	20.878
580000	3.670	11.025	15.740	580000	9.352	12.886	21.054
590000	9.100	9.485	10.150	590000	12.671	12.671	12.692
610000	3.200	2.978	2.070	610000	4.562	3.265	1.607
620000	4.000	3.750	3.940	620000	13.609	12.732	9.844
630000	33.590	35.461	35.880	630000	71.482	61.144	47.211
640000	5.450	6.871	8.840	640000	31.783	36.267	30.376
202400	17.190	17.247	25.440	202400	170.720	160.022	146.322

Tab. 1: Codes, names, and weights of commodity groups used in regression of German producer price indices on import and export price indices

[7] The component weights for the 1958-base import and export price indices fail to sum to 1000 owing to the unavailability of data for category 34 (ships & boats). This category is not represented in the other series.

provides for aggregation, this assumption is used in the present paper. It is hoped, however, that in future work this assumption can be relaxed and a more realistic specification adopted.

In an earlier paper [*Chipman*, 1978] the same model was applied but without consideration of lags. Monthly data were aggregated to quarterly data, and the internal quarterly price indices were regressed against the simultaneous quarterly import and export price-index data. The present paper replaces this by a formulation in terms of distributed lags, using a method recently proposed by *Corradi/Gambetta* [1974] which consists of approximating the lag distributions by spline functions – smooth functions consisting of smoothly joined polynominal segments.[2])

Owing to the large number of explanatory variables used in the present study, attention has also had to be paid to the problem of multicollinearity. Within the framework of the spline-lag technique developed in the next section, another technique has been imposed to deal with multicollinearity, borrowed from *Marquardt* [1970]. This consists in successively approximating the observation matrix by matrices of lower rank, and taking their generalized inverses. Graphical methods are then used to detect a rank at which the estimates stabilize as one varies the rank.[3])

The statistical techniques are described in detail in Section 2. The reader who is primarily interested in results is advised to proceed directly to Section 3.

Estimates of some of the lag distributions are shown in Figures 1–8. Among the features of particular interest are (1) the rapid response in the case of domestic petroleum products, iron & steel, non-ferrous metals, and machinery, road vehicles & other manufactures to changes in the corresponding international prices (2) the overshooting of these responses in the first two or three months, and (3) the more delayed response in the case of some products (e.g., textiles & clothing) or in the case of cross-effects.

It has been assumed thoughout that the international prices faced by the Federal Republic of Germany may be regarded as exogenous, i.e., uninfluenced (or at least not substantially influenced) by the German economy itself. A forthcoming study will exam-

---

[2]) This method generalizes the polynomial-lag approach of *Almon* [1965] and removes from the latter method the undesirable feature that erratic local behavior can affect the shape of the entire lag distribution. It is also considerably more economical in computer-storage capacity than *Shiller's* [1973] method of employing "smoothness priors". Shiller's method is simply not feasible in large-scale models such as this one, unless one is willing to aggregate the exogenous variables into at most nine or ten groups; and cf. *Ho* [1977] where Shiller's method has been successfully applied subject to this limitation. The spline-function technique was introduced in *Ouanes'* [1979] study.

[3]) This type of criterion was introduced by *Hoerl/Kennard* [1970b] in their pioneering work on ridge regression [*Hoerl/Kennard*, 1970a]. In connection with the Marquardt procedure used here, it also finds support in the numerical-analysis literature, which stresses the importance of measurement and rounding error when multicollinearity is present [cf. *Wedin*]. The approach also appears to find support in *Leamer's* [1973] Bayesian formulation of the multicollinearity problem. The ridge-regression and Marquardt procedures are two among several possible ways of perturbing least-squares estimates so as to obtain biased estimates with smaller mean-square error. [Cf. *Chipman*, 1964; *Hoerl/Kennard*, 1970a; *Marquardt; Goldstein/Smith; Bacon/Hausman*].

ine this hypothesis (as well as the maintained hypothesis that the number of tradable commodities produced at home exceeds or equals the number of primary factors of production) and subject them to test.[4])

2. Estimation of Distributed Lags by Spline Functions

2.1 The Basic Model

Letting y_{tj} stand for the value of the j-th endogenous variable at time t, and x_{ti} for the value of the i-th exogenous variable at time t, where $j = 1, 2, \ldots, m$ and $i = 1, 2, \ldots, k$, and $t = 1, 2, \ldots, n$, the basic model is

$$y_{tj} = \sum_{i=1}^{k} \sum_{l=0}^{L_i} x_{t-l,i}\, \beta_l^{ij} + \epsilon_{tj} \qquad (t = L+1, L+2, \ldots, L+T = n) \tag{2.1}$$

where $L = \max_{i=1,2,\ldots,k} L_i$ and $T = n - L$.[5]) Is is assumed that

$$E\,\epsilon_{tj} = 0, \quad E\,\epsilon_{tj}\,\epsilon_{t'j'} = v_{tt'}\,\sigma_{jj'}\,, \tag{2.2}$$

the expectations being conditional on the $x_{t-l,i}$. In matrix notation, (2.1) may be written

$$Y = XB + E = \sum_{i=1}^{k} X_i B_i + E \tag{2.3}$$

where $X = [X_1, X_2, \ldots, X_k]$, $B' = [B_1', B_2', \ldots, B_k']$,

$$Y = \begin{bmatrix} y_{L+1,1} & y_{L+1,2} & \cdots & y_{L+1,m} \\ y_{L+2,1} & y_{L+2,2} & \cdots & y_{L+2,m} \\ \vdots & \vdots & & \vdots \\ y_{L+T,1} & y_{L+T,2} & \cdots & y_{L+T,m} \end{bmatrix}, \quad E = \begin{bmatrix} \epsilon_{L+1,1} & \epsilon_{L+1,2} & \cdots & \epsilon_{L+1,m} \\ \epsilon_{L+2,1} & \epsilon_{L+2,2} & \cdots & \epsilon_{L+2,m} \\ \vdots & \vdots & & \vdots \\ \epsilon_{L+T,1} & \epsilon_{L+T,2} & \cdots & \epsilon_{L+T,m} \end{bmatrix}, \tag{2.4}$$

and

---

[4]) *Ouanes* [1979] has performed the *Sims* [1972] test of exogeneity by allowing the contemporaneous lag coefficients β_l^{ij} of (2.7) below to be estimated freely and postulating that the remaining ones β_l^{ij} $(1 \leqslant l < L_i)$ lie on a spline. His tests largely confirmed the exogeneity hypothesis. The other hypothesis referred to can be tested by testing the significance of certain balance-of-payments variables as additional explanatory variables in the regression, in accordance with the results of *Chipman* [1980].

[5]) More generally, one could replace L_i in (2.1) by L_{ij}, i.e., allow the assumed lag length to vary across endogenous as well as exogenous variables. This would require replacing L by $L_j = \max_{i=1,2,\ldots,k} L_{ij}$, and T by $T_j = n - L_j$, and necessitate a more cumbersome notation than that allowed by (2.3), (2.4), and (2.5). However, this would lead to the types of problems of efficient estimation singled out for analysis by *Zellner* [1962], which I prefer to avoid here (see footnote 9 below).

$$X_i = \begin{bmatrix} x_{L+1,i} & x_{Li} & \cdots & x_{L+1-L_i,i} \\ x_{L+2,i} & x_{L+1,i} & \cdots & x_{L+2-L_i,i} \\ \vdots & \vdots & & \vdots \\ x_{L+T,i} & x_{L+T-1,i} & \cdots & x_{L+T-L_i,i} \end{bmatrix}, \quad B_i = \begin{bmatrix} \beta_0^{i1} & \beta_0^{i2} & \cdots & \beta_0^{im} \\ \beta_1^{i1} & \beta_1^{i2} & \cdots & \beta_1^{im} \\ \vdots & \vdots & & \vdots \\ \beta_{L_i}^{i1} & \beta_{L_i}^{i2} & \cdots & \beta_{L_i}^{im} \end{bmatrix}, \tag{2.5}$$

X_i being of order $T \times (L_i + 1)$. Likewise, (2.2) may be written

$$\mathsf{E} E = 0, \quad \mathsf{E}(\text{col } E)(\text{col } E)' = \Sigma \otimes V \tag{2.6}$$

where "col E" denotes the $Tm \times 1$ column vector of the m columns of E, and $\Sigma = [\sigma_{jj'}]$ and $V = [v_{tt'}]$ denote the $m \times m$ contemporaneous covariance matrix and the $T \times T$ autocovariance matrix respectively.

We now postulate that the points on the lag distribution, (l, β_l^{ij}), $l = 0, 1, \ldots, L_i$, lie on a natural spline of degree $2\nu_i - 1$, with N_i knots κ_h^i, $h = 1, 2, \ldots, N_i$,[6]) so that they satisfy

$$\beta_l^{ij} = \sum_{h=0}^{\nu_i - 1} c_h^{ij} l^h + \sum_{h=1}^{N_i} c_{\nu_i-1+h}^{ij} (l - \kappa_h^i)_+^{2\nu_i - 1} \tag{2.7}$$

(where $x_+ = \max(x, 0)$), where the coefficients $c_{\nu_i-1+h}^{ij}$ satisfy

$$0 = \sum_{h=1}^{N_i} c_{\nu_i-1+h}^{ij} (\kappa_h^i)^r, \qquad r = 0, 1, \ldots, \nu_i - 1, \tag{2.8}$$

[cf. *Greville*, 1969, p. 3].[7]) We shall express the relations in matrix notations as follows. Define for $i = 1, 2, \ldots, k$ the $(L_i + 1) \times \nu_i$ Vandermonde matrix $P_i = [p_{lh}]$ $(l = 0, 1, \ldots, L_i; h = 0, 1, \ldots, \nu_i - 1)$ by

$$P_i = [p_{lh}] = [l^h] = \begin{bmatrix} 1 & 0 & 0 & \cdots & 0 \\ 1 & 1 & 1 & \cdots & 1 \\ 1 & 2 & 2^2 & \cdots & 2^{\nu_i-1} \\ \cdot & \cdot & \cdot & \cdots & \cdot \\ 1 & l & l^2 & \cdots & l^{\nu_i-1} \\ \cdot & \cdot & \cdot & \cdots & \cdot \\ 1 & L_i & L_i^2 & \cdots & L_i^{\nu_i-1} \end{bmatrix} \tag{2.9}$$

---

[6]) Referring to the preceding footnote, one could more generally replace ν_i, N_i, and κ_h^i by ν_{ij}, N_{ij}, and κ_h^{ij} respectively. This would require replacing the matrices P_i, Q_i, J_i, K_i, A_i, Φ_i, and Ψ_i below by P_{ij}, Q_{ij}, J_{ij}, K_{ij}, A_{ij}, Φ_{ij}, and Ψ_{ij} respectively, and of course dispensing with the notation of (2.24) – (2.30). This generalization is completely straightforward and is left to the interested reader [cf. *Ouanes*].

[7]) In both (2.7) and (2.8) we define $0^0 = 1$.

and the $(L_i + 1) \times (L_i + 1)$ lower-triangular matrix $Q_i = [q^i_{ll'}]$ $(l, l' = 0, 1, 2, \ldots, L_i)$ by

$$Q_i = [q^i_{ll'}] = [(l-l')_+^{2\nu_i-1}] = \begin{bmatrix} 0 & 0 & 0 & \ldots & 0 & 0 \\ 1 & 0 & 0 & \ldots & 0 & 0 \\ 2^{2\nu_i-1} & 1 & 0 & \ldots & 0 & 0 \\ \cdot & \cdot & \cdot & \ldots & \cdot & \cdot \\ l^{2\nu_i-1} & (l-1)^{2\nu_i-1} & (l-2)^{2\nu_i-1} & \ldots & 0 & 0 \\ \cdot & \cdot & \cdot & \ldots & \cdot & \cdot \\ L_i^{2\nu_i-1} & (L_i-1)^{2\nu_i-1} & (L_i-2)^{2\nu_i-1} & \ldots & 1 & 0 \end{bmatrix}. \tag{2.10}$$

Given a set of $N_i \leqslant L_i$ knots

$$\kappa_1^i < \kappa_2^i < \ldots < \kappa_{N_i}^i, \tag{2.11}$$

preselected from among the $L_i + 1$ integers $0, 1, \ldots, L_i$, we define the $N_i \times (L_i + 1)$ matrix J_i, for each $i = 1, 2, \ldots, k$, by

$$J_i = [\delta_{\kappa_h^i, l}] \qquad (h = 1, 2, \ldots, N_i;\, l = 0, 1, \ldots, L_i), \tag{2.12}$$

and the $(L_i + 1 - N_i) \times (L_i + 1)$ matrix K_i by

$$K_i = [\delta_{l'l}] \qquad (l' = 0, 1, \ldots, L_i,\, l' \neq \kappa_h^i;\, l = 0, 1, \ldots, L_i), \tag{2.13}$$

where $\delta_{l'l}$ is the Kronecker delta; together, J_i and K_i form the rows of the $(L_i + 1) \times (L_i + 1)$ identity matrix I_{L_i+1} corresponding to the lags that are and are not knots, respectively. Then the equations (2.7) and (2.8), which may be displayed in matrix notation as

$$\begin{bmatrix} \beta_0^{ij} \\ \beta_1^{ij} \\ \beta_2^{ij} \\ \cdot \\ \cdot \\ \cdot \\ \beta_{L_i}^{ij} \\ 0 \\ 0 \\ 0 \\ \cdot \\ \cdot \\ \cdot \\ 0 \end{bmatrix} = \begin{bmatrix} 1 & 0 & 0 & \ldots & 0 & (0-\kappa_1^i)_+^{2\nu_i-1} & (0-\kappa_2^i)_+^{2\nu_i-1} & \ldots & (0-\kappa_{N_i}^i)_+^{2\nu_i-1} \\ 1 & 1 & 1 & \ldots & 1 & (1-\kappa_1^i)_+^{2\nu_i-1} & (1-\kappa_2^i)_+^{2\nu_i-1} & \ldots & (1-\kappa_{N_i}^i)_+^{2\nu_i-1} \\ 1 & 2 & 2^2 & \ldots & 2^{\nu_i-1} & (2-\kappa_1^i)_+^{2\nu_i-1} & (2-\kappa_2^i)_+^{2\nu_i-1} & \ldots & (2-\kappa_{N_i}^i)_+^{2\nu_i-1} \\ \cdot & \cdot & \cdot & & \cdot & \cdot & \cdot & & \cdot \\ \cdot & \cdot & \cdot & & \cdot & \cdot & \cdot & & \cdot \\ \cdot & \cdot & \cdot & & \cdot & \cdot & \cdot & & \cdot \\ 1 & L_i & L_i^2 & \ldots & L_i^{\nu_i-1} & (L_i-\kappa_1^i)_+^{2\nu_i-1} & (L_i-\kappa_2^i)_+^{2\nu_i-1} & \ldots & (L_i-\kappa_{N_i}^i)_+^{2\nu_i-1} \\ 0 & 0 & 0 & \ldots & 0 & 1 & 1 & \ldots & 1 \\ 0 & 0 & 0 & \ldots & 0 & \kappa_1^i & \kappa_2^i & \ldots & \kappa_{N_i}^i \\ 0 & 0 & 0 & \ldots & 0 & (\kappa_1^i)^2 & (\kappa_2^i)^2 & \ldots & (\kappa_{N_i}^i)^2 \\ \cdot & \cdot & \cdot & & \cdot & \cdot & \cdot & & \cdot \\ \cdot & \cdot & \cdot & & \cdot & \cdot & \cdot & & \cdot \\ \cdot & \cdot & \cdot & & \cdot & \cdot & \cdot & & \cdot \\ 0 & 0 & 0 & \ldots & 0 & (\kappa_1^i)^{\nu_i-1} & (\kappa_2^i)^{\nu_i-1} & \ldots & (\kappa_{N_i}^i)^{\nu_i-1} \end{bmatrix} \begin{bmatrix} c_0^{ij} \\ c_1^{ij} \\ c_2^{ij} \\ \cdot \\ \cdot \\ \cdot \\ c_{\nu_i-1}^{ij} \\ c_{\nu_i}^{ij} \\ c_{\nu_i+1}^{ij} \\ c_{\nu_i+2}^{ij} \\ \cdot \\ \cdot \\ \cdot \\ c_{\nu_i+N_i-1}^{ij} \end{bmatrix} \tag{2.14}$$

may be written compactly in the form

$$\begin{bmatrix} \beta^{ij} \\ 0 \end{bmatrix} = \begin{bmatrix} P_i & Q_i J_i' \\ 0 & P_i' J_i' \end{bmatrix} c^{ij}, \tag{2.15}$$

where β^{ij} and c^{ij} denote the $(L_i + 1) \times 1$ and $(\nu_i + N_i) \times 1$ column vectors $[\beta_l^{ij}]$ and $[c_h^{ij}]$ respectively.

Denoting by

$$\gamma^{ij} = J_i \beta^{ij}, \text{ i.e., } \gamma^{ij} = [\gamma_h^{ij}] = [\beta^{ij}_{\kappa_h^i}] \qquad (h = 1, 2, \ldots, N_i), \tag{2.16}$$

the $N_i \times 1$ vector of lag coefficients at the knots, we have

$$\begin{bmatrix} \gamma^{ij} \\ 0 \end{bmatrix} = \begin{bmatrix} J_i P_i & J_i Q_i J_i' \\ 0 & P_i' J_i' \end{bmatrix} c^{ij} = A_i c^{ij}, \tag{2.17}$$

which defines the $(N_i + \nu_i) \times (\nu_i + N_i)$ matrix A_i. By the uniqueness theorem for natural splines [*Greville*, 1969, p. 6, Theorem 6.2], A_i is non-singular. Hence, from (2.15), (2.16), and (2.17) we have[8])

$$\beta^{ij} = \Phi_i \gamma^{ij}, \tag{2.18}$$

where

$$\Phi_i = [P_i, Q_i J_i'] \begin{bmatrix} J_i P_i & J_i Q_i J_i' \\ 0 & P_i' J_i' \end{bmatrix}^{-1} \begin{bmatrix} I_{N_i} \\ 0 \end{bmatrix}, \tag{2.19}$$

which defines the $(L_i + 1) \times N_i$ matrix Φ_i. This may be expressed equivalently as a set of $L_i + 1 - N_i$ independent linear restrictions on β^{ij} [cf. *Chipman/Rao*, 1964a], as follows. Premultiplying (2.19) by J_i we see that

$$J_i \Phi_i = I_{N_i}, \tag{2.20}$$

hence Φ_i is a right inverse of J_i, and thus the $(L_i + 1) \times (L_i + 1)$ matrix $\Phi_i J_i$ is idempotent of rank N_i. Premultiplying (2.18) by this latter matrix and using (2.20) and (2.16) we have $\Phi_i J_i \beta^{ij} = \beta^{ij}$, or

$$(I - \Phi_i J_i) \beta^{ij} = 0. \tag{2.21}$$

---

[8]) This may be contrasted with the case of the *Almon* [1965] lag in which the right side of (2.18) is replaced by $P_i c_*^{ij}$, where c_*^{ij} consists of the first ν_i elements of c^{ij} (see (2.7)). In both cases, the method consists of reparametrizing β^{ij} by a smaller-dimensional vector by means of a known transformation matrix (Φ_i or P_i) [cf. *Hamlen/Hamlen*]. As the referee has emphasized, and as might be obscured by the elaborate detail involved in spline-function estimation, it is simply a special case of linear reparametrization of the regression coefficients (or equivalently, of the imposition of linear restrictions on the regression coefficients).

Premultiplication of (2.21) by J_i yields the redundant equation $0 = 0$; to obtain our independent linear restrictions we therefore premultiply (2.21) by K_i to obtain

$$\Psi_i \beta^{ij} = 0, \tag{2.22}$$

where

$$\Psi_i = K_i [I - \Phi_i J_i] = K_i \left\{ I_{L_i+1} - [P_i, Q_i J_i'] \begin{bmatrix} J_i P_i & J_i Q_i J_i' \\ 0 & P_i' J_i' \end{bmatrix}^{-1} \begin{bmatrix} J_i \\ 0 \end{bmatrix} \right\}, \tag{2.23}$$

Ψ_i being an $(L_i + 1 - N_i) \times (L_i + 1)$ matrix. Since the $(L_i + 1) \times (L_i + 1)$ matrix $I - \Phi_i J_i$ is idempotent of rank $L_i + 1 - N_i$ [cf. *Chipman/Rao*, 1964b], we have $\Psi_i [I - \Phi_i J_i] = \Psi_i$, hence Ψ_i has rank $L_i + 1 - N_i$.

Noting, now, from (2.5) that the restrictions (2.18) and (2.23) apply to each column of B_i, and defining

$$\Gamma_i = J_i B_i, \tag{2.24}$$

we may express (2.18) and (2.22) for $j = 1, 2, \ldots, m$ as

$$B_i = \Phi_i \Gamma_i \quad \text{and} \quad \Psi_i B_i = 0 \tag{2.25}$$

respectively. Defining

$$Z_i = X_i \Phi_i, \quad Z = [Z_1, Z_2, \ldots, Z_k], \quad \Gamma = [\Gamma_1', \Gamma_2', \ldots, \Gamma_k'], \tag{2.26}$$

where Z_i is of order $T \times N_i$, as well as the $(\sum_{i=1}^{k} L_i + k) \times (\sum_{i=1}^{k} N_i)$ matrix

$$\Phi = \begin{bmatrix} \Phi_1 & 0 & \ldots & 0 \\ 0 & \Phi_2 & \ldots & 0 \\ \vdots & \vdots & & \vdots \\ 0 & 0 & \ldots & \Phi_k \end{bmatrix}, \tag{2.27}$$

we may write (2.3) in the form

$$Y = X\Phi\Gamma + E = Z\Gamma + E = \sum_{i=1}^{k} Z_i \Gamma_i + E. \tag{2.28}$$

Provided the $T \times \sum_{i=1}^{k} N_i$ matrix Z has rank $\sum_{i=1}^{k} N_i$, and that Z and the matrix V of (2.6) satisfy $Z = VM$ for some M, Γ may be estimated uniquely by its Gauss-Markoff estimator

$$\tilde{\Gamma} = (Z'V^{-}Z)^{-1} Z'V^{-}Y, \tag{2.29}$$

where V^- is any generalized inverse of V [cf. *Chipman*, 1977].[9]) B_i is then estimated by

$$\tilde{B}_i = \Phi_i \tilde{\Gamma}_i \qquad (i = 1, 2, \ldots, k). \tag{2.30}$$

2.2 Zero End-Point Constraints

We now introduce the additional end-point constraints

$$\beta^{ij}_{L_i} = 0 \qquad (i = 1, 2, \ldots, k;\ j = 1, 2, \ldots, m) \tag{2.31}$$

Given that (implicitly) we assume $\beta^{ij}_l = 0$ for $l = L_i + 1, L_i + 2, \ldots$, these constraints merely require that the entire lag distribution $(0 \leqslant l < \infty)$ be continuous. They may be effected by requiring for each exogenous variable, i, that the last (N_i-th) knot be equal to the lag length L_i, i.e., $\kappa^i_{N_i} = L_i$, so that the vanishing of the last row of B_i (see (2.5)) implies the vanishing of the last row of Γ_i (see (2.24)); then in the regression equation (2.28) we may delete the last column of each Z_i, i.e., replace Z_i by the $T \times (N_i - 1)$ matrix

$$Z_i^0 = Z_i \begin{bmatrix} I_{N_i-1} \\ 0 \end{bmatrix} = X_i \Phi_i \begin{bmatrix} I_{N_i-1} \\ 0 \end{bmatrix} = X_i \Phi_i^0 \qquad (i = 1, 2, \ldots, k), \tag{2.32}$$

where, in view of (2.26) and (2.19), Φ_i^0 is the $(L_i + 1) \times (N_i - 1)$ matrix

$$\Phi_i^0 = \Phi_i \begin{bmatrix} I_{N_i-1} \\ 0 \end{bmatrix} = [P_i, Q_i J_i'] \begin{bmatrix} J_i P_i & J_i Q_i J_i' \\ 0 & P_i' J_i' \end{bmatrix}^{-1} \begin{bmatrix} I_{N_i-1} \\ 0 \end{bmatrix}. \tag{2.33}$$

Computationally, this requires postmultiplying the $(L_i + 1) \times (\nu_i + N_i)$ matrix $[P_i, Q_i J_i']$ by the first $N_i - 1$ columns of the $(\nu_i + N_i) \times (\nu_i + N_i)$ matrix A_i^{-1} (see (2.17)). Like-

---

[9]) As indicated in footnote 5 above, the estimator (2.29) would no longer be efficient if disparities in lag length were introduced across endogenous variables. Since the referee has challenged the assertion that (2.50) is Gauss-Markoff, I present here a simple proof. Writing (2.49) as

$$\text{col}\, Y = (I \otimes Z^0)\, \text{col}\, \Gamma^0 + \text{col}\, E \tag{F.1}$$

and making use of (2.6), we see that the best linear unbiased estimator of col Γ^0 is given by

$$\text{col}\, \hat{\Gamma}^0 = [(I \otimes Z^0)' (\Sigma \otimes V)^- (I \otimes Z)]^{-1} (I \otimes Z^0)' (\Sigma \otimes V)^- \text{col}\, Y. \tag{F.2}$$

From well-known properties of Kronecker products this simplifies to

$$\begin{aligned} \text{col}\, \hat{\Gamma}^0 &= [\Sigma^{-1} \otimes Z^{0\prime} V^- Z^0]^{-1} [\Sigma^{-1} \otimes Z^{0\prime} V^-]\, \text{col}\, Y \\ &= [I \otimes (Z^{0\prime} V^- Z^0)^{-1} Z^{0\prime} V^-]\, \text{col}\, Y \\ &= \text{col}\, [(Z^{0\prime} V^- Z^0)^{-1} Z^{0\prime} V^- Y] \end{aligned} \tag{F.3}$$

yielding (2.50). It must be noted that $I \otimes Z^0$ is a block diagonal matrix whose diagonal blocks are all equal to Z^0, as opposed to being distinct as in Zellner's problem [*Zellner*, 1962] (or equivalently, as opposed to the elements of Γ^0 being subject to linear restrictions).

wise, defining the $(N_i - 1) \times (L_i + 1)$ matrix J_i^0 by

$$J_i^0 = [I_{N_i\text{-}1}, 0]\, J_i = [\delta_{\kappa_h^i, l}] \qquad (h = 1, 2, \ldots, N_i - 1;\ l = 0, 1, \ldots, L_i) \tag{2.34}$$

and the $(N_i - 1) \times 1$ vector $\gamma^{ij,0}$ and the $(N_i - 1) \times m$ matrix Γ_i^0 by

$$\gamma^{ij,0} = J_i^0 \beta^{ij} = [I_{N_i\text{-}1}, 0]\, \gamma^{ij},\ \Gamma_i^0 = J_i^0 B_i = [I_{N_i\text{-}1}, 0]\, \Gamma_i, \tag{2.35}$$

we see from (2.34), (2.33), and (2.20) that

$$J_i^0 \Phi_i^0 = I_{N_i\text{-}1}. \tag{2.36}$$

Expressing the constraints (2.31) in the form

$$\Gamma_i = \begin{bmatrix} I_{N_i\text{-}1} \\ 0 \end{bmatrix} \Gamma_i^0 \qquad (i = 1, 2, \ldots, k) \tag{2.37}$$

we see from (2.25), (2.37), and (2.33) that

$$B_i = \Phi_i^0 \Gamma_i^0 \qquad (i = 1, 2, \ldots, k) \tag{2.38}$$

hence, from (2.35),

$$(I_{L_0+1} - \Phi_i^0 J_i^0)\, B_i = 0. \tag{2.39}$$

Defining the $(L_i + 2 - N_i) \times (L_i + 1)$ matrix

$$\Psi_i^0 = K_i^0\, (I - \Phi_i^0 J_i^0), \tag{2.40}$$

where the $(L_i + 2 - N_i) \times (L_i + 1)$ matrix K_i^0 is formed by adjoining to K_i the row δ_{L_i} (the coordinate vector with 1 in the $(L_i + 1)$-th place) which was deleted from J_i to form J_i^0, i.e.,

$$K_i^0 = \begin{bmatrix} K_i \\ \delta_{L_i} \end{bmatrix}, \tag{2.41}$$

we may as before express the constraints on each column of B_i as a set of $L_i + 2 - N_i$ independent linear restrictions

$$\Psi_i^0 B_i = 0. \tag{2.42}$$

It is not hard to see that Ψ_i^0 is obtained from Ψ_i by replacing the last column of Ψ_i by zeros and adjoining to Ψ_i the additional row δ_{L_i}. Defining the

$(\sum_{i=1}^{k} L_i + 2k - \sum_{i=1}^{k} N_i) \times (\sum_{i=1}^{k} L_i + k)$ matrix

$$\Psi^0 = \begin{bmatrix} \Psi_1^0 & 0 & \dots & 0 \\ 0 & \Psi_2^0 & \dots & 0 \\ \vdots & \vdots & & \vdots \\ 0 & 0 & \dots & \Psi_k^0 \end{bmatrix}, \tag{2.43}$$

the entire set of restrictions (2.42) may be written as

$$\Psi^0 B = 0. \tag{2.44}$$

Defining now the $T \times (\sum_{i=1}^{k} N_i - k)$ matrix Z^0 and the $(\sum_{i=1}^{k} N_i - k) \times m$ matrix Γ^0 by

$$Z^0 = [Z_1^0, Z_2^0, \dots, Z_k^0] \text{ and } \Gamma^{0\prime} = [\Gamma_1^{0\prime}, \Gamma_2^{0\prime}, \dots, \Gamma_k^{0\prime}] \tag{2.45}$$

respectively, as well as the $(\sum_{i=1}^{k} L_i + k) \times (\sum_{i=1}^{k} N_i - k)$ matrix

$$\Phi^0 = \begin{bmatrix} \Phi_1^0 & 0 & \dots & 0 \\ 0 & \Phi_2^0 & \dots & 0 \\ \vdots & \vdots & & \vdots \\ 0 & 0 & \dots & \Phi_k^0 \end{bmatrix}, \tag{2.46}$$

we may write the constraints (2.38) as

$$B = \Phi^0 \Gamma^0, \tag{2.47}$$

and the transformation (2.32) may be written

$$Z^0 = X\Phi^0. \tag{2.48}$$

We then estimate Γ^0 from the regression model

$$Y = X\Phi^0\Gamma^0 + E = Z^0\Gamma^0 + E \sum_{i=1}^{k} Z_i^0\Gamma_i^0 + E \tag{2.49}$$

by

$$\hat{\Gamma}^0 = (Z^{0\prime}V^- Z^0)^{-1} Z^{0\prime}V^- Y. \tag{2.50}$$

Finally, we estimate each B_i by

$$\hat{B}_i = \Phi_i^0 \hat{\Gamma}_i^0 \qquad (i = 1, 2, \dots, k), \tag{2.51}$$

in accordance with (2.38), i.e.,

$$\hat{B} = \Phi^0 \hat{\Gamma}^0. \tag{2.52}$$

2.3 Rank Reduction and Hypothesis Testing

In the remainder of this section I shall assume that there is no serial correlation, so that the autocovariance matrix V of (2.6) reduces to the identity matrix of order T. (The symbol V will be used below to denote a different matrix.) The justification for this assumption rests not on its realism (which would not be possible to support) but on its robustness. Elsewhere [*Chipman*, 1979] I have shown that in at least some cases, least-squares estimation remains quite efficient in the presence of serial correlation. A much more serious problem than autocorrelation of residuals is multicollinearity among the explanatory variables.

If the matrix Z^0 of (2.48) is ill-conditioned, conventional Gauss-Seidel methods of computing the least-squares estimate (2.50) can prove to be highly inaccurate. The method to be followed here is to instead compute $\hat{\Gamma}^0$ by means of the singular-value decomposition of the $T \times K$ matrix Z^0 given by [cf. *Golub/Reinsch; Eckart/Young*, 1939]

$$Z^0 = UDV' \quad \text{where } U'U = V'V = I_K, \; D = \text{diag}\,(d_1, d_2, \ldots, d_K), \tag{2.53}$$

where we define $K = \sum_{i=1}^{k} (N_i - 1)$ (not to be confused with the matrix K_i of (2.13)), and the K diagonal elements of D are the (nonnegative) singular values of Z^0 (in descending order).[10]) Defining $D^\dagger = \text{diag}\,(d_1^\dagger, d_2^\dagger, \ldots, d_K^\dagger)$ where $d_i^\dagger = d_i^{-1}$ if $d_i > 0$ and $d_i^\dagger = 0$ if $d_i = 0$, the (unique) Moore-Penrose generalized inverse of Z^0, which coincides with $(Z^{0\prime}Z^0)^{-1}Z^0$ when $Z^{0\prime}$ has rank K (i.e., when $D \neq 0$ and $D^\dagger = D^{-1}$), is [cf. *Golub/Kahan*].

$$Z^{0\dagger} = VD^\dagger U'. \tag{2.54}$$

In practice it will always be the case – if only because of measurement error – that the singular values are all positive. However, *Marquardt* [1970, p. 601] has shown that if the length of the j-th column $\gamma^{j,0}$ of Γ^0 is subject to a particular a priori bound, namely

$$\frac{\gamma^{j,0\prime}\gamma^{j,0}}{\sigma_{jj}} < \sum_{i=r+1}^{K} \frac{1}{d_i^2}, \tag{2.55}$$

then the estimator

$$\hat{\gamma}^{j,0}(r) = Z_r^{0\dagger} y^j = VD_r^\dagger U' y^j \qquad (j = 1, 2, \ldots, m) \tag{2.56}$$

obtained by replacing D by the matrix D_r in which the $K - r$ smallest singular values have been replaced by zeros – where y^j is the j-th column of the matrix Y of (2.4) – will have lower mean-square error than the least-squares estimator

$$\hat{\gamma}^{j,0} = \hat{\gamma}^{j,0}(K) = VD^\dagger U' y^j = Z^{0\dagger} y^j = (Z^{0\prime}Z^0)^{-1} Z^{0\prime} y^j. \tag{2.57}$$

It is well known that the matrix Z_r^0 defined by

$$Z_r^0 = UD_r V' \tag{2.58}$$

---

[10]) These are the nonnegative square roots of the characteristic (eigen) values of the matrix $Z^{0\prime}Z^0 = VD^2V'$.

is the matrix of rank r that best approximates Z^0 among all $T \times K$ matrices of rank r, in terms of the Frobenius norm $\| Z_r^0 - Z^0 \| = \sqrt{tr\,(Z_r^0 - Z^0)'(Z_r^0 - Z^0)}$ [cf. *Golub/Kahan*, p. 220; *Eckart/Young*, 1936]. If Z^0 is ill-conditioned, for some $r < K$ the right side of (2.55) will be extremely large, and since in almost all economic applications one can think of (and most certainly in this one) one can impose very stringent a priori bounds on the regression coefficients, it can be said with confidence that by using the Marquardt procedure one can improve upon least squares.

Partitioning the orthogonal matrix V of (2.53) as $V' = [V_1', V_2', \ldots, V_k']$, where V_i is of order $(N_i - 1) \times K$, we obtain from (2.56) the estimator

$$\hat{\gamma}^{ij,0}(r) = V_i D_r^{\dagger} U' y^j \tag{2.59}$$

of the $(N_i - 1) \times 1$ vector $\gamma^{ij,0}$ of (2.35). This gives the lag coefficients $\hat{\gamma}_h^{ij} = \hat{\beta}_{\kappa_h^i}^{ij}$ for the regression of endogenous variable j on exogenous variable i at the $N_i - 1$ free knots κ_h^i, $h = 1, 2, \ldots, N_i - 1$. The remaining lag coefficients are obtained from (2.51) by the formula

$$\hat{\beta}^{ij}(r) = \Phi_i^0 \hat{\gamma}^{ij,0}(r) = \Phi_i^0 V_i D_r^{\dagger} U' y^j \tag{2.60}$$

or

$$\hat{B}_i(r) = \Phi_i \hat{\Gamma}_i^0(r) = \Phi_i^0 V_i D_r^{\dagger} U' Y. \tag{2.61}$$

Denoting by ϵ^j the j-th column of the matrix E of (2.4), it is clear from (2.60), (2.3), and (2.6) (recalling that the matrix V of (2.6) has been assumed to be equal to I) that the variance matrix of $\hat{\beta}^{ij}(r)$ is

$$\operatorname{Var} \hat{\beta}^{ij}(r) = \sigma_{jj} \Phi_i^0 V_i D_r^{\dagger 2} V_i' \Phi_i^{0\prime}. \tag{2.62}$$

To obtain an estimator of σ_{jj}, define the matrix

$$S(r) = [s_{jj'}(r)] = Y' [I_T - Z_r^0 Z_r^{0\dagger}]\, Y. \tag{2.63}$$

Denoting by U_r the first r columns of U, we have from (2.58) and (2.56)

$$S(r) = Y' [I_T - U_r U_r']\, Y. \tag{2.64}$$

If, now, we regard Z_r^0 as the "true" matrix of values of the exogenous variables rather than the actually observed matrix Z^0,[11]) then we have for the j-th column of Y

$$y^j = Z_r^0 \gamma^{j,0} + \epsilon^j = U D_r V' \gamma^{j,0} + \epsilon^j = [U_r D_r, 0]\, V' \gamma^{j,0} + \epsilon^j, \tag{2.65}$$

whence

$$[I - Z_r^0 Z_r^{0\dagger}]\, y^j = [I - U_r U_r'] \{[U_r D_r, 0]\, V' \gamma^{j,0} + \epsilon^j\} = [I - U_r U_r']\, \epsilon^j. \tag{2.66}$$

---

[11]) That is, for each rank r in turn, expectations are conditional on Z_r^0 rather than on Z^0. This seems reasonable inasmuch as Z^0 can be assumed to contain errors of measurement and rounding error. The criterion of robustness (stability of the estimates with respect to variations in r) discussed in sections 3.2 and 3.3 below is used both to validate this procedure as well as to estimate the best r from the data.

Accordingly,

$$E\, s_{jj'}(r) = E\,\epsilon^{j}{}' [I_T - U_r U_r'] \epsilon^{j'} = tr\{[I_T - U_r U_r'] \,E\,\epsilon^{j} \epsilon^{j'}{}'\} = (T-r)\,\sigma_{jj'}\,. \quad (2.67)$$

Thus, in terms of the interpretation of (2.65), the matrix (2.63) may be regarded as an unbiased estimator of $(T-r)\,\Sigma$, and thus

$$\hat{\sigma}_{jj'}(r) = y^{j}{}' [I_T - U_r U_r'] y^{j'} / (T-r) \quad (2.68)$$

may be regarded as an unbiased estimator of $\sigma_{jj'}$. Our estimator of the standard error of the estimated lag coefficient $\hat{\beta}_l^{ij}(r)$ is therefore

$$\text{S.E.}\{\hat{\beta}_l^{ij}(r)\} = \sqrt{\hat{\sigma}_{jj}(r)\, \delta_l \Phi_i^0 V_i D_r^{\dagger 2} V_i' \Phi_i^{0\prime} \delta_l'} \quad (2.69)$$

for $l = 0, 1, \ldots, L_i - 1$, where δ_l is a $1 \times (L_i + 1)$ coordinate vector with 1 in position l and zeros elsewhere; the corresponding t-ratio is of course $t = \hat{\beta}_l^{ij}(r) \,/\, \text{S.E.}\{\hat{\beta}_l^{ij}(r)\}$.

Likewise, the standard error of the sum of the estimated lag coefficients $\sum_{l=0}^{L_i-1} \hat{\beta}_l^{ij}(r) = \sum_{l=0}^{L_i} \hat{\beta}_l^{ij}(r)$ is given by

$$\text{S.E.}\{\sum_{l=0}^{L_i-1} \hat{\beta}_l^{ij}(r)\} = \sqrt{\hat{\sigma}_{jj}(r)\, \iota\, \Phi_i^0 V_i D_r^{\dagger 2} V_i' \Phi_i^{0\prime} \iota'} \quad (2.70)$$

where $\iota = (1, 1, \ldots, 1)$.

Finally, the F-statistic for testing the joint significance of all L_i estimated lag coefficients $\hat{\beta}^{ij}(r)$, $l = 0, 1, \ldots, L_i - 1$ (or equivalently, of all $N_i - 1$ estimated lag coefficients at the $N_i - 1$ free knots, $\hat{\beta}^{ij}_{\kappa_h^i} = \hat{\gamma}_h^{ij}$ for $h = 1, 2, \ldots, N_i - 1$) is given by

$$F\{\hat{\beta}^{ij}(r)\} = \frac{y^{j}{}' U_r D_r^{\dagger} V_i' [V_i D_r^{\dagger 2} V_i']^{-1} V_i D_r^{\dagger} U_r' y^{j}}{(N_i - 1)\, \hat{\sigma}_{jj}(r)}\,. \quad (2.71)$$

Under the null hypothesis $\beta^{ij} = 0$ this has the F distribution with $N_i - 1$ and $T - r$ degrees of freedom.

2.4 Adjustment for Weights

The rank-reduced estimation procedure just described is not invariant with respect to units of measurement. In the present study it has therefore been considered suitable to use as fundamental variables not the price indices themselves, but their numerators (price indices multiplied by the appropriate weights), i.e.,

$$x_{t-l,i} = \omega_i \pi_{t-l,i},\; y_{tj} = w_j\, p_{tj}\,, \quad (2.72)$$

where π_{ti} and p_{tj} are respectively the value of the price index in month t of the i-th international (import or export) commodity group and the j-th domestic commodity group, and ω_i and w_j are the corresponding weights in the total indices. The lag coefficients are derivatives of the form

$$\beta_l^{ij} = \frac{\partial y_{tj}}{\partial x_{t-l,i}} = \frac{w_j}{\omega_i} \frac{\partial p_{tj}}{\partial \pi_{t-l,i}} . \tag{2.73}$$

However, the reasonableness of the estimated magnitudes can be better assessed if expressed as elasticities, i.e.,

$$\frac{x_{t-l,i}}{y_{tj}} \frac{\partial y_{tj}}{\partial x_{t-l,i}} = \frac{\pi_{t-l,i}}{p_{tj}} \frac{\partial p_{tj}}{\partial \pi_{t-l,i}} = \frac{\omega_i}{w_j} \frac{\pi_{t-l,i}}{p_{tj}} \beta_l^{ij} . \tag{2.74}$$

Now, by definition of a price index, for months t and $t-l$ close to the base year we have $\pi_{t-l,i} \approx 100$ and $p_{tj} \approx 100$, so that our desired elasticity is given approximately by

$$\frac{x_{t-l,i}}{y_{tj}} \frac{\partial y_{tj}}{\partial x_{t-l,i}} \approx \frac{\omega_i}{w_j} \beta_l^{ij} . \tag{2.75}$$

The expression on the right in (2.75) will be referred to as the "elasticity form." The approximation will continue to be reasonable away from the base period provided $\pi_{t-l,i}$ and p_{tj} remain of the same order of magnitude, which will in practice be the case if the i-th exogenous and j-th endogenous variable refer to the same commodity group or to closely related commodity groups.

3. Empirical Results

3.1 The Data Set

The data used for this study are three series of Laspeyres price indices of imports and exports[12]) and of producer price indices for industrial products,[13]) with base years 1958, 1962, and 1970 respectively. Unpublished 1970-base data were furnished for the years 1968–1969, and following the recommendation of *Guckes* [1974] [see also *Rostin*] these were used to form a link with the 1962-base series in January 1968; the linkage-point chosen to link the 1958-base and 1962-base series was January 1962. A special problem presented itself with the producer price index, created by the value-added tax introduced in January 1968; following the recommendation of D. Gralla of the Statistisches Bundesamt, the 1962-base data for December 1967 were used to represent the 1962-base data for January 1968. A special problem also presented itself with the import price index, resulting from the fact that data for certain categories in 1958-base and 1962-base data

---

[12]) Published in the annual issues of Fachserie M, Reihe 1 up to 1975, and Fachserie 17, Reihe 8 from 1976 on. The 1961–62 and 1965 issues contain the 1958-base data from 1958–65; the 1967 and 1973 issues the 1962-base data from 1962–73; and the 1975, 1976, and 1978 issues the 1970-base data from 1970–78. The 1979 data have been obtained from current monthly issues of Fachserie 17, Reihe 8 [Statistisches Bundesamt, Wiesbaden].

[13]) Published in the annual issues of Fachserie M, Reihe 3 up to 1975, and Fachserie 17, Reihe 2 thereafter. The 1961 and 1963 issues contain the 1958-base data from 1958–63; the 1964 and 1967 (and 1970 and 1972) issues the 1962-base data from 1961–67 (and 1968–72); and the 1973, 1975, and 1978 issues the 1970-base data from 1970–78. The 1979 data have been obtained from current monthly issues of Fachserie 17, Reihe 2 [Statistisches Bundesamt, Wiesbaden].

were unpublished and no longer in the Bundesamt's files; proxy series had to be created for these categories, but in each case the resulting series was aggregated into a larger group in order to minimize the possible distortion.[14]) Finally, a few adjustments had to be made for minor changes in classification across base periods.[15])

In each of the three series (import, export, and producer prices), the price indices were multiplied by their respective weights for the three base years 1958, 1962, and 1970. After being thus set in "numerator form", for each mode of aggregation of the commodity groups the corresponding price-index series (for each of the three base years) were constructed by summing their components. The weights for the import and export price indices indicate the respective shares of the commodity groups in total imports and total exports during the base year; those for the producer price index indicate the share in (gross) value of national output. When import and export price indices were aggregated, the resulting weights therefore indicated the share of the commodity group in total trade, assuming (as is approximately the case) that trade is balanced during the base year. The

---

[14]) The three problem categories were 31 (structural-steel engineering products), 51 (fine ceramics), and 56 (paper and paper products). In the case of these three categories the 1962-base data are unpublished, and published data were recovered from the Statistisches Bundesamt's files only back to 1966; however, unpublished 1958-base data for categories 31 and 56 were recovered for the period January 1966 to February 1967. The following procedure was used: The entire 1958-base series, from January 1962 to January 1966, was multiplied by the ratio of the 1962-base data to 1958-base data for January 1966; denoting this series by a_t $(t = 1, 2, \ldots, 49)$, the constructed 1962-base proxy series is defined by $a_t^* = a_t R^{49-t}$ where R is the unique positive solution (by Descartes' Rule of Signs) of the equation

$$\sum_{t=1}^{12} a_t R^{49-t} - 1200 = 0.$$

(This constrains the average value of the index in 1962 to be equal to 100.) R was calculated by Newton's method and substituted in the above formula to obtain a_t^*.

This method was used for categories 51 and 56. In the case of category 51 (fine ceramics), no 1968 data were available, so the data for category 52 (glass & glassware) were used as a proxy, with category 51's weight. In the case of category 31 an alternative method was available and was the method used: unpublished 1962-base series were available for the aggregate of categories 22, 25, 27, 28, 29, 301 (products of drawing plants and cold rolling mills), 40, 53, 55, and 59 (see Table 1), and also for an aggregate of categories 302 (products of steel shaping), 31, 3205, 33, 36, 37, and 38. Data were also available for 30 = 301 + 302. From the three simultaneous equations defining these three aggregates (using the 1962 weights), it was possible to solve for categories 301, 302, and 31. Data for 31 were then smoothed by approximation by a cubic spline with knots placed at 6-month intervals, in order to remove the effects of rounding error.

[15]) A new category 50, consisting of office machines (501) and data-processing equipment (505), was broken out in the 1970-base series, 501 having previously been included largely under 32 (machinery) and 505 under 36 (electrical goods) in the earlier series (for the industrial classification system, see Statistisches Bundesamt [1970]). Limitation in availability of data dictated construction of slightly different groupings as between internal and external price indices (see Table 1). Another adjustment that had to be made to maintain consistency in classification was the transfer of fiberwood, mine timber, and telegraph poles from category 13 (forestry products) to category 53 (sawmill products) in the 1970-base import price index. Finally, the 1970-base producer price indices for coal and lignite underwent a change in composition in 1975; on the basis of unpublished data furnished for their subcomponents, the series for coal & lignite was recomputed for the period 1968–1974.

use of trade shares as weights can of course be (and has been) challenged as a matter of principle.[16]) Since even the finest subcategories for which data are available are constructed on this principle, it has seemed to me best to retain the principle for consistency; and even if trade shares as a measure of importance would be hard to defend from the standpoint of economic theory, the criterion can be defended on statistical grounds since higher weights indicate larger samples and thus more reliable data series.

In this study, linkage between base periods has always been carried out *after* aggregation, for each mode of aggregation. Since the earlier series have been linked to the latest (1970) series, the final data set used in the calculations reflected the 1970 weights. These weights were the ones used to make the adjustments described in section 2.4 to bring the estimated lag coefficients into "elasticity form".

3.2 Preliminary Calculations

Some preliminary aggregation was dictated by limitations of computer-storage capacity. Categories (29, 30, 31), (51, 52), (55, 56, 57), (61, 62), (63, 64) were grouped together for each of the three commodity series, and in addition two groupings (2131, 2132), (2107, 25) were formed for the import price index and one (215, 25) for the export price index. Import and export prices were not aggregated together. This brought the number of input-price indices down from 34 to 25 and the number of export-price indices down from 31 to 23, hence brought the number (k) of exogenous variables down from 65 to 48. Choosing a cubic spline ($\nu_i = 2$ for $i = 1, 2, \ldots, m$) with three free knots ($N_i = 4$ and zero end-point constraint), this brought the number of effective exogenous variables up to $3k = 144$. Choosing an 18-month lag ($L_i = L = 18$ for $i = 1, 2, \ldots, m$), the number of observations from January 1958 to December 1979 being $n = 264$, this gave $T = n - L = 246$. The order of the matrix Z^0 of (2.45) was then 246×144.

The results from this mode of aggregation were quite poor. The least-squares estimates were (as is to be expected when a high degree of multicollinearity is present) unrealistically large in absolute magnitude, even though they tended to have the "right signs", and there was little stability in estimates from rank to rank. This is not too surprising in view of the fact that the condition number of Z^0 (the ratio of its largest singular value to its smallest positive singular value – all singular values were positive) was $\kappa(Z^0) = 3{,}432{,}140.04$, showing that Z^0 was extremely ill-conditioned.

One feature of the results was, however, that lag coefficients for $l > 12$ were seldom statistically significant. In the second round of computations, therefore, the lag length L was reduced to 12 months.

3.3 "Final" Calculations

On the basis of a study of charts for the time series of import and export prices, various groupings were made, leading to the clustering indicated in Table 2. In many cases,

---

16) Cf. *Kravis/Lipsey* [1971], who have proposed using (and have used) shares in world trade as weights. One might also propose using weights corresponding to domestic consumption. There does not, remarkably, exist any economic theory of index numbers for import and export prices.

Import price indices	Export price indices	Producer price indices
G00 100000	G10 100000	
		G30 101000
		G30 103000
		G30 107000
G00 211000	G10 211000	G30 211000
G00 210700	G10 215000	G30 215000
	G10 210406	G30 210406
G00 216000		
G00 220000	G10 220000	G30 220000
G00 250000	G10 250000	G30 250000
G00 213100		
G00 270000	G10 270000	G30 270000
G00 213200		
G00 280000	G10 280000	G30 280000
G00 290000	G10 290000	G30 290000
G00 300000	G10 300000	G30 300000
G00 310000	G10 310000	G30 310000
G00 380000	G10 380000	G30 380000
G00 320005	G10 320005	G30 320005
G00 330000	G10 330000	G30 330000
G00 370000	G10 370000	G30 370000
G00 390000	G10 390000	G30 390000
G00 360000	G10 360000	G30 360005
G00 400000	G10 400000	G30 400000
G00 580000	G10 580000	G30 580000
G00 590000	G10 590000	G30 590000
G00 510000	G10 510000	G30 510000
G00 520000	G10 520000	G30 520000
G00 540000	G10 540000	G30 540000
G00 530005	G10 530000	G30 530000
G00 550000	G10 550000	G30 550000
G00 560000	G10 560000	G30 560000
G00 570000	G10 570000	G30 570000
G00 610000	G10 610000	G30 610000
G00 620000	G10 620000	G30 620000
G00 630000	G10 630000	G30 630000
G00 640000	G10 640000	G30 640000
G00 202400	G10 202400	G30 202400

Tab. 2: Grouping scheme used in the distributed-lag regression of domestic producer price indices on import and export price indices.*)
*) Code numbers refer to the codes listed in Table 1.

patterns as between import and export prices were remarkably similar, with turning points occurring during the very same month. In a few cases (e.g., electrical goods), the pattern of development of import and export prices was very dissimilar, so they were left unaggregated. Machinery showed a steady, smooth rise – possibly reflecting the heterogeneity of this industry and the smoothing effects of aggregation; other smooth risers were aggregated with machinery. Wood products showed similar tendencies. Most other categories exhibited pronounced fluctuations. The aggregation indicated by Table 2 greatly improved the conditioning of the resulting matrix Z^0, reducing its condition number to $\kappa\,(Z^0) = 169{,}135.2007$. The order of Z^0 was 252×72.

Knots were placed at months 0,4, and 8, the lag coefficients at 12 months being constrained to be zero; a cubic spline was used. There were $k = 24$ exogenous variables and $m = 20$ endogenous variables (see Table 2); in addition to the 20 basic endogenous variables, computations were performed for the two groups G30 100000 (electricity, city gas, and water) and G30 000000 (all products). Thus, a total of 528 lag distributions were estimated. Seven approximating observation matrices Z_r^0 were employed, including the original one $Z^0 = Z_{72}^0$, the rank being reduced by 9 at each step; thus, $r = 72,63,54,45,36,27$, and 18. A total of 4752 lag-distribution estimates $\hat{\beta}^{ij}\,(r)$ were therefore computed, along with t-ratios, estimates of the sum of lag coefficients $\sum_{l=0}^{12} \hat{\beta}_l^{ij}\,(r)$ and the corresponding t-ratios, and the F-statistic for testing the joint significance of all 12 estimated lag coefficients $\hat{\beta}_l^{ij}\,(r)$ (i.e., of all three estimated lag coefficients $\hat{\beta}_l^{ij}\,(r)$ at the free knots $l = 0,4,8$). Obviously, only a minute proportion of these 528 families of lag-distribution estimates can be displayed. I have chosen to display those which are of greatest practical interest and which at the same time appear convincing as estimates and provide a good illustration of the method employed.[17])

Eight families of lag distributions are depicted in Figures 1 to 8, and the corresponding estimates are shown in Tables 3.1 to 3.8.[18]) The first four relate the internal price of a commodity group to the external price of a comparable group, in the case of (1) petroleum, (2) iron & steel, (3) non-ferrous metals, and (4) machinery, road vehicles, and other manufactures. Not surprisingly, the most robust estimates are those for petroleum & petroleum products, differing very little from rank to rank, especially during the first four months. In all four of these cases, the rank estimates are quite stable for the inter-

---

[17]) The results for two groups, mining and chemicals & plastic products, were rather disappointing. In both cases the rank estimates were not very robust (particularly the case of mining). In the case of chemicals & plastic products, this may have resulted from the aggregation of (finished) plastic products and basic chemicals; in future work these will be disaggregated. In the case of mining, this may be due to unsatisfactory aggregates employed because of data limitations. Referring to Table 1, it will be observed that import category 210700 aggregates category 218 – a fuel (peat) – with non-fuels, and that export and domestic categories 210406 include mineral ores, crude petroleum & natural gas, and peat. Category 210406 is unavailable, and can be computed only by subtracting out the remaining components from the total index for mining products – leading to unacceptable rounding error unless smoothed or aggregated into a larger group. In the present instance (see Table 2) the decision (perhaps unfortunate) was made to aggregate it with salts and coal & lignite.

[18]) The computer-plotted graphs shown in Figures 1–8 are actually first-degree splines (polygons) linearly interpolating the values of the cubic splines at the knots.

mediate ranks $54 \geqslant r \geqslant 36$. The most surprising feature is the presence in all four cases of overshooting – this, despite the fact that the characteristics of the underlying data sets are quite different. This is most pronounced in the case of non-ferrous metals, where for $54 \geqslant r \geqslant 27$ we have $\sum_{l=0}^{1} \hat{\beta}_l^{ij}(r)\, \omega_i / w_j > 1$, i.e., a one-percent increase in the external price leads after one month to a greater than one-percent increase in the internal price. Assuming the model to be structurally stable [for discussion of this problem in the context of rational-expectations models, cf. *Lucas; Sims*, 1974], the sum of the lag coefficients measures the long-run equilibrium effect; *a priori* one would expect the elasticity for the own-commodity case to be between 0 and 1, which is the case in the intermediate ranks.

Figures 5 to 7 (and Tables 3.5 to 3.7) depict cases of cross-effects: (5) from petroleum to mining, (6) from iron & steel to steel semifinishes and products, and (7) from iron & steel to machinery, road vehicles, and other manufactures. The estimates for case (6) are quite robust in the interval $63 \geqslant r \geqslant 45$, displaying a unimodal density. The estimates for (6) are not very robust, those for (7) fairly robust; in both cases, the price effect is much more delayed than in the own-commodity case, in conformity with *a priori* expectations.

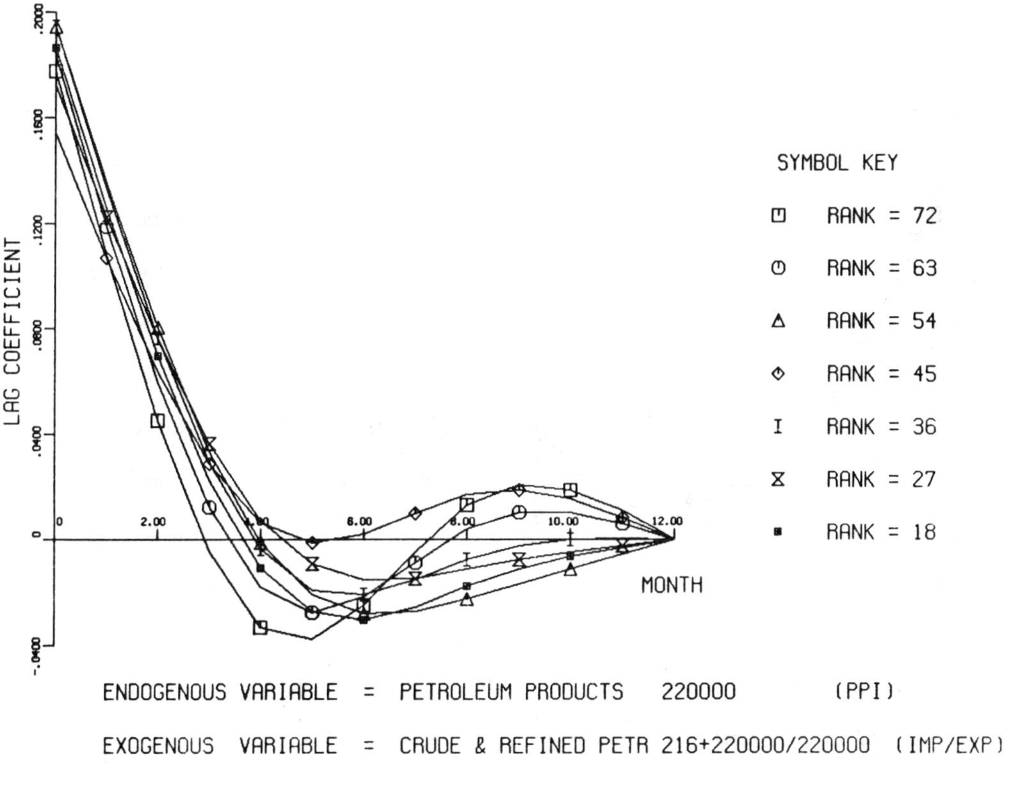

Fig. 1: Estimated lag distributions (in elasticity form) for the regression of domestic prices of petroleum products on international prices of crude petroleum & natural gas and petroleum products

Figure 8 (and Table 3.8) depict the own-effect of textiles and clothing; the estimates are very robust in the interval $54 \geqslant r \geqslant 36$. The lag length is also longer than in the case of petroleum, metals, and machinery, which again is in conformity with what one might expect *a priori*.

Finally, Table 4 displays the rank estimates of the sums of the lag coefficients for the regressions of the various internal prices on the external price index of petroleum and petroleum products. This shows the elasticity of the producer price index for all products with respect to the external petroleum price to be quite small – about .03. It must be kept in mind, however, that this is a partial elasticity; it is assumed that prices of coal, chemicals, etc., remain constant, whereas international petroleum prices undoubtedly exert a profound effect on other international prices. One would have to work with a global reduced-form model to take account of these effects.

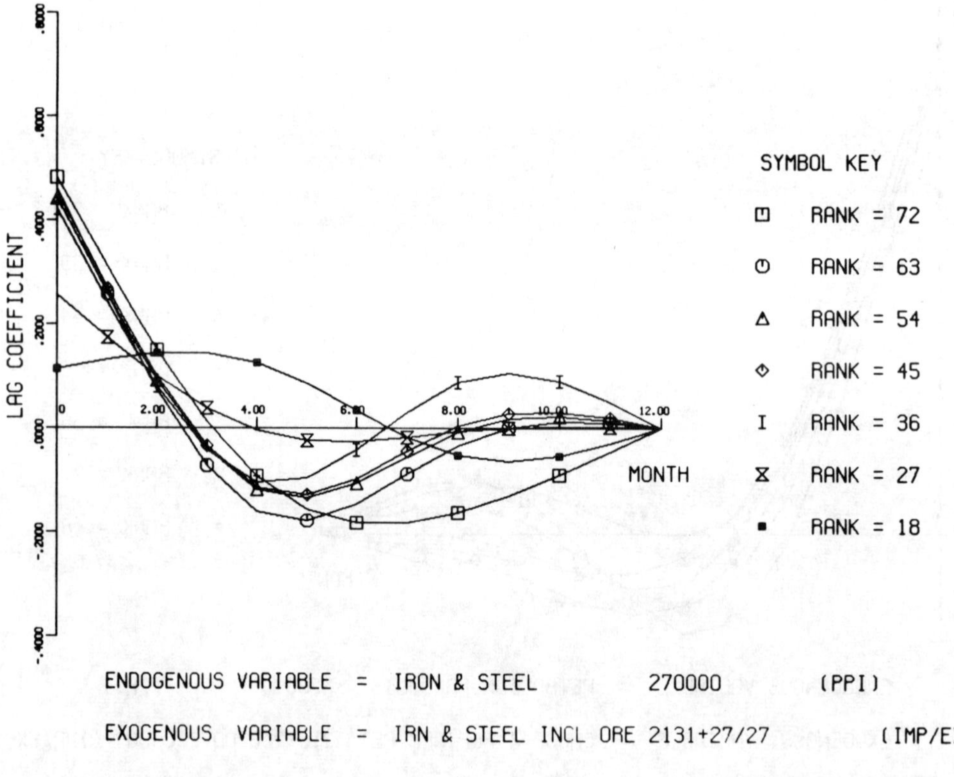

Fig. 2: Estimated lag distributions (in elasticity form) for the regression of domestic on international prices of iron & steel

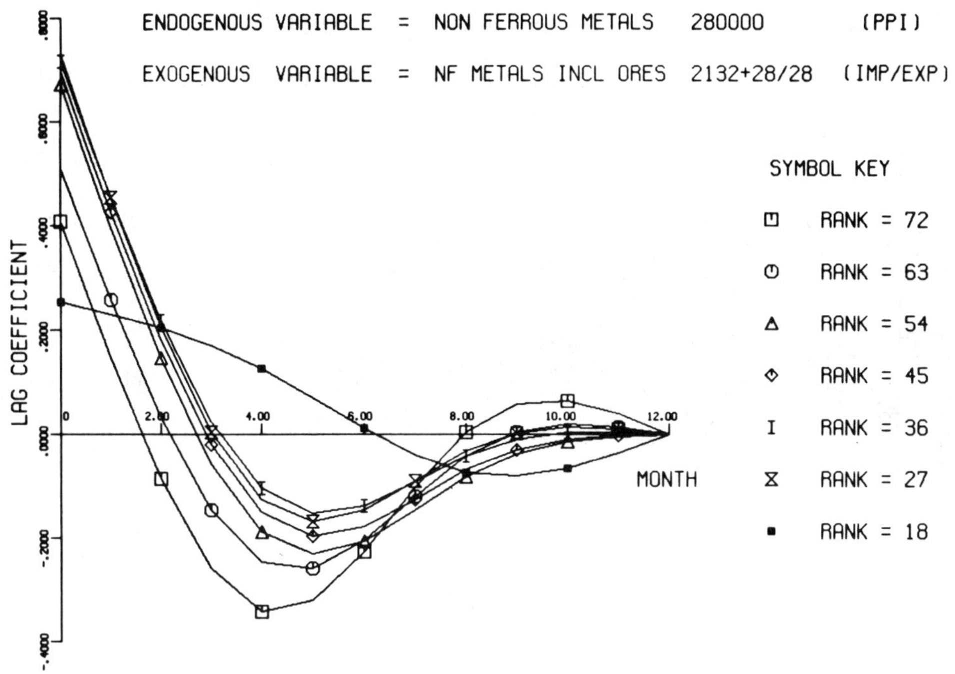

Fig. 3: Estimated lag distributions (in elasticity form) for the regression of domestic on international prices of non-ferrous metals

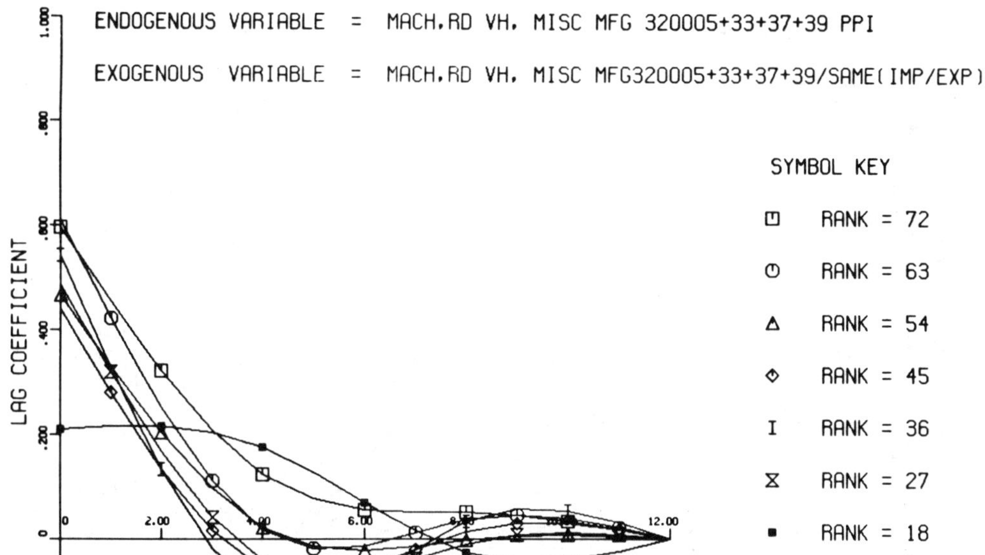

Fig. 4: Estimated lag distributions (in elasticity form) for the regression of domestic on international prices of machinery, road vehicles & miscellaneous manufacturing

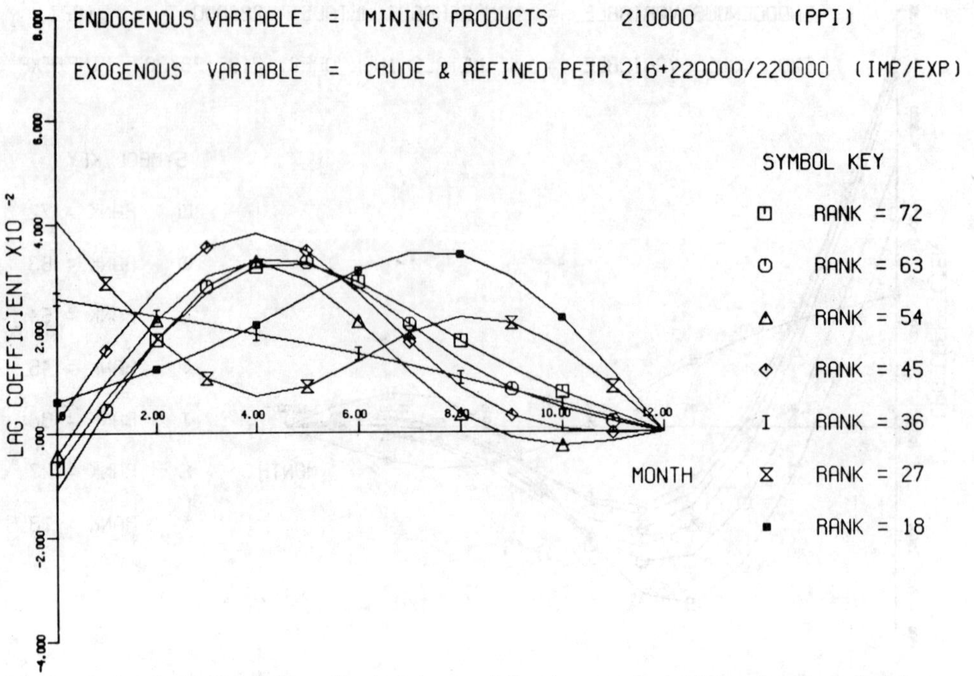

Fig. 5: Estimated lag distributions (in elasticity form) for the regression of domestic prices of mining products on international prices of crude petroleum & natural gas and petroleum products

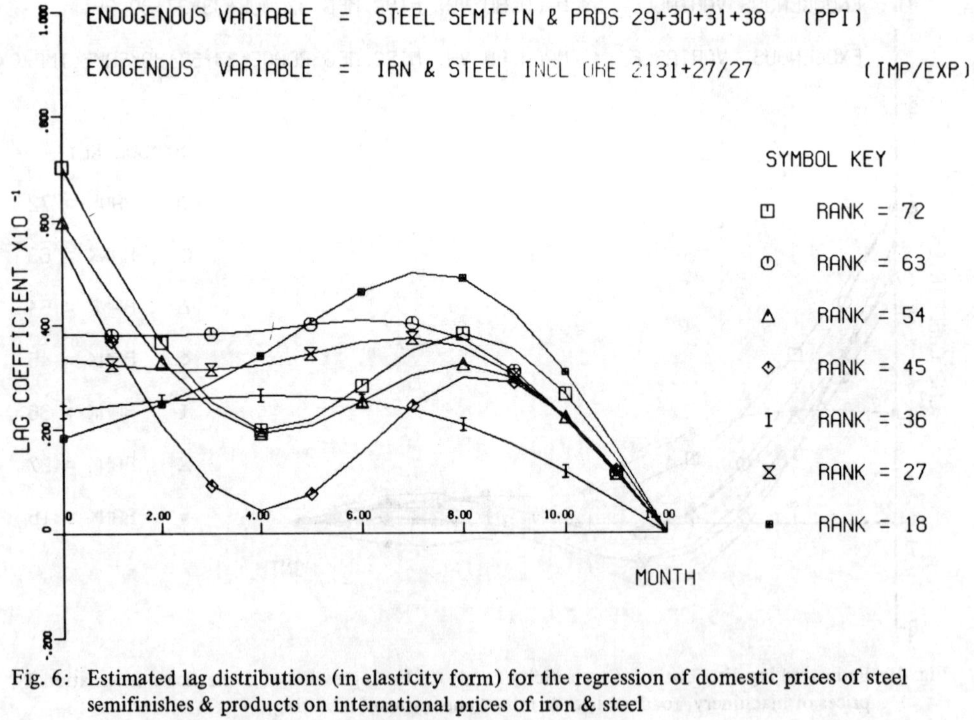

Fig. 6: Estimated lag distributions (in elasticity form) for the regression of domestic prices of steel semifinishes & products on international prices of iron & steel

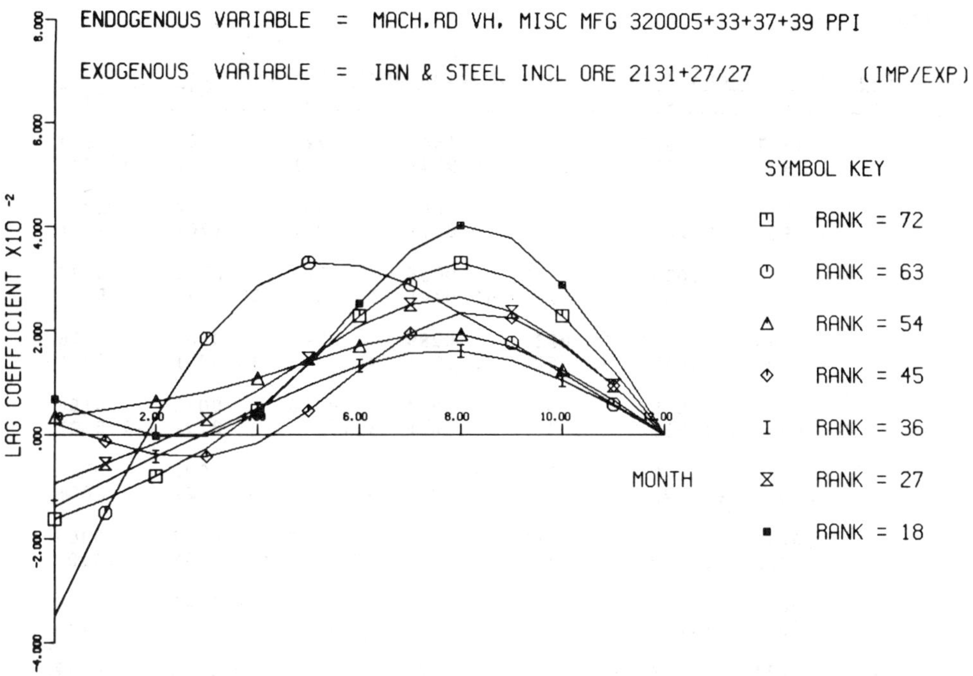

Fig. 7: Estimated lag distributions (in elasticity form) for the regression of domestic prices of machinery, road vehicles & miscellaneous manufacturing on international prices of iron & steel

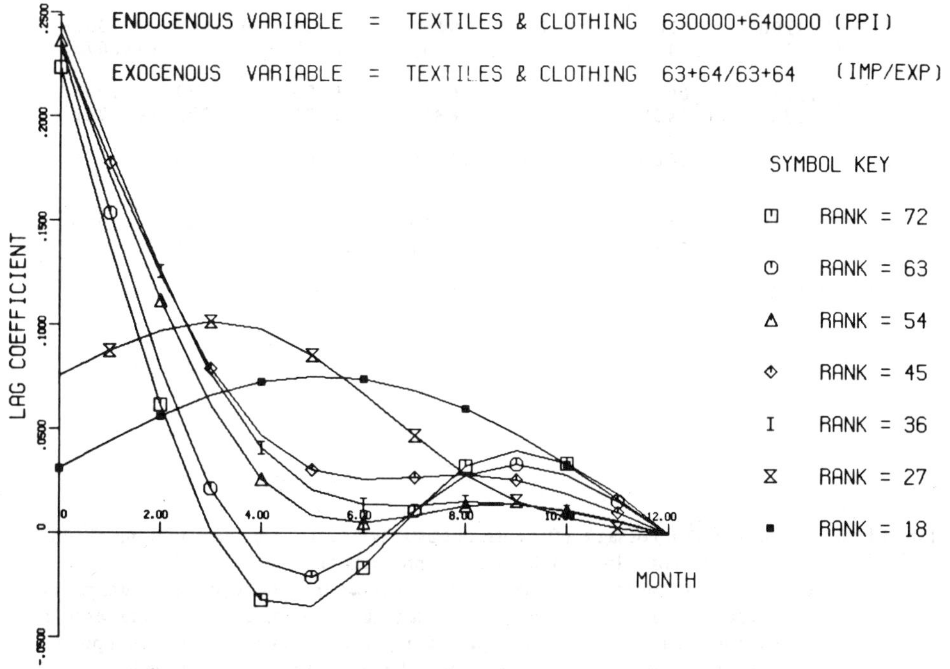

Fig. 8: Estimated lag distributions (in elasticity form) for the regression of domestic on international prices of textiles & clothing

Lag	Rank (r) of Approximating Observation Matrix						
ℓ	72	63	54	45	36	27	18
0	.1777	.1835	.1945	.1543	.1946	.1725	.1864
	(7.393)	(8.333)	(10.540)	(8.932)	(12.755)	(17.442)	(20.274)
1	.1080	.1187	.1353	.1069	.1331	.1224	.1257
	(5.998)	(8.203)	(11.347)	(9.867)	(16.406)	(23.170)	(28.144)
2	.0450	.0597	.0802	.0638	.0763	.0759	.0695
	(2.481)	(5.109)	(9.586)	(8.014)	(13.625)	(15.447)	(19.835)
3	-.0043	.0122	.0333	.0289	.0292	.0363	.0226
	(-.209)	(.915)	(3.852)	(3.197)	(3.449)	(5.038)	(3.871)
4	-.0332	-.0180	-.0013	.0064	-.0036	.0072	-.0106
	(-1.602)	(-1.232)	(-.137)	(.642)	(-.350)	(.879)	(-1.539)
5	-.0377	-.0275	-.0209	-.0012	-.0190	-.0092	-.0271
	(-2.206)	(-2.021)	(-2.279)	(-.129)	(-1.998)	(-1.312)	(-4.683)
6	-.0249	-.0218	-.0282	.0020	-.0210	-.0152	-.0303
	(-1.691)	(-1.758)	(-2.817)	(.255)	(-2.690)	(-2.808)	(-8.590)
7	-.0046	-.0086	-.0273	.0101	-.0152	-.0147	-.0254
	(-.257)	(-.654)	(-2.170)	(1.115)	(-1.985)	(-2.475)	(-9.147)
8	.0131	.0041	-.0223	.0173	-.0075	-.0112	-.0177
	(.596)	(.283)	(-1.529)	(1.605)	(-.851)	(-1.501)	(-4.219)
9	.0207	.0103	-.0167	.0189	-.0024	-.0077	-.0113
	(.950)	(.735)	(-1.193)	(1.783)	(-.271)	(-1.023)	(-2.392)
10	.0190	.0103	-.0111	.0154	-.0000	-.0049	-.0066
	(1.100)	(.946)	(-1.027)	(1.853)	(-.004)	(-.805)	(-1.675)
11	.0110	.0062	-.0056	.0086	.0000	-.0023	.0030
	(1.170)	(1.045)	(-.947)	(1.883)	(.119)	(-.705)	(-1.366)
12	.0000	.0000	.0000	.0000	.0000	.0000	.0000
Sum	.2898	.3291	.3102	.4313	.3649	.3490	.2721
	(2.553)	(3.933)	(4.516)	(12.212)	(10.669)	(12.268)	(28.771)
F	18.575	25.373	45.013	86.632	166.159	248.679	541.757

Tab. 3.1: Rank estimates $\hat{\beta}_l^{ij}$ (r) of lag coefficients (in elasticity form) of regression of domestic on international prices of petroleum & petroleum products.*)

*) The endogenous variable (j) is the domestic producer price index for petroleum products. The exogenous variable (i) is a weighted average (by trade shares) of price indices of imported crude petroleum and natural gas and imported and exported petroleum products. Figures in parentheses denote t-ratios, and F denotes the F-statistic for the joint significance of all 12 estimated lag coefficients.

Lag ℓ	Rank (r) of Approximating Observation Matrix 72	63	54	45	36	27	18
0	.4820 (7.643)	.4618 (10.338)	.4424 (10.627)	.4543 (11.532)	.4229 (11.700)	.2555 (9.962)	.1132 (12.518)
1	.3103 (8.558)	.2581 (9.809)	.2588 (11.293)	.2678 (13.608)	.2418 (13.825)	.1745 (13.103)	.1317 (13.964)
2	.1499 (4.840)	.0736 (3.879)	.0295 (7.002)	.0993 (11.834)	.0804 (8.903)	.0999 (9.051)	.1439 (14.367)
3	.0119 (.286)	-.0722 (-2.993)	-.0389 (-2.137)	-.0336 (-2.131)	-.0415 (-2.441)	.0380 (2.291)	.1438 (14.485)
4	-.0925 (-2.020)	-.1602 (-5.730)	-.1182 (-5.288)	-.1130 (-5.471)	-.1043 (-4.901)	-.0046 (-.244)	.1252 (14.681)
5	-.1553 (-4.105)	-.1786 (-7.044)	-.1349 (-6.801)	-.1282 (-7.256)	-.0968 (-5.504)	-.0240 (-1.579)	.0850 (13.291)
6	-.1820 (-6.262)	-.1461 (-6.888)	-.1061 (-6.985)	-.0971 (-8.580)	-.0415 (-4.146)	-.0256 (-2.651)	.0332 (4.787)
7	-.1810 (-5.178)	-.0890 (-3.997)	-.0559 (-3.456)	-.0448 (-3.871)	.0302 (3.071)	-.0171 (-1.591)	-.0171 (-1.700)
8	-.1611 (-3.528)	-.0336 (-1.286)	-.0086 (-.415)	.0035 (.203)	.0873 (5.433)	-.0065 (-.417)	-.0527 (-4.252)
9	-.1299 (-2.776)	-.0007 (-.028)	.0171 (.804)	.0280 (1.511)	.1056 (5.886)	.0000 (.000)	-.0639 (-5.269)
10	-.0909 (-2.433)	.0112 (.547)	.0226 (1.326)	.0308 (2.027)	.0895 (6.034)	.0023 (.171)	-.0542 (-5.735)
11	-.0467 (-2.274)	.0091 (.812)	.0146 (1.561)	.0190 (2.251)	.0505 (6.093)	.0019 (.246)	-.0306 (-5.952)
12	.0000	.0000	.0000	.0000	.0000	.0000	.0000
Sum	-.0853 (-.441)	.1334 (.775)	.3855 (2.798)	.4861 (6.195)	.8240 (12.176)	.4943 (8.031)	.5575 (11.350)
F	27.827	44.951	65.645	81.110	79.362	64.120	91.696

Tab. 3.2: Rank estimates $\hat{\beta}_l^{ij}$ (r) of lag coefficients (in elasticity form) of regression of domestic on international prices of iron and steel.*)

*) The endogenous variable (j) is the domestic producer price index for iron and steel. The exogenous variable (i) is a weighted average (by trade shares) of price indices of imported iron ore and imported and exported iron and steel. Figures in parentheses denote t-ratios, and F denotes the F-statistic for the joint significance of all 12 estimated lag coefficients.

Lag	Rank (r) of Approximating Observation Matrix						
ℓ	72	63	54	45	36	27	18
0	.4079 (5.647)	.5103 (10.533)	.6717 (14.470)	.6967 (17.265)	.7170 (18.154)	.7287 (19.256)	.2539 (14.682)
1	.1462 (2.838)	.2584 (8.119)	.3963 (14.705)	.4269 (18.836)	.4560 (20.653)	.4548 (22.665)	.2309 (17.326)
2	-.0859 (-2.028)	.0315 (1.202)	.1452 (6.858)	.1803 (9.925)	.2174 (14.215)	.2051 (18.503)	.2043 (14.643)
3	-.2587 (-5.880)	-.1453 (-4.841)	-.0574 (-2.056)	-.0196 (-.777)	.0232 (1.118)	.0035 (.205)	.1707 (10.807)
4	-.3426 (-7.403)	-.2469 (-7.626)	-.1873 (-5.920)	-.1497 (-5.174)	-.1043 (-4.350)	-.1259 (-5.857)	.1265 (8.372)
5	-.3205 (-7.356)	-.2583 (-8.879)	-.2292 (-8.389)	-.1953 (-7.798)	-.1512 (-7.522)	-.1682 (-8.807)	.0706 (6.634)
6	-.2252 (-5.546)	-.2045 (-7.857)	-.2050 (-9.717)	-.1773 (-9.444)	-.1374 (-9.889)	-.1457 (-11.642)	.0114 (1.743)
7	-.1019 (-2.417)	-.1208 (-4.159)	-.1456 (-6.507)	-.1249 (-6.651)	-.0913 (-6.178)	-.0900 (-10.723)	-.0403 (-4.046)
8	.0041 (.092)	-.0423 (-1.254)	-.0817 (-2.929)	-.0678 (-2.895)	-.0411 (-2.042)	-.0325 (-2.886)	-.0736 (-5.061)
9	.0578 (1.375)	.0035 (.108)	-.0381 (-1.340)	-.0293 (-1.218)	-.0096 (-.451)	.0017 (.132)	-.0808 (-5.279)
10	.0646 (2.001)	.0191 (.745)	-.0144 (-.633)	-.0093 (-.480)	.0037 (.217)	.0135 (1.253)	-.0660 (-5.356)
11	.0401 (2.298)	.0146 (1.043)	-.0039 (-.310)	-.0016 (-.146)	.0049 (.513)	.0105 (1.723)	-.0367 (-5.388)
12	.0000	.0000	.0000	.0000	.0000	.0000	.0000
Sum	-.6141 (-2.021)	-.1806 (-.971)	.2505 (1.712)	.5291 (4.420)	.8874 (14.517)	.8555 (23.158)	.7709 (24.394)
F	26.968	43.891	81.606	120.652	174.495	244.242	229.291

Tab. 3.3: Rank estimates $\hat{\beta}_l^{ij}$ (r) of lag coefficients (in elasticity form) of regression of domestic on international prices of non-ferrous metals.*)

*) The endogenous variable (j) is the domestic producer price index for non-ferrous metals. The exogenous variable (i) is a weighted average (by trade shares) of price indices of imported non-ferrous metal ores and imported and exported non-ferrous metals. Figures in parentheses denote t-ratios, and F denotes the F-statistic for the joint significance of all 12 lag coefficients.

Lag	Rank (r) of Approximating Observation Matrix						
ℓ	72	63	54	45	36	27	18
0	.5968	.6095	.4669	.4403	.5419	.4868	.2099
	(8.319)	(11.051)	(6.986)	(8.819)	(14.393)	(18.686)	(18.250)
1	.4543	.4227	.3300	.2797	.3277	.3201	.2153
	(8.372)	(12.447)	(8.620)	(9.798)	(15.664)	(21.669)	(19.176)
2	.3215	.2516	.2034	.1337	.1345	.1675	.2152
	(6.281)	(9.446)	(9.989)	(6.436)	(8.021)	(13.726)	(16.405)
3	.2085	.1116	.0976	.0170	-.0172	.0429	.2038
	(3.754)	(3.485)	(4.046)	(.617)	(-.730)	(2.561)	(14.207)
4	.1249	.0185	.0228	-.0558	-.1063	-.0395	.1756
	(2.283)	(.535)	(.755)	(-1.767)	(-3.951)	(-2.080)	(13.668)
5	.0771	-.0181	-.0144	-.0758	-.1206	-.0710	.1280
	(1.782)	(-.640)	(-.531)	(-2.848)	(-5.318)	(-4.454)	(16.063)
6	.0568	-.0132	-.0226	-.0574	-.0817	-.0644	.0704
	(1.900)	(-.646)	(-1.055)	(-3.252)	(-5.414)	(-6.096)	(16.524)
7	.0523	.0125	-.0140	-.0210	-.0198	-.0377	.0150
	(1.688)	(.530)	(-.601)	(-1.294)	(-1.473)	(-4.060)	(1.636)
8	.0517	.0380	-.0011	.0134	.0349	-.0090	-.0258
	(1.274)	(1.209)	(-.037)	(.601)	(1.915)	(-.719)	(-1.883)
9	.0456	.0469	.0062	.0296	.0588	.0073	-.0429
	(1.079)	(1.436)	(.205)	(1.236)	(2.997)	(.536)	(-2.981)
10	.0337	.0400	.0075	.0291	.0548	.0115	-.0398
	(.989)	(1.524)	(.309)	(1.482)	(3.406)	(1.038)	(-3.443)
11	.0178	.0226	.0047	.0173	.0321	.0078	-.0233
	(.946)	(1.562)	(.355)	(1.587)	(3.580)	(1.255)	(-3.650)
12	.0000	.0000	.0000	.0000	.0000	.0000	.0000
Sum	2.0409	1.5427	1.0871	.7501	.8391	.8223	1.1013
	(3.187)	(10.108)	(6.899)	(8.936)	(16.999)	(21.061)	(45.992)
F	30.675	57.016	36.343	41.369	173.166	266.566	710.374

Tab. 3.4: Rank estimates $\hat{\beta}_l^{ij}$ (r) of lag coefficients (in elasticity form of regression of domestic on international prices of machinery, road vehicles, and other manufactures.*)

*) The endogenous variable (j) is a weighted average of the domestic producer price indices for machinery (including office machines but not data-processing equipment), road vehicles, precision & optical goods, and musical instruments, toys, athletic & sporting goods, jewelry, etc. The endogenous variable (i) is a weighted average (by trade shares) of imports of iron ore and imports and exports of the same commodity categories as well as data-processing equipment. Figures in parentheses denote t-ratios and F denotes the F-statistic for the joint significance of all 12 estimated lag coefficients.

Lag ℓ	Rank (r) of Approximating Observation Matrix 72	63	54	45	36	27	18
0	-.0065	-.0107	-.0042	.0023	.0258	.0409	.0061
	(-.425)	(-.743)	(-.347)	(.208)	(2.659)	(5.515)	(.791)
1	.0063	.0044	.0096	.0158	.0241	.0288	.0090
	(.550)	(.463)	(1.235)	(2.259)	(4.680)	(7.265)	(2.429)
2	.0178	.0178	.0216	.0274	.0224	.0181	.0123
	(1.542)	(2.335)	(3.944)	(5.356)	(6.300)	(4.924)	(4.205)
3	.0268	.0279	.0300	.0356	.0207	.0104	.0160
	(2.028)	(3.217)	(5.289)	(6.118)	(3.848)	(1.923)	(3.307)
4	.0318	.0332	.0329	.0383	.0189	.0070	.0206
	(2.403)	(3.482)	(5.318)	(5.972)	(2.875)	(1.142)	(3.588)
5	.0321	.0326	.0292	.0348	.0169	.0087	.0260
	(2.944)	(3.679)	(4.872)	(6.031)	(2.798)	(1.666)	(5.399)
6	.0287	.0277	.0212	.0268	.0149	.0136	.0309
	(3.066)	(3.436)	(3.236)	(5.234)	(2.997)	(3.341)	(10.547)
7	.0233	.0206	.0116	.0172	.0127	.0189	.0341
	(2.039)	(2.407)	(1.414)	(2.944)	(2.598)	(4.250)	(14.726)
8	.0174	.0136	.0035	.0086	.0104	.0220	.0340
	(1.235)	(1.426)	(.362)	(1.244)	(1.849)	(3.936)	(9.721)
9	.0121	.0083	-.0011	.0032	.0079	.0208	.0296
	(.868)	(.906)	(-.124)	(.465)	(1.420)	(3.658)	(7.524)
10	.0077	.0046	-.0025	.0005	.0053	.0159	.0217
	(.696)	(.648)	(-.357)	(.102)	(1.209)	(3.508)	(6.624)
11	.0037	.0020	-.0018	-.0002	.0028	.0086	.0114
	(.616)	(.525)	(-.468)	(-.067)	(1.109)	(3.435)	(6.229)
12	.0000	.0000	.0000	.0000	.0000	.0000	.0000
Sum	.2011	.1818	.1500	.2103	.1827	.2136	.2516
	(2.780)	(3.339)	(3.333)	(9.251)	(8.400)	(10.012)	(31.979)
F	3.430	5.077	11.636	37.730	41.509	55.082	342.318

Tab. 3.5: Rank estimates $\hat{\beta}_l^{ij}$ (r) of lag coefficients (in elasticity form) of regression of domestic prices of mining products on international prices of petroleum & petroleum products.*)

*) The endogenous variable (j) is the domestic producer price index for mining products. The exogenous variable (i) is a weighted average (by trade shares) of the price indices of imported crude petroleum and natural gas and imported and exported petroleum products. Figures in parentheses denote t-ratios, and F denotes the F-statistic for the joint significance of all 12 estimated lag coefficients.

Lag ℓ	Rank (r) of Approximating Observation Matrix 72	63	54	45	36	27	18
0	.0702 (4.509)	.0383 (3.358)	.0599 (4.976)	.0552 (4.044)	.0235 (2.117)	.0335 (3.648)	.0184 (4.240)
1	.0524 (5.853)	.0380 (5.659)	.0457 (6.896)	.0368 (5.406)	.0245 (4.564)	.0324 (6.783)	.0214 (4.728)
2	.0367 (4.798)	.0379 (7.818)	.0331 (8.663)	.0208 (7.154)	.0254 (9.164)	.0316 (7.984)	.0247 (5.149)
3	.0251 (2.448)	.0381 (6.185)	.0238 (4.517)	.0092 (1.685)	.0261 (4.991)	.0314 (5.288)	.0288 (6.057)
4	.0198 (1.750)	.0389 (5.440)	.0193 (2.991)	.0044 (.615)	.0264 (4.039)	.0323 (4.795)	.0341 (8.333)
5	.0218 (2.328)	.0400 (6.183)	.0206 (3.593)	.0075 (1.229)	.0263 (4.861)	.0344 (6.330)	.0404 (13.176)
6	.0281 (3.918)	.0409 (7.542)	.0253 (5.755)	.0155 (3.970)	.0254 (8.260)	.0366 (10.584)	.0462 (13.920)
7	.0349 (4.046)	.0403 (7.080)	.0303 (6.463)	.0244 (6.077)	.0237 (7.830)	.0374 (9.677)	.0497 (10.305)
8	.0383 (3.393)	.0372 (5.569)	.0325 (5.432)	.0298 (5.046)	.0208 (4.223)	.0356 (6.331)	.0488 (8.207)
9	.0352 (3.045)	.0310 (4.677)	.0295 (4.801)	.0289 (4.494)	.0168 (3.045)	.0302 (5.008)	.0421 (7.248)
10	.0265 (2.876)	.0221 (4.229)	.0221 (4.492)	.0223 (4.245)	.0117 (2.576)	.0218 (4.440)	.0307 (6.783)
11	.0142 (2.796)	.0115 (4.014)	.0118 (4.346)	.0121 (4.132)	.0060 (2.370)	.0114 (4.185)	.0161 (6.561)
12	.0000	.0000	.0000	.0000	.0000	.0000	.0000
Sum	.4031 (8.444)	.4143 (9.421)	.3540 (8.879)	.2670 (9.828)	.2567 (12.347)	.3685 (16.711)	.4014 (17.047)
F	38.349	31.969	30.588	43.562	78.897	101.388	102.297

Tab. 3.6: Rank estimates $\hat{\beta}_l^{ij}$ (r) of lag coefficients (in elasticity form) of regression of domestic prices of steel semifinishes and products on international prices of iron and steel.*)

*) The endogenous variable (j) is a weighted average of the domestic producer price indices for foundry products, products of drawing plants and cold rolling mills and steel shaping, structural-steel engineering products, and iron, steel, sheet and metal goods. The exogenous variable (i) is a weighted average (by trade shares) of iron and steel imports and exports and iron-ore imports. Figures in parentheses denote t-ratios, and F denotes the F-statistic for the joint significance of all 12 estimated lag coefficients.

Lag	Rank (r) or Approximating Observation Matrix						
ℓ	72	63	54	45	36	27	18
0	-.0162	-.0348	.0035	.0022	-.0138	-.0094	.0068
	(-1.009)	(-3.067)	(.274)	(.147)	(-1.264)	(-1.357)	(2.503)
1	-.0124	-.0150	.0048	-.0012	-.0090	-.0057	.0026
	(-1.349)	(-2.235)	(.682)	(-.163)	(-1.704)	(-1.573)	(.917)
2	-.0081	.0033	.0063	-.0037	-.0043	-.0016	-.0002
	(-1.031)	(.689)	(1.551)	(-1.139)	(-1.553)	(-.549)	(-.058)
3	-.0026	.0184	.0082	-.0041	.0005	.0030	-.0001
	(-.250)	(2.997)	(1.466)	(-.674)	(.091)	(.659)	(-.025)
4	.0046	.0286	.0108	-.0015	.0051	.0084	.0043
	(.392)	(4.028)	(1.561)	(-.183)	(.790)	(1.647)	(1.688)
5	.0136	.0330	.0139	.0047	.0095	.0147	.0137
	(1.418)	(5.117)	(2.275)	(.687)	(1.783)	(3.576)	(7.091)
6	.0228	.0325	.0170	.0125	.0132	.0207	.0251
	(3.094)	(6.025)	(3.626)	(2.864)	(4.346)	(7.945)	(12.045)
7	.0030	.0287	.0191	.0195	.0156	.0251	.0352
	(3.382)	(5.077)	(3.817)	(4.382)	(5.218)	(8.604)	(11.623)
8	.0330	.0233	.0192	.0234	.0160	.0264	.0403
	(2.849)	(3.507)	(3.020)	(3.565)	(3.293)	(6.227)	(10.789)
9	.0303	.0176	.0169	.0224	.0142	.0237	.0377
	(2.553)	(2.664)	(2.577)	(3.140)	(2.614)	(5.213)	(10.334)
10	.0229	.0117	.0124	.0172	.0105	.0177	.0287
	(2.410)	(2.257)	(2.365)	(2.950)	(2.339)	(4.770)	(10.099)
11	.0122	.0059	.0066	.0093	.0056	.0094	.0154
	(2.343)	(2.064)	(2.266)	(2.863)	(2.218)	(4.570)	(9.983)
12	.0000	.0000	.0000	.0000	.0000	.0000	.0000
Sum	.1302	.1533	.1387	.1007	.0630	.1324	.2096
	(2.651)	(3.503)	(3.264)	(3.341)	(3.073)	(7.945)	(14.172)
F	4.112	13.478	5.352	6.588	11.788	31.202	98.733

Tab. 3.7: Rank estimates $\hat{\beta}_l^{ij}$ (r) of lag coefficients (in elasticity form) of regression of domestic prices of machinery, road vehicles and miscellaneous manufactures on international prices of iron & steel.*)

*) The endogenous variable (j) is a weighted average of the domestic producer price indices for machinery (including office machines but not data-processing equipment), road vehicles, precision & optical goods, and musical instruments, toys, athletic & sporting goods, jewelry, etc. The endogenous variable (i) is a weighted average (by trade shares) of price indices of imports of iron ore and imports and exports of iron & steel. Figures in parentheses denote t-ratios and F denotes the F-statistic for the joint significance of all 12 estimated lag coefficients.

Lag ℓ	Rank (r) of Approximating Observation Matrix 72	63	54	45	36	27	18
0	.2235 (8.789)	.2346 (11.544)	.2366 (15.594)	.2354 (16.233)	.2456 (18.445)	.0754 (16.774)	.0311 (21.679)
1	.1381 (8.117)	.1533 (13.785)	.1716 (18.623)	.1776 (24.278)	.1834 (26.789)	.0875 (16.373)	.0440 (20.973)
2	.0613 (3.760)	.0798 (8.367)	.1116 (16.020)	.1240 (27.382)	.1256 (26.717)	.0970 (16.151)	.0560 (20.383)
3	.0018 (.088)	.0216 (1.573)	.0614 (7.212)	.0791 (10.429)	.0766 (10.451)	.1014 (16.745)	.0658 (20.085)
4	-.0320 (-1.471)	-.0136 (-.864)	.0261 (2.722)	.0471 (4.986)	.0409 (4.728)	.0981 (18.981)	.0725 (19.855)
5	-.0348 (-1.818)	-.0211 (-1.561)	.0088 (1.022)	.0306 (3.642)	.0212 (3.003)	.0857 (23.916)	.0752 (19.206)
6	-.0163 (-1.065)	-.0092 (-.929)	.0050 (.689)	.0258 (4.299)	.0139 (3.396)	.0672 (19.781)	.0738 (17.811)
7	.0105 (.720)	.0110 (1.149)	.0086 (1.091)	.0270 (5.239)	.0137 (3.510)	.0468 (9.048)	.0687 (15.986)
8	.0327 (1.992)	.0282 (2.354)	.0134 (1.433)	.0285 (4.446)	.0153 (2.467)	.0286 (4.317)	.0600 (14.314)
9	.0400 (2.476)	.0336 (2.709)	.0145 (1.556)	.0260 (3.829)	.0145 (2.100)	.0158 (2.406)	.0480 (13.198)
10	.0341 (2.667)	.0283 (2.835)	.0117 (1.600)	.0195 (3.526)	.0111 (1.946)	.0079 (1.526)	.0334 (12.533)
11	.0193 (2.749)	.0159 (2.885)	.0065 (1.618)	.0104 (3.384)	.0060 (1.877)	.0031 (1.114)	.0171 (12.180)
12	.0000	.0000	.0000	.0000	.0000	.0000	.0000
Sum	.4781 (4.419)	.5623 (12.023)	.6758 (16.305)	.8309 (29.346)	.7677 (38.395)	.7146 (27.263)	.6456 (18.668)
F	28.711	108.921	174.265	477.092	621.830	306.914	159.377

Tab. 3.8: Rank estimates $\hat{\beta}_l^{ij}$ (r) of lag coefficients (in elasticity form) of regression of domestic on international prices of textiles & clothing.*)

*) The endogenous variable (j) is a weighted average of the producer price indices of textiles & clothing. The exogenous variable (i) is a weighted average (by trade shares) of price indices of imports and exports of textiles & clothing. Figures in parentheses denote t-ratios and F denotes the F-statistic for the joint significance of all 12 estimated lag coefficients.

Name of Commodity Category (j)	Rank (r) of Approximating Observation Matrix 72	63	54	45	36	27	18
Electricity, city gas, water	-.0707(-2.650)	-.0612(-2.998)	-.0420(-2.594)	-.0219(-2.314)	-.0356(-3.377)	-.0117(-1.214)	.0470 (13.314)
Electrity	-.0939(-3.478)	-.0720(-3.560)	-.0407(-2.474)	-.0104(-1.156)	-.0301(-3.020)	.0054 (1.359)	.0311 (9.267)
City gas	.1433 (1.235)	.0917 (1.042)	.0470 (.645)	.2059 (5.172)	.2076 (5.466)	.1126 (8.535)	.1331 (11.528)
Water	-.0598(-1.405)	-.0838(-2.441)	-.1126(-3.936)	-.2754(-18.095)	-.2452(-17.123)	-.2846(-17.373)	.0680 (6.870)
Mining products	.2011 (2.780)	.1818 (3.339)	.1500 (3.333)	.2103 (9.251)	.1827 (8.400)	.2136(10.012)	.2516 (31.979)
Petroleum products	.2898 (2.553)	.3291 (3.933)	.3102 (4.516)	.4313(12.212)	.3649(10.669)	.3490(12.268)	.2721 (28.771)
Quarrying products	.0589 (4.479)	.0607 (5.951)	.0423 (4.094)	.0069 (1.079)	.0442 (5.798)	.0218 (3.121)	-.0384(-12.414)
Iron & steel	.0213 (.424)	.0211 (.542)	.0106 (.338)	.0469 (3.145)	.0826 (5.173)	.0625 (3.692)	-.0643(-10.057)
Non-ferrous metals	.0620 (.515)	.1029 (1.107)	-.1318(-1.662)	-.1555(-4.133)	-.0701(-2.018)	-.0988(-3.432)	-.0772 (-6.182)
Steel semifinishes & products	.0378 (3.048)	.0336 (3.385)	.0647 (7.094)	.0542(10.512)	.0612(12.473)	.0600 (9.884)	.0108 (3.519)
Machinery, road vehicles, other manufactures	-.0306(-2.398)	-.0208(-2.107)	.0100 (1.033)	.0137 (2.386)	.0153 (3.153)	.0211 (4.595)	-.0194 (-4.963)
Electrical goods	.0565 (2.780)	.0511 (3.339)	.0421 (3.333)	.0591 (9.251)	.0513 (8.400)	.0600(10.012)	.0288 (6.414)
Chemicals & plastics	-.0532(-3.335)	-.0138(-1.119)	-.0044 (-.439)	.0204 (4.037)	.0296 (6.128)	.0197 (4.204)	.0013 (.723)
Rubber & asbestos	-.0913(-2.672)	-.0080 (-.298)	.0610 (2.862)	.1349(11.566)	.1457(13.363)	.1252(11.368)	.0443 (10.525)
Pottery & glassware	.0281 (1.477)	.0505 (3.496)	.0424 (3.428)	.0053 (.810)	.0127 (1.836)	-.0195(-7.598)	-.0105 (-3.731)
Wood products	-.0392(-3.193)	-.0063 (-.659)	-.0070 (-.764)	.0042 (.778)	.0223 (4.235)	.0190 (3.585)	.0035 (1.767)
Sawmill products	.0535 (3.515)	.0674 (5.398)	.1085 (8.690)	.1557(20.021)	.2010(19.598)	.1589(10.857)	-.0073 (-1.168)
Pulp, paper & products	.0477 (2.874)	.0327 (2.608)	.0041 (-.389)	.0276 (4.516)	.0345 (5.961)	.0405 (7.316)	.0630 (20.228)
Leather & leather products	-.0058 (-.263)	-.0012 (-.070)	.0143 (.887)	-.0045 (-.544)	-.0211(-2.758)	-.0242(-2.780)	.0150 (2.792)
Textiles & clothing	-.0267(-2.591)	-.0104(-1.337)	-.0213(-3.234)	-.0058(-1.708)	.0011 (.318)	-.0092(-1.710)	-.0141 (-5.714)
Food, beverages & tobacco	.0391 (2.161)	.0155 (1.052)	.0106 (.841)	-.0165(-2.773)	-.0315(-5.271)	-.0330(-6.514)	-.0352(-14.260)
All products	.0119 (1.188)	.0217 (2.848)	.0226 (3.523)	.0320 (8.441)	.0361(10.112)	.0315(10.197)	-.0000 (-.000)

Tab. 4: Rank estimates (and *t*-ratios) of the sum of lag coefficients $\sum_{l}^{11} \hat{\beta}_l^{ij}(r)$ (in elasticity form) of the regression of domestic producer price indices (*j*) on the price index (*i*) of imported crude petroleum & natural gas and imported and exported petroleum products.

References

Almon, Sh.: The Distributed Lag between Capital Appropriations and Expenditures. Econometrica **33**, 1965, 178–196.

Bacon, R.W., and *J.A. Hausman*: The Relationship between Ridge Regression and the Minimum Mean Square Error Estimator of Chipman. Oxford Bulletin of Economics and Statistics **36**, 1974, 115–124.

Chipman, J.S.: On Least Squares with Insufficient Observations. Journal of the American Statistical Association **59**, 1964, 1078–1111.

– : Statistical Problems Arising in the Theory of Aggregation. Applications of Statistics. Ed. by P.R. Krishnaiah. Amsterdam 1977, 123–140.

– : Towards the Construction of an Optimal Aggregative Model of International Trade: West Germany, 1963–1975. Annals of Economic and Social Measurement **6**, 1978, 535–554.

– : Efficiency of Least-Squares Estimation of Linear Trend when Residuals are Autocorrelated. Econometrica **47**, 1979, 115–128.

– : Exchange-Rate Flexibility and Resource Allocation. Flexible Exchange Rates and the Balance of Payments: Essays in Memory of Egon Sohmen. Ed. by J.S. Chipman and Ch.R. Kindleberger. Amsterdam 1980, 159–209.

Chipman, J.S., and *M.M. Rao*: The Treatment of Linear Restrictions in Regression Analysis. Econometrica **32**, 1964a, 198–209.

– : Projections, Generalized Inverses, and Quadratic Forms. Journal of Mathematical Analysis and Applications **9**, 1964b, 1–11.

Corradi, C., and *G. Gambetta*: The Estimation of Distributed Lags by Spline Functions. Empirical Economics **1** (1), 1975, 41–51.

Eckart, C., and *G. Young*: The Approximation of One Matrix by Another of Lower Rank. Psychometrika **1**, 1936, 211–218.

– : A Principal Axis Transformation for Non-Hermitian Matrices. Bulletin of the American Mathematical Society **45**, 1939, 118–121.

Goldstein, M., and *A.F.M. Smith*: Ridge-Type Estimators for Regression Analysis. Journal of the Royal Statistical Society [B], **36** (2), 1974, 284–291.

Golub, G., and *W. Kahan*: Calculating the Singular Values and Pseudo-Inverse of a Matrix. Journal of the Society for Industrial and Applied Mathematics, Series B (Numerical Analysis) **2** (2), 1965, 205–224.

Golub, G.H., and *C. Reinsch*: Singular Value Decomposition and Least Squares Solutions. Numerische Mathematik **14**, 1970, 403–420.

Greville, T.N.E.: Data Fitting by Spline Functions. Mathematics Research Center, United States Army, University of Wisconsin, Madison, MRC Technical Summary Report No. 893, 1968, (mimeographed).

– : Introduction to Spline Functions. Theory and Application of Spline Functions. Ed. by T.N.E. Greville. New York 1969, 1–35.

Guckes, S.: Zur Neuberechnung der Preisindices auf Basis 1970. Wirtschaft und Statistik, 1973, 691–693. English translation: A New Computation of the Price Indices on Base 1970. Studies on Statistics (28), 1974.

Hamlen, S.S., and *W.A. Hamlen*: Harmonic Alternatives to the Almon Polynomial Technique. Journal of Econometrics **7**, 1978, 57–66.

Ho, D.S.: An Econometric Study of the Relationship between International and Domestic Prices in the Japanese Economy. Ph.D. thesis, University of Minnesota, Minneapolis 1977.

Hoerl, A.E., and *R.W. Kennard*: Ridge Regression: Biased Estimation for Nonorthogonal Problems. Technometrics **12**, 1970a, 55–67.

– : Ridge Regression: Application to Nonorthogonal Problems. Technometrics **12**, 1970b, 69–82.

Kravis, I.B., and *R.E. Lipsey*: Price Competitiveness in World Trade. New York 1971.

Leamer, E.E.: Multicollinearity: A Bayesian Interpretation. Review of Economics and Statistics **55**, 1973, 371–380.

Lucas, R.E., Jr.: Econometric Testing of the Natural Rate Hypothesis. The Econometrics of Price Determination. Proceedings of a Conference held on October 30–31; 1970. Washington, D.C., 1970.

Marquardt, D.W.: Generalized Inverses, Ridge Regression, Biased Linear Estimation, and Nonlinear Estimation. Technometrics 12, 1970, 591–612.

Ouanes, A.: Econometric Study of the International Transmission of Inflation: The Case of West Germany. Ph.D. thesis, University of Minnesota, Minneapolis 1979.

Rostin, W.: Die Indices der Außenhandelspreise auf Basis 1970. Wirtschaft und Statistik, 1974, 387–394. English translation: Indices of Foreign Trade Prices, Base 1970. Studies on Statistics (30), 1974.

Samuelson, P.A.: Prices of Factors and Goods in General Equilibrium. Review of Economic Studies 21, 1953, 1–20.

Shephard, R.W.: Cost and Production Functions. Princeton, N.J., 1953.

Shiller, R.J.: A Distributed Lag Estimator Derived from Smoothness Priors. Econometrica 41, 1973, 775–788.

Sims, Ch.A.: Money, Income and Causality. American Economic Review 62, 1972, 540–552.

– : Distributed Lags. Frontiers of Quantitative Economics, Vol. II. Ed. by M.D. Intrilligator and D.A. Kendrick. Amsterdam 1974, 289–332.

Statistisches Bundesamt, Wiesbaden: Fachserie M, Preise, Löhne, Wirtschaftsrechnungen: Reihe 1, Preise und Preisindizes für Außenhandelsgüter; Reihe 3, Preise und Preisindizes für industrielle Produkte (Erzeugerpreise). Mainz 1958–1976.
Fachserie 17, Preise: Reihe 8, Preise und Preisindizes für die Ein- und Ausfuhr; Reihe 2, Preise und Preisindizes für industrielle Produkte (Erzeugerpreise). Mainz 1977–1979.

– : Systematisches Warenverzeichnis für die Industriestatistik, Ausgabe 1970. Mainz 1970.

Wedin, P.-Å.: On the Almost Rank Deficient Case of the Least Squares Problem. BIT Nordisk Tidskrift for Informationsbehandling 13 (3), 1973, 344–354.

Zellner, A.C.: An Efficient Method of Estimating Seemingly Unrelated Regressions and Tests for Aggregation Bias. Journal of the American Statistical Association 57, 1962, 348–368.

Quantitative Studies on Production and Prices

United States Demand for Material Imports: Distinguished by Regions of Supply

Georg Hasenkamp and *Anthony Y.C. Koo*[1])

1. Introduction

Today most supplying nations of raw materials are more than ever concious of their monopolistic or ologopolistic potential in "setting" prices and/or restricting supply. For this reason alone, the United States as one of the major user of materials, should learn more about the characteristics of her demand for material imports, and in particular about the degree of substitutability of a given material from various regions of supply. It is generally assumed that products of a given classification – which are supplied by various regions – are roughly of the same kind.[2]) This assumption suggests that the elasticity of substitution between a given material from the regional sources of supply might be very large. However, this assumption of (almost) perfect substitutability should be the subject matter of an investigation.

The question of this type of substitution possibility is relevant, because it is linked to a "degree of dependency" on the regions of supply: a perfect substitution possibility indicates also a low degree of dependency on the particular region of supply. Other indicators of such a "dependency" might also be the various price elasticities.

This paper is an attempt to fill part of this void. We base our analysis on one of the earliest and original work on this subject, namely *Armington* [1969a, 1969b]. In view of the broad data classification (or grouping) of materials, and the rather arbitrary classification of regions, our results should be considered as a demonstration of (one possible) method only.

2. Data

The United States Department of Commerce divides the US imports into five economic classes: crude materials, semi-manufactures, crude food stuffs, manufactured food stuffs and beverages, and finished manufactures. Imports of materials for our present purpose include those products which comprise the first two classifications: crude materials

---

[1]) The computations were performed by the first author at the University Bonn, with funds provided by the Deutsche Forschungsgemeinschaft.

[2]) For a list of references on the subject of estimating demand relationship for imports and exports exports, see *Cheng* [1959], *Leamer/Stern* [1970].

and semi-manufactures plus newsprint and burlap, which are normally included in finished manufactures. This paper makes use of unit value and quantity indexes of imports from 1923 to 1960. The data were first computed by *Adler/Schlesinger/Westerborg* [1952], and later brought up to 1960 by *Reimer* [1962].

Because of this broad classification, the composition of imports differs somewhat from one region to another. One example is lumber and newsprint. They constitute a substantial fraction of the United States imports from Canada. Little of it was imported from other regions, with the exception of pulpwood from Scandinavian countries. Another example is steel products: The *US* imports of semi-manufactures came largely from Europe, while imports of crude metals are from Latin America and the Overseas Sterling area.

The (physical) units of material imports are measured as value/unit value price index, and these are listed according to the regions of supply as follows, where the quantities x_i are measured in per capita terms:

x_1 = European Payments Union countries,
x_2 = Canada,
x_3 = Latin America,
x_4 = Overseas Sterling area,
x_5 = Rest of the world,
x_6 = other Europe.
(For regional classifications of countries see *Reimer* [1962].)

3. Method

In order to illustrate the applied simultaneous demand pattern for material imports, we start out with an aggregator function, which is specified to be of the form

$$y = (\Sigma\beta_i\,(x_i - z_i)^\rho)^{1/\rho} = (\Sigma\beta_i\,x_i^{*\rho})^{1/\rho} \qquad (1)$$

which is concave and homogeneous of degree 1 in the positive x_i^* variables $x_i^* = x_i - z_i$, under the parameter restrictions $0 < \beta_i < 1$, $\Sigma\,\beta_i = 1$, and $-\infty < \rho < 1$ for $\rho \neq 0$. The (positive and unobservable) variables z_i denote precommitted levels of the corresponding material imports. We note that the aggregator function is not homothetic in the (observable) variables x_i.[3]) Assuming that the levels of the x_i are determined by minimizing total expenditures (under exogenously determined positive prices p_i for x_i) to attain a given

[3]) The aggregate function may be interpreted as either a sub-utility or sub-production function; for the homothetic CES case we refer to *Sato* [1967]. *Armington* [1969a, 1969b] discussed the homothetic CES-type aggregator function to derive import demand functions; however, he does not present an empirical investigation. No multiplicative constant appears in expression (1) since such a parameter is not identified in a sub-utility or sub-production function. For a more general discussion of such subaggregates, existence and consistency within the aggregate utility or production function, we refer to *Green* [1964], and *Hasenkamp* [1980].

(positive) value for the aggregate material import y, we have a dual cost function of the form

$$C(p_1, \ldots, p_n; z_1, \ldots, z_n, y) = \Sigma\, p_i\, z_i + (\Sigma \beta_i' p_i^{\rho'})^{1/\rho'}\, y, \tag{2}$$

where $\beta_i' = \beta_i^{-1/(\rho-1)}$ and $\rho' = \rho/(\rho - 1)$. The system of (Hick's) demand functions follows by taking partial derivatives of the cost function with respect to prices, i.e., by Shephard's Lemma:

$$x_i = z_i + \beta_i' p_i^{\rho'-1} (\Sigma\, \beta_j' p_j^{\rho'})^{-1/\rho}\, y. \tag{3}$$

This demand function (3) represents a convenient tool to derive the elasticity of substitution σ_{ij} between x_i and x_j, for $i \neq j$:

$$\sigma_{ij} = -\frac{\partial \log (x_i/x_j)}{\partial \log (p_i/p_j)}\,. \tag{4}$$

This expression in (4) may be rewritten as

$$\sigma_{ij} = -\left(\frac{x_j}{x_i}\right)\left(\frac{p_i}{p_j}\right)\left(\frac{\partial (x_i/x_j)}{\partial (p_i/p_j)}\right) \tag{5}$$

$$= -\left(\frac{x_j}{x_i}\right)\left(\frac{p_i}{p_j}\right)\left(\frac{\partial (x_i/x_j)}{\partial (x_i^*/x_j^*)}\right)\left(\frac{\partial (x_i^*/x_j^*)}{\partial (p_i/p_j)}\right)$$

where

$$x_i^* = \beta_i' p_i^{\rho'-1} (\Sigma\, \beta_j' p_j^{\rho'})^{-1/\rho}\, y. \tag{6}$$

However, $\partial (x_i^*/x_j^*) / \partial (p_i/p_j)$ is easy to evaluate, so that expression (5) may be rewritten as

$$\sigma_{ij} = \sigma \left(\frac{x_j}{x_i}\right)\left(\frac{x_i^*}{x_j^*}\right)\left(\frac{\partial (x_i/x_j)}{\partial (x_i^*/x_j^*)}\right), \tag{7}$$

where $\sigma = 1/(1 - \rho)$ is the (constant) elasticity of substitution between the x_i^* and x_j^*. With some manipulations it is then possible to show that

$$\sigma_{ij} = \sigma \left(\frac{x_i^*}{x_i} a_j + \frac{x_j^*}{x_j} a_i\right) \tag{8}$$

where

$$a_j = \beta_j x_j^{*\rho} / (\beta_j x_j^{*\rho} + \beta_i x_i^{*\rho})\ .^{4)} \tag{9}$$

[4]) With some algebraic minipulations one can show that

$$w_i^* = \beta_i x_i^{*\rho} / (\Sigma\, \beta_k x_k^{*\rho}) = \beta_i' p_i^{\rho'} / (\Sigma\, \beta_k' p_k^{\rho'}) = p_i x_i^* / m^*$$

is the marginal budget share, where $m^* = (m - \Sigma\, p_j z_j)$. Thus we may rewrite a_j and a_i in (9) as

$$a_j = w_j^* / (w_j^* + w_i^*)$$

$$a_i = w_i^* / (w_j^* + w_i^*),$$

so that the elasticity of substitution σ_{ij} (8) may be calculated in terms of x_i, x_j, x_i^*, x_j^*, w_i^*, and w_j^*.

We note that $\sigma_{ij} = \sigma_{ji}$, and since the a_j and a_i are positive, $a_j + a_i = 1$, and since x_i^*/x_i as well as x_j^*/x_j are less than unity, it follows that the (non-constant) elasticity of substitution σ_{ij} satisfies

$$\sigma_{ij} < \sigma. \tag{10}$$

The estimation of the parameters for the aggregator function (1), and hence also for the elasticities of substitution (8), via the demand system (3) requires observations on the value of the sub-aggregate y. This, however, is rarely (if at all) the case. Instead, data on expenditures, hence total expenditures of imports and on prices are typically available. This suggests that we use the Marshallian system of demand functions,

$$x_i = z_i + (\beta_i' p_i^{\rho'-1} / (\Sigma\, \beta_k' p_k^{\rho'}))\,(m - \Sigma\, p_j z_j), \tag{11}$$

corresponding to the aggregator function (1) for estimation purposes. We note that the same parameters are involved in the elasticities of substitution (8) as in the demand function (11).

Building up from the system (11) we can obtain the following additional indicators of import "dependency" on the particular regions of supply: a) The expenditure elasticities indicate a change of import pattern over the regions of supply as the economic activity fluctuates. (Underlying this suggestion is the assumption that there exists a direct link between material imports and economic growth, for example.) b) The price elasticities, where a low own and cross price elasticity might indicate a larger "dependency" on a particular region of supply.

We note that the expenditure elasticities for (11) are given by

$$\eta_i = \gamma_i / w_i, \tag{12}$$

where $\gamma_i = \beta_i' p_i^{\rho'} / (\Sigma\, \beta_k' p_k^{\rho'})$ is the marginal budget share, and $w_i = p_i x_i / m$ is the budget share. The Cournot (uncompensated) price elasticities for (11) are given by

$$\eta_{ij} = -\gamma_i (p_j z_j / p_i x_i) - (\gamma_i \gamma_j / p_i x_i)\, \rho' \,(m - \Sigma\, p_k z_k) \tag{13}$$

for $i \neq j$, and by

$$\eta_{ii} = -1 + (1 - \gamma_i)\,((1 - \rho')\,(z_i / x_i) + \rho'). \tag{14}$$

Slutzky's (compensated) price elasticities follow as

$$\eta_{ij}^* = \eta_{ij} + \eta_i w_j. \tag{15}$$

The question comes up, which price elasticity – Cournot or Slutzky – is the more relevant one. These two alternative price elasticities provide *answers* to alternative questions: Under the Cournot price elasticities the total (import) expenditure m is held constant if the price of material imports from a region changes, i.e., as if there is a restriction on the value of imports. Under the Slutzky price elasticities the value of the quantity aggregate y is held constant, i.e., as if economic activity is held constant.

For estimation purposes we specified an additive disturbance term in the typical demand function (11), so that our model fits into the framework presented in *Malinvaud* [1972], to obtain Least Squares as well as Maximum Likelihood estimates. *Barten* [1963] and *Pollak/Wales* [1963] noted that the covariance matrix under the full system of demand functions is singular, due to the restriction $\Sigma p_i x_i = m$. Under the (plausible) assumption that the covariance matrix has the rank of the full system less unity, one (arbitrary) demand function will be dropped from the full system. Estimation also requires a specification for the z_i: We followed the suggestions presented in *Pollak* [1970] and *Phlips* [1972] to use the form

$$z_{i_t} = \lambda_i + \alpha_i x_{i_{t-1}}, \tag{16}$$

i.e., a "habit formation" type of a change for $\alpha_i \neq 0$.[5])

4. Results

For the present study we divided the time series into the Pre-War, 1923–1939, and the Post-War, 1946–1960, data. Separate estimation runs were made for each data set. We shall present only a summary of estimation results in the appendix, since these are only of minor interest once their significance and plausibility has been assured. Of more practical interest are the elasticities of substitution σ_{ij}, the expenditure elasticities η_i, the Cournot price elasticities η_{ij}, and perhaps the Slutzky (own) price elasticities η^*_{ij}. These elasticities are variable for each observation point, but we shall present the values for only the last observation point of each data set. All these elasticities are computed by using fitted values for the quantities x_i and x_i^* under the ML-parameter estimates. In Table 1 we present the elasticities of substitution σ_{ij}. Due to symmetry, only the upper right matrix is presented. Since the ratios x_i^*/x_i play such a decisive role in the computation of σ_{ij}, these ratios are presented on the diagonal elements of the matrix.

$i =$ \ $j =$	1	2	3	4	5	6
1	.4349	.3050	.3285	.2960	.3421	.2020
2		.3594	.3022	.2419	.3223	.1965
3			.4422	.2928	.3481	.1995
4				.3625	.3070	.1997
5					.4824	.2022
6						.2580

Tab. 1: Elasticities of Substitution $\sigma_{ij}, i \neq j$. Data base: 1946–1960, evaluated for 1960: σ = 7502

[5]) The "habit formation" parameters α_i really represent in this case an indication of an import pattern over time, which is not related to current price movements. Our specification of a constant parameter λ_i might indicate a shortcoming, since this expression could also reflect any possible institutional trade restrictions and their changes over time.

Even though the x_i^* variables are hypothetical concepts in the aggregator function (1), one would expect larger values for σ, say at least larger than unity, since the products are of such similar nature. Low values for σ in combination with low ratios for the x_i^*/x_i lead thus to rather low elasticities of substitution σ_{ij}. Thus, the "dependency" on material imports as distinguished by regions is larger than one would expect in intuitive grounds; at least in the short run, since we estimated a dynamic "habit-formation" type demand system.

a) Data base: 1923–1939, evaluated for 1939

i = \ j =	1	2	3	4	5	6
1	−0.4977	−0.1230	−0.0905	−0.1356	−0.1936	−0.0364
2	−0.1044	−0.3672	−0.0688	−0.1030	−0.1471	−0.0277
3	−0.1933	−0.1731	−0.6345	−0.1908	−0.2724	−0.0512
4	−0.1370	−0.1226	−0.0903	−0.4943	−0.1929	−0.0363
5	−0.0941	−0.0842	−0.0620	−0.0928	−0.3791	−0.0249
6	−0.0379	−0.0339	−0.0250	−0.0374	−0.0534	−0.1094

b) Data base: 1946–1960, evaluated for 1960

i = \ j =	1	2	3	4	5	6
1	−0.4338	−0.2342	−0.1560	−0.1114	−0.1149	−0.0147
2	−0.0884	−0.4631	−0.1289	−0.0930	−0.0950	−0.0121
3	−0.1093	−0.2381	−0.4904	−0.1133	−0.1168	−0.0149
4	−0.0896	−0.1952	−0.1300	−0.3648	−0.0958	−0.0122
5	−0.1193	−0.2597	−0.1730	−0.1235	−0.4893	−0.0163
6	−0.0538	−0.1389	−0.0926	−0.0641	−0.0682	−0.2023

Tab. 2: Cournot price elasticities η_{ij}

In Table 2 we present the Cournot price elasticities. The diagonal elements in this table indicate own price elasticities; off-diagonal elements indicate the (non-symmetric) cross price elasticities. Two results stand out: First, the relatively low own price elasticities, and second the low cross price elasticities. The low cross price elasticities confirm again the "dependency" on each region of supply, as was indicated above by the elasticities of substitution.[6]) This general pattern is repeated also by the Slutzky price elasticities, which we present in Table 3.

[6]) In two interesting papers, *Kemp* [1962] and *Kakwani* [1972], the question of a downward bias of price elasticities, given errors of measurements, has been investigated. In these papers a single (import) equation has been specified, with a parameter indicating the price elasticities. We deal with a system of equation, and it is not obvious whether their conclusions can be carried over to our specification.

data base	$i=$ 1	2	3	4	5	6
1923–1939	–.2829	–.2385	–.3759	–.2834	–.2033	–.0983
1946–1960	–.2742	–.1982	–.2530	–.2373	–.2896	–.1915

Tab. 3: Slutzky (own) price elasticities: η_{ii}^* evaluated at last observation point

data set	$i=$ 1	2	3	4	5	6
1923–1939	1.077	.8181	1.515	1.073	.7371	.2970
1946–1960	1.065	.8801	1.083	.8876	1.181	.6319

Tab. 4: Expenditure Elasticities η_i evaluated at last observation

In Table 4 we present the expenditure elasticities for the two data sets, evaluated at the last observation. This, we thought of more appropriate than evaluating these elasticities at some hypothetical mean expenditure and price situation. However, in order to indicate these elasticities for alternative years under the more relevant data set 1946–1960, we present in Table 5 additional information. It is interesting to note – for example for the results obtained with the 1946–1960 data – the relative constancy of these expenditure elasticities, except for x_1 (= European Payment Union Countries) and x_6 (= other Europe). During the Cold War years 1947 and 1950–1951 the elasticity falls for x_6, but rises for x_1; this is, given political circumstances reflected in the data, rather plausible. We also note that x_1 (= European Payment Union Countries), x_3 (= Latin America), and x_5 (= Rest of the World) are the main beneficiaries of an increase in material import expenditures of the United States. Canada, x_2, appears to play – rather surprisingly – a smaller role than anticipated on intuitive grounds.

year	$i=$ 1	2	3	4	5	6
1958	1.268	.8265	1.001	.9039	1.248	.7222
1952	1.096	.9171	1.065	.8011	1.225	.5521
1951	1.309	.9992	1.104	.6434	1.157	.5172
1950	1.301	.9429	1.038	.7510	1.124	.5605
1947	1.480	1.027	.8882	.6737	1.372	.3126

Tab. 5: Expenditure Elasticities η_i. For 1946–1960 data, alternative years.

Appendix: Parameter Estimates

In the table below we present the parameter estimates corresponding to the two data sets (i) 1923–1939; (ii) 1946–1960. We supply both the Maximum-Likelihood (ML) estimates and the Least-Squares (LS) estimates. Below the parameter estimates we present – whenever possible – the (asymptotic) standard errors in parenthesis. For each demand function the fit-measure R_i^2 was calculated as unity less the ratio of the residual variance to the variance of the dependent variable. The number of times for which $x_i - \hat{z}_i$ turned negative is denoted by N_1; more relevant however is N_2, the number of times for $\hat{x}_1 - \hat{z}_i$

turned negative. (The ^-symbol denotes "fits.") We do not present derived parameter estimates for the β_i's and for ρ; also, we do not present estimates for the λ_i's, since these parameters cannot be interpreted in a meaningful way. In the table: [a] denotes that the covariance matrix for parameter estimates turned singular. [b] denotes that R_i^2 was negative.

Parameter	1923–1939 ML	1923–1939 LS[a]	1946–1960 ML	1946–1960 LS
α_1	0.5727 (0.0126)	0.5805 –	0.4826 (0.0278)	0.4339 (0.0313)
α_2	0.6249 (0.01144)	0.6659 –	0.6029 (0.0141)	0.5893 (0.0169)
α_3	0.3256 (0.0605)	0.4198 –	0.5242 (0.0223)	0.5994 (0.0213)
α_4	0.5034 (0.02510)	0.5024 –	0.6223 (0.0195)	0.6544) (0.0245)
α_5	0.6955 (0.03975)	0.7018 –	0.4696 (0.0479)	0.4315 (0.0991)
α_6	0.8411 (0.4940)	1.0356 –	0.7186 (0.0307)	0.9051 (0.4041)
β'_1	0.3932 (0.00111)	0.2147 –	0.2487 (0.0014)	0.2896 (0.0151)
β'_2	0.2263 (0.02108)	0.1121 –	0.3924 (0.0314)	0.4334 (0.0357)
β'_3	0.4805 (0.03796)	0.2410 –	0.3382 (0.0488)	0.3042 (0.0500)
β'_4	0.3824 (0.05462)	0.2373 –	0.2008 (0.0381)	0.1965 (0.0475)
β'_5	0.3113 (0.03787)	0.2007 –	0.2973 (0.0276)	0.3398 (0.0554)
β'_6	0.0204 –	0.1564 –	0.0168 –	0.0051 –
R_1^2	0.9875	0.9704	0.8022	0.8031
R_2^2	0.9593	0.9235	0.9608	0.9632
R_3^2	0.8463	0.8397	0.7909	0.8113
R_4^2	0.9523	0.9347	0.8324	0.8280
R_5^2	0.9898	0.9772	0.9563	0.9485
R_6^2	0.5532	b	0.8707	0.7128
ρ'	0.3743 (0.1699)	−0.1199 –	0.2498 (0.1941)	0.2855 (0.3348)
N_1	4	7	0	5
N_2	0	0	0	0

Table

References

Adler, J.H., E.R. Schlesinger and *E.V. Westerborg*: The Pattern of United States Import Trade Since 1923. New York 1952.

Armington, P.S.: A Theory of Demand for Products Distinguished by Place of Production. International Monetary Fund, Staff Papers **XVI**, 1969a, 159–176.

– : The Geographic Pattern of Trade and the Effects of Price Changes. International Monetary Fund, Staff Papers **XVI**, 1969b, 179–201.

Barten, A.P.: Maximum Likelihood Estimation of a Complete System of Demand Equations. European Economic Review **1**, 1963, 7–73.

Brown, M., and *D. Heien*: The *S*-Branch Utility Tree: A Generalization of the Linear Expenditure System. Econometrica **40**, 1972, 737–748.

Cheng, H.S.: Statistical Estimates of Elasticities and Propensities in International Trade: A Survey of Published Studies. International Monetary Fund, Staff Papers **VII**, 1959, 107–158.

Gamaletsos, T.: Further Analysis of Cross-Country Comparidon of Consumer Expenditure Patterns. European Economic Review **4**, 1973, 1–20.

Green, H.A.J.: Aggregation in Economic Analysis. Princeton, NJ, 1964.

Hasenkamp, G.: A Demand System Analysis of Disaggregated Consumption. Göttingen 1980.

Kakwani, N.C.: On the Bias in Estimates of Import Demand Parameters. International Economic Review **13**, 1972, 239–244.

Kemp, M.C.: Errors of Measurement and Bias in Estimates of Import Demand Parameters. The Economic Record **XXXVIII**, 1962, 369–372.

Leamer, E.E., and *R.H. Stern*: Quantitative International Economics. Boston 1970.

Malinvaud, E.: Statistical Methods of Econometrics. Amsterdam 1972.

Mason, E.S.: An American View of the Raw Material Problem. Journal of Industrial Economics **I**, 1952–1953, 1–20.

Phlips, L.: A Dynamic Version of the Linear Expenditure Model. Review of Economics and Statistics **64**, 1972, 450–458.

Pollak, R.A.: Habit Formation and Dynamic Demand Functions. Journal of Political Economy **8**, 1970, 745–763.

Pollak, R.A., and *T.J. Wales*: Estimation of the Linear Expenditure System. Econometrica **37**, 1963, 611–627.

Reimer, R.D.: The United States Demand for Imports of Materials. Unpublished Ph.D. dissertation, Michigan State University, East Lansing 1962.

– : The United States Demand for Imports of Materials. Review of Economics and Statistics **56**, 1964, 307–312.

Sato, K.: A Two-Level Constant Elasticity of Substitution Production Function. Review of Economic Studies **34**, 1967, 201–218.

Quantitative Studies on Production and Prices © Physica-Verlag, Würzburg–Wien, 1983.

Relative Prices and Technical Change

Dale W. Jorgenson and *Barbara M. Fraumeni*[1])

1. Introduction

In this paper our objective is to analyze technical change and the distribution of the value of output for thirty-six industrial sectors of the U.S. economy. Our most important conceptual innovation is to determine the rate of technical change and the distributive shares of productive inputs simultaneously as functions of relative prices. We show that the effects of technical change on the distributive shares is precisely the same as the effects of relative prices on the rate of technical change.

Our methodology is based on a model of production treating substitution among inputs and changes in technology symmetrically. The model is based on a production function for each industrial sector, giving output as a function of time and of capital, labor, energy, and materials inputs. Necessary conditions for producer equilibrium in each sector are given by equalities between the distributive shares of the four productive inputs and the corresponding elasticities of output with respect to each of these inputs.

Producer equilibrium under constant returns to scale implies that the value of output is equal to the sum of the values of capital, labor, energy, and materials inputs into each sector. Given this identity and equalities between the distributive shares and the elasticities of output with respect to each of the inputs, we can express the price of output as a function of the prices of capital, labor, energy and materials inputs, and time. We refer to this function as the sectoral price function.

Given sectoral price functions for all thirty-six industrial sectors, we can generate econometric models that determine the rate of technical change and the distributive shares of the four productive inputs endogenously for each sector. The distributive shares and the rate of technical change, like the price of sectoral output, are functions of relative prices and time. We assume that the prices of sectoral outputs are transcendental logarithmic or, more simply, translog functions of the prices of the four inputs and time.

---

[1]) We are indebted to Peter Derksen for development of the software for transformation of the data to eliminate autocorrelation in the disturbances, as described in Section 3. We are grateful to Thomas Stoker for development and Christopher Holsing for implementation of the software used in obtaining the estimates presented in Section 4. All of the estimation was carried out by Holsing. We are indebted to Denise Gaudet and Nelda Hoxie for very able assistance in preparation of the data for estimation. Finally, we are grateful to Ernst Berndt, Frank Gollop, William Hogan, Edward Hudson, Lawrence Lau, and James Sweeney for valuable advice. Financial support for this research was provided by the Federal Emergency Management Agency and the U.S. Department of Energy. All errors remain the responsibility of the authors.

While technical change is endogenous in our models of production and technical change, these models must be carefully distinguished from models of induced technical change, such as those analyzed by *Hicks* [1932], *Kennedy* [1964], *Samuelson* [1965], *von Weizsäcker* [1962] and many others.[2]) In those models the biases of technical change are endogenous and depend on relative prices. In our models the biases of technical change are fixed, while the rate of technical change is endogenous and depends on relative prices.

As *Samuelson* [1965] has pointed out, models of induced technical change require intertemporal optimization, since technical change at any point of time affects future production possibilities. In our models myopic decision rules are appropriate, even though the rate of technical change is endogenous, provided that the price of capital input is treated as a rental price for capital services [for further discussion of myopic decision rules see *Jorgenson*, 1973]. The rate of technical change at any point of time is a function of relative prices, but does not affect future production possibilities. This vastly simplifies the modeling of producer behavior and greatly facilitates the implementation of our econometric models.

Given myopic decision rules for producers in each industrial sector, we can describe all of the implications of the theory of production in terms of the sectoral price functions. The sectoral price functions must be homogeneous of degree one in the prices of the four inputs, symmetric in the input prices and time, and nondecreasing and concave in the input prices. A novel feature of our econometric methodology is to fit econometric models of sectoral production and technical change that incorporate all of these implications of the theory of production.

The translog price functions that we employ to generate our econometric models cannot be monotone and concave for all possible input prices. However, we can assure concavity of these functions for any prices that result in nonnegative distributive shares for all four inputs, so that price effects on demands for productive inputs are nonpositive wherever the inputs themselves are nonnegative. This new methodology is based on the Cholesky factorization of a matrix of constant parameters in our econometric models associated with price effects. We have fitted these matrices subject to the condition that they must be negative semi-definite.

Under constant returns to scale the rate of technical change for each sector can be expressed as the negative of the rate of growth of the price of output, plus a weighted average of the rates of growth of the prices of the four inputs. We employ indexes of the rate of technical change and the four input prices that are exact for translog price functions. This important innovation assures consistency between the representations of technology that underly our measures of technical change and input prices and the representations that underly our econometric models.

Our most striking empirical finding is that the rate of technical change is predominately decreasing in the prices of capital, labor, and energy and increasing in the price of

[2]) A review of the literature on induced technical change is given by *Binswanger* [1978a]. Binswanger distinguishes between models, like ours and those of *Ben-Zion/Ruttan* [1978], *Lucas* [1967] and *Schmookler* [1966], with an endogenous rate of technical change and models, like those of *Hicks* [1932], *Kennedy* [1964], *Samuelson* [1965], *von Weizsäcker* [1962] and others, with an endogenous bias of technical change. Additional references are given by *Binswanger* [1978a].

materials. This pattern characterizes nineteen of the industries included in our study. The rate of technical change decreases with the price of capital in twenty-five industries, decreases with the price of labor in thirty-one industries, decreases with the price of energy in twenty-nine industries, and increases with the price of materials in thirty-three industries.

Our econometric models have been fitted to annual data for the period 1958–1974. Since 1973 the relative prices of capital, labor, energy, and materials in the United States have been altered radically as a consequence of the increase in the price of energy relative to the prices of other productive inputs. The sharp increase in the price of energy began with the run-up of world petroleum prices in late 1973 and early 1974 in the aftermath of the Arab Oil Embargo. Our econometric models reveal that slower productivity growth at the sectoral level after 1973 is associated with higher energy prices.

Our empirical findings on patterns of substitution are almost as clearcut as our findings on patterns of technical change. We find that the elasticities of the shares of capital with respect to the price of labor are nonnegative for thirty-three of our thirty-six industries, so that the shares of capital are nondecreasing in the price labor for thirty-three sectors. Similarly, elasticities of the share of capital with respect to the price of energy are nonnegative for thirty-four industries and elasticities with respect to the price of materials are nonnegative for all thirty-six industries. We find that the share elasticities of labor with respect to the prices of energy and materials are nonnegative for nineteen and for all thirty-six industries, respectively. Finally, we find that the share elasticities of energy with respect to the price of materials are nonnegative for thirty of the thirty-six industries.

2. Econometric Models

The development of our econometric model of production and technical change proceeds through two stages. We first specify a functional form for the sectoral price functions, say $\{P^i\}$, taking into account restrictions on the parameters implied by the theory of production.[3]) Secondly, we formulate an error structure for the econometric model and discuss procedures for estimation of the unknown parameters.

Our first step in formulating an econometric model of production and technical change is to consider specific forms for the sectoral price functions $\{P^i\}$:

$$\begin{aligned} q_i = \exp\Big[& \alpha_0^i + \alpha_K^i \ln p_K^i + \alpha_L^i \ln p_L^i + \alpha_E^i \ln p_E^i + \alpha_M^i \ln p_M^i + \alpha_T^i \cdot T \\ & + \frac{1}{2} \beta_{KK}^i (\ln p_K^i)^2 + \beta_{KL}^i \ln p_K^i \ln p_L^i + \beta_{KE}^i \ln p_K^i \ln p_E^i \\ & + \beta_{KM}^i \ln p_K^i \ln p_M^i + \beta_{KT}^i \ln p_K^i \cdot T + \frac{1}{2} \beta_{LL}^i (\ln p_L^i)^2 \\ & + \beta_{LE}^i \ln p_L^i \ln p_E^i + \beta_{LM}^i \ln p_L^i \ln p_M^i + \beta_{LT}^i \ln p_L^i \cdot T \end{aligned}$$

[3]) The price function was introduced by *Samuelson* [1953].

$$+\frac{1}{2}\beta^i_{EE}(\ln p^i_E)^2+\beta^i_{EM}\ln p^i_E\ln p^i_M+\beta^i_{ET}\ln p^i_E\cdot T$$
$$+\frac{1}{2}\beta^i_{MM}(\ln p^i_M)^2+\beta^i_{MT}\ln p^i_M\cdot T+\frac{1}{2}\beta^i_{TT}\cdot T^2\Big],$$
$$(i=1,2,\ldots,n).$$

For these price functions, the prices of outputs are transcendental or, more specifically, exponential functions of the logarithms of the prices of inputs. We refer to these forms as *transcendental logarithmic price functions* or, more simply, translog price functions,[4]) indicating the role of the variables that enter into the price functions.

The price functions $\{P^i\}$ are homogeneous of degree one in the input prices. The translog price function for an industrial sector is characterized by homogeneity of degree one if and only if the parameters for that sector satisfy the conditions:

$$\alpha^i_K+\alpha^i_L+\alpha^i_E+\alpha^i_M=1,$$
$$\beta^i_{KK}+\beta^i_{KL}+\beta^i_{KE}+\beta^i_{KM}=0,$$
$$\beta^i_{LK}+\beta^i_{LL}+\beta^i_{LE}+\beta^i_{LM}=0,$$
$$\beta^i_{EK}+\beta^i_{EL}+\beta^i_{EE}+\beta^i_{EM}=0,$$
$$\beta^i_{MK}+\beta^i_{ML}+\beta^i_{ME}+\beta^i_{MM}=0,$$
$$\beta^i_{KT}+\beta^i_{LT}+\beta^i_{ET}+\beta^i_{MT}=0,\qquad (i=1,2,\ldots,n).$$

For each sector the value shares of capital, labor, energy, and materials inputs, say $\{v^i_K\}$, $\{v^i_L\}$, $\{v^i_E\}$ and $\{v^i_M\}$, can be expressed in terms of logarithmic derivatives of the sectoral price function with respect to the logarithms of price of the corresponding input:

$$v^i_K=\alpha^i_K+\beta^i_{KK}\ln p^i_K+\beta^i_{KL}\ln p^i_L+\beta^i_{KE}\ln p^i_E+\beta^i_{KM}\ln p^i_M+\beta^i_{KT}\cdot T,$$
$$v^i_L=\alpha^i_L+\beta^i_{KL}\ln p^i_K+\beta^i_{LL}\ln p^i_L+\beta^i_{LE}\ln p^i_E+\beta^i_{LM}\ln p^i_M+\beta^i_{LT}\cdot T,$$
$$v^i_E=\alpha^i_E+\beta^i_{KE}\ln p^i_K+\beta^i_{LE}\ln p^i_L+\beta^i_{EE}\ln p^i_E+\beta^i_{EM}\ln p^i_M+\beta^i_{ET}\cdot T,$$
$$v^i_M=\alpha^i_M+\beta^i_{KM}\ln p^i_K+\beta^i_{LM}\ln p^i_L+\beta^i_{EM}\ln p^i_E+\beta^i_{MM}\ln p^i_M+\beta^i_{MT}\cdot T,$$
$$(i=1,2,\ldots,n).$$

Finally, for each sector the rate of technical change, say $\{v^i_T\}$, can be expressed as the negative of the rate of growth of the price of sectoral output with respect to time, hold-

4) The translog price function was introduced by *Christensen/Jorgenson/Lau* [1971; 1973]. The translog price function was first applied at the sectoral level by *Berndt/Jorgenson* [1973] and *Berndt/Wood* [1975]. References to sectoral production studies incorporating energy and materials inputs are given by *Berndt/Wood* [1979].

ing the prices of capital, labor, energy, and materials inputs constant. The negative of the rate of technical change takes the following form:

$$-v_T^i = \alpha_T^i + \beta_{KT}^i \ln p_K^i + \beta_{LT}^i \ln p_L^i + \beta_{ET}^i \ln p_E^i + \beta_{MT}^i \ln p_M^i + \beta_{TT}^i \cdot T, \quad (i = 1, 2, \ldots, n).$$

Given the sectoral price functions $\{P^i\}$, we can define the *share elasticities with respect to price*[5]) as the derivatives of the value shares with respect to the logarithms of the prices of capital, labor, energy, and materials inputs. For the translog price functions the share elasticities with respect to price are constant. We can also characterize these forms as *constant share elasticity* or CSE price functions,[6]) indicating the interpretation of the fixed parameters that enter the price functions. The share elasticities with respect to price are symmetric, so that the parameters satisfy the conditions:

$$\begin{aligned} \beta_{KL}^i &= \beta_{LK}^i, & \beta_{LE}^i &= \beta_{EL}^i, & & \\ \beta_{KE}^i &= \beta_{EK}^i, & \beta_{LM}^i &= \beta_{ML}^i, & & \\ \beta_{KM}^i &= \beta_{MK}^i, & \beta_{EM}^i &= \beta_{ME}^i, & & (i = 1, 2, \ldots, n). \end{aligned}$$

Similarly, given the sectoral price functions $\{P^i\}$, we can define the *biases of technical change with respect to price* as derivatives of the value shares with respect to time.[7]) Alternatively, we can define the biases of technical change with respect to price as derivatives of the rate of technical change with respect to the logarithms of the price of capital, labor, energy, and materials inputs.[8]) Those two definitions of biases of technical change are equivalent. For the translog price functions the biases of technical change with respect to price are constant; these parameters are symmetric and satisfy the conditions:

[5]) The share elasticity with respect to price was introduced by *Christensen/Jorgenson/Lau* [1971; 1973] as a fixed parameter of the translog price function. An analogous concept was employed by *Samuelson* [1973]. The terminology is due to *Jorgenson/Lau* [1982].

[6]) The terminology "constant share elasticity price function" is due to *Jorgenson/Lau* [1982], who have shown that constancy of share elasticities with respect to price, biases of technical change with respect to price, and the rate of change of the negative of the rate of technical change are necessary and sufficient for representation of the price function in translog form.

[7]) The bias of technical change was introduced by *Hicks* [1932]. An alternative definition of the bias of technical change is analyzed by *Burmeister/Dobell* [1969]. *Binswanger* [1974a] has introduced a translog cost function with fixed biases of technical change. Alternative definitions of biases of technical change are compared by *Binswanger* [1978b].

[8]) This definition of the bias of technical change with respect to price is due to *Jorgenson/Lau* [1982].

$$\beta^i_{ET} = \beta^i_{TE},$$

$$\beta^i_{LT} = \beta^i_{TL},$$

$$\beta^i_{ET} = \beta^i_{TE},$$

$$\beta^i_{MT} = \beta^i_{TM}, \qquad (i = 1, 2, \ldots, n).$$

Finally, we can define the *rate of change of the negative of the rate of technical change* β^i_{TT} $(i = 1, 2, \ldots, n)$ as the derivative of the negative of the rate of technical change with respect to time.[9]) For the translog price functions these rates of change are constant.

Our next step in considering specific forms of the sectoral price functions $\{P^i\}$ is to derive restrictions on the parameters implied by the fact that the price functions are increasing in all four input prices and the concave in the four input prices. First, since the price functions are increasing in each of the four input prices, the value shares are non-negative:

$$v^i_K \geqslant 0,$$

$$v^i_L \geqslant 0,$$

$$v^i_E \geqslant 0,$$

$$v^i_M \geqslant 0, \qquad (i = 1, 2, \ldots, n).$$

Under homogeneity these value shares sum to unity:

$$v^i_K + v^i_L + v^i_E + v^i_M = 1, \qquad (i = 1, 2, \ldots, n).$$

Concavity of the sectoral price functions $\{P^i\}$ implies that the matrices of second-order partial derivatives $\{H^i\}$ are negative semi-definite,[10]) so that the matrices $\{U^i + v^i v^{i'} - V^i\}$ are negative semi-definite, where:[11])

$$\frac{1}{P^i} \cdot N^i \cdot H^i \cdot N^i = U^i + v^i v^{i'} - V^i, \qquad (i = 1, 2, \ldots, n).$$

---

[9]) The rate of change of the negative of the rate of technical change was introduced by *Jorgenson/Lau* [1982].

[10]) The following discussion of share elasticities with respect to price and concavity follows that of *Jorgenson/Lau* [1982]. Representation of conditions for concavity in terms of the Cholesky factorization is due to *Lau* [1978].

[11]) The following discussion of concavity for the translog price function is based on that of *Jorgenson/Lau* [1982].

where:

$$N^i = \begin{bmatrix} p_K^i & 0 & 0 & 0 \\ 0 & p_L^i & 0 & 0 \\ 0 & 0 & p_E^i & 0 \\ 0 & 0 & 0 & p_M^i \end{bmatrix}, \quad V^i = \begin{bmatrix} v_K^i & 0 & 0 & 0 \\ 0 & v_L^i & 0 & 0 \\ 0 & 0 & v_E^i & 0 \\ 0 & 0 & 0 & v_M^i \end{bmatrix}, \quad v^i = \begin{bmatrix} v_K^i \\ v_L^i \\ v_E^i \\ v_M^i \end{bmatrix},$$

$$(i = 1, 2, \ldots, n),$$

and $\{U^i\}$ are matrices of constant share elasticities, defined above.

Without violating the nonnegativity restrictions on value shares we can set the matrices $\{v^i v^{i'} - V^i\}$ equal to zero, for example, by choosing the value shares:

$$\begin{aligned} v_K^i &= 1, \\ v_L^i &= 0, \\ v_E^i &= 0, \\ v_M^i &= 0. \end{aligned}$$

Necessary conditions for the matrices $\{U^i + v^i v^{i'} - V^i\}$ to be negative semi-definite are that the matrices of share elasticities $\{U^i\}$ must be negative semi-definite. These conditions are also sufficient, since the matrices $\{v^i v^{i'} - V^i\}$ are negative semi-definite for all nonnegative value shares summing to unity and the sum of two negative semi-definite matrices is negative semi-definite.

To impose concavity on the translog price functions the matrices $\{U^i\}$ of constant share elasticities can be represented in terms of their Cholesky factorizations:

$$\begin{bmatrix} \beta_{KK}^i & \beta_{KL}^i & \beta_{KE}^i & \beta_{KM}^i \\ \beta_{KL}^i & \beta_{LL}^i & \beta_{LE}^i & \beta_{LM}^i \\ \beta_{KE}^i & \beta_{LE}^i & \beta_{EE}^i & \beta_{EM}^i \\ \beta_{KM}^i & \beta_{LM}^i & \beta_{EM}^i & \beta_{MM}^i \end{bmatrix} = \begin{bmatrix} 1 & 0 & 0 & 0 \\ \lambda_{21}^i & 1 & 0 & 0 \\ \lambda_{31}^i & \lambda_{32}^i & 1 & 0 \\ \lambda_{41}^i & \lambda_{42}^i & \lambda_{43}^i & 1 \end{bmatrix} \begin{bmatrix} \delta_1^i & 0 & 0 & 0 \\ 0 & \delta_2^i & 0 & 0 \\ 0 & 0 & \delta_3^i & 0 \\ 0 & 0 & 0 & \delta_4^i \end{bmatrix} \begin{bmatrix} 1 & \lambda_{21}^i & \lambda_{31}^i & \lambda_{41}^i \\ 0 & 1 & \lambda_{22}^i & \lambda_{42}^i \\ 0 & 0 & 1 & \lambda_{43}^i \\ 0 & 0 & 0 & 1 \end{bmatrix},$$

$$= \begin{bmatrix} \delta_1^i & \lambda_{21}^i\delta_1^i & \lambda_{31}^i\delta_1^i & \lambda_{41}^i\delta_1^i \\ \lambda_{21}^i\delta_1^i & \lambda_{21}^i\lambda_{21}^i\delta_1^i + \delta_2^i & \lambda_{21}^i\lambda_{31}^i\delta_1^i + \lambda_{32}^i\delta_2^i & \lambda_{41}^i\lambda_{21}^i\delta_1^i + \lambda_{42}^i\delta_2^i \\ \lambda_{31}^i\delta_1^i & \lambda_{31}^i\lambda_{21}^i\delta_1^i + \lambda_{32}^i\delta_2^i & \lambda_{31}^i\lambda_{31}^i\delta_1^i + \lambda_{32}^i\lambda_{32}^i\delta_2^i + \delta_3^i & \lambda_{41}^i\lambda_{31}^i\delta_1^i + \lambda_{42}^i\lambda_{32}^i\delta_2^i + \lambda_{43}^i\delta_3^i \\ \lambda_{41}^i\delta_1^i & \lambda_{41}^i\lambda_{21}^i\delta_1^i + \lambda_{42}^i\delta_2^i & \lambda_{41}^i\lambda_{31}^i\delta_1^i + \lambda_{42}^i\lambda_{32}^i\delta_2^i + \lambda_{43}^i\delta_3^i & \lambda_{41}^i\lambda_{41}^i\delta_1^i + \lambda_{42}^i\lambda_{42}^i\delta_2^i + \lambda_{43}^i\lambda_{43}^i\delta_3^i + \delta_4^i \end{bmatrix},$$

$$(i = 1, 2, \ldots, n).$$

Under constant returns to scale the constant share elasticities satisfy symmetry restrictions implied by homogeneity of degree one of the price function. These restrictions imply that the parameters of the Cholesky factorizations $\{\lambda^i_{21}, \lambda^i_{31}, \lambda^i_{41}, \lambda^i_{32}, \lambda^i_{42}, \lambda^i_{43}, \delta^i_1, \delta^i_2, \delta^i_3, \delta^i_4\}$ must satisfy the following conditions:

$$\begin{aligned} 1 + \lambda^i_{21} + \lambda^i_{31} + \lambda^i_{41} &= 0, \\ 1 + \lambda^i_{32} + \lambda^i_{42} &= 0, \\ 1 + \lambda^i_{43} &= 0, \\ \delta^i_4 &= 0, \qquad (i = 1, 2, \ldots, n). \end{aligned}$$

Under these conditions there is a one-to-one transformation between the constant share elasticities $\{\beta^i_{KK}, \beta^i_{KL}, \beta^i_{KE}, \beta^i_{KM}, \beta^i_{LL}, \beta^i_{LE}, \beta^i_{LM}, \beta^i_{EE}, \beta^i_{EM}, \beta^i_{MM}\}$ and the parameters of the Cholesky factorizations. The matrices of share elasticities are negative semi-definite if and only if the diagonal elements $\{\delta^i_1, \delta^i_2, \delta^i_3\}$ of the matrices $\{D^i\}$ are non-positive. This completes the specification of our model of production and technical change.

The negative of the average rates of technical change in any two points of time, say T and $T-1$, can be expressed as the difference between successive logarithms of the price of output, less a weighted average of the differences between successive logarithms of the prices of capital, labor, energy and materials inputs, with weights given by the average value shares:

$$\begin{aligned} -\bar{v}^i_T = \ln q_i(T) - \ln q_i(T-1) - \bar{v}^i_K [\ln p^i_K(T) - \ln p^i_K(T-1)] \\ - \bar{v}^i_L [\ln p^i_L(T) - \ln p^i_L(T-1)] - \bar{v}^i_E [\ln p^i_E(T) - \ln p^i_E(T-1)] \\ - \bar{v}^i_M [\ln p^i_M(T) - \ln p^i_M(T-1)], \qquad (i = 1, 2, \ldots, n), \end{aligned}$$

where:

$$\bar{v}^i_T = \frac{1}{2}[v^i_T(T) + v^i_T(T-1)], \qquad (i = 1, 2, \ldots, n),$$

and the average value shares in the two periods are given by:

$$\begin{aligned} \bar{v}^i_K &= \frac{1}{2}[v^i_K(T) + v^i_K(T-1)], \\ \bar{v}^i_L &= \frac{1}{2}[v^i_L(T) + v^i_L(T-1)], \\ \bar{v}^i_E &= \frac{1}{2}[v^i_E(T) + v^i_E(T-1)], \\ \bar{v}^i_M &= \frac{1}{2}[v^i_M(T) + v^i_M(T-1)], \qquad (i = 1, 2, \ldots, n). \end{aligned}$$

We refer to the expressions for the average rates of technical change $\{\bar{v}^i_T\}$ as the *translog price indexes of the sectoral rates of technical change.*

Similarly, we can consider specific forms for prices of capital, labor, energy, and materials inputs as functions of prices of individual capital, labor, energy, and materials inputs into each industrial sector. We assume that the price of each input can be expressed as a translog function of the price of its components. Accordingly, the difference between successive logarithms of the price of the input is a weighted average of differences between successive logarithms of prices of its components. The weights are given by the average value shares of the components. We refer to these expressions of the input prices as *translog indexes of the price of sectoral inputs.* [12])

To formulate an econometric model of production and technical change we add a stochastic component to the equations for the value shares and the rate of technical change. We assume that each of these equations has two additive components.[13]) The first is a nonrandom function of capital, labor, energy, and materials inputs and time; the second is an unobservable random disturbance that is functionally independent of these variables. We obtain an econometric model of production and technical change corresponding to the translog price function by adding random disturbances to all five equations:

$$\begin{aligned}
v_K^i &= \alpha_K^i + \beta_{KK}^i \ln p_K^i + \beta_{KL}^i \ln p_L^i + \beta_{KE}^i \ln p_E^i + \beta_{KM}^i \ln p_M^i + \beta_{KT}^i \cdot T + \epsilon_K^i, \\
v_L^i &= \alpha_L^i + \beta_{KL}^i \ln p_K^i + \beta_{LL}^i \ln p_L^i + \beta_{LE}^i \ln p_E^i + \beta_{LM}^i \ln p_M^i + \beta_{LT}^i \cdot T + \epsilon_L^i, \\
v_E^i &= \alpha_E^i + \beta_{KE}^i \ln p_K^i + \beta_{LE}^i \ln p_L^i + \beta_{EE}^i \ln p_E^i + \beta_{EM}^i \ln p_M^i + \beta_{ET}^i \cdot T + \epsilon_E^i, \\
v_M^i &= \alpha_M^i + \beta_{KM}^i \ln p_K^i + \beta_{LM}^i \ln p_L^i + \beta_{EM}^i \ln p_E^i + \beta_{MM}^i \ln p_M^i + \beta_{MT}^i \cdot T + \epsilon_M^i, \\
-\, v_T^i &= \alpha_T^i + \beta_{KT}^i \ln p_K^i + \beta_{LT}^i \ln p_L^i + \beta_{ET}^i \ln p_E^i + \beta_{MT}^i \ln p_M^i + \beta_{TT}^i \cdot T + \epsilon_T^i, \\
& \qquad (i = 1, 2, \ldots, n),
\end{aligned}$$

where $\{\alpha_K^i, \alpha_L^i, \alpha_E^i, \alpha_M^i, \alpha_T^i, \beta_{KK}^i, \beta_{KL}^i, \beta_{KE}^i, \beta_{KM}^i, \beta_{KT}^i, \beta_{LL}^i, \beta_{LE}^i, \beta_{LM}^i, \beta_{LT}^i, \beta_{EE}^i, \beta_{EM}^i, \beta_{ET}^i, \beta_{MM}^i, \beta_{MT}^i, \beta_{TT}^i\}$ are unknown parameters and $\{\epsilon_K^i, \epsilon_L^i, \epsilon_E^i, \epsilon_M^i, \epsilon_T^i\}$ are unobservable random disturbances.

Since the value shares sum to unity, the unknown parameters satisfy the same restrictions as before and the random disturbances corresponding to the four value shares sum to zero:

$$\epsilon_K^i + \epsilon_L^i + \epsilon_E^i + \epsilon_M^i = 0, \qquad (i = 1, 2, \ldots, n),$$

so that these random disturbances are not distributed independently.

We assume that the random disturbances for all five equations have expected value equal to zero for all observations:

---

[12]) The price indexes were introduced by *Fisher* [1922] and have been discussed by *Tornquist* [1936], *Theil* [1965], and *Kloek* [1966]. These indexes were first derived from the translog price function by *Diewert* [1976]. The corresponding index of technical change was introduced by *Christensen/Jorgenson* [1970]. The translog index of technical change was first derived from the translog price function by *Diewert* [1980] and by *Jorgenson/Lau* [1982]. Earlier, *Diewert* [1976] had interpreted the ratio of translog indexes of the prices of input and output as an index of productivity under the assumption of Hicks neutrality.

[13]) The following formulation of an econometric model of production and technical change is based on that of *Jorgenson/Lau* [1982].

$$E\begin{pmatrix} \epsilon_K^i \\ \epsilon_L^i \\ \epsilon_E^i \\ \epsilon_M^i \\ \epsilon_T^i \end{pmatrix} = 0, \qquad (i = 1, 2, \ldots, n).$$

We also assume that the random disturbances have a covariance matrix that is the same for all observations; since the random disturbances corresponding to the four value shares sum to zero, this matrix is positive semi-definite with rank at most equal to four.

We assume that the covariance matrix of the random disturbances corresponding to the first three value shares and the rate of technical change, say Σ^i, has rank four, where:

$$V\begin{pmatrix} \epsilon_K^i \\ \epsilon_L^i \\ \epsilon_E^i \\ \epsilon_T^i \end{pmatrix} = \Sigma^i, \qquad (i = 1, 2, \ldots, n),$$

so the Σ^i is a positive definite matrix. Finally, we assume that the random disturbances corresponding to distinct observations in the same or distinct equations are uncorrelated. Under this assumption that the matrix of random disturbances for the first three value shares and the rate of technical change for all observations has the Kronecker product form:

$$V\begin{pmatrix} \epsilon_K^i(1) \\ \epsilon_K^i(2) \\ \vdots \\ \epsilon_K^i(N) \\ \epsilon_L^i(1) \\ \vdots \\ \epsilon_T^i(N) \end{pmatrix} = \Sigma^i \otimes I, \qquad (i = 1, 2, \ldots, n).$$

Since the rates of technical change $\{v_T^i\}$ are not directly observable, the equation for the rate of technical change can be written:

$$-\bar{v}_T^i = \alpha_T^i + \beta_{KT}^i \overline{\ln p_K^i} + \beta_{LT}^i \overline{\ln p_L^i} + \beta_{ET}^i \overline{\ln p_E^i} + \beta_{MT}^i \overline{\ln p_M^i} + \beta_{TT}^i \cdot \bar{T} + \bar{\epsilon}_T^i, \qquad (i = 1, 2, \ldots, n),$$

where $\bar{\epsilon}_T^i$ is the average disturbance in the two periods:

$$\bar{\epsilon}_T^i = \frac{1}{2}\,[\epsilon_T^i\,(T) + \epsilon_T^i\,(T-1)], \qquad (i = 1, 2, \ldots, n).$$

Similarly, the equations for the value shares of capital, labor, energy, and materials inputs can be written:

$$\bar{v}_K^i = \alpha_K^i + \beta_{KK}^i\,\overline{\ln p_K^i} + \beta_{KL}^i\,\overline{\ln p_L^i} + \beta_{KE}^i\,\overline{\ln p_E^i} + \beta_{KM}^i\,\overline{\ln p_M^i} + \beta_{KT}^i \cdot \bar{T} + \bar{\epsilon}_K^i,$$

$$\bar{v}_L^i = \alpha_L^i + \beta_{KL}^i\,\overline{\ln p_K^i} + \beta_{LL}^i\,\overline{\ln p_L^i} + \beta_{LE}^i\,\overline{\ln p_E^i} + \beta_{LM}^i\,\overline{\ln p_M^i} + \beta_{LT}^i \cdot \bar{T} + \bar{\epsilon}_L^i,$$

$$\bar{v}_E^i = \alpha_E^i + \beta_{KE}^i\,\overline{\ln p_K^i} + \beta_{LE}^i\,\overline{\ln p_L^i} + \beta_{EE}^i\,\overline{\ln p_E^i} + \beta_{EM}^i\,\overline{\ln p_M^i} + \beta_{ET}^i \cdot \bar{T} + \bar{\epsilon}_E^i,$$

$$\bar{v}_M^i = \alpha_M^i + \beta_{KM}^i\,\overline{\ln p_K^i} + \beta_{LM}^i\,\overline{\ln p_L^i} + \beta_{EM}^i\,\overline{\ln p_E^i} + \beta_{MM}^i\,\overline{\ln p_M^i} + \beta_{MT}^i \cdot \bar{T} + \bar{\epsilon}_M^i,$$

where

$$\bar{\epsilon}_K^i = \frac{1}{2}\,[\epsilon_K^i\,(T) + \epsilon_K^i\,(T-1)],$$

$$\bar{\epsilon}_L^i = \frac{1}{2}\,[\epsilon_L^i\,(T) + \epsilon_L^i\,(T-1)],$$

$$\bar{\epsilon}_E^i = \frac{1}{2}\,[\epsilon_E^i\,(T) + \epsilon_E^i\,(T-1)],$$

$$\bar{\epsilon}_M^i = \frac{1}{2}\,[\epsilon_M^i\,(T) + \epsilon_M^i\,(T-1)], \qquad (i = 1, 2, \ldots, n).$$

As before, the average value shares $\{\bar{v}_K^i, \bar{v}_L^i, \bar{v}_E^i, \bar{v}_M^i\}$ sum to unity, so that the average disturbances $\{\bar{\epsilon}_K^i, \bar{\epsilon}_L^i, \bar{\epsilon}_E^i, \bar{\epsilon}_M^i\}$ sum to zero:

$$\bar{\epsilon}_K^i + \bar{\epsilon}_L^i + \bar{\epsilon}_E^i + \bar{\epsilon}_M^i = 0, \qquad (i = 1, 2, \ldots, n).$$

The covariance matrix of the average disturbances corresponding to the equation for the rate of technical change for all observations, say Ω, is a Laurent matrix:

$$V\begin{pmatrix} \bar{\epsilon}_T^i\,(2) \\ \bar{\epsilon}_T^i\,(3) \\ \vdots \\ \bar{\epsilon}_T^i\,(N) \end{pmatrix} = \Omega,$$

where:

$$\Omega = \begin{bmatrix} \frac{1}{2} & \frac{1}{4} & 0 & \cdots & 0 \\ \frac{1}{4} & \frac{1}{2} & \frac{1}{4} & \cdots & 0 \\ 0 & \frac{1}{4} & \frac{1}{2} & \cdots & 0 \\ \vdots & \vdots & \vdots & & \vdots \\ 0 & 0 & 0 & \cdots & \frac{1}{2} \end{bmatrix}.$$

The covariance matrix of the average disturbance corresponding to each equation for the four value shares is the same, so that the covariance matrix of the average disturbances for the first three value shares and the rate of technical change for all observations has the Kronecker product form:

$$V \begin{pmatrix} \bar{\epsilon}_K^i\,(2) \\ \bar{\epsilon}_K^i\,(3) \\ \vdots \\ \bar{\epsilon}_K^i\,(N) \\ \bar{\epsilon}_L^i\,(2) \\ \vdots \\ \bar{\epsilon}_T^i\,(N) \end{pmatrix} = \Sigma^i \otimes \Omega, \qquad (i = 1, 2, \ldots, n).$$

Although disturbances in equations for the average rate of technical change and the average value shares are autocorrelated, the data can be transformed to eliminate the autocorrelation. The matrix Ω is positive definite, so that there is a matrix T such that:

$$T\Omega T' = I,$$

$$T'T = \Omega^{-1}.$$

To construct the matrix T we can first invert the matrix Ω to obtain the inverse matrix Ω^{-1}, a positive definite matrix. We then calculate the Cholesky factorization of the inverse matrix Ω^{-1},

$$\Omega^{-1} = LDL',$$

where L is a unit lower triangular matrix and D is a diagonal matrix with positive elements along the main diagonal. Finally, we can write the matrix T in the form:

$$T = D^{1/2}L',$$

where $D^{1/2}$ is a diagonal matrix with elements along the main diagonal equal to the square roots of the corresponding elements of D.

We can transform the equations for the average rates of technical change by the matrix $T = D^{1/2}L'$ to obtain equations with uncorrelated random disturbances:[14])

$$D^{1/2}L' \begin{pmatrix} \bar{v}_T^i(2) \\ \bar{v}_T^i(3) \\ \vdots \\ \bar{v}_T^i(N) \end{pmatrix} = D^{1/2}L' \begin{pmatrix} 1\ \overline{\ln p_K^i}(2) \ldots 2 - \frac{1}{2} \\ 1\ \overline{\ln p_K^i}(3) \ldots 3 - \frac{1}{2} \\ \\ 1\ \overline{\ln p_K^i}(N) \ldots N - \frac{1}{2} \end{pmatrix} \begin{pmatrix} \alpha_T^i \\ \beta_{KT}^i \\ \vdots \\ \beta_{TT}^i \end{pmatrix} + D^{1/2}L' \begin{pmatrix} \bar{\epsilon}_T^i(2) \\ \bar{\epsilon}_T^i(3) \\ \vdots \\ \bar{\epsilon}_T^i(N) \end{pmatrix}$$

$$(i = 1, 2, \ldots, n),$$

since:

$$T\Omega T' = (D^{1/2}L')\,\Omega\,(D^{1/2}L')' = I.$$

The transformation $T = D^{1/2}L'$ is applied to data on the average rates of technical change $\{\bar{v}_T^i\}$ and data on the average values of the variables that appear on the right hand side of the corresponding equation.

We can apply the transformation $T = D^{1/2}L'$ to the first three equations for average value shares to obtain equations with uncorrelated disturbances. As before, the transformation is applied to data on the average values shares and the average values of variables that appear in the corresponding equations. The covariance matrix of the transformed disturbances from the first three equations for the average value shares and the equation for the average rate of technical change has the Kronecker product form:

$$(I \otimes D^{1/2}L')\,(\Sigma^i \otimes \Omega)\,(I \otimes D^{1/2}L')' = \Sigma^i \otimes I, \qquad (i = 1, 2, \ldots, n).$$

To estimate the unknown parameters of the translog price function we combine the first three equations for the average value shares with the equation for the average rate of technical change to obtain a complete econometric model of production and technical change. We estimate the parameters of the equations for the remaining average value shares, using the restrictions on these parameters given above. The complete model involves fourteen unknown parameters. A total of sixteen additional parameters can be estimated as functions of these parameters, given the restrictions. Our estimate of the unknown parameters of the econometric model of production and technical change is based on the nonlinear three-stage least squares estimator introduced by *Jorgenson/Laffont* [1974].

3. Empirical Results

To implement the econometric models of production and technical change developed in Section 3 we have assembled a data base for thirty-six industrial sectors of the U.S. economy listed. For capital and labor inputs we have first compiled data by sector on the

---

[14]) The Cholesky factorization is used to obtain an equation with uncorrelated random disturbances by *Jorgenson/Lau* [1982].

basis of the classification of economic activities employed in the U.S. National Income and Product Accounts. We have then transformed these data into a format appropriate for the classification of activities employed in the U.S. Interindustry Transactions Accounts. For energy and materials inputs we have compiled data by sector on interindustry transactions among the thirty-six industrial sectors. For this purpose we have used the classification of economic activities employed in the U.S. Interindustry Transactions Accounts.[15])

For each sector we have compiled data on the value shares of capital, labor, energy, and materials inputs, annually, for the period 1958–1974. We have also compiled indexes of prices of sectoral output and all four sectoral inputs for the same period. Finally, we have compiled translog indexes of sectoral rates of technical change. For the Miscellaneous sector the rate of technical change is equal to zero by definition, so that the econometric model for the sector does not include an equation for the sectoral rate of technical change. There are sixteen observations for each behavioral equation since two period averages of all data are employed.

The parameters $\{\alpha^i_K, \alpha^i_L, \alpha^i_E, \alpha^i_M\}$ can be interpreted as average value shares of capital input, labor input, energy input, and materials input for the corresponding sector. Similarly, the parameters $\{\alpha^i_T\}$ can be interpreted as averages of the negative of rates of technical change. The parameters $\{\beta^i_{KK}, \beta^i_{KL}, \beta^i_{KE}, \beta^i_{KM}, \beta^i_{LL}, \beta^i_{LE}, \beta^i_{LM}, \beta^i_{EE}, \beta^i_{EM}, \beta^i_{MM}\}$ can be interpreted as constant share elasticities with respect to price for the corresponding sector. Similarly, the parameters $\{\beta^i_{KT}, \beta^i_{LT}, \beta^i_{ET}, \beta^i_{MT}\}$ can be interpreted as constant biases of technical change with respect to price. Finally, the parameters $\{\beta^i_{TT}\}$ can be interpreted as constant rates of change of the negative of the rates of technical change.

In estimating the parameters of our sectoral models of production and technical change we retain the average of the negative of the rate of technical change, biases of technical change, and the rate of change of the negative of the rate of technical change as parameters to be estimated for thirty-five of the thirty-six industrial sectors. For the Miscellaneous sector the rate of technical change is equal to zero by definition, so that these parameters are set equal to zero. Estimates of the share elasticities with respect to price are obtained under the restrictions implied by the necessary and sufficient conditions for concavity of the price functions presented in Section 3. Under these restrictions the matrices of constant share elasticities $\{U^i\}$ must be negative semi-definite for all industries. To impose the concavity restrictions we represent the matrices of constant share elasticities for all sectors in terms of their Cholesky factorizations. The necessary and sufficient conditions are that the diagonal elements $\{\delta^i_1, \delta^i_2, \delta^i_3\}$ of the matrices $\{D^i\}$ that appear in the Cholesky factorizations must be nonpositive. We present estimates subject to these restrictions for all thirty-six industrial sectors in Table 1.

---

[15]) Data on energy and materials are based on annual inter-industry transactions tables for the United States, 1958–1974, compiled by Jack Faucett Associates [1977] for the Federal Preparedness Agency. Data on labor and capital are based on estimates by *Fraumeni/Jorgenson* [1980].

Parameter	Industry							
	Agriculture Forestry & Fisheries		Metal Mining		Coal Mining		Crude Petroleum & Natural Gas	
α_K^i	.186	(.00620)	.232	(.0113)	.248	(.0135)	.486	(.0136)
α_L^i	.295	(.0122)	.314	(.0139)	.515	(.0110)	.113	(.00377)
α_E^i	.026	(.000718)	.0398	(.00301)	.125	(.00636)	.0579	(.00190)
α_M^i	.492	(.0173)	.414	(.0135)	.112	(.0288)	.343	(.0182)
α_T^i	– .00949	(.0637)	– .00306	(.0605)	.0323	(.0872)	.000985	(.0837)
β_{KK}^i								
β_{KL}^i								
β_{KE}^i								
β_{KM}^i								
β_{KT}^i	.00418	(.000778)	.00268	(.0142)	.00954	(.00169)	.00342	(.00170)
β_{LL}^i	– .970	(.0683)	–1.44	(.151)				
β_{LE}^i	– .0415	(.00593)	.0168	(.0254)				
β_{LM}^i	1.01	(.0671)	1.42	(.133)				
β_{LT}^i	.0353	(.00302)	.0432	(.00401)	.00971	(.00138)	.000277	(.000473)
β_{EE}^i	– .00178	(.000553)	– .000195	(.000578)	– .137	(.00862)		
β_{EM}^i	.0433	(.00647)	– .0166	(.0249)	.137	(.00862)		
β_{ET}^i	.00177	(.000235)	.000243	(.000688)	– .00433	(.000808)	.000979	(.000238)
β_{MM}^i	–1.05	(.0662)	–1.405	(.119)	– .137	(.00862)		
β_{MT}^i	– .0413	(.00334)	– .0461	(.00360)	– .0149	(.00362)	– .00468	(.00228)
β_{TT}^i	.000200	(.00803)	– .00120	(.00757)	.00426	(.0110)	.000491	(.0105)

Tab. 1: Parameter Estimates Sectoral Models of Production and Technical Change

Parameter	Industry							
	Nonmetallic Mining		Construction		Food & Kindred Products		Tobacco Manufacturers	
α^i_K	.290	(.0135)	.0735	(.00350)	.0595	(.00234)	.179	(.00719)
α^i_L	.333	(.0337)	.469	(.0185)	.167	(.00623)	.144	(.00686)
α^i_E	.0798	(.00214)	.0256	(.000905)	.0116	(.000746)	.00383	(.000404)
α^i_M	.297	(.0447)	.432	(.0228)	.761	(.00910)	.673	(.0135)
α^i_T	.0633	(.0347)	.0502	(.00809)	.0106	(.0142)	.0772	(.141)
β^i_{KK}								
β^i_{KL}								
β^i_{KE}								
β^i_{KM}								
β^i_{KT}	.00403	(.00169)	.000853	(.000438)	– .000718	(.000294)	.00289	(.000901)
β^i_{LL}			– .448	(.0483)			– .0709	(.0168)
β^i_{LE}			– .0517	(.00602)			.00281	(.00158)
β^i_{LM}			.500	(.0526)			.0681	(.0163)
β^i_{LT}	.000724	(.00422)	– .00579	(.00290)	– .000548	(.000781)	.00794	(.00125)
β^i_{EE}			– .00597	(.00106)			– .000112	(.000118)
β^i_{EM}			.0577	(.00697)			– .00270	(.00146)
β^i_{ET}	.00225	(.000268)	– .00142	(.000246)	.000133	(.0000935)	– .0000257	(.0000995)
β^i_{MM}			– .558	(.0577)			– .0654	(.0159)
β^i_{MT}	– .00700	(.00560)	.00636	(.00343)	.00113	(.00114)	– .0108	(.00191)
β^i_{TT}	.00610	(.00429)	.00379	(.00108)	.00132	(.00176)	.0140	(.0177)

Tab. 1: (Continued)

Parameter	Industry							
	Textile Mill Products		Apparel & Other Fabric. Textile Prod.		Lumber & Wood Products		Furniture & Fixtures	
α_K^i	.0739	(.00232)	.0446	(.00131)	.166	(.00506)	.0704	(.00299)
α_L^i	.221	(.00650)	.324	(.00819)	.295	(.0134)	.411	(.0122)
α_E^i	.0164	(.000675)	.00657	(.000231)	.0193	(.00113)	.0106	(.000486)
α_M^i	.689	(.00936)	.625	(.00956)	.519	(.0175)	.507	(.0155)
α_T^i	– .0133	(.0147)	– .00745	(.0347)	.00408	(.0412)	– .00687	(.0233)
β_{KK}^i					– .0896	(.0196)		
β_{KL}^i					– .178	(.0301)		
β_{KE}^i					– .0127	(.00418)		
β_{KM}^i					.280	(.0474)		
β_{KT}^i	.000457	(.000291)	.000693	(.000164)	.0145	(.00162)	.000122	(.000375)
β_{LL}^i			– .230	(.0257)	– .353	(.0819)	–1.56	(.0643)
β_{LE}^i			– .00880	(.00202)	– .0253	(.00768)	– .0625	(.00323)
β_{LM}^i			.239	(.0272)	.556	(.108)	1.62	(.0645)
β_{LT}^i	.00114	(.00178)	.00552	(.00116)	.0184	(.00367)	.0328	(.00196)
β_{EE}^i			– .000336	(.00130)	– .00181	(.00112)	– .00251	(.000276)
β_{EM}^i			.00913	(.00214)	.0398	(.0126)	.0650	(.00348)
β_{ET}^i	.000366	(.000217)	.000479	(0000517)	.00197	(.00380)	.00143	(.0000851)
β_{MM}^i			– .248	(.0288)	– .876	(.146)	–1.69	(.0648)
β_{MT}^i	– .00197	(.00208)	– .00669	(.00133)	– .0349	(.00497)	– .0344	(.00230)
β_{TT}^i	– .000516	(.00187)	– .00162	(.00436)	.000384	(.00517)	.000417	(.00292)

Tab. 1: (Continued)

Parameter	Paper & Allied Products		Printing Publishing & Allied Ind.		Chemicals & Allied Products		Petroleum Refining	
α_K^i	.119	(.00504)	.114	(.00412)	.138	(.00508)	.116	(.00583)
α_L^i	.276	(.0150)	.398	(.0152)	.218	(.00569)	.0792	(.00330)
α_E^i	.0328	(.00114)	.00857	(.000312)	.0945	(.00348)	.638	(.00600)
α_M^i	.572	(.0210)	.479	(.0195)	.549	(.0138)	.167	(.0107)
α_T^i	.0298	(.0371)	– .0124	(.0289)	.00607	(.0242)	.0203	(.0432)
β_{KK}^i								
β_{KL}^i								
β_{KE}^i								
β_{KM}^i								
β_{KT}^i	– .00101	(.000632)	.00154	(.000517)	– .00399	(.000637)	.00131	(.000731)
β_{LL}^i			– .402	(.0713)	– .102	(.0406)	– .312	(.0624)
β_{LE}^i			– .0268	(.00436)	.00183	(.0133)	.00205	(.0167)
β_{LM}^i			.429	(.0741)	.101	(.0474)	.310	(.0764)
β_{LT}^i	.00154	(.00188)	.0157	(.00304)	.00253	(.00157)	– .0000384	(.000593)
β_{EE}^i			– .00179	(.000452)	– .0000330	(.000483)	– .0000135	(.000221)
β_{EM}^i			.0286	(.00475)	– .00180	(.0128)	– .00203	(.0164)
β_{ET}^i	.000767	(.000143)	.00121	(.000152)	.00232	(.000640)	.00593	(.000764)
β_{MM}^i			– .457	(.0772)	– .0989	(.0562)	– .308	(.0910)
β_{MT}^i	– .00130	(.00264)	– .0185	(.00347)	– .000867	(.00237)	– .00721	(.00145)
β_{TT}^i	.00826	(.00463)	– .00188	(.00363)	.00337	(.00304)	.00272	(.00542)

Tab. 1: (Continued)

Parameter	Rubber & Misc. Plastic Products		Leather & Leather Products		Stone, Clay & Glass Products		Primary Metal Industries	
α_K^i	.106	(.00225)	.0507	(.00160)	.128	(.00520)	.0940	(.00446)
α_L^i	.283	(.00452)	.372	(.0105)	.416	(.0117)	.301	(.0172)
α_E^i	.0250	(.000427)	.00837	(.000523)	.0472	(.00130)	.0432	(.00270)
α_M^i	.586	(.00678)	.569	(.0116)	.409	(.0173)	.562	(.0241)
α_T^i	.0232	(.0437)	– .00966	(.0275)	.00972	(.0255)	– .00869	(.0302)
β_{KK}^i								
β_{KL}^i								
β_{KE}^i								
β_{KM}^i								
β_{KT}^i	– .00245	(.000282)	.0000824	(.000201)	– .00279	(.000652)	– .00157	(.000559)
β_{LL}^i	– .658	(.0301)	– .215	(.0627)	–2.06	(.122)		
β_{LE}^i	– .134	(.00505)	– .0142	(.00279)	– .108	(.0200)		
β_{LM}^i	.792	(.0316)	.229	(.0653)	2.17	(.136)		
β_{LT}^i	.0144	(.000832)	.00832	(.00214)	.0568	(.00329)	.00435	(.00215)
β_{EE}^i	– .0274	(.00216)	– .000936	(.000155)	– .00562	(.00189)		
β_{EM}^i	.162	(.00694)	.0151	(.00291)	.113	(.0219)		
β_{ET}^i	.00359	(.000122)	.000685	(.0000997)	.00287	(.000512)	– .0000721	(.000339)
β_{MM}^i	– .954	(.0337)	– .244	(.0680)	–2.28	(.152)		
β_{MT}^i	– .0155	(.00106)	– .00908	(.00228)	– .0568	(.00393)	– .00271	(.00302)
β_{TT}^i	.00585	(.00548)	– .00188	(.00343)	.00158	(.00319)	– .00123	(.00379)

Tab. 1: (Continued)

Parameter	Industry							
	Fabricated Metal Products		Machinery Except Electrical		Electrical Machinery		Motor Vehicles & Motor Vehicle Equipment	
α_K^i	.0969	(.00338)	.107	(.00194)	.102	(.00344)	.121	(.00403)
α_L^i	.370	(.00999)	.332	(.00442)	.362	(.00851)	.204	(.00618)
α_E^i	.0129	(.000308)	.0119	(.000227)	.0107	(.000414)	.00773	(.000201)
α_M^i	.520	(.0135)	.549	(.00604)	.525	(.111)	.667	(.0102)
α_T^i	.0224	(.0252)	.000389	(.0156)	.0113	(.0420)	.00787	(.0386)
β_{KK}^i								
β_{KL}^i								
β_{KE}^i								
β_{KM}^i								
β_{KT}^i	.00126	(.000424)	– .000343	(.000244)	.000801	(.000431)	.000981	(.000505)
β_{LL}^i	– .602	(.0240)	–2.05	(.111)	– .616	(.191)	– .350	(.0655)
β_{LE}^i	– .0431	(.00218)	– .120	(.00831)	– .0276	(.0103)	– .00435	(.00316)
β_{LM}^i	.645	(.0245)	2.17	(.118)	.643	(.201)	.354	(.0666)
β_{LT}^i	.0169	(.00134)	.0446	(.00243)	.0150	(.00457)	.0174	(.00248)
β_{EE}^i	– .00309	(.000315)	– .00699	(.000715)	– .00124	(.000575)	– .0000541	(.0000760)
β_{EM}^i	.0462	(.00248)	.127	(.00899)	.0289	(.0108)	.00441	(.00324)
β_{ET}^i	.00104	(.0000570)	.00289	(.000178)	.000901	(.000244)	.000330	(.000117)
β_{MM}^i	– .691	(.0251)	–2.30	(.125)	– .672	(.211)	– .359	(.0679)
β_{MT}^i	– .0192	(.00176)	– .0471	(.00262)	– .0167	(.00487)	– .0187	(.00272)
β_{TT}^i	.00407	(.00314)	.000205	(.00196)	.00244	(.00525)	.00235	(.00482)

Tab. 1: (Continued)

Parameter	Industry							
	Transportation Equipment & Ordinance		Instruments		Miscellaneous Manufacturing Industries		Transportation	
α_K^i	.0411	(.00291)	.139	(.00515)	.0995	(.00339)	.184	(.00670)
α_L^i	.396	(.00882)	.349	(.00729)	.350	(.00561)	.457	(.0126)
α_E^i	.00993	(.000352)	.00668	(.000151)	.0115	(.000290)	.0561	(.00304)
α_M^i	.553	(.0109)	.505	(.0122)	.539	(.00747)	.303	(.0222)
α_T^i	– .0153	(.0333)	.0191	(.0459)	.0123	(.0715)	– .0357	(.0138)
β_{KK}^i								
β_{KL}^i								
β_{KE}^i								
β_{KM}^i								
β_{KT}^i	– .00119	(.000365)	.000381	(.000646)	.00114	(.000425)	.000922	(.000839)
β_{LL}^i			–1.21	(.0336)	–1.02	(.076)		
β_{LE}^i			– .0230	(.00181)	– .0750	(.00635)		
β_{LM}^i			1.24	(.0335)	1.10	(.0774)		
β_{LT}^i	.00104	(.00111)	.0217	(.00105)	.0244	(.00177)	.00252	(.00158)
β_{EE}^i			– .000434	(.0000704)	– .00549	(.000950)		
β_{EM}^i			.0234	(.00188)	.0804	(.00723)		
β_{ET}^i	.000197	(.0000441)	.000460	(.0000332)	.00199	(.000140)	.000845	(.000381)
β_{MM}^i			–1.26	(.0335)	–1.18	(.0791)		
β_{MT}^i	– .0000465	(.00136)	– .0225	(.00161)	– .0276	(.00190)	– .000429	(.00278)
β_{TT}^i	– .00164	(.00417)	.00369	(.00575)	.00354	(.00895)	– .00243	(.00174)

Tab. 1: (Continued)

Parameter	Industry							
	Communications		Electric Utilities		Gas Utilities		Trade	
α^i_K	.403	(.0185)	.352	(.00940)	.229	(.00428)	.158	(.00996)
α^i_L	.431	(.0181)	.244	(.0114)	.192	(.00218)	.627	(.0357)
α^i_E	.0121	(.00118)	.259	(.0150)	.579	(.00582)	.0247	(.000658)
α^i_M	.154	(.0357)	.144	(.0330)	.000	(.000)	.190	(.0456)
α^i_T	– .0109	(.0344)	.0252	(.0251)	– .0133	(.0155)	– .00386	(.0171)
β^i_{KK}	– .757	(.109)						
β^i_{KL}	–1.08	(.109)						
β^i_{KE}	.0568	(.00728)						
β^i_{KM}	1.78	(.213)						
β^i_{KT}	.00397	(.00251)	– .00246	(.00118)	– .00453	(.000666)	.00135	(.00125)
β^i_{LL}	–1.55	(.106)					–1.48	(.120)
β^i_{LE}	.0813	(.00811)					– .0207	(.0119)
β^i_{LM}	2.55	(.207)					1.50	(.125)
β^i_{LT}	.00802	(.00279)	– .00460	(.00143)	.00883	(.000475)	.0492	(.00557)
β^i_{EE}	– .00427	(.000849)					– .000290	(.000325)
β^i_{EM}	– .134	(.0144)					.0210	(.0122)
β^i_{ET}	– .000350	(.000172)	.00999	(.00188)	.00621	(.00103)	.000192	(.000345)
β^i_{MM}	–4.20	(.409)					–1.52	(.131)
β^i_{MT}	– .0116	(.00512)	– .00294	(.00414)	– .0105	(.00151)	– .0508	(.00667)
β^i_{TT}	.00116	(.00432)	.00702	(.00315)	– .000823	(.00233)	.00116	(.00207)

Tab. 1: (Continued)

Parameter	Industry							
	Finance Insurance & Real Estate		Services		Government Enterprises		Miscellaneous	
α_K^i	.258	(.00971)	.106	(.00552)	.112	(.00755)	.595	(.00227)
α_L^i	.241	(.00886)	.558	(.0258)	.619	(.0405)	.350	(.00210)
α_E^i	.0164	(.00102)	.0214	(.000719)	.0332	(.00187)	.0000739	(.0000070)
α_M^i	.485	(.0172)	.315	(.0312)	.236	(.0405)	.0556	(.000661)
α_T^i	– .0198	(.0346)	– .0307	(.0502)	– .0106	(.0593)		
β_{KK}^i	– .0304	(.0178)						
β_{KL}^i	– .0561	(.0160)						
β_{KE}^i	– .00682	(.00186)						
β_{KM}^i	.0934	(.0324)						
β_{KT}^i	.00215	(.00201)	.00154	(.000691)	.00689	(.000947)		
β_{LL}^i	– .104	(.0489)			– .511	(.927)		
β_{LE}^i	– .0126	(.00598)			.0338	(.0425)		
β_{LM}^i	.172	(.0624)			.477	(.890)		
β_{LT}^i	.00954	(.0212)	.00877	(.00324)	.0373	(.0484)		
β_{EE}^i	– .00153	(.000783)			– .00223	(.00271)	– .000154	(.0000474)
β_{EM}^i	.0210	(.00764)			– .0315	(.0406)	.000154	(.0000474)
β_{ET}^i	.000942	(.000247)	.000238	(.0000901)	– .00202	(.00222)		
β_{MM}^i	– .287	(.0821)			– .446	(.853)	– .000154	(.0000474)
β_{MT}^i	– .0126	(.00368)	– .0105	(.00391)	– .0421	(.0464)		
β_{TT}^i	.00118	(.00433)	– .00374	(.00635)	– .00171	(.00787)		

Tab. 1: (Concluded)

Pattern of Biases	Industries
Capital Using Labor Using Energy Using Material Saving	Agriculture, metal mining, crude petroleum and natural gas, nonmetallic mining, textiles, apparel, lumber, furniture, printing, leather, fabricated metals, electrical machinery, motor vehicles, instruments, miscellaneous manufacturing, transportation, trade, finance, insurance and real estate, services.
Capital Using Labor Using Energy Saving Material Saving	Coal mining, tobacco manufactures, communications, government enterprises.
Capital Using Labor Saving Energy Using Material Saving	Petroleum refining.
Capital Using Labor Saving Energy Saving Material Using	Construction.
Capital Saving Labor Saving Energy Using Material Saving	Electric utilities.
Capital Saving Labor Using Energy Saving Material Saving	Primary metals.
Capital Saving Labor Using Energy Using Material Saving	Paper, chemicals, rubber, stone, clay and glass, machinery except electrical, transportation equipment and ordinance, gas utilities.
Capital Saving Labor Saving Energy Using Material Using	Food.

Tab. 2: Classification of Industries by Biases of Technical Change

Our interpretation of the parameter estimates reported in Table 2 begins with an analysis of the estimates of the parameters $\{\alpha_K^i, \alpha_L^i, \alpha_E^i, \alpha_M^i, \alpha_T^i\}$. The average value shares are nonnegative for all thirty-six sectors included in our study. The negative of the estimated average rate of technical change is negative in sixteen sectors, positive in nineteen sectors, and zero, by definition, in the Miscellaneous sector. Negative signs predominate only in transportation, communications, utilities, trade, and services. Positive signs predominate in the extractive industries and durable goods manufacturing industries. Nondurable goods manufacturing industries are almost evenly divided between positive and negative signs.

The estimated share elasticities with respect to price $\{\beta^i_{KK}, \beta^i_{KL}, \beta^i_{KE}, \beta^i_{KM}, \beta^i_{LL}, \beta^i_{LE}, \beta^i_{LM}, \beta^i_{EE}, \beta^i_{EM}, \beta^i_{MM}\}$ describe the implications of patterns of substitution among capital, labor, energy, and materials inputs for the relative distribution of the value of output among these four inputs. Positive share elasticities imply that the corresponding value shares increase with an increase in price; negative share elasticities imply that the value shares decrease with an increase in price; share elasticities equal to zero imply that the value shares are independent of price. It is important to keep in mind that we have fitted these parameters subject to the restrictions implied by concavity of the price function. These restrictions require that all the share elasticities be set equal to zero for eleven of the thirty-six industries. For eleven of the thirty-six industries the share elasticities for all inputs with respect to the prices of energy and materials inputs are set equal to zero. For thirteen of the thirty-six industries the share elasticities with respect to the price of labor input are set equal to zero. Finally, for thirty-three of the thirty-six industries the share elasticities for all inputs with respect to the price of capital input are set equal to zero. Of the three hundred sixty share elasticities for the thirty-six industries included in our study two hundred four are set equal to zero and one hundred fifty-six are fitted without constraint.

Our interpretation of the parameter estimates given in Table 1 continues with the estimated elasticities of the share of each input with respect to the price of the input itself $\{\beta^i_{KK}, \beta^i_{LL}, \beta^i_{EE}, \beta^i_{MM}\}$. Under the necessary and sufficient conditions for concavity of the price function for each sector, these share elasticities are nonpositive. The share of each input is nonincreasing in the price of the input itself. This condition together with the condition that the sum of all the share elasticities with respect to a given input is equal to zero implies that only two of the elasticities of the shares of each input with respect to the prices of the other three inputs $\{\beta^i_{KL}, \beta^i_{KE}, \beta^i_{KM}, \beta^i_{LE}, \beta^i_{LM}, \beta^i_{EM}\}$ can be negative. All six of these share elasticities can be nonnegative, and this condition holds for twelve of the thirty-six industries.

The share elasticity of capital with respect to the price of labor $\{\beta^i_{KL}\}$ is nonnegative for thirty-three of the thirty-six industries. By symmetry this parameter can also be interpreted as the share elasticity of labor with respect to the price of capital. The share elasticity of capital with respect to the price of energy $\{\beta^i_{KE}\}$ is nonnegative for thirty-four of the thirty-six industries. Finally, the share elasticity of capital with respect to the price of materials $\{\beta^i_{KM}\}$ is nonnegative for all thirty-six industries. These parameters can also be interpreted as the share elasticities of energy and materials with respect to the price of capital. Considering the elasticities of the share of labor with respect to the prices of energy and materials inputs, we find that the share elasticity with respect to the price of energy is nonnegative for nineteen of the thirty-six industries, while the share elasticity with respect to the price of materials is nonnegative for all thirty-six industries. These parameters can also be interpreted as share elasticities of energy and materials with respect to the price of labor. Finally, the share elasticity of energy with respect to the price of materials input is nonnegative for thirty of the thirty-six industries. This parameter can also be interpreted as the share elasticity of materials with respect to the price of energy.

We continue the interpretation of parameter estimates given in Table 1 with the estimated biases of technical change with respect to the price of each input $\{\beta^i_{KT}, \beta^i_{LT},$

$\beta^i_{ET}, \beta^i_{MT}\}$. These parameters can be interpreted as the change in the negative of the rate of technical change with respect to the price of each input or, alternatively, as the change in the share of each input with respect to time. The sum of the four biases of technical change with respect to price is equal to zero, so that we can rule out the possibility that all four biases are either all negative or all positive. Of the fourteen remaining logical possibilities, only eight actually occur among the results presented in Table 1. Of these, only three patterns occur for more than one industry. It is important to note that the biases of technical change are not affected by the concavity of the price function, so that all four parameters are fitted for thirty-five industries. For the Miscellaneous sector the rate of technical change is zero by definition so that all biases of technical change are set equal to zero.

We first consider the bias of technical change with respect to the price of capital input. If the estimated value of this parameter is positive, technical change is capital using. Alternatively, the rate of technical change decreases with an increase in the price of capital. If the estimated value is negative, technical change is capital saving and the rate of technical change increases with the price of capital. Technical change is capital using for twenty-five of the thirty-five industries included in our study of the biases of technical change; it is capital saving for ten of these industries. We conclude that the rate of technical change decreases with the price of capital for twenty-five industries and increases with the price of capital for ten industries.

The interpretation of the biases of technical change with respect to the prices of labor, energy, and materials inputs is analogous to the interpretation of the bias with respect to the price of capital input. If the estimated value of the bias is positive, technical change uses the corresponding input; alternatively, the rate of technical change decreases with an increase in the input price. If the estimated value is negative, technical change saves the corresponding input; alternatively, the rate of technical change decreases with the input price. Considering the bias of technical change with respect to the price of labor input, we find that technical change is labor using for thirty-one of the thirty-five industries included in our study and labor saving for only four of these industries. The rate of technical change decreases with the price of labor for thirty-one industries and increases with the price of labor for four industries.

Considering the bias of technical change with respect to the price of energy input, we find that technical change is energy using for twenty-nine of the thirty-five industries included in our study and energy saving for only six of these industries. The rate of technical change decreases with the price of energy for twenty-nine industries and increases for six industries. Finally, technical change is materials using for only two of the thirty-five industries included in our study and materials saving for the remaining thirty-three. We conclude that the rate of technical change increases with the price of materials for thirty-three industries and decreases with the price of materials for two industries.

A classification of industries by patterns of the biases of technical change is given in Table 2. The pattern that occurs with greatest frequency is capital using, labor using, energy using, and materials saving technical change. This pattern occurs for nineteen of the thirty-five industries included in our study. For this pattern the rate of technical change decreases with increases in the prices of capital, labor, and energy inputs and increases with the price of materials input. The pattern that occurs next most frequently is capital saving, labor using, energy using, and materials saving technical change. This pattern occurs for seven industries. The third most frequently occurring pattern is capital using, labor using, energy saving, and materials saving technical change. This pattern occurs for four industries. No other pattern occurs for more than one industry.

Our interpretation of the parameter estimates given in Table 1 concludes with rates of change of the negative of the rate of technical change $\{\beta^i_{TT}\}$. If the estimated value of this parameter is positive the rate of technical change is decreasing; if the value is negative the rate is increasing. For twenty-four of the thirty-five industries included in our study of the rate of change of the rate of technical change the estimated value is positive; for eleven industries the value is negative; for the remaining industry this parameter is set equal to zero, since the rate of technical change is zero by definition. We conclude that the rate of technical change is decreasing with time for twenty-four industries and increasing with time for eleven industries.

4. Conclusion

Our empirical results for sectoral patterns of production and technical change are very striking and suggest a considerable degree of similarity across industries. However, it is important to emphasize that these results have been obtained under strong simplifying assumptions. First, for all industries we have employed conditions for producer equilibrium under perfect competition; we have assumed constant returns to scale at the industry level; finally, we have employed a description of technology that leads to myopic decision rules. These assumptions must be justified primarily by their usefulness in implementing production models that are uniform for all thirty-six industrial sectors of the U.S. economy.

The most important simplification of the theory of production and technical change employed in the specification of our econometric models is the imposition of concavity of the sectoral price functions. By imposing concavity on the sectoral price functions we have reduced the number of share elasticities to be fitted from three hundred sixty or ten for each of our thirty-six industrial sectors to one hundred fifty-six or less than five per sector on average. All share elasticities are constrained to be zero for eleven of the thirty-six industries. The concavity constraints contribute to the precision of our estimates, but require that the share of each input be nonincreasing in the price of the input itself.

Although it might be worthwhile to weaken each of the assumptions we have enumerated above, a more promising direction for further research appears to lie within the framework provided by these assumptions. First, we can provide a more detailed model for allocation among productive inputs. We have disaggregated energy and materials into thirty-six groups – five types of energy and thirty-one types of materials – by constructing a hierarchy of models for allocation within the energy and materials aggregates. For this purpose we have assumed that each aggregate is homogeneously separable within the sectoral production function. We assume, for example, that the share of energy in the value of sectoral output depends on changes in technology, while the share of, say, electricity in the value of energy input does not.

The second research objective suggested by our results is to incorporate the production models for all thirty-six industrial sectors into a general equilibrium model of production in the U.S. economy. An econometric general equilibrium model of the U.S. economy has been constructed for nine industrial sectors by *Hudson/Jorgenson* [1974]. This model is currently being disaggregated to the level of the thirty-six industrial sectors included in our study. A novel feature of the thirty-six sector general equilibrium model will be the endogenous treatment of the rate of technical change for thirty-five of the thirty-six industries we have analyzed. A general equilibrium model will make it possible to analyze the implications of sectoral patterns of substitution and technical change for the U.S. economy as a whole.

References

Ben-Zion, U., and *V.W. Ruttan*: Aggregate Demand and the Rate of Technical Change. Induced Innovation. Ed. by H.P. Binswanger and V.W. Ruttan. Baltimore 1978, 261–275.

Berndt, E.R., and *D.W. Jorgenson*: Production Structure. U.S. Energy Resources and Economic Growth. Ed. by D.W. Jorgenson and H.S. Houthakker. Chapter 3, Washington 1973.

Berndt, E.R., and *D.O. Wood*: Technology, Prices, and the Derived Demand for Energy. Review of Economics and Statistics **56** (3), 1975, 259–268.

– : Engineering and Econometric Interpretations of Energy-Capital Complementarity. American Economic Review **69** (3), 1979, 342–354.

Binswanger, H.P.: The Measurement of Technical Change Biases with Many Factors of Production. American Economic Review **64** (5), 1974a, 964–976.

– : A Microeconomic Approach to Induced Innovation. Economic Journal **84** (336), 1974b, 940–958.

– : Induced Technical Change: Evolution of Thought. Induced Innovation. Ed. by H.P. Binswanger and V.W. Ruttan. Baltimore 1978a, 13–43.

– : Issues in Modeling Induced Technical Change. Induced Innovation. Ed. by H.P. Binswanger and V.W. Ruttan. Baltimore 1978b, 128–163.

Burmeister, E., and *A.R. Dobell*: Disembodied Technological Change with Several Factors. Journal of Economic Theory **1** (1), 1969, 1–8.

Christensen, L.R., and *D.W. Jorgenson*: U.S. Real Product and Real Factor Input, 1929–1967. Review of Income and Wealth, Series 16 (1), 1970, 19–50.

Christensen, L.R., D.W. Jorgenson and *L.J. Lau*: Conjugate Duality and the Transcendental Logarithmic Production Function. Econometrica **39** (4), 1971, 255–256.

– : Transcendental Logarithmic Production Frontiers. Review of Economics and Statistics **55** (1), 1973, 28–45.

Diewert, W.E.: Exact and Superlative Index Numbers. Journal of Econometrics **4** (2), 1976, 115–146.

– : Aggregation Problems in the Measurement of Capital. The Measurement of Capital. Ed. by D. Usher. Chicago 1980, 433–528.

Fisher, I.: The Making of Index Numbers. Boston 1922.

Fraumeni, B.M., and *D.W. Jorgenson*: The Role of Capital in U.S. Economic Growth, 1948–1976. Capital, Efficiency and Growth. Ed. by G.M. von Furstenberg. Cambridge 1980, 9–250.

Hicks, J.R.: The Theory of Wages. London 1932.

– : The Theory of Wages. 2nd edition. London 1963.

Jack Faucett Associates: Development of 35 Order Input-Output Tables, 1958–1974, Final Report. Washington, D.C., 1977.

Jorgenson, D.W.: Technology and Decision Rules in the Theory of Investment Behavior. Quarterly Journal of Economics 87 (4), 1973, 523–543.

Jorgenson, D.W., and *J.-J. Laffont*: Efficient Estimation of Non-Linear Simultaneous Equations with Additive Disturbances. Annals of Social and Economic Measurement **3** (4), 1974, 615–640.

Jorgenson, D.W., and *L.J. Lau*: Transcendental Logarithmic Production Functions. Amsterdam, 1982.

Kennedy, Ch.: Induced Bias in Innovation and the Theory of Distribution. Economic Journal **74** (295), 1964, 541–547.

Kloek, T.: Indexcijfers: enige methodologisch aspecten. The Hague 1966.

Lau, L.J.: Testing and Imposing Monotonicity, Convexity, and Quasi-Convexity Constraints. Production Economics: A Dual Approach to Theory and Applications, Vol. 1. Ed. by M. Fuss and D. McFadden. Amsterdam 1978, 409–453.

Lucas, R.E., Jr.: Tests of a Capital-Theoretic Model of Technological Change. Review of Economic Studies **34** (98), 1967, 175–180.

Samuelson, P.A.: Prices of Factors and Goods in General Equilibrium. Review of Economic Studies **21** (1), 1953, 1–20.

– : A Theory of Induced Innovation Along Kennedy-Weizsäcker Lines. Review of Economics and Statistics **47** (4), 1965, 343–356.

– : Relative Shares and Elasticities Simplified: Comment. American Economic Review **63** (4), 1973, 770–771.

Schmookler, J.: Invention and Economic Growth. Cambridge 1966.

Theil, H.: The Information Approach to Demand Analysis. Econometrica **33** (1), 1965, 67–87.

Tornquist, L.: The Bank of Finland's Consumption Price Index. Bank of Finland Monthly Bulletin **10**, 1936, 1–8.

Weizsäcker, C.C.v.: A New Technical Progress Function. Massachusetts Institute of Technology, 1962, unpublished manuscript, 23 pp.

Quantitative Studies on Production and Prices © Physica-Verlag, Würzburg–Wien, 1983.

Use of the Aggregator Function to Determine Import Shares in a Multi-Sectoral Model

Shinichiro Nakamura

1. Introduction

The demand for an input in the production process can be satisfied out of a domestic source, out of an imported source, or out of a mixture of these. With the exception of non-competitive imports, the last form of a mixture of sources may be the most usual pattern.

The aim of this work is to explain the shares of the imported inputs by use of an aggregator function. The inputs from domestic and imported sources are not a priori regarded as perfect substitutes, and an aggregator function is used to represent the substitution possibilities between them. This quantity aggregator function yields an aggregate measure for the total input which originated from the two sources.

Dual to the quantity aggregator function exists a price aggregator function which provides an aggregate price level of the aggregate input as a function of the price of the input from domestic source and the price of input from imported source. Then the cost-minimizing shares of imports are derived by applying Shephard's Lemma [*Shephard*, 1953] to the price aggregator function.

In Section 2 the assumptions about substitution between domestic inputs and corresponding imports as well as separability of the production function are discussed. In Section 3 the model is specified by a translog function. Section 4 gives the results of the empirical application of the model to the annual input-output tables for West-Germany, 1960–1974. Some concluding remarks are made in Section 5.

2. Inputs Differentiated by Sources and their Aggregator Function

2.1 Assumptions about Substitution Possibilities

Assumptions about the substitution possibilities between domestic inputs and corresponding imports are central to all empirical research on international trade: domestic inputs and corresponding imports can be regarded either as perfect substitutes (homogeneous inputs) – essentially indistinguishable – or as imperfect substitutes (heterogeneous inputs) with many similarities and some differences. The assumption of input heterogeneity or that imported inputs are merely imperfect substitutes for inputs from domestic sources may suggest a more realistic approach (see *Petri* [1976] for a further discussion on this point). Our analysis is based on the assumption of heterogeneity between the inputs from the two sources. Following *Armington* [1969], we regard the place of origin of inputs as their prime differentiating characteristic. We assume that domestic inputs and corresponding imports are imperfectly substitutable because of their difference in origin.

2.2 Production Function with Imports

Assume that there is one foreign country (the world market) which exports n products to one domestic country. The domestic country also produces n products. According to our assumptions made above, the imported n products are imperfect substitutes for the corresponding domestic products because of their difference in the place of origin. Hence we have altogether $2n$ products which are used as inputs in a producing sector of the domestic country. The production function for sector j in the domestic country is given by

$$XD_j = f_j\,(XD_{1j}, XM_{1j}, XD_{2j}, XM_{2j}, \ldots, XD_{nj}, XM_{nj}, K_j, L_j, t), \qquad j = 1, 2, \ldots, n, \tag{1}$$

where

XD_j: output of sector j,

XD_{ij}: input of domestic product i in sector j, $i = 1, \ldots, n$,

XM_{ij}: input of import i in sector j, $i = 1, \ldots, n$,

L_j: aggregate input of labor services in sector j,

K_j: aggregate input of capital services in sector j, and

t: time (used as a proxy for variables representing technical change).

The production function (1) is assumed to satisfy the usual conditions of monotonicity, continuity and quasi-concavity. We suppose that the domestic firm faces competitive input markets with strictly positive prices, and chooses an input bundle to minimize the cost of producing a given amount of output.

2.3 Separability in the Production Function

We assume that the production function (1) is weakly homogeneously separable in the input i of alternative sources (XD_{ij} and XM_{ij}) from the input k from alternative sources (XD_{kj} and XM_{kj}) and from K_j and L_j as well ($i, k = 1, \ldots, n$, $i \neq k$). This production function we rewrite as

$$\begin{aligned} XD_j &= F_j\,[g_{1j}\,(XD_{1j}, XM_{1j}, t), g_{2j}\,(XD_{2j}, XM_{2j}, t), \ldots, \\ &\qquad g_{nj}\,(XD_{nj}, XM_{nj}, t), K_j, L_j, t] \\ &= F_j\,(XX_{1j}, XX_{2j}, \ldots, XX_{nj}, K_j, L_j, t), \qquad j = 1, \ldots, n, \end{aligned} \tag{2}$$

where g_{ij} is the quantity aggregator function of the input i to the sector j and $XX_{ij} = g_{ij}\,(XD_{ij}, XM_{ij}, t)$ the aggregate quantity measure of input i used in sector j, $j = 1, 2, \ldots, n$. The aggregator function g_{ij} is supposed to satisfy the conditions of monotonicity, continuity, linear homogeneity and quasi-concavity in inputs. We note that the assumption of g_{ij} being homogeneous of degree one implies that shares of domestic inputs and imports are independent of the scale of demand for the aggregate of inputs.[1])

Homogeneous weak separability implies validity of the two-stage optimization procedure [see *Blackorby/Primont/Russell*, 173–214].

2.4 Price Aggregator Function

Dual to the quantity aggregator function g_{ij} exists a price aggregator function h_{ij} which gives the aggregate price level of the input i used in sector j:

$$PP_{ij} = h_{ij}\,(PD_i, PM_i, t), \qquad i, j = 1, \ldots, n, \tag{3}$$

where

PP_{ij}: aggregate price level of input i used in sector j,

PD_i: price of domestic input i, and

PM_i: price of import i.

The price aggregator function h_{ij} satisfies the usual conditions of monotonicity, continuity, concavity, and linear homogeneity in prices.

The price aggregate PP_{ij} and quantity aggregate XX_{ij} satisfy the condition of additive price aggregation [*Blackorby/Primont/Russell*, p. 206, Theorem 5.8]:

$$PP_{ij} \cdot XX_{ij} = PD_i \cdot XD_{ij} + PM_i \cdot XM_{ij}, \qquad i, j = 1, \ldots, n. \tag{4}$$

It is well known that there exists a one-to-one correspondence between h_{ij} and g_{ij} [see *McFadden*]. The subsequent analysis in this paper has been done using only the price aggregator function.

3. Model Specification and its Implications

3.1 Translog Price Aggregator Function

For purposes of estimation we must employ a specific functional form for the price aggregator function h_{ij}. Since our knowledge about substitution possibilities between domestic inputs and corresponding imports is rather limited, we choose a highly general form, namely the translog price aggregator function. This function places no a priori restrictions on the elasticity of substitution and can be interpreted as a second order approximation to an arbitrary twice-differentiable price aggregator function. We have

$$\begin{aligned} PP_{ij} = \exp\,[&\alpha_{Dij} \ln PD_i + \alpha_{Mij} \ln PM_i + 1/2\, \beta_{DDij} (\ln PD_i)^2 \\ &+ 1/2\, \beta_{MMij} (\ln PM_i)^2 + \beta_{DMij} \ln PD_i \cdot \ln PM_i \\ &+ \beta_{tDij} \ln PD_i \cdot t + \beta_{tMij} \ln PM_i \cdot t], \qquad i, j = 1, \ldots, n. \end{aligned} \tag{5}$$

---

[1]) In his analysis of US-Japan trade patterns *Petri* [1976] reports that for six of the thirteen sectors he analysed demand elasticities of imports were almost equal to unity. This finding is consistent with linear homogeneity of the aggregator function.

Linear homogeneity in prices implies the following restrictions on (5):

$$\begin{cases} \alpha_{Dij} + \alpha_{Mij} = 1, \\ \beta_{DDij} + \beta_{DMij} = 0, \\ \beta_{DMij} + \beta_{MMij} = 0, \\ \beta_{tDij} + \beta_{tMij} = 0, \qquad i, j = 1, \ldots, n. \end{cases} \tag{6}$$

Using Shephard's Lemma [*Shephard*, p. 11], from (5) we obtain the following value share functions for domestic inputs and imports:

$$SD_{ij} = \frac{PD_i \cdot XD_{ij}}{PP_{ij} \cdot XX_{ij}} = \frac{\partial \ln PP_{ij}}{\partial \ln PD_i} \tag{7a}$$

$$= \alpha_{Dij} + \beta_{DDij} \ln PD_i + \beta_{DMij} \ln PM_i + \beta_{tDij} \cdot t$$

$$= \alpha_{Dij} + \beta_{DDij} \ln (PD_i / PM_i) + \beta_{tDij} \cdot t \qquad \text{(from (6))},$$

$$SM_{ij} = \frac{PM_i \cdot XM_{ij}}{PP_{ij} \cdot XX_{ij}} = \frac{\partial \ln PP_{ij}}{\partial \ln PM_i} \tag{7b}$$

$$= \alpha_{Mij} + \beta_{DMij} \ln PD_i + \beta_{MMij} \ln PM_i + \beta_{tMij} \cdot t$$

$$= 1 - \alpha_{Dij} + \beta_{DDij} \ln (PM_i / PD_i) - \beta_{tDij} \cdot t \qquad \text{(from (6))}, \quad i, j = 1, \ldots, n,$$

where SD_{ij} (SM_{ij}) is the value share of domestic input i (import i) in the cost of input i in sector j, and $SD_{ij} + SM_{ij} = 1$.

Concavity of the price aggregator function implies that the parameter β_{DDij} are not larger than the product of SD_{ij} and SM_{ij} (for a derivation of this condition, see *Nakamura* [1981]):

$$\beta_{DDij} - SD_{ij} \cdot SM_{ij} \leqslant 0. \tag{8}$$

3.2 Implications of Parameters

The parameters $\{\beta_{DDij}, \beta_{DMij}, \beta_{MMij}\}$ can be interpreted as constant share elasticities [*Jorgenson/Fraumeni*]. Given the translog price aggregator function (5), the elasticity of substitution between domestic input i and import i used in sector j (σ_{DMij}) is calculated as [*Uzawa*, p. 213]:

$$\sigma_{DMij} = \frac{H_{ij} \cdot (\partial^2 H_{ij} / \partial PD_i \cdot \partial PM_i)}{(\partial H_{ij} / \partial PD_i) \cdot (\partial H_{ij} / \partial PM_i)} = \frac{\beta_{DMij} + SD_{ij} \cdot SM_{ij}}{SD_{ij} \cdot SM_{ij}} \tag{9}$$

$$= \frac{-\beta_{DDij}}{SD_{ij} \cdot SM_{ij}} + 1 \qquad \text{(from (6))}, \quad i, j = 1, \ldots, n.$$

From (9) we can now derive the following implications for the elasticity of substitution σ_{DMij}[2]):

$$\begin{cases} \text{if } \beta_{DDij} > 0, \text{ then } 0 \leqslant \sigma_{DMij} < 1, \\ \text{if } \beta_{DDij} < 0, \text{ then } \sigma_{DMij} > 1, \text{ and} \\ \text{if } \beta_{DDij} = 0, \text{ then } \sigma_{DMij} = 1, \qquad i, j = 1, \ldots, n. \end{cases} \tag{10}$$

If β_{DDij} is positive, the elasticity of substitution is smaller than one and the value share of domestic product i increases with an increase in its price. If β_{DDij} is negative, the elasticity of substitution is greater than one and the value share of the domestic product decreases with an increase in its price. If β_{DDij} is zero, the elasticity of substitution is equal to one and the value share is independent of price changes.

The parameters $\{\beta_{tDij}, \beta_{tMij}\}$ can be interpreted as constant biases of technical change with respect to price [*Jorgenson/Fraumeni*]. If β_{tDij} is positive, the value share of domestic product i increases with time, holding the prices of the domestic product and imports constant: domestic product using (import saving) technical change. If β_{tDij} is negative, the value share of domestic product decreases with time, holding the prices of domestic product and imports constant: domestic product saving (import using) technical change. If β_{tDij} is zero, the value share is independent of time: no biases of technical change.

The effect of biases of technical change on the aggregate price level can be easily seen by taking the derivative of the logarithm of (5) with respect to time and using (6):

$$\frac{\partial \ln PP_{ij}}{\partial t} = \beta_{tDij} \ln (PD_i / PM_i), \qquad i, j = 1, \ldots, n. \tag{11}$$

If $\beta_{tDij} \neq 0$, the aggregate price level PP_{ij} changes with time for constant PD_i and PM_i and $PD_i \neq PM_i$.

4. Empirical Results

4.1 Estimation of the Parameters

The model described in Section 3 was applied to the annual input-output tables of West Germany for 1960–1974 [*Frerichs*, et al.]. Table 1 shows the sectoral classification of the tables. The model was applied to individual cells of the input-output tables. The estimation of the model was made for 101 of the 144 cells of the 12 sectors input-output table excluding the 43 cells with import shares smaller than one per cent for the whole period.[3]) We use the price indices of domestic outputs and imports corresponding to the input-output table with $PD_i = PM_i = 1$ for 1970.

[2]) By monotonicity, SD_{ij} and SM_{ij} are positive.

[3]) An almost zero import share can be regarded either as a result of almost perfect substitutability between a domestic input and its imported counterpart or as that of almost perfect complementarity between them. Since the relative prices PD_i/PM_i (i = 01, . . . , 12) showed a considerable change over the observation period (see Tab. 2), it seems more reasonable to see the almost zero import share as an indication of almost perfect complementarity. It can be said that for the 43 cells excluded from the analysis, the elasticity of substitution is almost equal to zero.

01 Agriculture	Agriculture, forestry, fishing, gardening
02 Energy & Mining	Electricity, gas and water, coal mining, iron ore mining, potash and rock salt mining, petroleum extraction
03 Chemicals	Chemicals, building materials, petroleum refining, rubber and asbestos manufactures, fine ceramics, glass, plastic manufactures
04 Iron & steel, NFM	Iron and steel, iron and steel foundries, steel drawing and cold rolling mills, non-ferrous metals, steel forging
05 Machinery & vehicles	Constructional steel, machinery, vehicles, aerospace, shipbuilding
06 Electrical goods	Electrical engineering, precision engineering and optics, hardware and metal goods, musical instruments, toys, jewelry, sport articles
07 Paper & textiles	Saw mills and wood processing, cellulose and paper, timber manufactures, paper and board manufactures, printing, leather, textiles, clothing
08 Food	Grain milling, edible oils and margarine, sugar, brewing and malting, tobacco manufactures, other food and beverages
09 Construction	Construction
10 Trade & Commerce	Wholesaling, retailing
11 Transportation & communications	Railway, Shipping, waterways and harbours, other transports, communications
12 Other services	Banks and insurances, rented dwellings

Tab. 1: Classification of Production Sectors

	*PX*01	*PM*01	*PX*02	*PM*02	*PX*03	*PM*03	*PX*04	*PM*04
1962	103.2	97.6	97.0	92.5	100.2	92.4	99.2	95.4
1964	107.3	102.3	97.9	92.7	98.9	87.8	101.2	102.7
1966	115.2	106.8	102.5	93.8	100.4	86.7	106.7	116.9
1968	105.8	99.8	104.1	99.1	99.9	87.9	100.3	116.8
1970	107.8	98.6	108.2	95.8	101.6	85.6	115.8	127.4
1972	122.2	99.4	120.9	102.6	106.5	84.0	115.1	112.5
1974	127.7	131.9	140.3	251.9	142.7	138.8	149.7	160.4

	*PX*05	*PM*05	*PX*06	*PM*06	*PX*07	*PM*07	*PX*08	*PM*08
1962	105.9	98.0	103.8	97.0	104.3	97.3	103.7	97.1
1964	108.4	101.7	105.1	99.0	107.9	104.0	105.8	103.9
1966	114.1	104.8	109.7	102.9	113.2	106.9	109.7	107.3
1968	113.2	107.1	106.8	99.0	112.1	103.4	108.6	97.8
1970	128.3	105.9	116.3	97.5	119.1	104.9	112.3	103.7
1972	143.1	109.7	124.1	95.8	127.9	110.3	121.2	107.1
1974	163.7	115.9	139.2	102.2	154.0	137.3	138.2	146.2

Tab. 2: Changes in Prices of Domestic Outputs and Imports (1960 = 100)

We obtain the estimation equation by adding a random disturbance term with expected value equal to zero to (7a). The equation was estimated for the above 101 cells by OLS for the period 1960–1974 [see *Nakamura*]. It turned out that the coefficient of determination R^2 was rather low ($R^2 \leqslant \cdot 60$ for 47 cells). We estimated the value share functions, and for a considerable part of the cells analysed the value shares did not show any significant change over the observation period. Hence, a low R^2 is not necessarily a result of misspecification but may be an indication of approximately constant value shares with respect to price variation and time.

We tested the concavity condition (8) for the translog price aggregator function (5), using estimates of β_{DDij} and SD_{ij} for all observations. We could not reject the concavity condition (8) for 91 of the 101 cells analysed for all observations at a 5 per cent level of significance (for details of the test procedure and results, see *Nakamura* [1981]). We conclude that the translog price aggregator function is well behaved for 91 of the 101 cells. In 4.2 and 4.3 we limit our analysis to those 91 cells.

Evaluating the result that for 10 cells the condition of concavity is not satisfied, one should keep in mind that our test was made under the assumptions of weak separability of the underlying production function in the form of (2) and of a specific functional form of the price aggregator function. In addition, our data is rather aggregated in that a sectoral output consists of a number of heterogeneous products (see Tab. 1). Hence it is not appropriate to conclude from the above result that for these 10 cells the assumption of cost-minimization does not hold. A more general test of the assumptions should be made by use of more disaggregated data.

4.2 Elasticity of Substitution

Table 3 classifies the 91 cells with the well-behaved translog price aggregator function by patterns of substitution between domestic inputs and corresponding imports implied by the estimates of constant share elasticities (see (10)). From Table 3 it is seen that for 72 of the 91 cells for which the concavity condition is not rejected, the share elasticities β_{DDij} are not significantly different from zero (at a 5 per cent level). For 13 of the 19 cells for which the share elasticities are significantly different from zero, the share elasticities are significantly positive. For the remaining 6 cells the share elasticities are significantly negative. These results imply, i) for 72 of the 91 cells the elasticity of substitution σ_{DMij} is not significantly different from unity, ii) for 13 of the 91 cells the elasticity of substitution is significantly smaller than one, and iii) for 6 of the 91 cells the elasticity of substitution is significantly larger than one. We can say that for 78 of the 91 cells domestic inputs and corresponding imports tend to be quite substitutable and that for the remaining 13 cells they are slightly substitutable.

We next test the hypothesis of constancy of the elasticities of substitution (CES). From above it follows that for 72 of the 91 cells the hypothesis of CES is not rejected (these 72 cells have an elasticity of substitution which is not significantly different from one). For the remaining 19 of the 91 cells we test the CES hypothesis using the estimates for the elasticity of substitution (for details of the test procedure see *Nakamura* [1981]). It turned out that for 17 of the above 19 cells in which the elasticity of substitution was significantly different from one, the hypothesis of CES could not be rejected at a 5 p.c.

estimates of β_{DDij}	cell (input-output)[1]								number of cells
$\hat{\beta}_{DDij} < 0$ ($\hat{\sigma}_{DMij} > 1$)	03/06	05/08	05/09	12/02	12/04	12/06			6
$\hat{\beta}_{DDij} \approx 0$ ($\hat{\sigma}_{DMij} \approx 1$)	01/01	01/06	01/07	01/08	01/09	01/12	02/04	02/08	72
	02/11	03/01	03/04	03/05	03/07	03/09	03/10	03/11	
	03/12	04/01	04/08	04/09	04/11	05/02	05/03	05/04	
	05/05	05/06	05/10	05/11	06/02	06/06	06/07	06/08	
	06/09	06/12	07/01	07/02	07/05	07/08	07/09	07/10	
	07/11	07/12	08/01	08/06	08/07	08/11	08/12	09/05	
	09/06	09/08	09/11	11/01	11/02	11/03	11/04	11/05	
	11/06	11/07	11/08	11/09	11/10	11/11	11/12	12/01	
	12/03	12/05	12/07	12/08	12/09	12/10	12/11	12/12	
$\hat{\beta}_{DDij} > 0$ ($0 < \hat{\sigma}_{DMij} < 1$)	01/03	01/11	02/01	02/02	02/03	03/03	03/08	04/05	13
	06/05	07/03	07/06	07/07	08/08				

[1]) 01 Agriculture
02 Energy & mining
03 Chemicals
04 Iron & steel, NFM
05 Machinery & vehicles
06 Electrical goods
07 Paper & textile
08 Food
09 Construction
10 Commerce
11 Transport
12 Other services

Tab. 3: Share Elasticities and Patterns of Substitution

year	05/08 $\hat{\sigma}_{DM}$	05/08 standard error	05/09 $\hat{\sigma}_{DM}$	05/09 standard error
1960	3.22076	.466428	5.82738	1.56394
1961	3.22523	.441128	4.81176	1.05701
1962	3.35167	.461194	4.48873	.959071
1963	3.67655	.554924	4.60405	1.10545
1964	4.03970	.660622	4.57737	1.17315
1965	4.33227	.726343	4.31530	1.08147
1966	4.94539	.922807	4.28252	1.13434
1967	6.37060	1.53712	4.47816	1.35922
1968	8.87057	2.93181	4.54770	1.50443
1969	10.0968	3.38550	4.12290	1.23384
1970	7.72326	1.55165	3.41509	.778136
1971	8.51158	1.61094	3.20936	.686020
1972	9.75338	1.80418	3.04990	.620635
1973	11.3806	2.15809	2.90874	.564233
1974	13.0922	2.77132	2.77347	.509730

Tab. 4: Elasticity of Substitution

level of significance. The exceptions were cells 05/08 and 05/09. For these two cells the elasticity of substitution showed a significant change in its value over the observation period. Table 4 shows the development of the elasticity of substitution for these two cells with its standard errors. It is found that in both cells the elasticities of substitution are larger than one and that they show different developments over time: for 05/08 an increasing tendency is observed while for 05/09 the contrary is the case.

$\hat{\sigma}_{DM}$ / CES, VES		$0 < \hat{\sigma}_{DM} < 1$	$\sigma_{DM} \approx 1$	$\sigma_{DM} \approx 1$
VES	2			2
CES	89	13	72	4

Tab. 5: Estimation Results of Elasticity of Substitution

Table 5 summarizes our estimation results of the elasticity of substitution. From this table we can see that for 89 of the 91 cells, for which the translog price aggregator function is well behaved, the elasticity of substitution is constant, and that for 85 of these 89 cells the elasticity is not larger than one.

4.3 Biases of Technical Change

Table 6 classifies the 91 cells by the patterns of biases of technical change implied by the estimates of constant biases of technical change. From the table we see that for 58 of the 91 cells the constant biases of technical change are significantly different from zero.

estimates of β_{tDij}	cell (input-output)[1])	number of cells
$\hat{\beta}_{tDij} < 0$	01/01 01/06 01/08 01/11 02/03 03/01 03/03 03/05 03/06 03/07 03/08 03/09 03/10 03/12 04/01 04/05 04/09 05/05 05/10 06/05 06/06 06/09 06/12 07/01 07/03 07/06 07/07 07/12 08/01 08/06 08/07 08/12 11/01 11/02 11/03 11/04 11/05 11/06 11/07 11/09 11/10 11/12 12/01 12/02	44
$\hat{\beta}_{tDij} \approx 0$	01/09 02/01 02/04 02/08 03/04 03/11 04/11 05/02 05/06 05/09 05/11 06/02 06/07 06/08 07/05 07/08 07/09 07/10 07/11 08/08 08/11 09/05 09/06 09/11 11/08 11/11 12/04 12/05 12/06 12/07 12/09 12/10 12/11	33
$\hat{\beta}_{tDij} > 0$	01/03 01/07 01/12 02/02 02/11 04/08 05/03 05/04 05/08 07/02 09/08 12/03 12/08 12/12	14

[1]) 01 Agriculture
02 Energy & mining
03 Chemicals
04 Iron & steel, NFM
05 Machinery & vehicles
06 Electrical goods
07 Paper & textile
08 Food
09 Construction
10 Commerce
11 Transport
12 Other services

Tab. 6: Biases of Technical Change

The estimation results indicate the existence of biases of technical change for 58 of the 91 cells. We can say that for these 58 cells the aggregate price level PP_{ij} changes with time under unchanged PD_i and PM_i (see (11)). For 44 of these 58 cells technical change is domestic input saving. For the remaining 14 cells technical change is import saving.

Limiting our discussion to agriculture, energy, and manufacturing sectors (sectors 01 to 08), we find that the rates of increase in prices of domestic products were higher than those of corresponding imports with the exception of sector 04 (Iron & steel, nonferrous metals) at least until 1972 (see Tab. 2). Of the above 44 cells with domestic inputs saving technical change 30 cells refer to inputs, whose domestic prices increased with higher rates than import prices. We can say that the behavior of price and biases of technical change observed for the 30 cells is consistent with the induced innovation hypothesis and neutral innovation possibilities.

5. Concluding Remarks

In this paper we have presented a model designed to deal with the problem of explaining import shares in an input-output model. The empirical results for the West German input-output tables 1960–1974 provide support for the procedure developed in this paper. They imply the existence of a well-behaved price aggregator function representing substitution possibilities between domestic inputs and corresponding imports for 91 of the 101 cells analysed. Our analysis of the estimates of the elasticity of substitution between domestic inputs and corresponding imports suggests that for 89 of the above 91 cells the elasticity of substitution is constant over the observation period. Of these 89 cells the constant elasticity of substitution is one for 72 cells, smaller than one for 13 cells, and larger than one for 4 cells. The estimates of the constant biases of technical change indicate the existence of biases of technical change for 58 of the 91 cells. We conclude that a CES function with the elasticity of substitution not larger than one incorporating biases of technical change gives the representative form of the aggregator function for domestic inputs and corresponding imports for the West German input-output tables 1960–1974.

Our analysis in this paper has been limited to the case of two countries, because our date sources do not give imports by countries of origin. We can apply our model to the more general case of m ($>$ 2) countries by a slight modification. In *Nakamura* [1981] a model for m ($>$ 2) countries has been developed. An interesting future study would be the application of a three-countries version of our model to the imports of West Germany from EC member countries and those from the rest of the world.

References

Armington, P.S.: A Theory of Demand for Products Distinguished by Place of Production. IMF Staff Papers **15** (1), 1969, 159–176.

Blackorby, C., D. Primont, and *R.R. Russell*: Duality, Separability, and the Functional Structure: Theory and Economic Applications. New York 1978.

Frerichs, W., et al.: Die Datenbasis zum Disaggregierten Prognosesystem II (Referenzperiode 1960–1974). Institut für Gesellschafts- und Wirtschaftswissenschaften, University of Bonn, Bonn 1979.

Jorgenson, D.W., and *B.M. Fraumeni*: Substitution and Technical Change in Production. Quantitative Studies on Production and Prices. Ed. by W. Eichhorn et al. Würzburg–Wien 1982 (this volume).

McFadden, D.: Cost, Revenue and Profit Functions. Production Economics: A Dual Approach to Theory and Applications. Ed. by M. Fuss and D. McFadden. Amsterdam 1978, 1–101.

Nakamura, S.: Use of the Aggregator Function to Determine Import Shares in a Multi-Sectoral Model. Discussion Paper No. 115. Institut für Gesellschafts- und Wirtschaftswissenschaften, University of Bonn, Bonn 1981.

Petri, P.: A Multilateral Model of Japanese-American Trade. Advances in Input-Output Analysis. Ed. by K.R. Polenske and J.V. Skolka. Cambridge, Mass., 1976, 461–492.

Shephard, R.W.: Cost and Production Functions. Princeton 1953.

Uzawa, H.: Production Functions with Constant Elasticities of Substitution. Review of Economic Studies **29** (81), 1962, 291–299.

Author Index

Subject Index

List of Contributors

Bosworth, Derek L.,
Department of Economics, University of Loughborough, Loughborough, Leicestershire LE 11 3 TU, England.

Buhl, Hans Ulrich,
Institut für Wirtschaftstheorie und Operations Research, University of Karlsruhe, D–7500 Karlsruhe, Federal Republic of Germany.

Chipman, John S.,
Department of Economics, University of Minnesota, Minneapolis, MN 55455, U.S.A.

Dawkins, Peter J.,
Department of Economics, Warwick University, Warwick, England.

Diewert, W. Erwin,
Department of Economics, University of British Columbia, Vancouver, B.C. V6T 1W5, Canada.

Eichhorn, Wolfgang,
Institut für Wirtschaftstheorie und Operations Research, Universität Karlsruhe, D–7500 Karlsruhe Federal Republic of Germany.

Färe, Rolf,
Department of Economics, Southern Illinois University, Carbondale, Ill. 62901, U.S.A.

Fraumeni, Barbara M.,
Department of Economics, Boston College, Boston, MA, U.S.A.

Gleissner, Winfried,
Münchener Rückversicherungs-Gesellschaft, D–8000 München, Federal Republic of Germany.

Hasenkamp, Georg,
Sozialökonomisches Seminar, Universität Hamburg, D–2000 Hamburg, Federal Republic of Germany.

Henn, Rudolf,
Institut für Statistik und Mathematische Wirtschaftstheorie, Universität Karlsruhe, D–7500 Karlsruhe, Federal Republic of Germany.

Hildenbrand, Kurt,
Institut für Gesellschafts- und Wirtschaftswissenschaften, Universität Bonn, D–5300 Bonn, Federal Republic of Germany.

Jorgenson, Dale W.,
Department of Economics, Harvard University, Cambridge, MA 02138, U.S.A.

Kischka, Peter,
Institut für Statistik und Mathematische Wirtschaftstheorie, Universität Karlsruhe, D–7500 Karlsruhe, Federal Republic of Germany.

Koo, Anthony Y.C.,
Department of Economics, Michigan State University, MI, U.S.A.

Lovell, C.A. Knox,
Department of Economics, University of North Carolina, Chapel Hill, NC. 27514, U.S.A.

Mak, King-Tim,
Department of Quantitative Methods, University of Illinois at Chicago Circle, Chicage, Ill. 60680, U.S.A.

Neumann, Klaus,
Institut für Wirtschaftstheorie und Operations Research, Universität Karlsruhe, D–7500 Karlsruhe, Federal Republic of Germany.

Nakamura, Shinichiro,
Institut für Gesellschafts- und Wirtschaftswissenschaften, Universität Bonn, D–5300 Bonn, Federal Republic of Germany.

Pallaschke, Diethard,
Institut für Statistik und Mathematische Wirtschaftstheorie, Universität Karlsruhe, D–7500 Karlsruhe, Federal Republic of Germany.

Parkan, Celik,
Faculty of Commerce, University of Calgary, Calgary, Alberta, Canada.

Primont, Daniel,
Department of Economics, Southern Illinois University, Carbonale, Ill. 62901, U.S.A.

Shephard, Ronald W. †,
Department of Industrial Engineering and Operations Research, University of California, Berkeley, CA 94720, U.S.A.

Teusch, Wolfgang,
Abteilung Wirtschafts- und Sozialwissenschaften, Universität Dortmund, D–4600 Dortmund, Federal Republic of Germany.

Zieschang, Kimberly D.,
U.S. Bureau of Labor Statistics, Washington, D.C., 20212, U.S.A.